Doing Sociology of Education

Social Research and Educational Studies Series

Series Editor
Robert G. Burgess,
Senior Lecturer in Sociology,
University of Warwick.

Social Research and Education Studies Series: 6

Doing Sociology of Education

Edited by
Geoffrey Walford

 The Falmer Press

(A member of the Taylor & Francis Group)
London, New York and Philadelphia

UK The Falmer Press, Falmer House, Barcombe, Lewes, East Sussex, BN8 5DL

USA The Falmer Press, Taylor & Francis Inc., 242 Cherry Street, Philadelphia, PA 19106-1906

First published 1987

Library of Congress Cataloging in Publication Data

Doing sociology of education.

  (Social research and educational studies series; 6)
  Includes index.
1. Educational sociology—Research. I. Walford, Geoffrey. II. Series.
LC191.D64 1987 370.19′072 87-6860
ISBN 0-85000-145-6
ISBN 0-85000-146-4 (pbk.)

Jacket design by Caroline Archer

Typeset in 11/13 Garamond by
Imago Publishing Ltd, Thame, Oxon

Printed in Great Britain by Taylor & Francis (Printers) Ltd, Basingstoke

Contents

Contents

Series Editor's Preface

The purpose of the *Social Research and Educational Studies* series is to provide authoritative guides to key issues in educational research. The series includes overviews of fields, guidance on good practice and discussions of the practical implications of social and educational research. In particular, the series deals with a variety of approaches to conducting social and educational research. Contributors to this series review recent work, raise critical concerns that are particular to the field of education, and reflect on the implications of research for educational policy and practice.

Each volume in the series draws on material that will be relevant for an international audience. The contributors to this series all have wide experience of teaching, conducting and using educational research. The volumes are written so that they will appeal to a wide audience of students, teachers and researchers. Altogether, the volumes in the *Social Research and Educational Studies* series provide a comprehensive guide for anyone concerned with contemporary educational research.

The series will include individually authored books and edited volumes on a range of themes in education including: qualitative research, survey research, the interpretation of data, self-evaluation, research and social policy, analyzing data, action research, the politics and ethics of research.

In recent years social and educational researchers have begun to discuss the relationship between the problems, processes and procedures of their investigations. Geoffrey Walford has brought together a number of British sociologists of education who work in different traditions of their subject: ethnographers, action researchers, survey researchers and theorists among many others. Together they tell us about the way in which research in the sociology of education is conceived, designed, funded, conducted, analyzed, written and published. This 'behind the scenes' view of sociology of education will be of value to students, teachers and researchers who evaluate the published studies.

Robert Burgess
University of Warwick

Introduction: The Research Process

Geoffrey Walford

Academic subject areas are not static monolithic entities, but shifting amalgamations of sub-groups and traditions. The frontiers of the discipline are stretched, and the contents shaped and defined by those with power and influence to do so. Disputes arise as to what should be included within the discipline and what rejected. Changes in the external environment raise new questions, new methods, new theoretical frameworks and new potential audiences for the subject area, each of which can be used as a resource by those wishing to influence the nature and development of the subject.

Within the sociology of education, one of the most recent developments has been the growing interest in the study of the ways in which academic subject areas have been defined and fought over within schools (for example Goodson, 1983, 1985; Cooper, 1985; McCulloch et al., 1984; Walford, 1985). These authors have shown the ways in which subjects have become accepted and established as the result of the work of substantial interest groups which have been involved in the continuance and promotion of the various areas. Change within the subject has been shown to occur as one or other of these interest groups gains dominance and its concerns are promoted. The territory is shaped and the frontiers maintained by conflict between these various interest groups.

It is unfortunate that while we now have several excellent studies of the process of change within school subjects, such as mathematics (Cooper, 1985), science (Layton, 1973; Waring, 1979) and environmental studies (Goodson, 1983), the various accounts that purport to outline the shifts and conflicts within the sociology of education itself have been less useful. There has been a tendency for authors to present a partial history; the elements selected in such a way as to bolster the particular position or view of the writer. In particular, there has been a tendency to view the development of the sociology of education in Britain since the war as a fairly linear process with a succession of new theoretical perspectives, problems and methods supplanting the old. In particular, as Burgess (1984a, p. 122) notes:

> There are now numerous reviews that chart the transition from the 'old' or 'traditional' sociology of education which dominated the disciplines in the 1950s and 1960s with its concern for social stratification and social mobility to the 'new' sociology of education in the 1970s which through the work of Michael F.D. Young and others introduced such questions as: what counts as education? What does it mean to be educated? As such, this change in perspective found sociologists exploring new territory as schools, classrooms and school curricula became the site for sociological research. Structural functionalism was replaced by symbolic interactionism and with this changing theoretical perspective came a change in methodology as the social survey was quickly replaced by participant observation and unstructured interviews.

The next stage in the 'linear model' of the development of the sociology of education then sees the original emphasis of the 'new' sociology of education on the construction and transmission of knowledge as being widened into a variety of classroom studies based upon various micro-level theoretical perspectives such as symbolic interactionism and ethnomethodology using a variety of qualitative research methods.

If the shift from this 'old' to the 'new' sociology of education was to be seen as the first paradigm shift, then the next had to be the recognition that classrooms and the activities within them could not be understood in isolation from the wider society. The stress on the individual had to be replaced by one on the collectivity through various forms of neo-Marxism, perhaps first the 'harder' neo-Marxism associated with Althusser (1971) or Bowles and Gintis (1976), with their emphasis on correspondence (and with Althusser an attack on all empirical research methods), and then, later, the rather 'softer' viewpoint of such writers as Willis (1977) or Apple (1979, 1982), who opened the possibility of contradiction and resistance and based their work largely on participant observation. The final stage of the development is always least clear. For some, feminism was the next major influence, while for others it was the move towards policy relevance, or the developments of structuralism that were important. The essence was a continuing process of the 'new' replacing the 'old' in terms of theory, method and audience.

The problem with such outlines of the development of the sociology of education is quite simply that they do not cover the majority of research and publications in what most people would accept as the sociology of education. A rapid review of sociological books on education and articles published in the sociological and educational academic journals shows that the bulk of such publications do not follow the neat progression implied by the 'stages of development' model. This is not to deny that the model is a fairly reasonable indication of how the discipline has been presented to others at the various historical periods since the war. The 'best known' research at any period has certainly followed this pattern. The partial dependence that the sociology of education has had on teacher education to provide an audience for its work, for example, has meant that what has been 'in fashion' has been influenced by changing perceptions of what constitutes teacher education. The rapid expansion of classroom research, for example, was heavily influenced by the demands for 'greater relevance' in the early 1970s. The Open University has also played a major part in the promotion of 'fashionable' work in British sociology of education. Since the early 1970s it has published a succession of courses in the area, each with a different emphasis, from the symbolic interaction and classroom orientation of early courses through to the more Marxist and education policy orientation of recent work. The Open University units and readers which form the core of each course have been widely used by students and their teachers in many universities and colleges, and have often been viewed as authoritative summaries of the field. It should also be remembered that sociology of education has not been the only academic subject area to experience these changes in fashion. They are also clearly evident in the parent discipline of sociology, and several other sub-disciplinary areas have also passed through similar changes. The sociology of deviance is one area to show a fairly similar shift in fashion from traditional criminology, through interactionist perspectives to various forms of critical criminology, neo-Marxism and feminism.

What has often been forgotten is that while changes in fashion can be newsworthy, and indeed the news-reporters may amplify the changes to generate interest (for example, The Open University), the majority of researchers do not follow changes of fashion. They usually go on wearing their old clothes, watching each succeeding generation don the current fad. They are aware that if they wait long enough their old clothes may come back into fashion, and that few of the new innovations are actually new anyway. Thus, within the sociology of education, political arithmetic and the social survey did not die in 1970, in fact, some of the leading protagonists were about to embark on a major new study (Halsey, Heath and Ridge, 1980, 1984). The old issues of social class inequality, home/school relations and educational achievement may have been developed and refined since the early days of sociology of education, but they have never ceased to be areas of active research and are experiencing something of a resurgence in wider interests at the moment (for example, Rogers, 1986; Reynolds, 1985). In the same way, there are those who find symbolic interactionism profitable (Woods, 1983) many years after the death of the perspective had been announced (Sharp and Green, 1975). Nor, of course, were the 'new' developments always actually new. As Burgess (1986, p. 202) notes, Floud and Halsey, back in 1961, had expressed their disappointment at the lack of sociological work on the curriculum, a view backed by Stenhouse as early as 1963. In a similar way the roots of symbolic interactionism and the ethnographic case study lay with the Chicago School of Sociology between the two world wars (Bulmer, 1984), while those who looked to Marx or Gramsci could hardly be called up to date.

This is not the place to investigate the structuring process undergone by the sociology of education. My aim here is only to indicate that the linear model of the repeated overthrow of one paradigm by another is inadequate. The problem with it is not only that it fails to take account of the wide variety of research that has been regularly conducted since the war, but also that it tends to overemphasize the differences between the various forms of research and research methods. Functionalism is contrasted with Marxism, quantitative methods contrasted with qualitative methods and the social survey contrasted with the ethnographic case study. Now at the level of theoretical perspective there may well, of course, be a fundamental conflict, but at the level of research method there are similarities as well as differences. There are many elements of the process of conducting research in the sociology of education that are common to the various methods used. Whether the researcher is using postal questionnaires, interview surveys, unstructured interviews or participant observation there are basic similarities to the process that would be recognised by all. Some of these similarities are explored in the chapters of this book.

Fundamentally, doing research is a profoundly pragmatic and down-to-earth activity. Individuals and groups try as best they can to grapple with the innumerable problems that confront them in their task, working within practical, personal, financial and time constraints imposed upon them to produce research reports which are as sound and propitious as possible. Where text books on research methods usually give normative advice on how research should proceed in an 'ideal' environment, the real world of research is one of constraint and compromise. The nature of the various compromises to be made will vary with the research project and may well change in importance as the research progresses. Finance is nearly always a major constraint which necessitates some compromise to be made between what the researcher would ideally wish to do, and what is possible. In social survey research, for example, the amount of funding crucially influences the possible sample size, but it also constrains the amount of pilot work conducted, the efforts made to reduce non-response, the depth of analysis of the data that is possible and so on. In a somewhat similar way, in ethnographic research financial compromises can determine the amount of time spent in the field, the extent to which interviews can be fully transcribed and the extent to which the observer can truly participate in the life-style of those he or she is studying. Time is also a fundamental constraint that impinges on all research. This is not just time in the field or time gathering data, but also extends into the analysis stage, the development of theory and the writing and publication of research reports. It is always possible for the researcher to gather more data, follow up more references, do more detailed statistical analysis, refine a developing theory, re-write a chapter draft once again and so on, but in each case a line has to be drawn and a decision taken to stop, or no report would ever get published. Few researchers are ever entirely happy with their own work once it is in cold print, for they recognise that a trade-off had to be made in terms of quality for their work ever to get to that stage. This particular stark conflict faces all researchers whether involved in qualitative or quantitative work and perhaps especially those involved in the development of theory. Providing they have a good library, the latter, however, are not usually faced by the myriad of practical problems that beset those involved in empirical work. The empirical researcher is often overwhelmed by the daily round of research problems, each one of which, although trivial, must be overcome or dealt with in some way. For an ethnographer the problem of access may be personified by the teacher who refuses to allow the observer into the classroom, while for those involved with social surveys it may involve the construction of an adequate sampling frame or the threat of a boycott of questionnaires by a trade union's members. With longitudinal work, whether it be qualitative or quantitative, the researcher is forced to deal with the inappropriateness and inadequacies of data gathered in an earlier social context and often for different purposes than those for which the data are now to be used. Here, as elsewhere, decision and compromise are the essence of the research process.

Further compromises that must sometimes be made if research is to be conducted and published involve complicated questions of politics and ethics. Here it is not simply a matter of the choice between 'overt' and 'covert' research, for such a dichotomy is a gross simplification of the reality of the continuous decision-making process that accompanies research. Even in the most 'open' of research procedures, where there is sustained negotiation between researchers and researched, it is quite impossible to avoid all political and ethical problems. The essence of research, after all, is concerned with the uncovering of what is not known, and that cannot be predicted in advance. Should the researcher only publish what those researched wish to be known, or might there be some occasions when the public's 'need to know' has priority? Indeed, some authors go further than this, agreeing with Becker (1964) that 'A study that purports to deal with social structure ... inevitably will reveal that the organization or community is not all it claims to be, not all it would like to be able to feel itself to be. A good study, therefore, will make someone angry'. Such dilemmas have only recently begun to be discussed in research methods text books. Many of the textbooks still widely used in both undergraduate and postgraduate teaching present a model of conducting research which is akin to following a recipe from a cook-book.

The aim of the contributions collected together in this book is to get 'beneath the surface' (Fletcher, 1974) of some of the ways in which research is currently conducted in the sociology of education. Each of the authors has been involved with a major research project and here reflects not only upon the trials and tribulations, problems and promises of that particular piece of research, but on the links between what is possible in research and personal idiosyncrasies and circumstances. Research is revealed as a much more complicated

process than many would expect, sometimes more messy and dis-
organized, sometimes constrained in ways unexpected, but always
challenging to the researcher and, hopefully, to the reader.

The book seeks to place itself in what is becoming a strong
tradition of books concerned to allow the reader to appreciate the
practical and human aspects of doing research in the social sciences.
In sociology and ethnography the genre has a respectable history
going back at least to the publication of *Middletown in Transition* in
1937 (Lynd and Lynd). The Guide to Further Reading at the end of
this book gives a list of some of the major previous contributions in
the area, but it is generally agreed that the collection by Hammond
(1964) was of key significance, even though some of the articles now
seem somewhat cautious and constrained. Within British sociology
one of the earliest similar collections of accounts was that edited by
Colin Bell and Howard Newby in *Doing Sociological Research*
(1977). They consciously set out to produce a British version of
Hammond's work, which would describe the process of doing research and unveil some of the idiosyncrasies of person and circumst-
ance which they saw as being at the heart of the enterprise. However, while the articles in Hammond (1964) had been cautious, some
of the articles in the collection by Bell and Newby (1977) might
have been chosen for their sensational value. One contributor conducted covert research in scientology meetings and then used private
mailing lists for a sample survey; another had to deal with all the
problems of negotiating with the Home Office and the Official
Secrets Act in researching prisoners in a high security prison; while
Bell himself recounted the problems of conducting a large scale
restudy with three researchers, two of whom were directly from
undergraduate study and the third with limited postgraduate experience, living a long distance from the university base and the project
director. In such circumstances the problems of conducting research
were bound to dominate the articles. Bell later went on to co-edit
two further similar collections of reflexive accounts (Bell and Encel,
1978; Bell and Roberts, 1984) and a collection on feminist research
was published by Roberts (1981).

Few of the articles in these collections on sociological research
were concerned with sociology of education. Indeed the only article
on education intended for inclusion in Bell and Newby (1977) was
not published due to possible libel actions and a modified version
has only recently appeared (Punch, 1986). Nevertheless there have
now been several collections (the most important of which are those
by Shipman (1976) and Burgess (1984b) which present the practical

and human side of doing educational research and the sociology of education. This book seeks to develop this tradition established in Britain by Bell and others whilst, at the same time, presenting accounts from authors representing a wide range of methodological perspectives and substantive issues.

The collection includes chapters which describe the conduct of large-scale surveys, as well as others which are concerned with small-scale ethnographic case studies. Other chapters concentrate on the process of conducting more theoretical and policy-based work, while accounts of action research and the process of dissemination of research are also included. As might be expected the range leads to considerable differences in the style and tone of the various chapters, but all of the authors are united in their concern to illuminate the personal activity of conducting research, structured as it is by the numerous constraints and opportunities that surround the researcher.

The Chapters

The first five chapters are all concerned with various aspects of the process of doing ethnographic or field research. The first chapter, by Andy Hargreaves, gives an account of the way in which he conducted research in two middle schools. He describes the ways in which the research area was shaped and developed by changing circumstances and by changing theoretical interests. In particular, a planned second phase to the work had to be abandoned because of the effective withdrawal of support by one of the schools. An unusual feature of the chapter is a section where Hargreaves looks at the process of writing up the work for a doctoral degree, and the way in which this was influenced by changing personal circumstances. He also shows that the process of converting the thesis into a book was not without its problems — the constraints imposed by publishers differ considerably from those demanded by university examiners.

The problems of gaining and maintaining access are also prominently featured in the chapter by Geoffrey Walford which is concerned with ethnographic fieldwork in two major independent boarding schools. The chapter concentrates on the conflicts that arise and the compromises that have to be made in adopting various fieldwork roles. He emphasizes that the only fieldwork roles that are initially open to researchers are ones that are recognized and accepted by those with whom the researcher interacts. While these can be modified and negotiated over time, the roles adopted restrict the possible areas of research.

The following chapter by Robert G. Burgess presents an almost unique analysis of the problems and possibilities inherent in conducting an ethnographic 'restudy'. The original study of a Catholic comprehensive secondary school was conducted in the mid 1970s, initially for a doctoral degree and later for a book. Contact with the school was maintained after the end of the study, and a decade later the opportunity was taken to return to the school. Burgess discusses in detail the extent to which these two fieldwork sites were in fact the 'same', and looks at the constraints and advantages of conducting 'longitudinal' ethnographic research.

In the fourth chapter Andrew Pollard returns us to middle schools. His chapter is concerned with the methods that he used to gain information from 9 to 12-year-old children about their social world. Again, the study was originally undertaken for a doctoral degree, but with the major difference that the work was conducted on a part-time basis, and that the children involved were pupils at the school where Pollard taught. This posed particular problems and many unique advantages, but also imposed restrictions on the form of research that was possible. A particular feature of the research was the use of a group of these pupils as 'research assistants' advising the researcher, interviewing each other, and interviewing other children in their year group. The strengths and weaknesses of this 'collaborative triangulation' are examined.

The chapter by Denis Gleeson and George Mardle provides an account of the research procedures used in their study of a local Further Education College. The research was based on a period of participant observation in one college. The authors provide some insights into the theoretical and practical problems involved in conducting such case study research. They consider problems of entry, building research relationships and testing the validity of data, and discuss the ways in which their research caused them to modify their initial assumptions and premises. They give particular emphasis to the constraints put upon researchers by those who are researched and the way they found that as one new channel of information opened, so another previously established channel would close. Somewhat unusually, they also consider the process of writing up their research.

Chapter 6 discusses the very different area of action research in sociology of education, which has a long and distinguished pedigree and includes the Educational Priority Area research which followed the Plowden Report. In this chapter Judith Byrne Whyte reports on the Girls Into Science and Technology (GIST) project which was based in ten schools in Manchester. The project had the twin aims of trying to understand the reasons for girls dropping scientific and technical subjects and simultaneously attempting to reduce this drop-out and modify the sex-stereotyping of subject choice. She focuses on four research issues. First, the tensions between action and research goals; second, the ethical framework for researcher/ teacher relationships; third, the appropriateness of the methodology used in this particular context; and finally, the way that GIST has been reported and disseminated, and the implications for policy-oriented research.

The issues of reporting and dissemination are of central importance to the chapter by Neville Bennett. His book *Teaching Styles and Pupil Progress* was published in an orgy of press and academic coverage in the mid–1970s and was the subject of much controversy. Briefly, the book reported findings from a study of a relatively small, but representative, sample of teachers and their pupils in Lancashire and Cumbria. It examined teaching styles and found that on standardized tests of arithmetic, English and reading children who were exposed to formal or mixed teaching showed greater gains than those exposed to informal methods. Bennett discusses the problems of dissemination of research in such a highly charged policy area, concentrating particularly on the role of the media in the process. The second part of the chapter is concerned with theoretical developments relating to the study of teaching and learning in classroom settings. Bennett now sees studies of teaching styles as being unlikely to lead to improvements in teaching, and regards them as a theoretical cul-de-sac. He outlines some of his more recent work based on a task model where children are seen as constructivist learners operating within complex social settings.

Controversy also greeted the publication of the research with which chapter 8 is concerned. Jane Steedman writes about a statistical study to investigate the progress of a national sample of children as they passed through comprehensive or selective schools. The study was based upon the National Child Development Study longitudinal data set which contains information on children born in Great Britain in one week in 1958. Information is available on a wide range of topics for the early years of life, at 7, at 11, at 16, and at 18, thus enabling progress as well as performance to be evaluated. Steedman discusses the factors that made the study worth doing, the constraints on design of the study dictated by the data set, other practical difficulties, the influences that operated to make the reports take the form they did, and the reception that the findings were given. The problems of relating research to policy questions are also considered.

Chapter 9, by four researchers at the Centre for Educational Sociology, University of Edinburgh, is also concerned with large-scale statistical survey work. Here the data base is a series of national postal surveys of school leavers in Scotland conducted on a regular basis since the early 1970s. The paper describes the development of the Scottish survey series, focusing particularly on the relationship between the aims of government and the technical means required by researchers. The authors explain the various difficulties of obtaining sampling frames and adequate response rates, and show that these problems lead to an over-optimistic account of the school system. They argue that even with high coverage rates, significant biases towards optimism remain in the data obtained. This alienation of young people from a survey on schooling, and other topics, may well be a function of their alienation from schooling itself.

The next chapter is different again, in that its author, Ronald King, is one of the few researchers in the sociology of education to have substantial experience of both quantitative and qualitative research. His past work ranges from a large-scale survey with over seventy secondary schools and 7500 pupils to detailed ethnographic work in infants' school classrooms. King gives an account of the ways in which each of his five major projects was conducted and argues that there is no best method in the sociology of education, only suitable and feasible methods. He sees it as the task of the sociology of education to deliver the 'sociological news' — empirically realized interpretations of what has been shown to happen — and to use whatever methods are appropriate in that task.

The final three chapters of the book are more concerned with the process of doing theoretical work in the sociology of education — a process very rarely discussed in any of the literature. Graham Vulliamy's work on music education was one of the first attempts to theorize about the school curriculum to be influenced by the 'new' sociology of education and M.F.D. Young's *Knowledge and Control*. Vulliamy shows the ways in which developing theory, in his case, was greatly influenced by aspects of his own biography and by the writings of others. Ideas were clarified through conflict with other theorists, and the scope of the theory enlarged in response to more Marxist critiques to link with wider interests in dominant ideologies. The creation of theory thus emerges as a very personal enterprise, in which developments are highly circumscribed by disciplinary, institutional and biographical factors.

This aspect of the interaction of the personal with the process of doing research is echoed in chapter 12 by Miriam E. David, who gives an account of her various research experiences and her growing commitment to feminism. Her early research was concerned with the analysis of large-scale statistical survey data, first at the level of administration of data collection and low level analysis of data for a study of mental illness, and later, with greater responsibility, for a study into gambling as a social activity. This was followed by a case study of decision making in local education authorities based largely on semi-structured interviews, then a related study of budgetary processes in four school districts in the U.S.A. Taking each of these studies in turn, David shows the ways in which sexism intruded into the research at every stage. Her developing feminism has led her to use an explicitly feminist perspective in her more recent work. She argues for a non-sexist approach to both methodology and analysis where all biases on the basis of sex are eliminated and where research, whilst being sensitized to the problems of sexism, is sex-neutral or sex-blind.

The final chapter by Patricia Broadfoot widens the discussion to include a consideration of the compromises that sociology of education as an academic discipline is increasingly making to accomodate to a changing social context. Broadfoot uses her account of her own involvement in research into pupil profiling to discuss the different kinds of theory being generated by sociologists of education. These are, first, that which emanates from and extends sociological questions about the nature of social life as evinced in the educational process and, second, that theory which seeks to apply social scientific methods to a specific initiative or problem. Broadfoot argues that sociologists of education are likely to find themselves increasingly tied to substantive topic areas rather than to the base discipline, and that this will lead to a changed relationship between practice and theory. This changing context may mean that sociologists of education will once again have a chance to operate in close partnership with policy makers, but it will be a changed sociology of education where there will be not only new kinds of theory but also new ways of making theory. Her vision is that of a sociology of education where theory is more applied and integrally connected in both its generation and purpose with practice itself.

The chapters in this book are thus concerned with a wide range of research, and one of the aims of this collection is to illustrate the diversity of methods and substantive topic areas that is to be found within current sociology of education. A more important aim, however, is to provide a set of accounts of the process of conducting research, written by the authors of recent and significant studies, where each author reflects critically on that research process. It is hoped that the publication of such accounts will be helpful to students, teachers, lecturers, and all those who use academic research, helping them to understand how research is produced and thus being in a better position to evaluate its findings and recommendations. It is also hoped that the collection will be of significant interest to fellow researchers in sociology of education, for the publication of reflexive accounts of real research, which illustrate the constraints and opportunities of research and the ways in which these influence the final reports, should lead to greater discussion and openness about the process of doing sociology of education. It is hoped that this book will thus, in a modest way, help to generate more high quality research in the sociology of education.

References

ALTHUSSER, L (1971) *For Marx*, London, New Left Books.

APPLE, M.W. (1979) *Ideology and Curriculum*, London, Routledge and Kegan Paul.

APPLE, M.W. (Ed.) (1982) *Cultural and Economic Reproduction in Education*, London, Routledge and Kegan Paul.

BECKER, H.S. (1964) 'Problems in the publication of field studies', in VIDICH, A., BENSMAN, J. and STEIN, M.R. (Eds) *Reflections on Community Studies*, New York, Wiley.

BELL, C. and ENCEL, S. (Eds) (1978) *Inside the Whale. Ten personal accounts of social research*, Rushcutters Bay, New South Wales, Pergamon Press.

BELL, C. and NEWBY, H. (Eds) (1977) *Doing Sociological Research*, London, Allen and Unwin.

BELL, C. and ROBERTS, H. (Eds) (1984) *Social Researching. Politics, Problems, Practice*, London, Routledge and Kegan Paul.

BOWLES, S. and GINTIS, H. (1976) *Schooling in Capitalist America*, London, Routledge and Kegan Paul.

BULMER, M. (1984) *The Chicago School of Sociology*, Chicago, Chicago University Press.

BURGESS, R.G. (1984a) 'Exploring frontiers and setting territory: Shaping the sociology of education', Review Essay, *British Journal of Sociology*, 35, 1, pp. 122–137.

BURGESS, R.G. (1984b) (Ed.) *The Research Process in Educational Settings: Ten Case Studies*, Lewes, Falmer Press.

BURGESS, R.G. (1986) *Sociology, Education and Schools*, London, Batsford.

COOPER, B. (1985) *Renegotiating Secondary School Mathematics: A Study of Curriculum Change and Stability*, Lewes, Falmer Press.

FLETCHER, C. (1974) *Beneath the Surface. An Account of Three Styles of Sociological Research*, London, Routledge and Kegan Paul.

FLOUD, J. and HALSEY, A.H. (1961) 'Introduction' in HALSEY, A.H., FLOUD J. and ANDERSON, C.A. (Eds) *Education, Economy and Society*, New York, Free Press.

GOODSON, I.F. (1983) *School Subjects and Curriculum Change*, Beckenham, Croom Helm.

GOODSON, I.F. (Ed.) (1985), *Social Histories of the Secondary Curriculum: Subjects for Study*, Lewes, Falmer Press.

HALSEY, A.H., HEATH, A.F. and RIDGE, J.M. (1980) *Origins and Destinations*, Oxford, Oxford University Press.

HALSEY, A.H., HEATH, A.F. and RIDGE, J.M. (1984) 'The political arithmetic of public schools' in WALFORD G. (Ed.) *British Public Schools: Policy and Practice*, Lewes, Falmer Press.

HAMMOND, P.E. (Ed.) (1964) *Sociologists at Work*, New York, Basic Books.

LAYTON, D. (1973) *Science for the People*, London, Allen and Unwin.

LYND, R.S. and LYND, H.M. (1937) *Middletown in Transition*, New York, Harcourt Brace.

MCCULLOCH, G., JENKINS, E. and LAYTON, D. (1984) *Technological Revolution? The Politics of School Science and Technology in England and Wales since 1945*, Lewes, Falmer Press.

PUNCH, M. (1985) *The Politics and Ethics of Fieldwork. Muddy Boots and Grubby Hands*, London, Sage.

REYNOLDS, D. (Ed.) (1985) *Studying School Effectiveness*, Lewes, Falmer Press.

ROBERTS, H. (Ed.) (1981) *Doing Feminist Research*, London, Routledge and Kegan Paul.

ROGERS, R. (Ed.) (1986) *Education and Social Class*, Lewes, Falmer Press.

SHARP, R. and GREEN A. (1975) *Education and Social Control*, London, Routledge and Kegan Paul.

STENHOUSE, L. (1963) 'A cultural approach to the study of the curriculum', *Pedagogisk Forskning*, 3, pp. 120–134. Reprinted in STENHOUSE, L. (1983) *Authority, Education and Emancipation*, London, Heinemann.

WALFORD, G. (1985) 'The construction of a curriculum area: science in society', *British Journal of Sociology of Education*, 6, 2, pp. 155–171.

WARING, M. (1979) *Social Pressures and Curriculum Innovation: a study of the Nuffield Foundation Science Teaching Project*, London, Methuen.

WILLIS, P. (1977) *Learning to Labour*, Farnborough, Saxon House.

WOODS, P. (1983) *Sociology of the School: An Interactionist Viewpoint*, London, Routledge and Kegan Paul.

YOUNG, M.F.D. (1971) (Ed.) *Knowledge and Control*, London, Collier-Macmillan.

1 Past, Imperfect, Tense: Reflections on an Ethnographic and Historical Study of Middle Schools

Andy Hargreaves

> When at the first I took my pen in hand,
> Thus for to write, I did not understand
> That I at all should make a little book
> In such a mode; nay, I had undertook
> To make another, which when almost done,
> Before I was aware, I this begun.

So wrote John Bunyan in 'The Author's Apology for His Book' at the commencement of *The Pilgrim's Progress*. I have some sympathy with how he felt. Except amongst the most inflexible, the process of social research is, like the skills of navigating among the Trukese 'argonauts' of the South Pacific described by Gladwin (1964), one which involves a continuous process of *ad hoc* adjustment and realignment, major and minor changes of course and speed, appropriate responses to the onset of unexpected adversity, and so on. Unlike the Trukese, however, who almost invariably succeed in reaching their desired destination, for the social researcher it is often not just the route that changes, but the destination too. When the research voyage must be undertaken alone, as ethnography and historical enquiry commonly are, and with the minimum of appropriate previous experience, as is the case with the majority of higher degree students, it presents not just technical challenges but deeply personal ones too. The purpose of a research biography is to unfold and retrieve the technical, personal and social aspects of this ever-changing research process, not just as a procedure for expiating methodological sins (though there is something to be said for that), but for illustrating how irremediably social (a point of strength as well as weakness) the process of social research actually is.

This research biography is of a doctoral study of *English Middle Schools* (Hargreaves, 1985) published in revised form as *Two Cultures of Schooling: the case of middle schools* by Falmer Press in 1986. This was not just a study of middle schools as such. It also sought to examine, clarify and develop links between 'micro and macro' levels of analysis in the sociology of education — using middle schools as a critical case. Much of the emphasis of the final thesis was therefore directed towards showing and developing links between theory and evidence, school and society, policy and practice, and history and ethnography. Yet when the study commenced, no such theoretical ambitions were entertained. 'Micro-macro' integration was not an issue within the study. Indeed, at this time, it was scarcely an issue of theoretical importance within the subdiscipline at all. More than this, in substantive terms, the original study was not even meant to be about middle schools. I scarcely knew what they were, in fact. This research biography, therefore, is a retrospective attempt to chart the changing course of this study amid strong and often cross-cutting theoretical currents in the subdiscipline; and in the context of shifting practical interests and possibilities, too. Like all biographies, the account is a selective one. Fuller (though of course, still not exhaustive) accounts of the fieldwork — particularly of the issues involved in doing comparative ethnography — are available in the methodological appendix to the original thesis. Here I want to focus more on issues bearing upon the overall course and direction of educational research projects and in particular those encountered in the process of analysis and writing up.

Origins

My study, supported by an SSRC studentship at the University of Leeds, began as a rather abstractly phrased venture to explore the 'relationship between different kinds of educational experience and different individual constructions of reality'. It was my contention that the structure of people's educational experience in terms of classification and framing (Bernstein 1971) would significantly affect the ways in which they later construed and responded to other life experiences. My 'critical case', as I would now call it, for testing this thesis would be an examination of the educational backgrounds and experiences of politically radical and non-radical students in higher education. This proposal did not directly follow from any specific interests I had been pursuing in the sociology of education component of my undergraduate sociology degree at Sheffield University three years earlier. Apart from some discussion of the deschoolers and Jackson and Marsden's *Education and the Working Class* (1962) the sociology of education course I studied was predominantly concerned with issues of educational access and opportunity within a rather atheoretical tradition of political arithmetic. This was much less attractive to me than work in sociology more generally which engaged more directly with and tried to make sense of people's everyday experience — the writings of Schur, Szasz, Matza, Douglas and Lemert in 'social problems' and radical and humanistic traditions in 'social psychology'. When, as a result of a 'chance' conversation with a fellow student, I 'discovered' the 'new sociology of education' (Young 1971) and other related work (D. Hargreaves, 1967; Barnes, Britton & Rosen, 1968) during study for my Postgraduate Certificate in Education, I felt, at last, that I had begun to find ways of linking experientially-directed approaches in sociological theory to the process of education in particular.

My research proposal, constructed during primary teaching in the following year, drew heavily on Michael Young's and Basil Bernstein's contributions to *Knowledge and Control* (1971), and over the first few weeks I expanded my knowledge of interpretive sociology by reading widely in sociolinguistics, phenomenology (Schutz, 1973), ethnomethodology (e.g., Turner, 1974) and more eclectic interpretive syntheses (e.g., Berger and Luckman, 1966), as well as early attempts at interpretive forms of educational inquiry (e.g., Hammersley, 1974). Through this, I developed a heightened resolve to adopt a broadly qualitative approach to whatever it was I eventually chose to study: I wanted very much to get inside the 'black box' of schooling. In addition, though, I was now also aware that notwithstanding all its other advantages, interpretive sociology, particularly ethnomethodology, often neglected the role that power and constraint played within and upon social interaction. Though my unease was, at that stage, an inchoate one, in retrospect I can see that the seeds of my later, more extended, theoretical interest in 'micromacro' integration had now been sown.

Following this theoretical review, a substantive focus for the research now had to be chosen. Because of the decline of 'student militancy' as a public issue at the time and because of my developing interest in the analysis of *school* processes in particular (a result of my initial reading) — these things, together with my supervisor's advice, led to my dropping the initial interest in higher education students. Instead, drawing on my own brief experience and dilemmas as a primary teacher of trying to operate something my head called an 'integrated day' curriculum, and recognising that what classroom research there was to date had tended to be concerned mainly with *secondary* education, I settled upon a comparative case study of a 'traditional' and 'progressive' primary school with a view to examining how the educational experiences of the pupils in each of the schools subsequently affected their response to and interpretation of secondary education. Already, while the theoretical problem had remained constant, the empirical one had now changed very substantially.

Selecting Cases

For fieldwork purposes, I wanted to select two contrasting primary schools which would differ on progressive/traditional lines. There were no existing relevant survey data to help guide this selection (a common problem of case study), so I drew up a number of observable characteristics such as type of building (open-plan or classroom-based), degree of emphasis on ritual (types of assemblies, regulations regarding school uniform), and openness or closedness of the timetable, as possible criteria for the initial selection.

Both wider preliminary sampling (to identify the eventual cases which would best approximate to the initial criteria) and the whole problem of gaining access to schools were potentially difficult given that I was based in a *sociology* (not an education) department, with little continuing contact with schools. When my supervisor informed me that he was a member of the joint governing body of two adjacent middle schools feeding into a common upper school, this therefore seemed an ideal opportunity to circumvent these difficulties, and to bypass other more formal and time-consuming procedures of getting into schools too (involving formal consent of the LEA, etc.). If I had not been able to 'case the joints' (Schatzman & Strauss, 1973) myself, I had been able to do so vicariously through my supervisor and thereby establish some grounds for typicality. At the same time, while access to the schools was not yet absolutely guaranteed, my supervisor's connection with them seemed to make acceptance very likely. Similarly, his involvement in local politics and his role as a (somewhat influential) parent in the receiving upper school, cleared the way for the head of that school to grant formal permission for me to do some small-scale follow-up work there later in the year. At this stage, I was extremely pleased with how well this informal network appeared to be serving me. Access had been secured — the 'Hierarchy of Consent' (Dingwall, 1981) had been bypassed.

A typed research outline prepared for an initial 'clearing' meeting with the two headteachers involved, contained several references to 'middle schools' and 'middle years of childhood', but these were inserted very much at my supervisor's suggestion. At the time, their inclusion seemed to me to be largely cosmetic. I had yet to appreciate the distinctive difficulties such schools encountered by virtue of their middle school status. In addition to these references to middle school issues, I promised anonymity, offered assurances that I had no research interest in 'invidiously comparative' rates of educational achievement, and stressed the research's focus on curriculum process. The second part of the outline then listed the methods I proposed to use during the study.

While both heads expressed some worries about the dangers of comparison, the problems of generalizability (they used the term 'validity') of case study research, and my underestimation of the importance of differences in size between the two schools, they nonetheless welcomed me warmly into their schools for the approaching summer term. I would have to secure the formal approval of their staffs, of course, and this was subsequently done at staff meetings in each school where I outlined my research intentions and dealt with questions and queries. But for all practical purposes it seemed to me that satisfactory access had now been gained. Fieldwork 'proper' could commence. At this stage of the research, following the selection of cases and the gaining of access, I was not aware of any imminent shift in the focus of the study. But it would soon become strongly apparent during the fieldwork that the choice of cases and the arrangements for access would have huge ramifications for the ensuing direction of the study.

Fieldwork

In describing the fieldwork, I want to pursue the implications of these two issues for the course of the research in some detail. My account of the fieldwork is therefore highly selective, and those who wish to look at other important aspects of the fieldwork in this study — the problems of doing comparative ethnography, the arrangements for sampling within the field, my own field role, etc.

— should again consult the thesis appendix. Here, the briefest summary of such issues must suffice.

Background

Fieldwork took place during the whole of the summer term, 1975. Though apparently briefer than many other school ethnographies which stretch to a period of a year or more (e.g. Willis, 1977; Woods, 1979; Ball, 1981; Burgess, 1983), the intensity of the fieldwork (five days per week) meant that the overall field-work time of a little over sixty days was not dissimilar from and in some cases greater than a number of other studies (e.g. Hammersley, 1984; Delamont, 1984). Were the intention to undertake a full-blown ethnography of one particular school, I would still regard this as rather brief. The aim, however, was to try and identify contrasts and links between different settings and to that end, *depth* of exploration was to some extent sacrificed for *breadth* of coverage. All research involves such trade-offs, and given its place within a wider research programme, I do not regard the duration of fieldwork in the study as unjustifiably short.

A mixture of methods was adopted. I wished to gain access to a variety of natural settings in which curriculum was discussed and enacted, to get an awareness of the contextual variability of actions and accounts within the schools; and to relate pupils' and teachers' stated perspectives to their classroom practice. This, it seemed to me, called for observation of a range of natural settings — classroom interaction, staff meetings, parents' evenings, etc. — and interviews with the leading participants — heads, teachers and pupils.

Examining such a range of settings across two schools entailed making difficult decisions about data sampling within the field. As Hammersley and Atkinson, (1983, p. 46) point out, there are three dimensions to consider within such sampling: *time, people* and *context*. The sampling of *contexts* has just been examined; time and people will be dealt with now. In terms of *time* within the school year, given the initial research intention to follow a group of pupils through into secondary (upper school) in the autumn term, the fieldwork had to be compressed into the summer term. This explains the unusually intensive nature of the fieldwork programme. I suspected that kind of intensity might create difficulties: insufficient time out of the field for analytical reflection on the data, for progressive focusing on to more closely defined issues, for sampling of contexts according to emerging theoretical concerns and so on (Glaser and Strauss, 1967). Most of the analysis was, as a result, done *after* fieldwork, not during it. For these reasons, I would not normally recommend such a research strategy to other fieldworkers. However, even with the benefit of hindsight, it is difficult to see, given the overall research purpose at the time, how things might reasonably have been otherwise.

Within the summer term, I allocated my time between the two schools according to an overlapping time frame (Schatzman and Strauss, 1973), undertaking three whole days fieldwork in each school in turn, so that all days, times of day and points of term were covered in each case.

In terms of *people*, I devoted the majority of my classroom observation time (around 75 per cent) to the third and fourth year groups, the ones closest to the point of upper school transfer, a major element of my initial research interest. To the extent that my final account of Riverdale's and Moorhead's curricula and their participants' perception of it is more comprehensive for the third and fourth year groups, that is in part because of this initial research emphasis.

Twenty fourth year pupils (ten boys, ten girls), about to transfer to upper school, were also selected from each school at random, for interviewing. Both heads were interviewed, as were all thirteen staff at Riverdale middle school. No more than a 50 per cent staff sample could be interviewed there. Given that it was not yet known which particular factors would have the strongest bearing on differences in teachers' perspectives, this sample was therefore selected at random.

My fieldwork role was less than that of a fully fledged participant but something more than entirely non-participant too (a term which, as Burgess (1982) points out, is in any case rather misleading, since the most fly-like, wall-bound observers tend to get drawn into the proceedings of the field from time to time). My overall aim was to minimize any participant role that approximated to that of teacher, since I needed to build open relationships with both teachers *and* pupils. Relationships of the latter kind often require fieldworkers to ditch their practical teaching role (D. Hargreaves, 1967)[1]. My general strategy was to offer auxiliary help, particularly towards the end of fieldwork when most of my data had been collected, by accompanying school trips, supervising pupils going to the swimming baths and so forth. It seemed only fair to offer some practical assistance, however small, in return for the school's readiness to accommodate my research interests. What kind of person would a social researcher be who felt no such guilt nor the need to appease it in some way! Similarly, I offered individual pupils help with their schoolwork when it was sought, provided this was on a small scale and that it helped rather than hindered good field relations. Broadly speaking, then, this was the methodological approach I adopted within the school case studies.

For reasons of space, this outline has been a somewhat cursory one. But there are two issues arising from the fieldwork that I do want to discuss in more detail, for they were ones that had a major bearing on the course and direction of the study. The first concerns issues that were opened up as a result of the exploratory nature of the methodological approach, and its capacity to identify central (and from the researcher's point of view, unexpected) problems and concerns of the participants involved. The second concerns issues and possibilities that were closed down as the original access arrangements rebounded upon later fieldwork opportunities.

1. The 'Discovery' of Middle Schools

A commonly remarked advantage of ethnography and of case study work in particular is its relative openness compared to other methodological approaches; its sensitivity to the meanings, concerns and interpretations of participants in the field. More than any other method, ethnography does not prejudge what the most important research issues are going to be. It does not question people about matters which may not concern them. It does not impose its own limited frameworks of meaning and interpretation on the participants through closed schedules, attitude scales, questionnaires, etc. based on pre-existing hypotheses. Ethnography, that is, suffers little from the 'outsider's arrogance' that is often attributed by people in schools to those researchers who, for a brief time, come and work among them.[2]

Of course, ethnographers do not and probably should not commence their work with a blank conceptual sheet, with no theoretical starting points in mind. But, sensitively conducted, the ethnographic approach should not only allow such starting points to be clarified, refined and tested, but should also enable new and unexpected issues in the field to emerge: necessitating the consideration and development of other theories where appropriate (Glaser and Strauss, 1967).

In my own research, this kind of process led to a radical shift in the overall direction and focus of the project. Substantively, the project began as a comparative study of 'traditional' and 'progressive' primary schools and the effects of the differing educational experience they offered on pupils' subsequent response to their common upper school education. The first seeds of doubt about the appropriateness of this focus were first sown in my mind when I presented an outline of my research intentions to staff meetings at each of the two schools before 'fieldwork proper', as it were, commenced. In these presentations, I described the study as being of primary schools, as if the word 'primary' were synonymous with 'middle'. For this misjudgement, I received a number of interjections from the teacher audience of 'middle', 'not primary; middle', 'it's a middle school'. Clearly, there were sensitivities here, aspects of teacher identity connected with middle school status that were very important.

The doubts that these initial reactions generated were further reinforced through later observational and interview work. In whole school curriculum meetings at one of the middle schools, for instance, there were references to and long discussions about 'the agony of the middle school; the basic dilemma', of staff having to choose between specialist and generalist teaching roles. During observation, differences in curriculum, setting, timetabling and even architecture between the 'top' and 'bottom' ends of the schools became strongly apparent. And in interview, a number of staff talked at length about the problems of their middle school's year system, the way it segregated staff in the upper and lower years respectively. As one teacher at Riverdale Middle put it —

> the first and second years come into very little contact with the third and fourth years. In this school, it's very much first and second — stop — third and fourth, which I personally don't think is a good thing. . . . .
> First and second years, I think we feel aggrieved that the third and fourth years are helped out as much as possible. You know, any extra staff then they get it. And yet, we're battling down here with the larger classes and we get very little help.

Similarly, a teacher at Moorhead stated that —

> I feel that the school is not integrated. There's definitely a second year, and a gap, and a third year and a gap, and a fourth year. And I don't think we work together.

Statements of this kind then, along with the evidence of observation and the discussion I witnessed in curriculum meetings, alerted me to the significance of middle schooling and divisions within the middle school as an issue of importance for the participants involved. This evidence, it should be borne in mind, emerged within the field and was not, through the pursuit of strongly prefixed concerns, 'forcibly extracted' through questioning etc. The importance of this distinction and its implications for the ways in which 'middle schooling' became one of the central issues of the research, can be seen by examining the structure and conduct of the staff interviews.

The teacher interviews were mainly constructed around a set of initial theoretical starting points. They were teachers' perceptions of and preferences regarding curriculum and pedagogy. Many of the categories in the schedule sought to identify teachers' perspectives on *curricular* matters, *pedagogical* matters and on their own *career* position (Esland, 1971), and, within the broad area of curriculum choice, to tease out their views on the *selection*, *organization* and *pacing* of classroom knowledge (Bernstein, 1971). In many respects then, the interview schedule was tightly structured, the questions were pre-set, the categories based on existing theory and so on. Yet many of the questions — on strengths, weaknesses, likes, dislikes and problems, for example — were of a deliberately general nature — designed to get at matters of high priority to the teachers themselves, rather than what might otherwise be contrived responses to questions on educational issues to which they may have previously given very little thought. Interviewing strategies of this sort have been criticized elsewhere by David Hargreaves (1978), who has argued that they can create apparent uncertainty and confusion in teachers' responses. Hargreaves takes issue in particular with a study by Sharp and Green (1975) which claimed to identify a number of uncertainties and a degree of confusion in the perspectives of a group of infant teachers. This, argues Hargreaves, appears to have resulted largely from the somewhat insensitive questions the teachers were asked: strange, difficult, abstract and decontextualized ones. While these may have been fair criticisms of the particular study Hargreaves was criticizing, I want to suggest that as a more general rule, there would be dangers in running together criticisms about *difficulty* and *strangeness* in questions like 'How does one notice what stage a child is at?' with other criticisms about *abstractness* and *decontextualization*[3]. For it is perfectly possible to put 'abstract', 'decontextualized' questions to teachers such as 'what do you regard as your greatest strengths as a teacher?', and perfectly possible these will yield sensible and expansive responses on issues which are important and relevant to those teachers, without these questions being at all 'difficult' or 'strange'. Questions which are easy and familiar do not also have to be concrete and contextualized. Indeed, to the extent that they possess the latter two characteristics, they always carry with them the danger of putting words, issues and priorities into teachers' mouths.

This brings me to the importance of the relatively general and open questioning strategy I adopted in my own study. For very many of the teachers' stated views on the year system, ability grouping, subject specialism, discipline and so on, which form the basis for later theoretical understandings of the middle school and of different types of teacher culture within it, were in fact given in response to general questions and not to specific prompts about middle school issues. These emerged very much as the teachers' own central concerns. It was this kind of methodological approach that produced the shift in the study's substantive focus towards middle school issues.

2. *The Termination of the Second Phase*

A further change of research focus was occasioned not by methodological openness, but by field closure, by the effective withdrawal of fieldwork opportunities which had actually been granted earlier. Paul Atkinson (1982) has proposed the intriguing methodological hypothesis that ease of access to the field is, by virtue of its sponsorship by (and therefore, presumably, perceived usefulness to) those in positions of power, inversely related to the quality of field relations. What might seem like an initial blessing can ultimately turn out to be a methodological curse. Though substantial work would need to be done to establish the exact conditions under which this hypothesis held, my own fieldwork experiences offer some support for it.

Although my supervisor's status as governor of the two schools certainly smoothed the process of access to the field, his association with my work, the access he would have to and use he might be able to make of any information I collected, created a basis of deep and continuing mistrust and suspicion among certain members of the Riverdale staff — the smaller of the two schools whose governors were therefore more visible, and the school where there were the strongest forms of conflict and unease between members of staff and the head about curricular policy. There was, said Mr. Pool, the seconded deputy head, a certain resentment on the part of some of the staff about my connection with this governor and about the fact that, notwithstanding my attendance at a staff meeting where staff approval for the project had been sought, a general sense that it was presented to them by the head as a 'fait accompli'.

Even so, in most cases, I was able to overcome the obstacles to trust and rapport posed by the nature of my access to the field. All the staff in the lower years, with the exception of Mr. Button (a teacher who had been temporarily moved there from years 3 and 4), were open and welcoming when I visited their bays, and enthusiastically suggested I accompany them on a lower school residential visit to the Yorkshire Dales. In the upper years Mrs. Weaver, the acting deputy, seemed happy to act as guide (an important initial informant) and explain the unfamiliar 'culture' of the school, its curriculum and organization, to someone as young and inexperienced as I; Miss Rogers, trained in and keen on drama, saw in me someone who had sympathy with her egalitarian and libertarian educational values; and Mr. Driver, a graduate scientist still in the process of writing up his Ph.D., responded to me very much as a fellow researcher and a defender of high academic standards (hence his 'knowing', disparaging remarks about his non-graduate colleagues, the obviousness of which it was assumed I would share). Even so, the most sensitive aspects of school life were withheld from me (most notably, an open and bitter conflict between staff and head about the following year's curriculum arrangements) lest it 'got back' to my supervisor. And, despite all efforts to the contrary, throughout the research I remained unable to mollify two particular members of staff in Riverdale's upper years. Mrs. Spencer, who was engaged in a protracted dispute with the head over promotion, referred to me throughout as 'CIA' and was guardedly vague in most of her interview responses. And Mr. Button, an Open University student who publicly voiced his worry in my first meeting with the school staff that I might be engaged in that kind of 'blame the teacher' approach to educational enquiry which characterized the writings of John Holt and others in the late 60s and early 70s, asked several times while he was being observed if he could glance at my fieldnotes; seeming somewhat disappointed when he could find no incriminating comments therein.

In numerical terms, these may only have been minor setbacks in the overall establishment of trust and rapport, but they might serve as lessons to other ethnographers who would do well, when offered the bait of easy access through having close contact with highly placed 'gatekeepers', to consider the implications it might subsequently have for their field relations. The importance of that advice becomes particularly evident when the second phase of the middle school research is examined.

The second phase of fieldwork, it will be recalled, was meant to involve interviews with and some observation of pupils from Riverdale and Moorhead who had just transferred to the upper school in the autumn term. Permission for this had, through an interview with the head, already been verbally agreed in summer, 1975. But when I returned in October to formalize the acceptance and clarify the conditions of my fieldwork, the head's attitude now struck me as very different: 'cagey', as I wrote in my field notes. I went on, 'he stated that interviews would have to be subject to parental approval: this could cause serious delay and difficulties' (Fieldnotes 14.10.75). The apparent about-turn in attitude towards the research and the strong and unexpected line he now appeared to be adopting in relation to parental consent was inexplicable to me at the time. My supervisor, however, offered a possible reason for this shift when he explained that the parental 'scotch' may have been a consequence of his own recent interference as a parent, when he 'raised a fuss' about them ignoring parents during the option choice process in which his own son had just been involved (Fieldnotes 15.10.75). Certainly the head's carefully phrased explanation of his changed position in terms of parental approval would offer some support for this interpretation of events. The resulting parental letter which, despite several requests, I was never allowed to see, yielded only a 50 per cent response rate. In a lengthy and heated conversation with the senior mistress, deputed by the head to handle this matter, I sought information on the reasons for refusal, requested permission to visit the parents myself to explain my purpose and so on, but all to no avail. Despondent, I endeavoured for a few days to press on interviewing the remainder of the sample regardless, but when the additional constraint that interviews must only take place in the lunch hour was imposed and some pupils unsurprisingly failed to turn up, it was obvious that there was little point in continuing. With a feeling of intense irritation and deep personal failure, I left the field, virtually data-less. There are issues here of access procedures and their consequences for field-relations, which would merit close consideration by others about to embark on ethnographic projects. Supervisors and intending graduate students please take note!

Despite the collapse of this phase of the research, however, I was not at a loss for alternative courses of action. Most of the middle school data awaited analysis, and much of it still needed to be transcribed. More than this, I had in the meantime become aware of the virtual absence of any research literature on what had, during the course of fieldwork, emerged as perhaps the most central and unexpected theme of the research: middle schools and middle schooling. I became anxious to know something about the nature, the background, the origins of this little-studied institution and so I turned to historical study in order to place the ethnography in some kind of context. At first, as I searched through back copies of the West Riding's *Schools Bulletin* for teachers in Leeds Reference Library, this historical investigation was but a minor accompaniment to the dominant ethnographic theme. After being made aware by Paul Sharp of Leeds University School of Education, of the existence of stored West Riding correspondence and memoranda within Leeds Education Museum, however, it began to occupy a major role within the thesis; one which would have important implications for the conduct of the ethnographic analysis too.

Because of methodological openness and field closure, then, the direction of the research had shifted dramatically. It was now concerned with middle schools, not primary schools. And instead of its initial preoccupation with the perspectives and experiences of transferring pupils, it began to focus on the links between middle school policy and practice. Moreover, as the substantive concerns shifted, so too did some of the theoretical ones, most notably during data analysis and writing up.

Analysis and Write-up

My first attempts at data analysis scored rather higher on theoretical creativity than they did on methodological exactitude. The second half of the 1970s was an exciting time for those working in British sociology of education. It was a time when many different approaches and perspectives were advanced. Yet amid all this excitement — and indeed as part of it — it seemed to me that there was a need for better theoretical coordination and clearer empirical support. A paper I wrote on classroom coping strategies (1978) was an attempt to achieve this, but while many of the theoretical insights that emerged during this exercise arose very much from the field work, the process of emergence was a somewhat mysterious one. It was not that the data were selected to illustrate any preconceived theory, but the principle of selection was governed more by an impetus towards creating interesting theoretical patterns, than by a concern for testing the accuracy, or the validity of theoretical claims.

At this time, as I was developing my work on coping strategies and sorting through historical data, I was also lecturing in a college of education. Here the hours committed to student contact made the sustained pursuit of any research difficult and what I tended to do, as one form of economy, was to try and secure as much overlap as possible between my teaching and research commitments. The (old style) B.Ed. courses I taught in sociology of education examined different sociological perspectives on education, and my attempt to compare and in some respects reconcile these grew out of my teaching needs as much as my research needs at this time, culminating in a renewed attempt at theoretical synthesis towards the end of my appointment (Hargreaves, 1980). Together, these theoretical interests along with the pressures of time and teaching drew me more into theory and away from my ethnographic data at this point (though I continued to busy myself with sorting historical documents).

It was my move to the Open University, the greater opportunity for research it gave me and conversations with my colleague and near neighbour, Martyn Hammersley, there that began to change my orientation towards data analysis. This methodological influence combined at the time with another set of influences deriving from a new course which was being produced at the Open University while I was there: E353 *Society, Schooling and the State*. This course, which contained and presented many new developments in Marxist sociology of education, particularly in explaining the relationship between education and the state, seemed to offer all kinds of possibilities for interpreting my historical data on middle school policy. At the same time, though, I was becoming increasingly concerned about the importance of methodological rigour in data analysis. These two influences created an enormous tension in my work at the time and absorbed a great deal of my time and energy in attempting to reconcile them.

Searching for a principle to organize a mass of documentary data, one strategy I eventually adopted in an attempt to explain the determination of middle schools was to focus on comprehensive reorganization in three West Riding districts with *contrasting* policy outcomes. This, I felt, would make detailed empirical analysis manageable while providing the strongest possible test for any theoretical claims — either pre-existing or emergent. The process by which that analysis came to be produced was both a tortuous and personally tormenting one, though. There was the initial mismatch between a broadly chronological empirical account of middle schools and a preferred Marxist theory organized around the notion of over-determination; then the shelving of a proposed paper to the annual sociology of education conference at Westhill College, Birmingham, because the theory and evidence could not be made to fit; the (initially reluctant) consideration of alternative 'macro' paradigms in a desperate search for a more appropriate theoretical framework; the struggle to reconcile competing theoretical frameworks each of which accounted for parts of the data only; and the eventual theoretical synthesis of Marxist and pluralist elements as the best framework available to explain the evidence to hand. The eventual shift was a substantial one: entailing not just technical adjustments to parts of the argument, but a major shift of theoretical allegiance too.

This is an appropriate point, perhaps, to note some remarks made by Sara Delamont (1984) about the dangers of writing up research projects within different frameworks from the ones in which those projects were situated when first planned. According to Delamont (1984, p.17), 'bad ethnographic writing comes from taking data collected within one frame of reference and writing it up using a different one'. I should like to take issue with this contentious claim. If Delamont wishes ethnographers to guard against squeezing their data into what subsequently becomes fashionable theoretical apparel, no matter how ill-fitting and unbecoming the final 'look', then this is an understandable and justifiable caution. But if she is rejecting the consideration of new or previously unencountered theoretical frameworks after the conclusion of fieldwork, however relevant or enlightening they might be — her caution is both unnecessary and unhelpful. It seems to treat 'writing up' as little more than a mere technical 'rounding off' of a concluded analytical project. To be fair, Delamont (1984, p. 29) herself later states that she was still analyzing data as she was writing up, but even this observation fails to recognize that analysis is, or should be, a constituent feature of the writing-up process itself. To divorce writing up from or simply tack it on to the research process; to confine theoretical development and exploration only to certain stages of the research process; to foreclose the possibility of newly confronted alternative theories providing better explanations of one's evidence than those with which one had set out; to arrogate to oneself the certainty that new and more enlightening theoretical explanations of one's data cannot challenge and bring about some shift in one's central value assumptions and theoretical allegiances; to cast one's research adrift from all the theoretical currents and developments of the time and regard these as somehow outside of or separate from the research process — all this seems to me a position which can be sustained only by the most single-minded and inflexible of educational researchers.

There are, it is true, 'slaves' to theoretical fashion, who will avidly take on almost every new trend, no matter how bizarre and incongruous it looks in their own particular project. There are also those — the philistines of social research — who will determinedly stand aside from or heap scorn upon changes of theoretical fashion, no matter how well such fashions might, on closer inspection, suit their own body of data. But the shrewdest social researchers, aware of the strengths and limitations of their own bodies of data, will watch the changes in theoretical fashion, make judicious selections from them, and experiment until they have secured the best possible fit, tailored in neatness, elegance, and indeed accuracy, to their own particular data requirements.

No doubt, I have set up a metaphor of educational research here which can easily and entertainingly be used against me (theoretical jumble? dirty linen? Emperor's new clothes? etc.). But for me, the tensions between theory and evidence, the movements between and combination of different theoretical frameworks — sometimes out of 'playfulness' (Woods 1985), sometimes out of sheer desperation in search of more adequate explanations of the data (long after those data had in fact been collected) — were an absolutely integral feature of the whole research process; central to its growth and development. In this sense, a number of papers I produced on social theory in education (Hargreaves, 1980, 1982, 1985) were not diversions from the research task but absolutely integral to it; a way for me of resolving what were at the time major theoretical puzzles in order to explain more satisfactorily the evidence that lay before me. And this was increasingly true not just of the historical work, but of the ethnographic work also.

I began to apply the same stringent criteria of searching for disconfirming cases during the course of the historical analysis and the like to the ethnographic analysis as well. My first serious attempt at this was made in a paper analyzing aspects of staff decision-making at Riverdale; a paper whose contents, by and large, did not appear in the final book and thesis (Hargreaves, 1981). In that paper, the novel theoretical construct — contrastive rhetoric — was created by combining and applying various differing theories — interactionist and Durkheimian theories of deviance, theories of symbolization in mass media research, and Marxist theories of hegemony — to describe and explain a practice whereby the head quickly focused staff discussion down to 'safe', manageable issues by setting up stylized images of outrageous and extreme practice in other schools, ruling out all they stood for by implication. Throughout this process of theory construction, there was a constant movement between data and theory, testing for alternative theories, looking for disconfirming cases in the data (hence the formulation of another construct — 'extremist talk'), as the notion of contrastive rhetoric slowly evolved through interim stages of 'going to extremes', 'making contrasts', etc.

At Oxford, where I took up my next post, the same kind of process continued — although the necessity of yet another job move impelled by the insecurities of temporary appointment that have become such a depressing feature of academic careers in the 1980s, incurred yet more inevitable delays in writing up. There, my twin preoccupation with theoretical 'playfulness' and methodological rigour were, if anything, probably reinforced by my working with David Hargreaves who shared many of my concerns. When the final process of writing up took place between the summer of 1983 and Christmas 1984, the first implication of adopting this more rigorous analytic stance was that what was to have been just a brief illustrative description of organizational divisions within the middle schools as a prelude to the main analysis of coping strategies, now expanded into three chapters on the year system, setting and specialism. I sought to cross reference data on the same phenomenon (e.g., interviews and staffroom seating patterns in relation to an argument about the insulated nature of different year groups); to back up qualitative indicators with quantitative ones where possible (e.g., on teaching time allocations to different year groups); and to link localized case study findings to national survey evidence — some of it collated and compared for the first time — where available and appropriate (e.g., on the distribution of setting), in order to deal with questions of case study typicality and raise pertinent problems in relation to the validity of survey indicators. All this methodological craftsmanship took space: already I was up to chapter 12 (out of seventeen).

In the ensuing chapters, as I sought to explain the reasons for these organizational divisions, I turned my attention to the biographies and perspectives, cultures and careers of middle school teachers. This was also a response to criticisms made of my first outlines of coping strategies theory that it tended to neglect the cultures and perspectives which informed teachers' strategic choices (Pollard, 1982), and it drew upon a developing corpus of work on teachers' life histories and careers that had been extensively discussed and debated at a conference I attended on 'Teachers' Lives and Careers' at St. Hilda's College, Oxford. At first, this biographical work was to take up but one chapter, concentrating on four strikingly contrasting illustrative cases with sprinklings of supportive quotations from other teachers where appropriate. A prototype for this — a case study of one teacher — was presented in an Open University unit on middle schools (Hargreaves 1983). But as I tried to add supportive quotations to my main four cases, however, it became clear that in many instances the examples were not of the same analytic type at all. In frustration, I conceded that the only way to ensure that valid categories were being employed, that theories were being generated according to stringent methodological procedure, was to conduct an analysis which exhausted all the cells, accounting for all teachers interviewed — Glaser and Strauss's (1967) constant comparative method, applied in retrospect. The outcome of this was not only four chapters instead of one, but an analysis which now located the middle school's organizational problems in the cultural inheritance of the staff — either 'academic-elementary' or 'developmental' in character — rather than in the (initially preferred notion of the) age-phase pattern (primary or secondary) of their previous training and experience.

During the course of the historical analysis I had increasingly come to recognize that much of the problem of micro-macro integration was not so much theoretical as empirical, of establishing the links between different settings, of identifying the unacknowledged historically grounded conditions of teachers' actions. Now, through the analysis of teacher interviews I was increasingly seeing the connection between biography and history — between private troubles and public issues, as Mills (1959) called them. In retrospect, these connections between policy and practice, history and biography seem to me rather more obvious, but at the time their discovery and their construction was a source of great excitement. I worked furiously, intensively, manically. I read newly written extracts aloud to uninterested but tolerant friends and acquaintances. The adrenalin flowed. The empty spaces in each of my puzzles (one theoretical — 'micro-macro'; one substantive — middle schools), were rapidly beginning to fill. The pictures were becoming clearer. I felt a vast sense of breakthrough as the results of painstaking empirical analysis on ethnographic, historical and statistical data, and of protracted theoretical puzzlement were becoming apparent. It was not a perfect picture — there were still many gaps, many unavailable pieces — but it was more clearly defined, more coherent and in some respects more dramatic than I had hoped (and feared) for a long time. Methodological craftsmanship and theoretical creativity; building technique and landscape design, I was coming to appreciate, were not competing kinds of expertise, not preferred modes of scholarship, as they are so often portrayed as being (e.g., Ball, 1984). They were, rather, mutually reinforcing analytical skills. Attention to the methodological skills of building produced technically sound, but aesthetically dull landscapes. Concentration on landscape design to the exclusion of construction skills, produced improbable and unstable theoretical edifices. The important thing, I began to realize, was to combine the two types of skill and help each contribute to the other.

In retrospect, it seems to me that these things were equally true of the historical and the ethnographic work alike. Like Hammersley (1984a), what strikes me now, after having undertaken both historical and ethnographic study, is not so much the differences — though there are differences — between the two enterprises, but the similarities:

— the importance of comparative method (in comparing three LEA divisions, two schools, different types of teacher);
— the importance of searching for disconfirming cases (of finding LEA divisions which did not establish middle schools, or where middle schools were established but were not the most administratively expedient option; of looking for ex-primary teachers employed in the 'secondary' end of the middle school and seeing what distinguished them from ex-primary teachers in the primary end;
— the difficult but fascinating relationship between theory and evidence (the combination of Marxism and pluralism to explain the historical data; the addition of biographical elements to the theory of coping strategies; the identification of two cultures in middle school teaching — academic-elementary and developmental, the development of a notion of situational vulnerability to explain the hyper-adaptability of middle-school-trained teachers);
— the awareness of how accounts are shaped by the context in

which they are presented (Sir Alec Clegg's different presentation of the case of the middle school to 'The Guardian'
on the one hand, and to the Ministry of Education during a
Conservative government on the other; the discrepancy between the kinds of accounts teachers present in interview, as
compared to staff discussion);

— the fear of being excluded from vital sources of data (un-
noted telephone calls to the Ministry of Education; staff
disputes with the head) — and so on.

All this analytical development led to changes in the format of the
final empirical chapter on coping strategies which, compared with
its original exploratory formulation (Hargreaves, 1978) now drew
more widely on empirical support, was a little more cautious in its
theoretical claims, and was, in accordance with the preceding thesis
design, now constructed on a basis of explicit contrast between the
two schools. Ironically, though, looking back, although this was one
of the first major theoretical developments to emerge during the
course of the thesis, at the time of write-up it occurred very late, in
the face of severe pressures of time and mounting tiredness. It is a
matter of some regret that coping strategies theory has not been
developed all that much further from its earlier formulations —
although I suspect (and here I would agree with Delamont) that the
available data would not have allowed very much more progress to
be made here anyway.

By now, having ranged over history and ethnography, theory
and evidence, policy and practice, culture and constraint, and so on,
the thesis was, in its attempt to achieve theoretical breadth on a
reasonably firm methodological foundation, becoming very long. I
had intended to extend the explanation still further to look at how,
in the occupational culture of teaching as a whole, teachers rely
almost exclusively on classroom experience and how this restricts
them to the business of coping, and not transforming. I also wanted
to examine some of the differences between the schools in terms of
the parallels between teacher-pupil and headteacher-staff relations.
Limitations of space, time and sheer exhaustion, however, meant
that two chapters on these issues regrettably had to be deleted,
although versions of them are published elsewhere (A. Hargreaves,
1981, 1984). Ten years had passed, 150000 words had been written.
I had yet another new job, at Warwick, to start. Enough was
enough!

Thesis into Book Won't Go

I shall not say too much about the conversion of the thesis into the book. Many of the problems — restrictions of length, publishers' aversions to methodological appendixes, etc. — have been well discussed by Ball (1984). Here, I want to comment on two issues only: the publishers' perceived needs of the market and the implication of this for the nature, quality and integrity of the product.

My own thesis was completed and available for publication at a risky time for educational publishing. The decline in numbers in teacher education and the erosion of 'the disciplines' within it has had a strong bearing on the kinds of manuscripts publishers are now prepared to accept. I had held a contract with one major publisher for several years, but by the time the manuscript was ready they were unwilling to publish it for two reasons. First, the study was about middle schools, and since middle schools were on the decline there would not now be much of a market for books about them, would there? While I could perceive the market sense of this, it also struck me that there was a cruel irony at work here. For it seems that if an institution is placed under political threat and begins to suffer decline, the economics of educational publishing dictate that there will be no public forum for consideration of the research and writing that may be essential to its defence (save for the official publications of the DES and HMI). Secondly, my publishers, like many major educational publishers now, were increasingly reluctant to publish pieces of empirical research, as such. Introductory texts, 'potboilers' on current educational issues — these were the kinds of lower risk products they were interested in taking in a precarious market. Accordingly, I was asked if I could set about writing an introductory book on transfer and liaison, using my data as illustrative material. Some of my colleagues have, I know, been persuaded into adopting this strategy, but I remain doubtful of its benefits. For one thing, it seems to me that the best parts of such books are those which remain closest to the original purpose of the studies from which they are drawn — the remaining parts (historical background, etc.) included to meet the 'coherence' of the introductory format tend to come across as relatively bland, forced and contrived. Academically, such books, it seems to me, succeed despite rather than because of their introductory packaging.

More importantly still, I worry about the collective implications of this market strategy for the standard of academic work that is produced, and for the extent to which educational research, its findings and the evidence on which it is based is open to public inspection. As some of the major consumers of educational writing, intending and serving teachers deserve to be given the opportunity to inspect the evidence and the reasoning on which current educational arguments are based. Where educational research and ethnographic research in particular is used merely to 'illustrate' more general arguments for which it was perhaps never designed, the result will likely be either a community of misled and misinformed teachers, or more probably (for teachers are not that easily fooled) discredit and disrespect for the integrity of the research enterprise. Here Delamont's earlier criticisms would be very apt — ethnography as loose illustration, ill-becoming the argument around which it is draped.

Falmer Press (publishers of the book) I am glad to say, have a more enlightened approach to printing empirical research than many of their competitors. But the signing of a contract does not complete the writing of the book. At 150 000 words, the thesis was too long to be published in anything approaching its entirety. I considered producing two books — one on history and policy, one on ethnography and practice — and the entrepreneur and careerist in me saw the sense in it: less work, two separate and identifiable markets, an extra publication for the curriculum vitae, etc. But I very much wanted a study which would try to indicate and demonstrate links *between* policy and practice, which would get teachers to reappraise their school experience but move beyond it, outside it, into politics, into the past, as part of that appraisal. This was the most distinctive contribution I felt my work could make and I could not let market inducements override it. Of such things are spoilt careers probably made.

So it had to be one book. This meant cuts. And, like major surgery without anaesthetic, they hurt! Every nip and tuck felt like the removal of some vital organ. What was it, then, that was removed? Entire chapters were excised. Three theory chapters and a chapter on middle school ideology were condensed into the introduction and into a number of short, ensuing introductory sections. Some theory was built more explicitly into the analysis of the empirical data, but the extended analyses of Marxism and pluralism, micro-theory and macro-theory, etc., which underpinned the final discussion had to be omitted. Two other complete chapters were removed. One considered the relationship between individual actions and collective state pressures in the formulation of middle school policy. Though important, this seemed to be not absolutely essential to understanding the connection between policy and practice. The final, and to others perhaps the most surprising, exclusion was the chapter on coping strategies. A colleague suggested this strategy to me and though initially surprised by it, I soon saw its sense — it was a very long chapter and did not add a great deal to versions of the argument I had already published elsewhere. The book contained only one major addition to the thesis: an extended conclusion including a rather heavily prescriptive section on the future of middle schools (an inclusion which I attribute to my time in Oxford, much of which was spent working closely with experienced teachers and alongside David Hargreaves who was himself then being drawn increasingly into the sphere of policy debate). In the academic community, we often wish to stand aloof from the political implications of our findings: to maintain a stance of disinterest and detachment. Yet we are also aware that other people *will* draw conclusions from what we do, and that is why, if only in self-defence, we perhaps have a duty, *once the research has been done*, to spell out, in terms of our own values, where we think the findings might lead. In addition to this, most of those of us who work in educational research operate not only in an academic community, but in a professional educational community too. Here we do carry responsibilities to share with teachers what we see as the practical, professional and political implications of our work. It does not prejudice or compromise the validity of our research to debate its implications with our colleagues in schools. Indeed, they have a right to expect that we should do so. It is because of such thoughts that the book (and to a lesser extent, the thesis) closes on a strongly prescriptive note.

Conclusion

As a result of reorientations and adjustments made before, during and after the ethnographic fieldwork, therefore, the concern of the thesis (and book) had shifted from a focus on progressive and traditional primary schooling (and before that, on student militancy), to an historical and ethnographical investigation of English middle schools as an instance of 'micro-macro' integration. This is a very substantial shift indeed, but one which I regard not as a weakness or an aberration, but as integral to the flexible and ongoing nature of educational research as a social process, where theory, evidence and the difficult relationship between them are a constant subject of personal and intellectual struggle — right up to the point where the final word of the research report has been written.

The study is now past. It is certainly imperfect. And, in intellectual terms, I have always experienced it as tense (though often creatively so). Unlike Bunyan's Pilgrim, I am sure I shall never reach the Celestial City of Sociological Understanding. In any case, I am increasingly convinced that like Santa Claus, tooth fairies, the noiseless car and the clear desk, that place is but one of those myths with which human beings feel the need to comfort themselves from time to time. Social research can never be 'above' or entirely cleansed of imperfections. What matters is that we come to terms with them. All the same, though the status of the destination remains uncertain, I do know that the journey, tortuous as it has been, has at all times been a challenging one. I can only hope that despite or perhaps because of the difficulties I am a better sociologist for having made it. Next time, I'll take someone with me!

Notes

1. There are conditions under which these difficulties can be significantly eased, of course. Teaching within an insulated, low status part of the school — as in the 'Newsom' department researched by Burgess (1983, p. 84) — can lead to relaxed colleaguial expectations and awareness of academic and disciplinary standards, and thus to an easier environment for building good fieldwork relations with pupils whom one also teaches. Equally, where a teacher-researcher, as full-participant, has a continuous, extensive and long-standing teaching relationship with a group of pupils, this relationship can be developed in such a way as to facilitate rather than impede good field relations (see Pollard, this volume). It was not possible to create either of these conditions in my own study.
2. The term is McNamara's (1980). Ironically, he applied it to ethnography.
3. It is interesting that while Hargreaves criticizes Sharp and Green for not really explaining what 'confusion' and 'inadequacy' means, for assuming that we can fill in from our common sense what these things are, he commits exactly the same error with regard to his notions of difficulty and strangeness.

Acknowledgements

This paper has been revised in the light of helpful comments from Bob Burgess, Martyn Hammersley, John Scarth and Geoffrey Walford.

References

ATKINSON, P. (1982) 'The Atkinson hypothesis', *Ethnography*, 5, June, Milton Keynes, Open University.

BALL, S. (1981) *Beachside Comprehensive*, Cambridge, Cambridge University Press.

BALL, S. (1984) 'Beachside reconsidered: Reflections on a methodological apprenticeship', in BURGESS, R.G. (Ed.) *The Research Process in Educational Settings: Ten Case Studies*, Lewes, Falmer Press.

BARNES, D., BRITTON, J. and ROSEN, H. (1968) *Language, Learner and the School*, Harmondsworth, Penguin.

BERGER, T. and LUCKMANN, T. (1966) *The Social Construction of Reality*, Harmondsworth, Penguin.

BERNSTEIN, B. (1971) 'On the classification and framing of educational knowledge', in YOUNG, M.F.D. (Ed.) *Knowledge and Control*, London, Collier-Macmillan.

BUNYAN, J. (1965) *The Pilgrim's Progress*, Harmondsworth, Penguin.

BURGESS, R. (1982) *Field Research: A Sourcebook and Field Manual*, London, Allen and Unwin.

BURGESS, R. (1983) *Experiencing Comprehensive Education*, London, Methuen.

DELAMONT, S. (1984) 'The Old Girl Network: reflections on the fieldwork at St. Lukes', in BURGESS, R. (Ed.) *The Research Process in Educational Settings*, Lewes, Falmer Press.

DINGWALL, R. (1981) 'Practical ethnography', in PAYNE, G., DINGWALL, R., PAYNE, J. and CARTER, M. (Eds) *Sociology and Social Research*, London, Routledge and Kegan Paul.

ESLAND, G. (1971) 'Teaching and learning as the organization of knowledge' in YOUNG, M.F.D. (Ed.) *Knowledge and Control*, London, Collier-MacMillan.

GLADWIN, T. (1964) 'Culture and logical process', in GOODENOUGH, W. (Ed.) *Explorations in Cultural Anthropology*, New York, McGraw-Hill.

GLASER, B. and STRAUSS, A. (1967) *The Discovery of Grounded Theory*, Aldine, Chicago.

GOODSON, I. and BALL, S. (Eds) (1985) *Teachers' Lives and Careers*, Lewes, Falmer Press.

HAMMERSLEY, M. (1974) 'The organization of pupil participation', *Sociological Review*, 22, 3, pp. 355–68.

HAMMERSLEY, M. (1984a) 'Making a vice of our virtues: some notes on theory in ethnography and history', in GOODSON, I. and BALL, S. (Eds) *Defining the Curriculum*, Lewes, Falmer Press.

HAMMERSLEY, M. (1984b) 'The researcher exposed: A natural history', in BURGESS, R.G. (Ed.) *The Research Process in Educational Settings: Ten Case Studies*, Lewes, Falmer Press.

HAMMERSLEY, M. and ATKINSON, P. (1983) *Ethnography; Principles in Practice*, London, Tavistock.

HARGREAVES, A. (1978) 'The significance of classroom coping strategies', in BARTON, L. and MEIGHAN, R. (Eds) *Sociological Interpretations of Schooling and Classrooms: a reappraisal*, Driffield, Nafferton Books.

HARGREAVES, A. (1979) 'Strategies, decisions and control: interaction in a middle school classroom', in EGGLESTON, J. (Ed.) *Teacher Decision Making in the Classroom*, London, Routledge and Kegan Paul.

HARGREAVES, A. (1980) 'Synthesis and the study of strategies: a project for the sociological imagination' in WOODS, P. (Ed.) *Pupil Strategies*, London, Croom Helm.

HARGREAVES, A. (1981) 'Contrastive rhetoric and extremist talk: teachers hegemony and the educationist context', in BARTON, L. and WALKER, S. (Eds) *Schools, Teachers and Teaching*, Lewes, Falmer Press.

HARGREAVES, A. (1982) 'Resistance and relative autonomy theories: problems of distortion and incoherence in recent Marxist sociology of education', *British Journal of Sociology of Education*, 3, 2, pp. 107–126.

HARGREAVES. A. (1983) 'The case of middle schools', Unit 19, E205 *Conflict and Change in Education*, Milton Keynes, Open University.

HARGREAVES, A. (1984) 'Experience counts, theory doesn't: how teachers talk about their work', *Sociology of Education*, 57, 4.

HARGREAVES, A. (1985) 'The Micro-Macro Problem in the Sociology of Education', in BURGESS, R.G. (Ed.) (1985) *Issues in Educational Research*, Lewes, Falmer Press.

HARGREAVES, A. (1986) *Two Cultures of Schooling*, Lewes, Falmer Press.

HARGREAVES, D.H. (1967) *Social Relations in a Secondary School*, London, Routledge and Kegan Paul.

HARGREAVES, D.H. (1978) 'Whatever happened to symbolic interactionism?' in BARTON, L. and MEIGHAN, R. (Eds) *Sociological Interpretations and Schooling and Classrooms: a reappraisal*, Driffield, Nafferton Books.

JACKSON, B. and MARSDEN, D. (1962) *Education and the Working Class*, Harmondsworth, Penguin.

LABOV, W. (1973) 'The logic of non-standard English' in KEDDIE, N. (Ed.), *Tinker, Tailor ...*, Harmondsworth, Penguin.

LACEY, C. (1970) *Hightown Grammar*, Manchester, Manchester University Press.

McNAMARA, D. (1980) 'The outsider's arrogance: The failure of participant observers to understand classroom events', *British Educational Research Journal*, 6, 2, pp. 113–25.

MILLS, C.W. (1959) *The Sociological Imagination*, Harmondsworth, Penguin.

POLLARD, A. (1982) 'A model of classroom coping strategies', *British Journal of Sociology of Education*, 3, 1, pp. 19–37.

SCHATZMAN, A. and STRAUSS, A. (1973) *Field Research: Strategies for a Natural Sociology*, Engelwood Cliffs, New Jersey, Prentice-Hall.

SCHUTZ, A. (1973) *Collected Papers I*, The Hague, Martinus Nijhoff.

SHARP, R. and GREEN, A. (1975) *Education and Social Control*, London, Routledge and Kegan Paul.

TURNER, R. (1974) *Ethnomethodology*, Harmondsworth, Penguin.

WILLIS, P. (1977) *Learning to Labour*, Farnborough, Saxon House.

WOODS, P. (1979) *The Divided School*, London, Routledge and Kegan Paul.

WOODS, P. (1985) 'Ethnography and theory construction in educational research', in BURGESS, R. (Ed.) *Field Methods in the Study of Education*, Lewes, Falmer Press.

YOUNG, M.F.D. (1971) *Knowledge & Control*, London, Collier-Macmillan.

2 Research Role Conflicts and Compromises in Public Schools

Geoffrey Walford

It is now widely accepted that fieldwork roles in ethnography are not fixed, but gradually change and develop as a result of negotiations between the researcher and those who are the subjects of the research. The researcher does not simply choose an appropriate role and adhere to it throughout the project, nor is it possible to think in terms of a single role no matter how dynamic, for a variety of roles must be adopted which will vary with the different individuals with whom the researcher interacts. There have been several attempts to analyze the development of field roles. Janes (1961), for example, describes five separate phases through which he perceives roles may pass: newcomer, provisional acceptance, categorical acceptance, personal acceptance and imminent migrant. Oleson and Whittaker (1967), on the other hand, emphasize the process of exchange between researcher and researched and discuss four phases through which they perceive the process to develop. One of the clearest examples of change within research roles is given by Burgess (1984, p. 85) where he uses the framework proposed by Janes to show the way his own role relationships with three school staff changed over the first six months of fieldwork at Bishop McGregor School.

This greater realism about research roles is a clear improvement on earlier typologies put forward by Gold (1958) and Junker (1960), which are still widely discussed in research methods textbooks even though they have long been the targets of criticism (see, for example, Hammersley and Atkinson (1983, p. 96) and Collins (1984)). From my own fieldwork experience, however, the present literature still does not adequately describe the process of role definition, negotiation and renegotiation. In this chapter I wish to emphasize one simple factor — that the only fieldwork roles initially open to researchers are ones that are recognized and accepted by those with whom the researcher interacts. Those who are to be the subjects of research abhore uncertainty in the role definitions of others as nature abhores a vacuum, and will automatically assign a role to a researcher. Over a period of time it may be possible to 'educate' the subjects of research and develop new role possibilities, but the researcher initially is restricted in the choice of his or her roles by the knowledge, experiences and expectations of those to be studied. This can be a major limitation on what can be accomplished in ethnographic research.

This chapter is not a full natural history of my research. I aim to discuss a number of items related to research roles that I feel may be of interest to others conducting research. I took on a range of accommodative roles, roles which restricted what it was possible for me to do and observe, but the only reasonable ones which were possible for me to adopt, in the time limits of the research, if I was to remain at the schools.

The Research in Question

This paper is concerned with some ethnographic fieldwork conducted in 1981 and 1982 in two of the major British public schools. Four weeks in the summer of 1981 were spent in the first school and the whole of the summer term of 1982 was spent in the second. In both schools I aimed to be an open researcher. Staff and pupils knew that I was at the school for the specific purpose of writing a book about public schools. In the first school, I did no teaching, but in the second I taught two sets of lower form boys — six periods a week for the first half of term and three thereafter. During this time I lived in accommodation provided by the schools on the school sites. In both schools my research method was eclectic. I talked with boys, girls, masters, wives, secretaries, other staff and headmasters. I became involved with the various aspects of school and community life, including sports, visits, drinking at the local pub, dinner parties, and other activities. I observed lessons, chapel, meals, sports and meetings of masters, parents and prefects. I also conducted eighty taped semi-structured interviews with academic staff.

At the end of the fieldwork I had two boxes of questionnaires, a drawer of tape-recorded interviews, about 800 pages of A4 notes, twenty hours of tape-recorded notes and comments, and a pile of documentation about two feet high. Only a small proportion of this material has been directly used in publications! The main publications have been a full-length book on *Life in Public Schools*, (Walford, 1986a), two journal articles on girls in boys' schools and on reproduction of social class (Walford, 1983 and 1986b), and an article in a collected volume about the changing experiences of public schoolmasters (Walford, 1984).

Background to the Project

One of the first questions that teachers asked me was whether I had attended a public school as a boy. In fact, I had not and had worked my way through the state maintained system until I found myself taking a physics degree at the University of Kent at Canterbury. My first contact with the independent sector came when I was twenty-three and working for a doctorate at that same university. Even that long ago I found the grant rather too small to fully support a reasonable lifestyle so, when my supervisor told me that a local minor public school wanted someone to teach mathematics part-time for two terms, I willingly took on the task. I am sure that I learnt far more from those twenty-two 14 and 15-year-old 'bottom set' boys than they did from me, for my lessons were noisy and chaotic. I yelled at them and threatened them and they fired paper missiles back at me. Eventually we came to a compromise but I was more than grateful that the room I taught in was physically isolated from the rest of the teaching rooms and only accessible by an external stairway. Educational though the experience was to me, the school struck me as a strange institution, for I could never understand why it was that parents were prepared to pay a considerable amount of money for their boys to be taught by an incompetent and untrained part-timer, rather than send them to local authority schools which had better facilities and equipment and fully trained staff.

I intended to teach in 'normal' schools and a few months after hearing the disastrous mathematics results of my twenty-two boys, I started a PGCE at Oxford. As I had already had some experience of the independent sector and was also well qualified it seemed 'appropriate' to the department that I should do my teaching practice term in one of the local and prestigious public boarding schools.

By the end of that year I wanted to study for a higher degree in sociology and was fairly sure that I could get funding for two years. I needed a job to tide me over for two terms. A public boarding school, with its cheap accommodation supplied for teachers, good teaching conditions and ample facilities seemed an obvious choice. I received confirmation of funding for my higher degree on the very day I started teaching at another of the major public boarding schools, so from the first day I knew that my permanent position was only a temporary one. The staff I worked with were up to date and enthusiastic, they gave me help when I requested it, but otherwise left me to teach in the way I felt best.

This background of my association with public schools was important for the development of the research project. It meant that after I had been appointed as lecturer in sociology of education at Aston University in 1979, and the time came for me to think about conducting new research, trying to understand the micro-world of the public school was an immediate first thought. I wanted to attempt an ethnographic study, and public boarding schools had many factors which made them specifically interesting. Perhaps the most important of these was the role that these schools have played in reproducing our inegalitarian society and educating the sons of the affluent to take their place in social, economic and political elites. The research on the culture of these schools was limited and out of date. There had been a flurry of research activity in the early 1960s which found its way into print later on in the decade. This included Wakeford's (1969) study of a school at which he had originally been a pupil and which was based on research conducted in 1962 and 1963. Weinberg (1967) based his work on a larger sample of schools, while Kalton (1966) surveyed statistically all schools in the Headmasters' Conference. The deluge of publications on boarding schools by Royston Lambert and his colleagues was based on extensive survey and observational work at about the same time (Lambert, Hipkin and Stagg, 1969; Lambert, Millham and Bullock, 1970 and 1973; Lambert and Woolfe, 1968).

For girls' independent schools the data was a little more up to date. Sara Delamont's study of girls' public schools in Edinburgh was conducted in the early 1970s (Delamont, 1973, 1976a and b, 1984a and b), while Mallory Wober's account of girls' boarding schools, which was part of the Lambert research, was published in 1971. However, by the 1980s some twenty years had passed since the studies of boys' schools and, according to commentators from within the schools, much had changed in that time (Rae, 1981; Thorn, 1978).

I had a number of other 'foreshadowed problems' (Hammersley and Atkinson, 1983) beside that of documenting the lives of the various inhabitants of the schools and trying to see how this fitted with social reproduction. I had done some work on sexism in science textbooks (Walford, 1980 and 1981) and I had become interested in aspects of gender reproduction as well as class reproduction. The fact that many of these public schools had recently admitted girls, usually only into the sixth form, gave rise to a whole host of questions about the changing role of these schools in the reproduction of gender.

A further major foreshadowed problem was the whole area of the links between the state maintained and the private education sectors. I knew that a number of public schoolmasters had been very influential in curriculum development especially in the sciences, mathematics, economics and classics. I was interested in the nature of school knowledge and the way that, where a selection of knowledge was made by public schoolteachers, it was likely to favour these pupils at the expense of pupils in local authority schools. I hoped to be able to interview teachers who had been involved in curriculum development, writing of textbooks and examination work and document curriculum changes which would show how 'objective' curriculum content actively favoured and embodied the assumptions of the ruling class and ruling gender.

I will show, later in the chapter, that only some of these problem areas actually came to fruition, and that some were eased out as others took their place.

Gaining Access

Initial access to independent schools has to be negotiated through the headteacher of the individual school, but gaining and maintaining access in ethnographic work is a process so that, even when initial permission has been granted by the headteacher, negotiations must be conducted with all those involved over what the researcher is allowed to see or do. My 'credentials' as someone who had taught at a public boarding school in the past were vital at all stages of the negotiation process. Gaining access to conduct research in the two public schools was not easy, and I am fairly sure that anyone without some previous contact with the public school sector would not even have been able to gain initial access.

It took a considerable time to eventually gain permission to conduct research in the first school. My original intention was to spend time in three of the major public boarding schools. I wanted to study boarding schools because that would allow me to conduct a 'mini-community study' in what was virtually a 'total institution' (Goffman, 1961), and I wanted to study the most prestigious of the Headmasters' Conference schools because of their key roles in curriculum development and in the reproduction of social elites. I excluded such schools as Eton and Winchester because I was interested in the similarities of experience rather than differences, which left me with about thirty schools to choose from. It didn't seem to matter very much which I chose from these. In letters to headmasters I stressed that I was particularly interested in the public schools as an alternative to the state system and that I was gathering information to write a book. 'I wish to describe in detail the experiences of teaching, learning and living in a public school from the rather different points of view of the masters and the boys.' I stressed that I was 'interested in the similarities of experience rather than the differences, which would mean that it would not be my intention to identify the schools studied in any publication or to make any comparison between them.' The letter continued with an outline of my own academic and teaching history in which I mentioned by name the three schools in which I had taught and gave the names of four referees. I initially asked to visit the schools for a period of about six weeks, hoping that I would be able to extend this once actually there. I made no mention of the word 'sociology'. I had five refusals.

My interview with the headmaster of the first school to express interest lasted only twenty minutes, but I experienced it as being far longer and more nerve-racking than any of the interviews I had had for academic appointments. He was extremely sharp and shrewd and demanded precise answers to a range of questions about my purposes and methodology. I had envisaged presenting myself as an open ethnographer and thus had prepared only a fairly flimsy outline of the sort of areas in which I was interested — I intended, in true ethnographic style, to develop my research strategy once actually in the school. The headmaster, however, had a rather different view of how research should be conducted, where questions are tightly framed, questionnaires or interview schedules developed, and representative samples drawn from populations. It quickly became obvious that the role of 'open ethnographic researcher' was one which he would not entertain. This was the first occasion when it became clear to me that possible research roles were structured by the definitions of others. At the time I had no intention of systematically interviewing a sample of boys, as it seemed unlikely to me that any particularly useful information could be gained from schoolboys by multiple one-off interviews of this type. Yet I found myself discussing random sampling, possible sample bias and interview schedules. The headmaster also spent time checking the question 'Are you one of us?' where my background of teaching in the schools was clearly of major importance. This was also the occasion of the first appearance of what I came to know as 'the ghost of Royston Lambert'. As I shall explain later, the ghost was to haunt me throughout the research.

By the end of the interview I had been forced to agree that six weeks (which I actually thought was far too short) was too long, and had compromised with a period of four weeks. I was to send him more details in writing of the topic areas I wished to cover in interviews with masters and boys, while he was to contact my academic and public school referees. These references were evidently convincing, for an invitation to conduct the research soon followed.

It is worth spending time considering my problems of access because it raises a number of questions with regard to the responsibilities of researchers to the wider research community. My experience was in direct contrast to that of Delamont (1984a) who states that she had no problems whatever about obtaining access to research on girls' public schools. Part of the difference is undoubtedly due to the fact that I was asking to be accommodated by the school (which would be paid for, of course) while Delamont only wished to visit during the daytime, but I feel that 'the ghost of Royston Lambert' had a far greater debilitating effect. Royston Lambert started his research on boarding education while a Fellow of King's College, Cambridge, where he founded and directed the government-financed Research Unit into Boarding Education between 1964 and 1968. When Lambert moved to Devon in 1968 to become headmaster of the progressive Dartington Hall School some of the research team moved with him to form the Dartington Research Unit. The original study was very wide-ranging, covering sixty-six boarding schools in England and Wales, for boys or coeducational. One in three of Headmasters' Conference boarding schools were included. A sub sample of seven schools (five of them HMC) were 'studied minutely during a period of observation and survey lasting in each at least a term or more'. In these schools '(the headmasters) welcomed us into their communities, gave us unrestricted freedom in them, housed and fed us, entertained us and gave us unremitting help, information, material and guidance' (Lambert and Millham, 1968). The output of the two research units has been prodigious. Lambert (1975) lists six books, eight sections of books and sixteen pamphlets or articles which resulted from the research, but only one of these is really widely known. In 1968 Lambert and Millham published *The Hothouse Society* which was described as a 'by-product' of the main research study. It was based on written comments by boys and girls at boarding schools provided in answer to questionnaires, in diaries and in other writings. The pupils' own words are used to describe the boredom and pettiness of life at the schools, their own cynicism and what they see as masters' hypocrisy. An underworld of bullying, drink, drugs and gambling is uncovered, followed by a chapter on 'problems' and a further one on 'sex in single sex schools' where a flourishing homosexual life is described in some schools. The book was a considerable public success, later being republished by Penguin, but the schools, quite understandably, were horrified.

For some masters this horror was compounded when the First Report of the Public Schools Commission, using Lambert's research, was to argue that the public boarding schools should make about half their boarding places available to 'children with special boarding needs' which would ensure that they became more academically comprehensive and less socially divisive. He who had seemed a supporter had turned traitor.

During my research and subsequently I have talked with many schoolmasters who had been closely involved with the Lambert research. Almost without exception they felt that he and the team had been dishonest and had tricked them. 'He came looking for trouble and found it'; 'the boys fed him with exactly the sort of comments he wanted — and he lapped it up'; 'the bad bits all came from one very run-down and antiquated school' were typical comments. They accused him of 'rigging the questions'; being 'obsessively concerned with homosexual activity amongst the boys'; and of 'not giving a fair report' but only including 'all the sensational bits'. I am obviously in no position to judge whether these accusations are true (I personally doubt it), my point is that whenever one of the headmasters or schoolmasters had read this book, I had to fight against its effect in order to gain access or interviews. The negative effect of previous research had even become enshrined in the Headmasters' Conference official *Manual of Guidance* (1978) which notes: 'Experience shows that headmasters can be too trusting in regard to enquiries made by researchers and sociologists. Evidence obtained in so-called confidence may be used several years later, in ways totally different from those intimated at the time of original approach'. Faced with the 'ghost of Royston Lambert', I am quite sure that I would have not obtained the degree of access and help that I did without being able to point to my own previous experience of teaching in public boarding schools.

It is also worthy of note that, once into the system, it was very easy to be given permission to conduct research in other schools. The headmaster of the second school simply telephoned the headmaster of the first for a reference and let me loose for a whole term with hardly a question as to what I was going to be doing. I felt I had joined the 'old boy network' myself.

Ethnography in Practice

When doing fieldwork ethnographers construct a variety of different types of field notes. Burgess (1984) uses the terms substantive, methodological and analytic field notes, while Hammersley and Atkinson (1983) describe ways of recording observational data, interviews and documents and recommend the development of a fieldwork journal to include notes on emerging ideas and theories, a running account of the conduct of the research and a record of the ethnographer's own personal feelings and experiences. The notes I made whilst in public schools are best described as substantive, methodological and reflexive. For the latter I used a small pocket tape recorder and the range of material included was from early formulations of theories to shouts of anger, agony and self-pity. At the end of any traumatic experience I would simply talk all my anxiety into the tape recorder, and I would recommend that every ethnographer do this simply for the therapeutic effect alone. That it is also a record of the experience of doing ethnography, which might be used in accounts such as this, is a bonus.

Numerous researchers have now written about the emotional and psychological stresses that are a part of doing ethnographic research. Johnson (1975), for example, tells us about his own physical pain and sickness which were a constant accompaniment of fieldwork and we now know that even the pathsetting anthropologist, Malinowski (1967), experienced severe stress and anxiety during his fieldwork with the Trobriani Islanders. Junker (1960) sees one of the main problems as that of striking a balance between being a 'good friend' and a 'snooping stranger', for the 'subjects' of the research do not ask for research to be conducted on them. Researchers have to use whatever social skills they can muster to convince people that they are 'on their side' and can be treated as a friend. The researcher asks about personal plans, feelings and failures and, like a good friend, promises not to tell anyone else, but the relationship is not reciprocal. The researcher does not tell his or her secrets to those being interviewed, for the objective is not friendship at all but information — a cache of data that can be stored away and analyzed later. Quite simply, the ethnographer *is* a 'snooping stranger' but one who has to conceal that identity behind a mask of friendship in order to gain information.

Recently there have been a number of personal accounts about ethnographic research in schools which have indicated similar anxieties. Hammersley (1984), for example, writes of stress, loneliness and fear of personal inadequacy. My own experiences of doing research in public schools were, if anything, worse. Most researchers doing fieldwork in Britain do so on a part-time basis. Each morning they leave their homes and drive to the 'fieldwork site' knowing that whatever happens during the day they will be able to return at night to the warm security of their home, family and friends. In my case I lived at the schools and there was no escape from being 'the person who was writing a book about public schools'. Whilst at the schools I ate most of my meals with staff in the communal facilities provided largely for unmarried masters and in the main research school I lived communally with about twelve unmarried masters. Even in the local pub it was inevitable that people connected with the school would be around. This made the research experience more like that of a community study than that of most school ethnographers (see Bell, 1977), but it was a community study being conducted by a single lonely individual rather than with a group who could share their ideas and pains. Moreover, the community was one where there was considerable submerged hostility to my presence.

At the end of the first week I returned to Birmingham for a day. On the train journey away from the school I wrote:

> I, even already, feel the continued turning stomach beginning to subside. I've had continuous sleepless nights, diarrhoea and churning stomach for all of the week.

It did get better as time went on and I became less fearful of being thought incompetent or making a mistake which could lead to my being thrown out. But I always felt anxious and worried about the next person I was going to interview or having to push my way into groups of pupils who often did not want me to be there. For most of the participants in the school I *was* and felt myself to be a 'snooping stranger' which was a role I did not enjoy.

I got most open hostility from pupils, rather than staff, who would usually, fairly early on in any discussion, ask a question something similar to 'Are you pro- or anti-public schools?' I tried to answer such questions as truthfully as I could which necessitated unpacking the question to discuss the various aspects with which I was concerned. To pupils who had clear ideas about their own answers to these questions this seemed like an evasion and sometimes led to lively argument with the older pupils. The pupils were always polite and well-mannered but, like most young people, tended to see problems in clear-cut terms, and were thus often suspicious of me. Most of the time at the schools it was possible to almost forget just how right-wing most of the pupils were, but there were many times when I was jolted into such a recognition. While observing one lesson, for example, one boy joked about the National Front being the right way to run the country. Not only did the teacher not make any comment, but neither did any of the other boys in the class. On another occasion I asked one pupil who I knew quite well whether there was anyone who was left wing in his House. The ferocity of 'no, certainly not' was stunning.

Hostility from staff was less open. I wrote in my fieldwork diary:

> It is not that the people are not helpful — they are, and are as helpful as I could or should expect. But I feel that behind that mask of gentlemanliness there lurks a deep suspicion of educational research in general and of this sort of research in particular.

Many of the staff were far more critical and questioning about public schools than were the pupils, but they still wanted to know how the research was going to help them. They were fed up with innumerable MSc and MEd theses that tied up many teachers yet were never of any use to teachers, and demanded that I explain how my research might help others if not themselves. Public schoolmasters are busy people and an undercurrent that I felt and recorded in my fieldwork diary was:

> A really annoying part of doing this sort of work is that everyone you meet believes that you have found yourself a really cushy job. (This includes other academics who have not done this sort of work.) A number of masters have been really fairly angry that someone should be able to 'come and have a nice holiday at the beginning of the summer' and at the same time take up their valuable time and stop them from working.

Researchers are not unaffected by such comments, and while I was quite clear that I had not found myself 'a cushy job' I realized that it was important to ensure that staff and pupils knew that I was actually keeping myself busy. Most ethnographic fieldwork techniques which involve simply talking, observing and listening to people in pubs, common rooms, classrooms and homes were simply not seen as work by others. The role of ethnographer was not one which masters were prepared to accept as legitimate. I thus undertook systematic interviewing with masters as much to show staff that I was doing something — collecting real, solid data — as for the data themselves. They expected me to take on their view of what a researcher was and that was someone who interviewed and asked specific replicable questions rather than someone who in Delamont's (1984a) terms 'lurked' about the school often with no clear function. The roles I adopted were not freely chosen, but the result of the expectations of others.

Not all of the staff were hostile. Many of them were very open and helpful and some clearly enjoyed the experience of being interviewed. For others the interviews acted something akin to therapy, as I fell into a 'good listener' role. Housemasters, especially, it seemed to me, really appreciated the chance to talk about their experiences with someone who was knowledgeable about the school, yet outside it. I tried to interview housemasters in the evening so that I could have another chance of being in houses when all the boys were there and see just how involved the man was with the affairs of the house. They were usually very pleasant occasions with food being offered and gin and tonic flowing liberally, but they were still a strain for me because I had to ensure that I did not say too much about my own views, which could frequently be in opposition to those of the person I was interviewing, or about the views of other masters in the school. Housemasters frequently asked me to draw comparisons between the way they conducted their house and the way other housemasters organized theirs, for they simply did not know. One of the peculiarities of the boarding house system is that each house is very isolated from the others. Housemasters will only very rarely enter the house of another housemaster and will never enter the boys' part of another house. Housemasters did not know the real extent of fagging, smoking and drinking, for example, in other houses. By the end of the research period I found myself in the unique position of having visited all of the houses and having eaten in most. I had much 'guilty' knowledge that was of interest to others. I found the strain of being evasive and of simply continuously 'being nice' to everyone, extremely exhausting.

In short, the roles that were available to me were not planned, but the only suitable roles that were available to me within the time limits of the research that would enable me to gather data. Just as Peshkin (1984) found in his fieldwork in a fundamentalist Christian community, the roles were all accommodative and the effect of maintaining these roles was exhaustion.

Compromise in Fieldwork Roles and Areas of Research

Both of my periods of research in schools were fairly short, and I initially attempted to cover a wide range of foreshadowed problems. I recognise now that the range of problems was far too great to be satisfactorily covered in such a short time and that this meant that with many of the people I met I was unable to develop greatly the initial role in which they placed me. With pupils I was rarely able to negotiate any role beyond those of 'teacher', 'adult/authority figure', 'snooping stranger', 'left-wing troublemaker' or whatever other role was initially cast for me. With the schoolmasters, on the other hand, I was interacting with them for a far longer period and with some I was able to move beyond their first assessments of my role.

This had a great effect on the final subject matter of the study. When I first started the research project I was much more interested in how the pupils experienced the school rather than the masters; I was interested in what the schoolmasters could tell me about curriculum development, but I did not feel that their own experiences would be particularly worthy of study. In the end, much of the book (Walford, 1986a) and one article (Walford, 1984) were concerned with masters, and the only publication about curriculum was a paper on a very peripheral area (Walford, 1985).

My interest in schoolmasters was forced upon me by the schoolmasters themselves and by the limited types of research role open to me. At the very first staff meeting I attended there was a discussion about how a large amount of money was to be spent. One master, who I had not even spoken to before, passed a note to me which read, 'This is a v. political area of debate'. I had not expected a consensus world, but here was conflict near the surface begging to be uncovered. The pressures from senior staff in particu-

lar to push me into a research role with which they were accus-
tomed, ensured that I quickly started to conduct systematic interviews with a sample of staff. I found that a number of the younger
masters, on interview, were prepared to accept the research role of
critic and confidant. They were still suspicious of what I was doing,
but welcomed the chance to talk to an outsider and wanted to
ensure that what I wrote would not be a whitewash. They told me
about problems of pay and housing, about 'the winter of discon-
tent', about masters being eased out of their jobs, and about the
pressures from the school on wives and families. They wanted me to
know, and I felt almost obliged to ensure that their voices were
heard, as they were in the article on 'the changing professionalism of
public schoolmasters' (Walford, 1984). In a similar way a considerable amount of space in the book (Walford, 1986a) was devoted to
schoolmasters, including a chapter on housemasters.

Like Hammersley (1984) I found that doing ethnographic research on these teachers led me to modify my initial perspectives on
them. I was originally not particularly well-disposed to people who
could devote their entire lives to children of the affluent (I justified
my own periods teaching in public schools as part of a 'finding out'
process and temporary). But the empathy that is a prime requisite
for ethnographic work led me to modify my feelings. Hammersley
(1984) describes the problems as:

> I therefore found myself facing a severe dilemma, especially
> since empathy tends to lead to sympathy. The very process
> of gaining and maintaining access also pushed me in the
> direction of sympathy for the teachers; one cannot constant-
> ly present an image of agreement, friendliness and under-
> standing without strong pressures towards such feelings.

Part of the eventual emphasis on teachers was also due to
corresponding lack of data in other areas. I soon found, for example,
that it would not be possible to write very much on curriculum
development within public schools because, although I interviewed
several textbook writers and others heavily involved, each case was
idiosyncratic and thus would have been impossible to write about
without identifying individuals involved and thus the research
schools. My major problem, however, was that I had great difficulty
in gaining useful information from pupils.

The headmaster of the first school wanted me to interview a
random sample of boys. I saw no reasonable way of organizing this
and thought at the time that it would probably lead to little useful

data. The essence of ethnography after all, I argued, is that information is gained over a period of time once trust has been established rather than through interviews with strangers. I preferred to try a less structured approach, but in practice I found it very difficult to meet and talk with pupils except on a superficial level. Quite simply there was no suitable role for me to adopt and no time to develop any. Some researchers have suggested that it is possible for adult observers to fully participate in the world of the school by taking on the role of the pupil (e.g. Spindler, 1974; Llewellyn, 1980), but I did not find this possible. I spent time 'following' pupils and sitting with pupils in lessons, but I always felt uneasy and aware that I was observing rather than participating. The Junior Common Room appeared to offer a good place to meet older pupils, but the opening hours were so short that they were more interested in getting the maximum number of half pints into them than in talking with a weird adult who was pushing his way into their territory. I was automatically a 'weird adult' because no other adult roles were available to me in the JCR. Any other adult in there was automatically in an authority role, which I wished to avoid. While ony a few of the pupils were openly hostile, it was often made clear to me that they would rather I was elsewhere. Those who wished to talk with me were obviously unrepresentative.

I felt that the ethical problems of ethnography were also of greater concern when it came to pupils. None had given informed consent to be part of the study — I had simply forced my way into their lives with few of the common courtesies. Somehow exploiting what 'social graces' I had with other adults to encourage them to give me data seemed less offensive than doing the same with pupils. The guilt at 'ripping people off' for data was worse with pupils.

Younger boys were usually much more willing to talk and, like those in Burgess' school (1985), saw the exercise as a chance for fame and wished to have their names in the resulting book. But there was still no role that I could conveniently fill. I was able to talk with boys at breaks and over lunch, but these were rushed affairs and I found I would spend more time explaining to boys what I was doing rather than asking them questions. The houses were the obvious places to gather such informal data, yet the only adult roles available are housemaster, assistant housemaster or tutor and matron, all of whom have clear authority positions over the boys. An adult cannot simply 'hang around' the house watching what is going on, listening and asking questions, any more than a researcher could do this in a private home. It is an invasion of privacy and perceived as such by pupils. Several housemasters allowed me access to their houses 'at any time I wanted', an invitation which I only accepted if the boys themselves seemed happy for me to be there, but in practice when one of the housemasters found me talking with the head of house and a prefect at 12.30 in the morning it was clear that I had overstayed my welcome. He acted coolly and calmly, but next day I found that the 'news' had swept through the staff.

I thought that it might be easier to make contact with pupils if I did some teaching in the second school. I hoped to take the role of teacher with a small number of pupils in which I could then relax into 'friendly teacher' and then 'friend' role as the term progressed. I took on two groups for a total of six periods a week. However, I had to ensure that my role with the schoolmasters was that of 'competent teacher and researcher' rather than 'incompetent educationalist' so I had to ensure that I could keep order and cover the work. My 'rules of the game', which were meant to be fairly generous, kept the younger group completely docile for half a term — I had quite clearly terrified them without meaning to, and it was only when I stopped teaching them in the second half of term that I could become friendly with any of them. The older group saw through my imitation thunder more easily. I learned more from this group, but I am not convinced that all the extra work that I caused myself by wanting to teach (my physics was *very* rusty) was actually worthwhile in terms of additional data from pupils. It helped at first to establish myself with teachers into the 'fellow teacher' role, but when I gave up teaching three of my six periods because 'it was taking up too much of my time', I felt my reputation plummet, as it was clear to the staff that I would never be able to cope as a *real* teacher. In fact, I felt my 'teacher' role to be always in some doubt. The head of department initially treated me as a 'trainee teacher' and sat at the back of the lesson until he was convinced that I would not do the pupils too much harm. I felt he was also quite happy to take one class back after half-term.

The role of 'observer' is recognized within classrooms. Both teachers and pupils are reasonably happy with the idea that someone should come into the classroom to view either teaching or pupil behaviour. I found, however, that the role of observer is only acceptable within tightly defined circumstances. One weekend I simply wished to observe what was going on in the main quadrangle of the school. I sat in a corner, and almost everyone who passed either gave me a strange look or came over to ask me what I was doing. There was simply no acceptable role that I could take on which would allow me to sit and observe in the main quadrangle. Watching cricket, on the other hand, seemed designed to help me out. Although I have never been able to understand the game and dreaded people asking me questions about how it was going, the 'cricket fan' was a role that served me well.

Staff found assigning a role to me particularly difficult at times of social activity. I often used to go for a drink or two in one of the local pubs with some of the schoolmasters and, perhaps because I was there, the topic of conversation would often come round to the school. I was asked several times, 'Are you on duty or off duty?' Was I going to force them to be careful about what they said at every occasion when I was around? Surely I could compartmental-ize my research role? Yet, of course, I could not do so, but had to force myself out of hiding in the comfort of my rooms to intrude once more upon their privacy.

In the second school, in near desperation for some sort of usable data from the pupils, I fell back on questionnaires and issued a short version of the one used by Lambert (Lambert, Bullock and Millham, 1970). There was no way I could issue it to sixth form pupils just at 'A' level time, so I compromised by giving it to the whole of the first and second years of the school (13–15-year-olds). It was much more informative than I had hoped and had the additional benefit of leading to many more informal discussions with the boys. I wish I had given it to them earlier in the term and to boys at the first school.

The dearth of information from pupils led to a de-emphasis on their experiences in the book. Other topics that replaced this were forced upon me during fieldwork. I was aware of the introduction of girls into former boys only schools, and was interested in the ways in which this related to class and gender reproduction, but I had not given a thought to the experiences of female teachers in these schools. I was shaken out of my complacency when I read the list of staff in the first school which, under the heading 'masters', listed several Mrs and Miss names. What was life like for these female 'masters'? They were more than pleased to tell me, although much of the data could not be used in the end for fear of identifying individuals. Sandra Acker's (1980) article on 'Women, the other academics' alerted me to the way that wives of academics can play a vital support role in their careers. It became obvious that a similar process was occurring in public schools and that wives had a vital role to play in 'assisting' housemasters in particular. I remember being annoyed when Janet Finch's excellent book *Married to the Job* was published in 1983 and showed how widespread the problem was — I had hoped I was on to something fairly new.

Conclusion

In this chapter I have tried to indicate some of the compromises that I felt forced to make during fieldwork and their effects on the final content of published work. I found that while some negotiation of roles was possible over a long period, the roles open to me were severely restricted by the expectations of those being researched. Moreover, throughout the time at the schools I felt obliged to present an 'overarching role' which was somewhat in conflict with my own feelings. As Spencer (1973) who studied West Point Military Academy suggests, there is an implicit, if not explicit, assumption made that the researcher will not directly attempt to harm the institution. Royston Lambert and his colleagues had, to the minds of most of the schoolmasters I spoke to, betrayed the trust the schools had put in them and had 'shown his true colours' only after leaving the schools. Throughout my research I felt that an unspoken gentlemen's agreement had been assumed on the part of most of the staff in the schools. I also felt myself cast in the role of 'sympathetic researcher' — maybe not wholeheartedly in favour, but SDP rather than Labour or anything worse. Once again those being researched forced me to adopt a role which was shaped by their expectations. If I had not been prepared to take on such a role I would have neither obtained nor maintained access or legitimacy.

The ethical problems of such role-taking are considerable, for the line between personal restraint in putting forward one's own ideas and deliberate deception is a fine one. In my writing on public schools I have attempted to describe and analyze those schools in as fair, balanced and honest a way as possible. While ends cannot justify means, I hope that headmasters, staff and pupils will not feel that I have betrayed their trust in what I have written. I dread becoming another 'ghost' for future academic researchers to have to fight against, for public schools are far too important to be left unresearched in the future, and need to be open to researchers with a wide range of attitudes towards them.

Acknowledgements

I am grateful to Robert Burgess and Andrew Pollard for helpful comments on an earlier draft of this chapter, and to the headmasters, staff and pupils of the two research schools who allowed me to enter their lives on a temporary basis.

References

ACKER, S. (1980) 'Women: The other academics', *British Journal of Sociology of Education*, *1*, (1) pp. 81–91.

BALL, S.J. (1984) 'Beachside reconsidered: Reflections on a methodological apprenticeship', in BURGESS, R.G. (Ed.) *The Research Process in Educational Settings: Ten Case Studies*, Lewes, Falmer Press.

BELL, C. (1977) 'Reflections on the Banbury restudy', in BELL, C. and NEWBY, H. (Eds) *Doing Sociological Research*, London, George Allen and Unwin.

BURGESS, R.G. (1984) *In the Field: An Introduction to Field Research*, London, George Allen & Unwin.

BURGESS, R.G. (1985) 'The whole truth? Some ethical problems of research in a comprehensive school', in BURGESS, R.G. (Ed.) *Field Methods in the Study of Education*, Lewes, Falmer Press.

COLLINS, H.M. (1984) 'Researching spoonbending: concepts and practice of participatory fieldwork', in BELL, C. and ROBERTS, H. (Eds) *Social Researching*, London, Routledge and Kegan Paul.

DELAMONT, S. (1973) *Academic Conformity Observed: Studies in the Classroom*, Unpublished Ph.D. thesis, University of Edinburgh.

DELAMONT, S. (1976a) 'The girls most likely to: Cultural reproduction and Scottish elites', *Scottish Journal of Sociology*, *1*, pp. 29–43.

DELAMONT, S. (1976b) *Interaction in the Classroom*, London, Methuen.

DELAMONT, S. (1984a) 'The old girl network: Recollections on the fieldwork at St. Luke's', in BURGESS, R.G. (Ed.) *The Research Process in Educational Settings: Ten Case Studies*, Lewes, Falmer Press.

DELAMONT, S. (1984b) 'Debs, dollies, swots and weeds: classroom styles at St. Luke's', in WALFORD, G. (Ed.) *British Public Schools: Policy and Practice*, Lewes, Falmer Press.

FINCH, J. (1983) *Married to the Job*, London, George Allen & Unwin.

GOFFMAN, E. (1961) *Asylums*, New York, Doubleday.

GOLD, R.L. (1958) 'Roles in sociological fieldwork', *Social Forces*, *36*, pp. 217–223.

HAMMERSLEY, M. (1984) 'The researcher exposed: A natural history', in BURGESS, R.G. (Ed.) *The Research Process in Educational Settings: Ten Case Studies*, Lewes, Falmer Press.

HAMMERSLEY, M. and ATKINSON, P. (1983) *Ethnography: Principles in Practice*, London, Tavistock.

HEADMASTERS' CONFERENCE (1978) *Manual of Guidance*, London, HMC.

JANES, R.W. (1961) 'A note on the phases of the community role of the participant observer', *American Sociological Review*, 26 (3), pp. 446–450.

JOHNSON, J. (1975) *Doing Field Research*, New York, Free Press.

JUNKER, B.H. (1960) *Field Research: an Introduction to the Social Sciences*, Chicago, Chicago University Press.

KALTON, G. (1966) *The Public Schools*, London, Longmans.

LAMBERT, R. (1966) *The State and Boarding Education*, London, Methuen.

LAMBERT, R. (1968a) 'Religious education in the boarding school', in JEBB, D.P. (Ed.) *Religious Education*, London, Darton, Longman and Todd.

LAMBERT, R. (1968b) 'The future of boarding in modern society' in ASH, M. (Ed.) *Who Are the Progressives Now?* London, Routledge and Kegan Paul.

LAMBERT, R. (1975) *The Chance of a Lifetime? A Study of Boarding Education*, London, Weidenfeld and Nicolson.

LAMBERT, R., BULLOCK, R. and MILLHAM, S. (1970) *A Manual to the Sociology of the School*, London, Weidenfeld and Nicolson.

LAMBERT, R., MILLHAM, S. and BULLOCK, R. (1973) 'The informal social system' in BROWN, R.K. (Ed.) *Knowledge, Education and Cultural Change*, London, Tavistock.

LAMBERT, R., HIPKIN, J. and STAGG, S. (1968) *New Wine in Old Bottles?*, Occasional Papers in Social Administration, 28, London, Bell.

LAMBERT, R. and MILLHAM, S. (1968) *The Hothouse Society*, London, Weidenfeld and Nicolson.

LAMBERT, R. and WOOLFE, R. (1968) 'Need and demand for boarding education', in *Public Schools Commission, First Report*, Vol. 2, Appendix 7, London, HMSO.

LLEWELLYN, M. (1960) 'Studying girls at school: the implications of a confusion' in DEEM, R. (Ed.) *Schooling for Women's Work*, London, Routledge and Kegan Paul.

MALINOWSKI, B. (1967) *A Dairy in the Strict Sense of the Term*, London, Routledge and Kegan Paul.

OLENSEN V. and WHITTAKER, E. (1967) 'Role-making in participant observation: processes in the researcher-actor relationship', *Human Organizations*, 26 (4), pp. 273–281.

PESHKIN, A. (1984) 'Odd man out: the participant observer in an absolutist setting', *Sociology of Education*, 57, pp. 254–264.

RAE, J. (1981) *The Public School Revolution*, London, Faber and Faber.

SPENCER, G. (1973) 'Methodological issues in the study of bureaucratic elites: A case study of West Point', *Social Problems*, 21 (1) pp. 90–103.

SPINDLER, G. (Ed.) (1974) *Education and Cultural Process: Towards an Anthropology of Education*, New York, Holt, Rinehart and Winston.

THORN, J. (1978) 'The new public schoolboy', *Spectator*, 16 December, p. 15.

WAKEFORD, J. (1969) *The Cloistered Elite. A Sociological Analysis of the English Boarding School*, London, Macmillan.

WALFORD, G. (1980) 'Sex bias in physics textbooks', *School Science Review* 62, pp. 220–227.

WALFORD, G. (1981) 'Tracking down sexism in physics textbooks', *Physics Education 16*, pp. 261–265

WALFORD, G. (1983) 'Girls in boys' public schools: A prelude to further research', *British Journal of Sociology of Education 4* (1), pp. 39–54.

WALFORD, G. (1984) 'The changing professionalism of public school teachers', in WALFORD, G. (Ed.) *British Public Schools: Policy and Practice*, Lewes, Falmer Press.

WALFORD, G. (1985) 'The construction of a curriculum area: science in society', *British Journal of Sociology of Education 6* (2), pp. 155–171.

WALFORD, G. (1986a) *Life in Public Schools*, London, Methuen.

WALFORD, G. (1986b) 'Ruling-class classification and framing', *British Educational Research Journal* 12(2), pp. 183–195.

WEINBERG, I. (1967) *The English Public Schools*, New York, Atherton.

WOBER, M. (1971) *English Girls' Boarding Schools*, London, Allen Lane.

3 Studying and Restudying Bishop McGregor School

Robert G. Burgess

It all began under the fireplace in the Merston teachers' centre in October 1972, for this was my initial encounter with the headmaster of Bishop McGregor School[1]. As we sat beneath the fireplace at the back of a crowded meeting we briefly chatted about what we both did and I was invited to visit Bishop McGregor School. Little did I think that this casual conversation was an important research encounter which would result in research projects, a research career and a research relationship that would span fifteen years until the head retired from the school.

In the early 1970s I graduated with a degree in sociology which I had taken three years after a teachers' certificate course. As a qualified teacher with a sociology degree I was eager to teach social studies in a secondary school and so headed for the classroom. However, this was not to last for long as I was wooed back to university with the promise of an SSRC [now ESRC] postgraduate award in the newly established Department of Sociology at the University of Warwick. Here, I wanted to bring together my interests in sociology and education to study the raising of the school leaving age; a policy issue that many of my former colleagues were then grappling with in their classrooms.

Having just left the world of schools and classrooms it was not my intention to re-enter it, and in any case much of the work associated with the raising of the school leaving age was taking place in an administrative setting. As a consequence, I did not arrange a visit to McGregor School for two months. On 8th December 1972 I first went into McGregor School where I spent a morning with the head before being taken around the school by two pupils. At the end of my visit, which involved meeting teachers and pupils, I was taken back to the head's room where I was invited to come back to the school if I ever wanted to do research.

Automatically, I thanked the head for his assistance, but inwardly I thought 'some chance' as at that time I had no wish to conduct a school study. Yet within weeks I was persuaded by my supervisors to put a proposal to the head of this school for a short one-term project on how the McGregor staff were handling the raising of the school leaving age. I recall that I was not over-enthusiastic, as McGregor was a Roman Catholic school and while I had worked in a Church school I had little knowledge of the Catholic faith, having been brought up in the non-conformist tradition. For me, studying a Catholic school added to my problems. It was enough to handle the study of a school, let alone a Catholic school where a researcher would have to come to terms with the ways in which Catholicism permeated the school structure. I agreed to go into McGregor as access appeared easy, but I thought I would leave after one term's pilot work to do a 'proper' study in a county school.

Looking back at this early encounter I am struck by the good fortune that I had in meeting the head of Bishop McGregor School[2], as my research experiences within that school have not only generated research projects but also books, articles, and conference presentations that are based on McGregor research[3]. In turn, I am also struck by my own naivete as a young researcher who at that time was unaware how to turn this opportunity to my advantage. Indeed, now that I am coming to the end of my current project in McGregor I can look back at a vast array of pupils, teachers, situations and events that I have had an opportunity to observe and on which to write. But we might ask: what has been learned from a research experience covering fifteen years in one school?

Beginnings: A Tale of Two Projects

When I began my research in Bishop McGregor School in May 1973 the research focus was on the raising of the school leaving age (ROSLA). A clean-cut policy with a clear line of curriculum development backed by national projects — or at least that was the rhetoric at the time. Yet in McGregor School I quickly found there was little talk of ROSLA or of ROSLA projects, as teachers were more concerned with how they might cope with Peter Vincent and Terry Nicholls who were notorious troublemakers in the school's

Newsom department where pupils who were caught up in ROSLA were located[4]. This was ROSLA work in action and it contained an important lesson for me as a researcher — namely that individuals seldom talk about the research topic in the terms anticipated by the researcher. It is, therefore, the researcher's task to go beyond the everyday routine that happens right in front of everybody.

I joined the Newsom department as a part-time teacher doing research and immediately went on the timetable to teach classes on a Tuesday afternoon and on Thursday mornings — the times are etched into my memory to this day as I acquired experience of 'teaching' Newsom pupils (see Burgess, 1983, especially pp. 123–146). Certainly, my presence was welcomed by the Newsom staff who were glad for a further pair of hands to deal with Peter Vincent and to 'entertain' a group of pupils who were unwilling participants in the school scene. This was field research in the raw — getting your hands dirty in real research.

At the time of my first study I was still very close to being a teacher. My initial concern was with my teaching and whether the pupils were learning anything from my lessons. Yet I also found teaching Newsom pupils difficult and at one stage in the first term thought about asking to teach another group as I had doubts about whether anything beneficial was happening in the classroom beyond fieldwork experience for me[5]. However, when I talked to the teachers and to the pupils about other classes it was apparent that my lessons were very similar to those of other teachers. The classroom encounters were, therefore, an important base for my research. However, I soon found that there were a number of other settings where research could be conducted: in school assembly, in the staff common room at breaks and after school, in department meetings and by following up school-wide events that occurred throughout the school year. The study that was presented as a Ph.D. thesis (Burgess, 1981b) and subsequently published as a book (Burgess, 1983) was divided into two parts: part one on social relations in the school and part two on Newsom pupils and their teachers. In short, it focused on some sets of social relations that were involved in the comprehensive experience and the way the school worked.

In the intervening years between finishing the fieldwork and publishing my study I kept in touch with Bishop McGregor School by visiting the school and the headteacher and maintaining links with some of the staff. I had enjoyed my early field experience at McGregor School. I had found it fascinating terrain and wanted to keep up with the changes that occurred. For me, McGregor was a touch-stone for secondary education: a small-scale situation where it had been possible to observe some of the key processes of secondary schooling in the 1970s. Almost ten years on I felt I needed further field experience, as by summer 1982 I had prepared two books on research, was in the midst of writing *In the Field* (Burgess, 1984a) — a textbook devoted to field research that was lavishly illustrated by my McGregor School experience, and was engaged in developing ways to examine critically the experience of doing ethnographic studies in schools.

All this work provided me with an opportunity to reflect on my first study and on ethnographic work in schools. Certainly, I shared some of David Hargreaves' views (Hargreaves, 1980) about the lack of a cumulative tradition in this branch of the sociology of education where researchers appeared very fleet of foot, being ready to move on to 'new' territory before working through the substantive, methodological and theoretical issues involved. Yet there was a further issue here — nobody apart from Lou Smith in the USA had attempted to do a restudy of a school they had initially studied (Smith and Keith, 1971; Smith *et al.*, 1983). Certainly, this was a well established tradition among fieldworkers studying communities with such celebrated accounts as *Middletown* (Lynd and Lynd, 1929) and *Middletown in Transition* (Lynd and Lynd, 1937) in the USA and the Banbury studies in Britain (Stacey, 1960; Stacey *et al.*, 1975). This was the kind of study that I wanted to do, as I thought that a further study of McGregor School would allow me to follow up some of the themes that I had started to examine in the 1970s.

In the summer of 1982 I approached the head of McGregor School with the suggestion that I start a follow up study. I explained that this would allow me to continue my analysis of school organization, of headship, and of the pastoral and academic organization of the school. In addition, I indicated that I would want to conduct a detailed study of one particular part of the school that I had not looked at before, given the fact that there was no longer a Newsom department in McGregor. At this time the first study had yet to be published and the head was very guarded. He wanted to wait and see the reception of the first study. He also wanted to consult his staff before agreeing to let me back into the school to do research. He also added forcibly: 'You know what they always say: "Never look back and never go back". You learn by your mistakes and move on somewhere else. I've always found that sound advice'. We spent some time considering alternative projects that I had in mind

— on other schools, on headship and on teacher unions. At this stage a second McGregor study looked unlikely and it seemed probable that I would have to look elsewhere to start a new project.

Almost a year had elapsed by June 1983 (five months before my first study was published) when a letter arrived from the head at McGregor School in which he indicated that plans were in hand to grant McGregor School community college status and he wondered if I would like to monitor the second stage of their development. We met and discussed the possibilities for research and I agreed that I would monitor the transition from school to community college if he would allow me to look at some of the issues I had examined in the first study. In short, I was following Lawrence Stenhouse's advice of doing something for the sponsor and something for myself in negotiating the terms for this new project (Stenhouse, 1984). This was immediately agreed and I came away from McGregor with the feeling that fieldwork could begin once the school had been granted community college status in the autumn. Meanwhile, there were other issues to confront.

As a postgraduate student in the 1970s I had been given a studentship before gaining research access, while in the 1980s I had gained access before I had funds available to conduct the study. I knew that if the restudy was to be successfully conducted, funding would be essential as the fieldwork had to be fitted around teaching and administrative work that I now had at the Warwick department where I had obtained a post at the end of my fieldwork in 1974. Unlike the 1970s where fieldwork was my only task, this project had to be fitted alongside other commitments within the university and outside it. I decided that the restudy, like the first study, would involve observation, participant observation, unstructured interviews and the collection of documentary evidence. Such a project would generate field notes, documents that would need filing, and tape-recordings that would have to be transcribed — as a consequence a part-time secretary would be essential. A successful bid was made to the University of Warwick Research and Innovations Fund Sub-Committee so that fieldwork could start in November 1983. In addition, another grant for a further period of fieldwork was obtained from the university, and the Nuffield Foundation provided a grant for the final phase of the project. These grants have been used principally to provide secretarial support: the research secretary has provided essential liaison with the school by keeping a diary of school meetings and events, and making appointments for me to meet teachers. She has also transcribed tape-recorded interviews and field notes and established files — all of which had to be done from the beginning of this project.

With the start of fieldwork in November 1983 I began to re-establish my bearings in the school by attending meetings with the head and by going into school for staff meetings and joining teachers in the common room at breaks. I was aware that there might be some difficulties here, as I had had a discussion with Margaret Stacey from the Warwick department about her restudy of Banbury and she had particularly made the point that there is a tendency for the fieldworker to go back to those groups with whom work had been done in the past (a point that Bell (1977) had criticized). Furthermore, she indicated that when you went back for a second time you went with a reputation not only as someone who had done research but also as someone who had written about the school. She warned me that I needed to monitor carefully the groups with whom I re-established contact and to watch for situations where people used my analyses to explain events. For it was her experience that research projects developed sets of mythologies that became incorporated into the lives of those studied.

In the early days of my return to McGregor I found that I quickly re-established my links with the English Department, as Paul Klee, who had been a probationary teacher and a key informant in the previous study, (Burgess, 1985b) was now head of the department. In addition, this department had subsequently recruited a number of teachers who were feminists, who were actively involved with teacher unions and who frequently discussed politics. It was a group with whom I could settle in the staff common room. However, they often joked that they had enough problems being seen by staff as 'a bunch of left-wing trendies' and now they had a sociologist sitting with them! Yet from this base I got back into the McGregor staff, meeting 'old' acquaintances as well as being introduced to other teachers. In addition, newly appointed community college staff quickly became acquainted with me in the 1980s in a manner similar to newly appointed Newsom staff in the 1970s. However, some caution was apparent as the newly appointed Deputy Head for Community subsequently told me that he had telephoned the head prior to our first interview to see if he could tell me everything that was being planned — a situation that he indicated had received positive support from the head. Similarly, senior staff who were known to be seeking promotion often asked at the end of interviews when their material would be published. When I replied that publication might take five years a smile flickered across their faces and one teacher said 'Oh good, I should be out of here by then'.

I was now back in McGregor School to do the restudy but the question that soon arose was: is it the same school in the restudy?

The Study and the Restudy: The Importance of Social Context

There is a tendency in the literature on long term research and on restudies to make the assumption that research is conducted in the same location (Foster *et al.*, 1979), but this fails to take account of changes in space and time and underplays the importance of social context — a point that is readily apparent in many ethnographic studies and which has been the subject of much criticism (Burgess, 1982b, 1986c).

At first glance it might appear that the Bishop McGregor School I am studying in the 1980s is the same place that I studied in the 1970s. However, even the physical site has changed, since there has been a further phase of building. A library and sixth form study area are now located on what were lawns. A new theatre and chaplaincy centre is now a dominant feature of the site. The result is a much more physically crowded site with less space between blocks. Even the names of some of the original blocks have changed to reflect changes in use that have occurred in the intervening period. Such changes have implications for the pattern of interaction during the day but there is also the issue of dual use of the site whereby adults and pupils (or 'students' as they are now called by some staff since the advent of community college status) share the same facilities; a situation that gives rise to territorial disputes between the school staff and the community staff that are reminiscent of the disputes over territory that took place between house staff and departmental staff in the 1970s (Burgess, 1983, pp. 52–83).

While some of the teachers who worked in the school in the 1970s are still there, many have changed their position. Some of my informants who were probationary teachers in the first study are now heads of departments, while two teachers who were heads of departments are now senior teachers. Some departments still contain many people who were there in the 1970s, while others have had a complete change of staff. The senior staff have now formed themselves into a senior management team which never existed in the

1970s and which currently consists of the head and his three deputies. Of this team only the head and a deputy head who has been promoted from the position of head of house were in the first study.

On this basis, it would appear that there is some continuity between the first and second studies. Yet we need to recall that those in the first study (including the head) had relatively little experience of comprehensive education. Now the head of Bishop McGregor School has seventeen years experience of being in that school and is now the senior comprehensive school head in the authority. He also has broad experience of work in the authority, in his union and in local and national committees concerned with Catholic education. Similarly, many teachers who have remained at McGregor School have a wider range of experience on which to draw. The passing of time has made a mark upon them.

The time period of the two studies has also to be taken into account. The first study took place in a school that was gradually building its roll to a total of 1269 pupils during the academic year 1973–4. In the 1980s, pupil rolls at McGregor School, in common with other secondary schools, are falling rapidly with the result that McGregor now has just over 1000 pupils on roll; a situation that has implications for staffing. In the early 1970s, recruitment of staff was a major issue, and in 1973 ten probationary teachers joined the school, while in 1974 teacher mobility was such that twenty-five teachers left the school for jobs elsewhere, promotion being relatively easy to obtain. In the 1980s the story is very different. Community college status has not provided a vast new range of jobs. The two full-time community posts have gone to people from outside McGregor School, as did the post of Deputy Head for Community. The only way in which McGregor staff have benefited is through temporary contracts on an additional scale post for one or two terms to give them an opportunity to do some planning for the community college. In addition, three teachers have obtained an extra permanent scale post for taking on community responsibilities. Beyond that McGregor School has two teachers allocated to its staffing to reflect community involvement, but these staff are not identifiable as their time is allocated to the timetables of existing staff who are prepared to work with adults. The result is that each year McGregor School has to go through an exercise concerning the internal deployment of staff and the possibility of teacher redeployment. While staff common room discussions in the 1970s were dominated by who might get promoted, in the 1980s the period from March to June is dominated by gloom and despondency concerning who might get redeployed.

It is against this background that the focus of my research is different in terms of style and strategy. In the 1970s, with no shortage of teacher posts and a demand for extra teachers, there was no concern expressed by the head or the teacher unions to me going on the timetable and being allocated a class while doing my research. Indeed, this was a strategy used by several sociologists who had formerly been teachers (Hargreaves, 1967; Lacey, 1970; Ball, 1981). However, I was aware that the social, economic and political context of schooling in the 1980s did not even make this a possibility — even if I had had the time to do continuous fieldwork, teaching classes would not have been a possibility as it would quickly be seen as a way of taking a teacher's job and would have aligned me with the management against the unions. A series of different locations therefore had to be selected to conduct my research.

Research strategies do not merely rely on a series of practical arrangements, as the strategies that are used depend much on the researcher and the theoretical and substantive interests of the research. My interests in the 1970s were shaped by my sociological training, which resulted in a symbolic interactionist perspective being used, while my recent experience as a school teacher influenced my focus on school organization and on courses for 'the less able' — an interest that also developed out of a policy initiative to raise the school leaving age to 16. In the 1980s I am a different researcher from the 1970s. I have read much more widely since my postgraduate days, not only in the sociology of education but also more broadly in sociology and related disciplines where ethnographic studies are conducted. My research is, therefore, shaped not only by the changing circumstances in McGregor School but by my own interests and by debates that are taking place within sociology and educational studies. Clearly, a major change in the shape and substance of sociology since the 1970s has been the impact of feminism which has resulted in gender-related questions being posed in many empirical studies. Such questions were not asked in the first study (as in many other school studies conducted during that period (Delamont, 1984)). However, gender has been an issue raised by teachers in the school and used in the second study (Burgess, 1986f). Furthermore, my interest in teachers and teaching has led me towards a teacher-focused project in the 1980s rather than a teacher-pupil project. While this does reflect my changing research interests, it is also a compromise. As I indicated earlier, the second project has been wedged between other duties, with the result that I have only been able to attend McGregor School for a day or two each week. These short periods together with an absence of teaching duties in the school really made it too difficult to research pupils. A teacher-centred project was, therefore, most appropriate. The result is that some of the issues in the second study are different from those in the first study and require different kinds of access.

Two areas that I had always been critical about in my first study concerned my analysis of senior teachers, including the head-teacher, and in turn my lack of knowledge of the process by which teachers were appointed. Accordingly, I negotiated access to spend one day a week for a whole term with the headteacher so as to follow up my study of school headship, and in turn I also obtained permission from the head to sit in on all the teacher job interviews that took place during the two-year fieldwork period; a vast number given the restructuring of the staff that took place. At the time I agreed that the head would introduce me to people who were interviewed and ask if they had any objection to my research presence at their interview. In these circumstances no individual ever objected, but I was subsequently told by those teachers who gained appointments that my presence stimulated discussion and specula-tion among the candidates about what I was doing. On this basis, the candidates at interview were not fully informed of my research intentions. However, I am still not sure what alternative tactics could have been used, as job interviews cannot be prefaced by research statements.

In negotiating access and doing fieldwork I am aware that it is not only my knowledge of research that has increased during the last ten years but also that of the head and his staff. When I first discussed the possibility of an observational study with the head in 1973 he had not read either of the then widely accessible studies by Hargreaves (1967) and Lacey (1970) and thought that an ethnogra-phy would look something like the kinds of studies conducted by John Barron Mays who had used survey-based methods to look at schooling in Liverpool (Mays, 1962). Now, in the 1980s, the head has read draft copies of all my publications that directly relate to McGregor School and has received copies of many of the books and articles in which I make reference to the first Bishop McGregor study. Similarly, many staff have now read my study and have some appreciation of observation and participant observation and how it is conducted — perhaps this explains the lack of questions that have been raised in the second study about what I am doing when I sit in meetings or talk to staff in the common room. Furthermore, some teachers have indicated that they now appreciate what might happen to a transcribed interview, whereas before they were relatively ignorant about what constituted an ethnographic study. But we might ask: what implications does this have for the conduct of an ethnographic study? How does it influence the data that are collected? What ethical issues are raised? It is to some of these issues that we now turn.

The Practice of Sociological Research

(a)   Doing Participant Observation

Accounts of ethnographic studies indicate that the researcher is central to the research. Here, the researcher obtains first hand information about a situation through direct experience, through sharing in the experience of a situation by means of being a participant observer and doing participant observation (cf. Becker, 1958). Indeed, the characteristic task of the participant observer is well summarized by Becker and his colleagues when they state:

> The participant observer follows those he studies through their daily round of life, seeing what they do, when, with whom, under what circumstances and querying them about the meaning of their actions. (Becker *et al.*, 1968, p. 13).

Such a statement focuses on what the participant observer does rather than upon the characteristics of the participant observer. Yet within my studies I have become very aware of the truth of Casagrande's remark that the researcher engaged in fieldwork needs to work closely with a group of informants:

> the successful outcome of field research depends not only on the anthropologist's own skills, but also on the capabilities and interests of those who teach him their ways. (Casagrande, 1960, p. x).

On this basis, much would seem to depend not only upon the researcher but also on the quality of relationships between the researcher and those who are researched (cf. Burgess, 1985a).

In conducting my studies I have attempted to come to terms with understanding the characteristics of field relations and the relations between researcher and researched (Burgess, 1984a, 1985b, 1986b) but through the study and restudy I have also become more aware of the way in which the characteristics of the researcher influence the conduct of participant observation. For example, if we take a variable such as age we need to consider how this influences social research (cf. Finch, 1986). Here, we might ask: how does the age of the researcher influence the kind of activities one engages in? How does age influence the kinds of informants that one works with?

Certainly, it has become apparent to me that age and status have influenced my activities and the people I work with. When I conducted my first study in the school I was 26. In one's mid-20s it is easy to associate with other teachers in that age group but not with senior teachers. Indeed, it is not just a question of age but also a question of status. I had at that time come from being a scale two teacher who had responsibility for the social studies and sociology department in a girls' secondary modern school. In these circumstances, it was possible on the basis of my age and former teacher status to indicate in discussions with probationary teachers that I knew what it was like to have to wade through piles of marking and to handle 'difficult' pupils. Similarly, when talking to people who were responsible for a subject area or for a small department I could say that I knew what it was like juggling with a small capitation allowance. However, at that stage, such comments would not cut much ice with heads of houses or with a deputy head or with the head who were very much aware of my former teacher status and my lowly student status as a postgraduate. One head of department (who had trained as a mature student teacher) asked me in a rather patronizing way, 'Are you going to train to be a teacher then?' However, it came as a surprise to be told that I had qualified as a teacher a year before him! Indeed, when other teachers asked me this question I talked about my teaching experience, which resulted in them finding out that I had more teaching experience than they did (cf. Beynon, 1983). This was an asset among junior teachers with whom I found it easy to associate in the 1970s as I could identify with them. The first study of Bishop McGregor School was, therefore, seen principally through the eyes of those who were starting teaching or beginning a new job in McGregor School (Burgess, 1983).

When I returned to McGregor School in the 1980s I was 36. Gone were the beginning teachers. Indeed, it was common for those who were perceived as the 'young' members of staff on scale one and scale two posts to have five and six years teaching experience respectively. Indeed, a scale two teacher with six years teaching experience had wide classroom experience, had been a sixth-form tutor and had taken on considerable pastoral responsibilities as a deputy head of year. My former scale two status had less resemblance to such teachers' duties. Yet I did not want to be seen as a senior lecturer from Warwick University so I had to find a way in. Here, age helped again. Some of the people who I had known as probationary and beginning teachers in the 1970s were still in the school. Many had gained promotion internally with the result that they were now in the middle management in the school. This was strategically useful, as their position in the school structure eased my passage in meetings with senior teachers who I had not encountered before and also provided introductions to junior staff within their respective departments. Here, my university status as the chairperson of a department is never referred to, although I am often asked for advice about courses for which staff might apply when they wish to take a first degree or a taught master's course. Indeed, unlike Ronald King, who was involved in a Dr. King-Mrs Pink relationship with teachers (King, 1978, 1984), I am known as Bob Burgess to all the teachers with whom I work. However, it amuses me that many higher education staff who supervize teaching practice students or who come to talk to sixth formers are treated deferentially by several staff including the head.

Yet it is not just age and status that influences relationships with teachers but also gender. At the time of my first study, gender issues were not questioned by many sociologists and as a consequence I did not consider the influence of sex and gender on the conduct of my research in the way in which sociologists such as Roberts (1981), Oakley (1981) and Morgan (1981, 1986) have subsequently suggested. Nevertheless, I did make sure that I studied a co-educational school and that I talked to men and women teachers and to boys and girls rather than researching the all-male world of schools that had been portrayed by Hargreaves (1967) and Lacey (1970). In the second study I have been more conscious of gender as an issue not only in sociology and the sociology of education but also among the staff at McGregor School where by the mid-1980s questions of sexism and equal opportunities are frequently discussed by teachers. It is on this basis that I have had to consider how my self-presentation will open up these areas for discussion by men and women teachers.

As other researchers have indicated (e.g., Jenkins, 1984) it is much easier for a male researcher to get access to the world of men and boys than that of girls and women. The culture of the staff common room at McGregor is a masculine world where sport dominates. At the centre of the common room is a pool table which one woman likened to a giant phallus in the centre of the room. The activity and much of the talk is dominated by sport — a topic on which I have relatively little knowledge and no skill. In these terms, when women criticize the way in which the common room is dominated by talk of masculine sports and by the way in which the men organize sports competitions among themselves I am able to join them in their criticism for I find it a very 'macho' sports-dominated world. In part, this has helped me to earn credibility among women teachers who have been willing to share with me numerous examples of the way in which women are put down by men and undervalued in the school. For example, at the beginning of one term a woman teacher had been coming into school and had passed a window cleaner en route who had called out to her 'Hello gorgeous, how are you?' The teacher he had selected for this verbal abuse was Jenny Ball, a feminist who had reported him to the school administrative officer with a suggestion that his firm should no longer be hired.

At the pre-term staff meeting the head had referred to this at the end of the meeting which I recorded in my field notebook in the following terms:

> With a smile on his face the head said, 'And the last word I think should go to Mrs. Ball who might like to tell us how she was greeted on her arrival at school'.
>
> Jenny Ball who was sat next to me indicated a reluctance to say anything. But many staff (especially the men) were shouting 'Come on!' Jenny said 'Well I was coming in to school past the administrative block this morning when the window cleaner shouted out 'Hello gorgeous'. Many teachers laughed when she continued by saying that she had complained about it to the administrative officer. Alan Jones quickly said, in a mincing tone: 'It happened to me as well!', at which everyone laughed. Jenny turned to me and said 'You can put that down in your book. By bringing it up in that way the boss has ridiculed it.'

Later that day Jenny took the opportunity to talk to me further about this situation. She said that since the meeting several men on the staff had said to her 'Hello gorgeous' to see how she would respond. Jenny explained that she had told the window cleaner to 'get stuffed' but she would like to have said far more to him and to her male colleagues who were not prepared to treat sexism seriously. It is through discussions such as this that I have been able to establish my credibility with women on the staff. This has allowed me access to issues of central concern to women teachers which have been taken up in conversations with them. However, I have also had to maintain relationships with their male 'macho' colleagues. In these terms, questions can be raised about the authenticity of the participant observer and the extent to which participant observation involves a somewhat schizophrenic existence.

Alongside my ascribed roles, the role of 'researcher' also helps me to get to know some staff. For example, in my first study I found that teachers who were new to McGregor often sought me out to discover things about the school. Certainly, this was the case with Ron Ward, a new head of house, who wanted to check up on aspects of the way in which McGregor worked in terms of discipline and standards (see Burgess, 1983, pp. 52–83). Similarly, a new teacher to the Newsom department who joined the school after the start of my work took the opportunity to discuss his experience of classes with me to see if my teaching experience in the Newsom department was similar to his own. It was these discussions that he claimed helped him to understand Newsom work and which helped me to construct the process of becoming a Newsom teacher (Burgess, 1983, pp. 190–197). Similarly, in the second study I have got to know new members of staff especially well. In particular, Chris Cousins, who was appointed as the Deputy Head (Community) after my fieldwork had commenced, has spent many hours talking to me about the school and his work within it. In part, I think this is because I am seen by him and by many other teachers as a repository of knowledge about the way the school operates. Furthermore, discussions about his work have provided an opportunity for him to reflect upon his own practice and for me to begin to understand how a deputy head teacher sets about establishing community education within a comprehensive school. While this involves a degree of reciprocity in fieldwork, it also highlights the way in which the researcher is cast in the role of expert, having stayed longer in the school than all pupils and many staff.

Doing participant observation therefore involves the researcher not only in a process of considering the relationships that are established with others but also in considering the role that he or she plays within a particular study; a situation that also occurs when conducting interviews and conversations.

(b) Talking to Teachers: Interviews and Conversations

For many researchers, including those who conduct ethnographic or case studies, the interview is a major strategy that is used (cf. Oakley, 1981; Burgess, 1984a; Finch, 1984; Stenhouse, 1984; Measor, 1985). Within all these accounts it is apparent that researchers are not attempting to follow the so-called 'good' practice that has been portrayed in methods textbooks by Goode and Hatt (1952) or by Moser and Kalton (1971). Instead, their aim is to be involved in non-hierarchical work so that they can share the perceptions that their informants have of the social world.

Within my own work at McGregor School I have attempted to move from interviews more towards conversations with the individuals with whom I work. The discussions that I enter into with individuals are therefore less artificial, although many are still tape-recorded. In all cases discussions are only established with individuals who I have got to know through my participation in the school. For example, in the first study, pupils were only interviewed in groups after I had worked with them in the classroom (see Burgess, 1983, especially part two, 1984a). Furthermore, I attempt to share in the discussion with those with whom I work as shown in the following transcript of a tape-recorded talk with Maggie Childs about the way in which gender influenced appointments in the pastoral system. Here, rather than moving straight to direct questions from me, we talked about the way in which women were treated by the staff in general and the senior staff in particular. She remarked:

> MC: To me personally the boss has always been very supportive and I got promotion very quickly, and you know, he's encouraged me very much when I have been applying for jobs, and I know that he knows I've got what I want and he is very pleased for me. But then he does throw out these comments [sexist comments] that annoy people.
>
> RB: Yes, publicly.
>
> MC: And yet, I don't think he is like that really, but you get sometimes — I think it is more that he is thinking about

certain people who are getting fixed ideas about where he is going to put them.

RB: Yes, certainly I am aware — I picked it up when he gives examples of model things that he thinks that people could do. He said at a meeting, 'Boys could learn to do needlework' and the audience laughed, and then he said 'and the girls should learn how to do car maintenance'. I thought, 'Very good too'.

MC: (laughs) Yes.

RB: You know, he seemed to be slightly embarrassed at his — he realized what the game was in terms of the examples. Yes, and I have noticed that he does tend to sort of give very fixed notions when he is publicly speaking by saying, 'Well, we will have a woman as head of first year and men will be in the upper school'.

MC: Yes.

RB: And I heard Phil [Deputy Head] even take it further; he uses this phrase, 'It is important to have a Mother figure'.

MC: Aah, that really annoyed a lot of people.

RB: Yes, does that annoy you?

MC: Yes, it does. I think it is a very sexist ... (laughs). Well what image in your mind do you have of mother figures? Really nice and rounded, in their fifties and perhaps a grandmother as well, and you know, I think it is a load of nonsense. I think if you have a man who is good with the younger children, there is no reason why a man shouldn't be head of first year. I know it generally does tend to be women, but I don't see why there should be any reason why a man couldn't do the job just as well. And it is my personal feeling that we need a lot of women in the upper school especially. Women are generally tougher, maybe because they perhaps have to fight harder initially to get the respect of the people, because I think a lot of them tend to think 'Oh, well a woman will be softer'. There are, I think, many instances when their discipline is often a lot better than men's. I have said this more than once. But I personally believe that a woman in the upper school is necessary.

RB: We have moved over to talking about the pastoral side, which is very neat. That is where I intended to go, talking about the pastoral side of the school, and there are sort of many new ideas floating around now. We have been through a whole set of debates about the pastoral organization. What are your views on the pastoral set-up in the school and the way you hoped it would go?

MC: What I hoped it would . . .?

RB: What you hoped, really hoped it would look like when the discussions started. What were your — what are your — what were your views? This is regardless of what the outcome is now.

MC: I hoped we would have a year system. I don't — I don't particularly like the idea of — the boss keeps on about the idea of a first year house. I think there is a danger that he's trying to, maybe trying to isolate them a bit too much. But I mean, there are some schools that are not purpose-built. You often might have the first years even coming on a separate site, aren't they? And I don't think that's a very good thing, and I think in his efforts to go on about, 'We must set the standards in the first year' etc., etc., etc. Not that I am arguing with *that*. I think the danger is that he is almost wanting to keep them isolated from everybody else and that worries me. How was it . . .? It is all very confusing, isn't it?

RB: Mmmm.

MC: I think, he has got no choice. He will change to a year system in September. Whether he puts the most suitable people to the most suitable year is very difficult, and you could argue, well, how are people to know when this school has always had a house system before?

Within this extract I do not just pose questions but discuss situations that have occurred in the school which leads into questions, comments and further points of discussion not only from me but also from Maggie Childs. In this way, the topic of pastoral care, the reorganization of the pastoral system and the way in which women are used within the system arises naturally out of our conversation and is put in its social context. However, even in this situation the talk lacks some spontaneity as research and data collection influences the pattern the discussion takes. Often, my conversational style involves a degree of manipulation as I 'encourage by naivete' (Stenhouse, 1984), but this becomes much more difficult in situations that I have witnessed first hand or in situations where the speaker assumes that I have a detailed knowledge given my long term association with the school and its members. In turn, I find that conducting conversations of this kind often puts me in the situation of talking to individuals who are on opposite sides. Maintaining relationships with such diverse groups and keeping the channels of communication open constitute but one of the many dilemmas that face the researcher during such encounters with informants drawn from different areas of the school.

Some Dilemmas for the Researcher

The kind of long term project that has been discussed involves two case studies that are separated by ten years. In these circumstances several issues arise that are relevant to many case studies but of particular importance where restudies are concerned.

(a) Time

As I have indicated, the time period has an influence on the social context within which the study is set. Yet there is a further issue. Many informants assume that I have a detailed knowledge of the school and its members across the decade. In some cases, individuals have started to discuss situations that assume a knowledge that I do not possess. In these circumstances I have had to ask them to explain the events to which they are making reference, for without that information I would be unable to make sense of their remarks. It is, therefore, important that the researcher should be able to establish briefly some of the significant changes that have occurred in the intervening period by using documentary records. In addition, individuals drawn from different areas of the school and who are from different levels in the school hierarchy can be used to 'fill in' details on some of the situations that have occurred and provide essential background data on current events. In this respect, documentary evidence both written and oral is an essential resource. However, this cannot overcome the problem that some people have arrived in the school and departed during the intervening period — where it is argued that they have had a significant impact on events. It is important to trace these developments through interviews with others.

(b) Informants

The importance of working with individuals in some depth has already been emphasized. In turn, the advantage of working with individuals who were previously studied is considerable. Some can take you back into 'old' social networks, while others will provide the researcher with introductions to new sets of colleagues with whom they have established relationships in the intervening period. Yet given the process of research it is also important to establish relationships with new informants. At first glance, this may appear to be a relatively straightforward process but it may be that some of your 'old' informants have indicated that they do not approve of some of those with whom you wish to work. Moving from study to restudy may therefore involve dropping or at least loosening 'old' ties and sets of relationships in order to move successfully into 'new' areas of study.

(c)   The Research Focus

The process of social research is such that it is never static. Even when the same researcher conducts both studies, topics will emerge in the second study on which data were not collected in the original study. In some cases, this may be overcome by re-reading some of the earlier field notes to see if material can be drawn upon that will shed light on the current issues. However, the advantage of conducting a restudy comes from being able to conduct comparisons between aspects of the two studies.

(d)   The Influence of Study on Restudy

For anyone who returns to an initial field of study there are several different levels of existence — Bishop McGregor in the 1970s, Bishop McGregor in the 1980s and Bishop McGregor in the published study. Certainly when the study has been widely read in the institution this may have several influences. First, individuals are no longer 'naive' informants. They have some idea of the researcher's task and the way in which the data that are collected might be used. In some situations, this has resulted in individuals being more guarded and asking for comments to be considered 'off the record' or for the tape-recorder to be switched off. Yet in other cases individuals have openly discussed and critically evaluated the work of others knowing that it might be reported in a published study. Secondly, the researcher finds that parts of the analysis from the original study have passed into the folklore of the institution. For example, my analysis of the relationships between house staff and department staff and the social divisions between them is now referred to as an established fact. In these circumstances, my work has helped to reinforce a point of view which was drawn on by those who wished to change the house system. Thirdly, terms that have been coined in the study are taken up and used to explain social situations when they had not been used before. In particular, I find that the head frequently uses phrases about 'negotiating the curriculum' and 'defining situations' that were never part of his vocabulary prior to the publication of the study. Finally, some staff are prepared to make political capital out of the previous study; especially when the researcher is present in the school. Certainly, this has been the case regarding my analysis of the school curriculum and the lack of curriculum development in McGregor School. Some teachers who want developments in this area have used my study to point out to the head and to others that this is a 'blind spot' in McGregor School. However, some teachers who were initially charged with curriculum responsibilities have maintained some 'distance' between themselves and the restudy.

Conclusion

For those considering conducting ethnographic studies and restudies I turn finally to the question of the merits and demerits of conducting case studies in this way. This approach has been well used among social anthropologists (Mead, 1956; Firth, 1959; Epstein, 1979). Here, the advantages have been argued in terms of the researcher being able to follow up topics concerned with continuity and change whereby theoretical issues that were developed in the initial study can be followed up in the restudy. To this can be added fieldwork experience whereby different approaches can be used on the same site and the strengths and limitations of strategies that are 'normally' used in 'one-shot' case studies can be assessed. As far as the collection of data is concerned, depth can be added to the initial material and new substantive concerns can be developed that are based upon or developed from core data that were collected some years earlier. Finally, new issues can be explored in relation to a research location with which the researcher already has a familiarity.

Alongside these issues it is important to consider the impact of research upon those that are researched. Teachers have access to the monograph, and to the texts and papers which utilize the McGregor

School study. In addition, they also have access to the reviews that not only discuss the study but also criticize the character of the school, its pattern of organization (Lambert, 1984; Roy, 1983) and individuals; especially the head (Lacey, 1984). On this basis it is essential to consider the impact that a study may have on the lives and careers of individuals. The initial McGregor study was not published until ten years after the fieldwork was completed, partly due to the issues that were to be discussed in the second part of the study where teachers' difficulties in teaching were to be graphically portrayed. I had feared that this could be used against teachers and waited until all those involved were no longer in the school. Now with a restudy similar problems emerge; especially as a wider span of years are taken to examine some teachers' careers. However, I would now argue that it is important to attempt to disseminate this material sooner so that it is of use to practitioners and to policy makers. Nevertheless, the teachers are identifiable to themselves even beneath the pseudonyms, for if this was not possible questions might legitimately be posed about the quality of the study. There is also the question of familiarity and the extent to which I am 'all too familiar' (Delamont, 1981) with McGregor School and with the participants. Here, the advantage of familiarity is also a disadvantage, as the researcher has to be able to question the routine and to look behind the everyday events that occur in the school and classroom.

For some researchers, the way around some of these problems would be to commission another fieldworker to go into the institution. However, the researcher would need not only to be acceptable to me but also to the head and teachers in McGregor School. Furthermore, what kind of person would need to be selected? Someone like me? Someone like I thought I was ten years ago? Someone with similar sociological skills and educational interests to me or someone with different skills and interests? The difficulties encountered when others have been engaged in restudies (e.g., Lewis, (1951) on Tepotzlan, and Bell, (1977) on Banbury) dissuaded me from taking this approach. However, I did resolve that even if I conducted the study, critical scrutiny and a reflexive stance towards my own research practice would be essential. Certainly, studying and restudying Bishop McGregor has helped me to develop methodological insights on the use of interviews and conversations (see Burgess, 1985, 1986c), the use of documentary evidence (Burgess, 1985d) and the development of 'observational' strategies in schools and classrooms (Burgess, 1986b). Secondly, it has helped me to study 'new' issues that confront schools in the 1980s but which are set in the same location. In this respect, data on teachers' appointments have been extended and the analysis developed (cf. Burgess, 1986a). Thirdly, my long term involvement with the school has also led to a consideration of the ways in which some of the research material can be used by teachers as well as other researchers to enhance their professional practice (Burgess, 1985d; Burgess and Burgess, 1985). Finally, my involvement with McGregor School has been more than a brief encounter in a research career, for my association with the school, the head, and many of the staff has been a major part of my life. This poses a problem that other researchers engaged in short term studies have identified, namely the problem of 'getting out'. But I have often asked myself, do I really want to 'get out' of McGregor School or could it be used as a research base for further studies? Already, I have embarked on another McGregor-based investigation by interviewing the head on a regular basis through to his retirement in 1987. For me, this started as an offshoot of the restudy, but deep down a further question haunts me: is this the third study of Bishop McGregor School?

Acknowledgements

The initial study of Bishop McGregor School was made possible by an SSRC (now ESRC) postgraduate studentship, while the restudy has been generously supported by grants from the University of Warwick Research and Innovations Fund Sub-Committee and the Nuffield Foundation. I am grateful to all these funding bodies for making the studies possible. I am also indebted to the staff and governors of Bishop McGregor School who have been generous with their time and permitted a sociologist to return to talk to them on numerous occasions. An earlier draft of this paper was read and discussed by some McGregor staff who raised many useful points. I have also received many helpful comments from Stephen Ball, Hilary Burgess, Lou Smith and Geoffrey Walford that have been used in revising this paper for publication. Finally, I am greatly indebted to Fiona Stone and Sue Turner who have provided first rate secretarial support on this project and without whom much of the work could not have been possible.

Robert G. Burgess

Notes

1. As in the research projects, all names used in this article are pseudonyms.
2. In several ethnographic studies, chance meetings have played a major role. For a classic example see Whyte's encounter with Doc in *Street Corner Society* (WHYTE, 1981).
3. The books that have been directly based on the first McGregor study are:
   Experiencing Comprehensive Education: A Study of Bishop McGregor School (BURGESS, 1983);
   In the Field: An Introduction to Field Research (BURGESS, 1984).
   Articles and chapters in books that directly focus on the McGregor research include:
   'The practice of sociological research: some issues in school ethnography' (BURGESS, 1982a, revised in BURGESS, 1986d);
   '"It's not a proper subject: It's just Newsom"' (BURGESS, 1984b);
   'The whole truth? Some ethical problems in the study of a comprehensive school' (BURGESS, 1985a);
   'In the company of teachers: key informants in the study of a comprehensive school' (BURGESS, 1985b);
   'Documenting pastoral care: strategies for teachers and researchers' (BURGESS, 1985d);
   'Collecting and conducting conversations in educational research' (BURGESS, 1986c);
   'Research methodology' (BURGESS, 1986e);
   'Doing participant observation' (BURGESS, 1986f).
   In addition, the McGregor work is also referred to in the following unpublished conference papers: BURGESS, 1979, 1981a, 1985c, 1986a, 1986b and in the following books: BURGESS 1986g, 1986h.
4. For a further discussion of these pupils, see BURGESS, 1983; especially part two.
5. For a discussion on the ways in which my initial encounters with Newsom pupils helped to stimulate research questions, see BURGESS, 1983, pp. 123–146.

References

BALL, S.J. (1981) *Beachside Comprehensive: A Case Study of Secondary Schooling*, Cambridge, Cambridge University Press.
BECKER, H.S. (1958) 'Problems of inference and proof in participant observation', *American Sociological Review*, 23, 6, pp. 652–660.
BECKER, H.S., GEER, B. and HUGHES, E.C. (1968) *Making the Grade*,

New York, John Wiley.

BELL, C. (1977) 'Reflections on the Banbury restudy', in BELL, C. and NEWBY, H. (Eds.) *Doing Sociological Research*, London, Allen & Unwin.

BEYNON, J. (1983) 'Ways in and staying in: Fieldwork as problem solving', in HAMMERSLEY, M. (Ed.) *The Ethnography of Schooling: Methodological Issues*, Driffield, Nafferton.

BURGESS, H. and BURGESS, R.G. (1985) 'Collaborative research and the curriculum', paper prepared for ESRC conference on Sociology and the Teacher, St. Hilda's College, Oxford (September).

BURGESS, R.G. (1979) 'Gaining Access: Some problems and implications for the participant observer', SSRC conference on Participant Observation, University of Birmingham, (September).

BURGESS, R.G. (1981a) 'Ethical Codes and Field Relations', paper prepared for the 41st Annual Conference of the Society for Applied Anthropology, University of Edinburgh, (April).

BURGESS, R.G. (1981b) *An Ethnographic Study of a Comprehensive School*, PhD thesis, University of Warwick.

BURGESS, R.G. (1982a) 'The practice of sociological research: some issues in school ethnography' in BURGESS, R.G. (Ed.) *Exploring Society*, London, British Sociological Association.

BURGESS, R.G. (Ed.) (1982b) *Field Research: A Sourcebook and Field Manual*, London, Allen & Unwin.

BURGESS, R.G. (1983) *Experiencing Comprehensive Education: A Study of Bishop McGregor School*, London, Methuen.

BURGESS, R.G. (1984a) *In the Field: An Introduction to Field Research*, London, Allen & Unwin.

BURGESS, R.G. (1984b) '"It's not a proper subject: it's just Newsom"', in GOODSON, I.F. and BALL, S.J. (Eds.) *Defining the Curriculum*, Lewes, Falmer Press.

BURGESS, R.G. (1985a) 'The whole truth? Some ethical problems in the study of a comprehensive school', in BURGESS, R.G. (Ed.) *Field Methods in the Study of Education*, Lewes, Falmer Press.

BURGESS, R.G. (1985b) 'In the company of teachers: key informants and the study of a comprehensive school', in BURGESS, R.G., (Ed.) *Strategies of Educational Research: Qualitative Methods*, Lewes, Falmer Press.

BURGESS, R.G. (1985c) 'Conversations with a purpose? The ethnographic interview in educational research', paper prepared for British Educational Research Association's Annual Conference, University of Sheffield, (August).

BURGESS, R.G. (1985d) 'Documenting pastoral care: strategies for teachers and researchers', in LANG, P. and MARLAND, M. (Eds.) *New Directions in Pastoral Care*, Oxford, Basil Blackwell.

BURGESS, R.G. (1986a) 'Points and posts: teacher careers in a comprehensive school', paper presented for British Educational Research Association's conference, Comprehensive Schooling in the 1980s, King's College, University of London, (February).

BURGESS, R.G. (1986b) '"Observing" schools and classrooms', paper prepared for Classroom Research and Professional Practice conference, Faculty of Education, University of the West Indies, St. Lucia, West Indies, (April).

BURGESS, R.G. (1986c) 'Collecting and conducting conversations in educational research', *Bulletin of Educational Development and Research* (forthcoming).

BURGESS, R.G. (1986d) 'The practice of sociological research: some issues in school ethnography', in BURGESS, R.G. (Ed.) *Exploring Society*, 2nd edn., London, Longman.

BURGESS, R.G. (1986e) 'Research methodology', in HARALAMBOS, M. (Ed.) *Developments in Sociology*, Volume 2, Ormskirk, Causeway Press.

BURGESS, R.G. (1986f) 'Doing participant observation', Working Paper for Department of Environmental Science, Queen Mary College, University of London.

BURGESS, R.G. (Ed.) (1986g) *Key Variables in Social Investigation*, London, Routledge and Kegan Paul.

BURGESS, R.G. (1986h) *Sociology, Education and Schools: An Introduction to the Sociology of Education*, London, Batsford.

CASAGRANDE, J. (Ed.) (1960) *In the Company of Man*, New York, Harper and Row.

DELAMONT, S. (1981) 'All too familiar? A decade of classroom research', *Educational Analysis*, 3, 1, pp. 69–83.

DELAMONT, S. (1984) 'The old girl network: recollections on the fieldwork at St. Luke's', in BURGESS, R.G. (Ed.) *The Research Process in Educational Settings: Ten Case Studies*, Lewes, Falmer Press.

EPSTEIN, T.S. (1979) 'Mysore villages revisited', in FOSTER, G.M., SCUDDER, T., COLSON, E. and KEMPER, R.V. (Eds.) *Long Term Field Research in Social Anthropology*, London, Academic Press.

FINCH, J. (1984) '"It's great to have someone to talk to": the ethics and politics of interviewing women', in BELL, C. and ROBERTS, H. (Eds.) *Social Researching: Politics, Problems, Practice*, London, Routledge and Kegan Paul.

FINCH, J. (1986) 'Age', in BURGESS, R.G. (Ed.) *Key Variables in Social Investigation*, London, Routledge and Kegan Paul.

FIRTH, R. (1959) *Social Change in Tikopia: Restudy of a Polynesian community after a generation*, New York, Macmillan.

FOSTER, G., SCUDDER, T., COLSON, E. and KEMPER, R.V. (Eds.) (1979) *Long Term Field Research in Social Anthropology*, London, Academic Press.

GOODE, W. and HATT, P. (1952) *Methods of Social Research*, London, McGraw Hill.

HARGREAVES, D.H. (1967) *Social Relations in a Secondary School*, London, Routledge and Kegan Paul.

HARGREAVES, D.H. (1980) 'Classrooms, schools and juvenile delinquency', *Educational Analysis*, 2, 2, pp. 75–87.

JENKINS, R. (1984) 'Bringing it all back home: an anthropologist in Belfast', in BELL, C. and ROBERTS, H. (Eds.) *Social Researching: Politics, Problems, Practice*, London, Routledge and Kegan Paul.

KING, R. (1978) *All Things Bright and Beautiful? A Sociological Study of Infants' Classrooms*, Chichester, John Wiley.

KING, R. (1984) 'The man in the Wendy house', in BURGESS, R.G. (Ed.) *The Research Process in Educational Settings: Ten Case Studies*, Lewes, Falmer Press.

LACEY, C. (1970) *Hightown Grammar: the School as a Social System*, Manchester, Manchester University Press.

LACEY, C. (1984) 'In the works' (review of BURGESS, R.G. *Experiencing Comprehensive Education*), *The Times Educational Supplement*, 17th February.

LAMBERT, K. (1984) Review of BURGESS, R.G. *Experiencing Comprehensive Education*, *Educational Review* 36, 3, pp. 330–331.

LEWIS, O. (1951) *Life in a Mexican Village: Tepoztlan Restudied*, Urbana, University of Illinois Press.

LYND, R.S. and LYND H.M. (1929) *Middletown: A Study in Contemporary American Culture*, New York, Harcourt Brace Jovanovich.

LYND, R.S. and LYND, H.M. (1937) *Middletown in Transition*, New York, Harcourt Brace Jovanovich.

MAYS, J.B. (1962) *Education and the Urban Child*, Liverpool, Liverpool University Press.

MEAD, M. (1956) *New Lives for Old: Cultural Transformation — Manus 1928–1953*, New York, William Morrow.

MEASOR, L. (1985) 'Interviewing: a strategy in qualitative research', in BURGESS, R.G. (Ed.) *Strategies of Educational Research: Qualitative Methods*, Lewes, Falmer Press.

MORGAN, D.H.J. (1981) 'Men, masculinity and the process of sociological enquiry', in ROBERTS, H. (Ed.) *Doing Feminist Research*, London, Routledge and Kegan Paul.

MORGAN, D.H.J. (1986) 'Gender', in BURGESS, R.G. (Ed.) *Key Variables in Social Investigation*, London, Routledge and Kegan Paul.

MOSER, C.A. and KALTON, G.K. (1971) *Survey Methods in Social Investigation*, 2nd edn., London, Heinemann.

OAKLEY, A. (1981) 'Interviewing women: a contradiction in terms', in ROBERTS, H. (Ed.) *Doing Feminist Research*, London, Routledge and Kegan Paul.

ROBERTS, H. (1981) (Ed.) *Doing Feminist Research*, London, Routledge and Kegan Paul.

ROY, W. (1983) 'Curricular dead brought back to life' (review of BURGESS,

R.G. *Experiencing Comprehensive Education*), *The Teacher*, 16th December.

SMITH, L.M. and KEITH, P.M. (1971) *Anatomy of Educational Innovation: An Organizational Analysis of an Elementary School*, New York, John Wiley.

SMITH, L.M., PRUNTY, J.J., DWYER, D.C. and KLEINE, P.M. (1983) *Innovation and Change in American Education, Kensington Revisited: A Fifteen Year Follow up of an Innovative Elementary School and its Faculty* (Final Grant Report in six volumes to the National Institute of Education).

STACEY, M. (1960) *Tradition and Change: A Study of Banbury*, Oxford, Oxford University Press.

STACEY, M., BATSTONE, E., BELL, C. and MURCOTT, A. (1975) *Power, Persistence and Change: A Second Study of Banbury*, London, Routledge and Kegan Paul.

STENHOUSE, L. (1984) 'Library access, library use and user education in academic sixth forms: an autobiographical account', in BURGESS, R.G. (Ed.) *The Research Process in Educational Settings: Ten Case Studies*, Lewes, Falmer Press.

WHYTE, W.F. (1981) *Street Corner Society*, 3rd edn., Chicago, University of Chicago Press.

4 Studying Children's Perspectives — A Collaborative Approach

Andrew Pollard

Introduction

In this chapter I reflect on and discuss some of the processes and issues involved in trying to gather data on the perspectives of children regarding their school lives. For illustrative material the paper draws on some of my own experiences when collecting data from 9 and 11-year-old children in the middle school in which I was a full-time teacher — a position which, of course, posed particular problems as well as offering some almost unique advantages. The study was a major element of a part-time research project undertaken for a PhD. A general methodological account of the study is available (1985a) and many of the substantive findings have also been published in a book called *The Social World of the Primary School*, (1985b).

Methodologically the study has been considered to have been unusual in that I enlisted the support of a group of 11 to 12-year-old children to help me collect data about the perspectives of their peers. A lunchtime club was formed and took the name of MID (Moorside Investigations Department). The children advised me and collaborated with me. They interviewed each other and other children in their year-group. They commented on my analysis as it unfolded. I do not believe that I would have been able to gather the data I did without this support for, in essence, I experienced a type of collaborative sponsorship of myself as the researcher by the children who were being researched.

My main findings with regard to the children were that their social structure and culture were both highly formed and socially sophisticated and that three different types of groups were discernible — 'Goodies', 'Jokers' and 'Gangs'. I suggested that children from these different types of groups had distinctive views on the value of school, on the legitimacy of teacher authority, and on each other. I also argued that the children in each type of group typically developed particular ways of coping with their school experiences. These, in simple terms, can be summarized as the strategies of conformity, negotiation and rejection respectively.

The present paper has been written looking back on this study, and I have been able to construct an account of its methodological development and of the issues involved more reflectively than was possible during the period of fieldwork. I frankly acknowledge that, at that time, intuition and pragmatism were considerable methodological resources and that my main strategy, of enlisting a group of the children almost as research assistants, had only a little of the tidy rationality which is implied by the label of 'collaborative triangulation' which I give to it in the final part of this paper. By reflecting on such realities I hope that the paper will contribute towards the work of others who may be able to plan their research strategies rather more carefully.

The chapter is organized in three parts. In the first part the issue of the validity of children's accounts is considered. Some researchers have seen this as a problem when working with young children and I therefore thought that it was essential to face it directly. In the second part the critical question of achieving trust, so that the cultural gaps between adults and children can be bridged, receives particular attention. In part three the interview strategy of 'collaborative triangulation' is specifically illustrated and discussed.

Part 1: Taking Children Seriously

The validity of children's accounts is something that has often been doubted. Of course, this issue is always of concern to interpretive sociologists whatever the age of those with whom they are working and arguably it is just as important in work with adults as it is in studies of children. Indeed, I would assert that, in principle, there is no difference in either the issue to be faced or in the procedures which become necessary to deal with it. In any type of interpretive work there is a fundamental assumption that a relationship between subjective perceptions and action exists, but I recognize that it may be felt that the case of work with children puts a particular strain on this assumption. Indeed, it is the case that a great deal of research by developmental psychologists, particularly of the Piagetian school, has, up to the late 1970s, produced and reinforced a widely held belief in children's egocentricity and limitations prior to their passage through certain developmental stages. Such research implicitly undercuts the validity of child perspectives and may have been responsible for the fact that, as Ball (1985) has observed, ethnographic researchers have generally 'shied away' from work with young children. Ball suggests that the field has been dominated by psychologists who. . . .

> from their positivistic stance share none of the participant observer's worries about making culturally invalid interpretations of the world of those being studied (Ball 1985, p. 47).

Ball is perhaps a little unfair to more recent psychologists here, for there is now a growing body of psychological research which takes children's meanings and perceptions more seriously and demonstrates the existence of particular forms of social understanding and competence at even very young ages — a development which was popularized by books such as Donaldson (1978), McGurk (1978) and Asher and Gottman (1981). It seems increasingly clear that children both have considerable social understanding and are capable of increasing their social competence at a very rapid rate, especially in social situations which are meaningful to them (Richards and Light, 1986). These developments in psychology reinforce the views of the few interpretive sociologists who have worked with young children and who have also argued strongly that children have considerable interpretive competence. For instance, MacKay (1973) underpinned his studies on socialization by suggesting that interpretive types of sociology . . .

> make children available as beings who interpret the world as adults do, ... and that they . . . . transform a theory of deficiency into a theory of competency (1973, p. 31).

Silvers (1977) made the same basic point and asserted that children's accounts should be explored as . . . . 'entirely reasonable and fully practical to their purposes at hand' (1977, p. 136).

If work on children's accounts is to be carried out, then this basic assumption about the rationality and interpretive competence of children must be adopted, but of course, this is not to deny that both the nature of subjective data and the relationship between words and actions need to be closely monitored, as with research with adults. Indeed it is the responsibility of the researcher to consider these issues in any sort of interpretive work.

These issues were raised many years ago by Dean and Whyte (1958) in their paper entitled 'How do you know if the informant is telling the truth?'. As they argued, it must be recognized as a base position that the researcher can only obtain the subject's perspective as made available in the particular data-gathering situation. Data then has to be evaluated and judged by the researcher. A number of factors might be considered — 'ulterior motives' held by the subjects, 'bars to spontaneity', 'desires to please' or particular 'idiosyncratic factors' which might affect the interview situation. When considering the relationship between what is said and more objective data on actions, other sets of criteria and information can be applied — the plausibility of the account, the reliability of the subject, knowledge of the subject's existing perceptions, but, above all, comparison with other sorts of data. The strongest source of evidence about validity then, is triangulation.

In my own study I was thus concerned to attempt to make observations of actual behaviour as well as collecting accounts and perspectives from a range of participants, so that triangulation of data would be possible. However, it is clear that even if this is done it must still involve the researcher in making judgments. For instance, children are no less prone to exaggerate than adults when in the company of others whom they wish to impress or in situations in which they might wish to recoup dignity, and this was something of which I had to be aware in my study. I felt, though, that such bravado could still yield good data, as in the example below. This arose in a conversation between a 'gang' group of children and myself after they had been 'done' (told off) by the headteacher.

> *Robert:* What I'll do, right, if he tells me to stay in, ... I'll walk straight out ... an' go home. I would, I'd go.
> *A.P.:* (Laughs)
> *Robert:* No joke, I would, if he stopped me I'd hit him, I'd hit him.
> *Nigel:* Yea, if Mr. Smith got a cane I'd take it off him and break it in half.
> *A.P.:* Would you?
> *Malcolm:* I'd take it home to me Dad.
> *A.P.:* What would he do?
> *Malcolm:* He'd come back and cane Smith.
> *A.P.:* Well, what do you think is going to happen?

Sarah: Nowt, he wouldn't put us in for all the time. I've been in loads of times by him and he's threatened me like this lots of times but he hasn't done it.

Malcolm: No, he don't mean it.

Nigel: No, it's all poppycock. He's a stupid, big beady-eyed. If he touches me or makes one mark on me I'll get him done by the cops.

Observations of the children over a long period and other accounts showed no evidence that the headteacher's authority was in fact challenged in any of the ways which the children suggested above, but this does not diminish the interest, and indeed, the validity of the data for building up an understanding of specific issues. It shows clearly both the absence of any semblance of legitimacy to the head's authority in the eyes of this particular group of children and it also illustrates the more general sense of the headteacher's ineffectiveness which these children had developed.

Of course, it is probably the case that children are more likely than adults to engage in the types of creative fantasy which are connected with their play and this again calls for judgment. One very clear example of this I came across was that of the 'Scorpion Gang'. The transcript below was produced when one of their members, Carl, was interviewed by another child, Paul, who was a member of the investigating group which worked with me.

Paul: Can you tell me all about your gang?

Carl: Well, I can't tell you about everything, 'cos some of it's highly classified top secret.

Paul: Well, it won't get out from here.

Carl: Well, I can tell you a bit about this gang that we've got now. ... We've got a head, n' a second, — he has to sign all the contracts and file the files and the stamp to seal so none of the letters can be revealed 'n given to other agents, so the top secret stuff can't get put into someone else's stuff. So without this stamp on, everyone will say, 'It's not valid', — it has to be stamped. .....In our gang we've got Jonathan, Patrick, Neil and me and some other agents which I can't tell you about like, and we've all got a code name for all of us — that's the same but the code numbers are different.

Paul: Can you tell us the code names?

Carl: Well, I can't tell you everything, some of it's highly classified top secret. Anyway there's code names on all our calling cards and our papers — it's called 'Scorpion'. We've

> done 'Operation Army' and we're on Scorpion now. It's on the main stamp. Then we've got lots of codes to send messages 'n that, and we've got a headquarters and shoulder-holsters. Some of the messages are in invisible ink so spies from other gangs don't know what to get. Most of us, ... we've all got organization levels, some are 5, 3, 2. I've got organization level 6. We've all got qualifications. I've got six, drawing, baseball, jokes, poetry, go-kart racing and one that I just can't mention.

Some details of this account undoubtedly stemmed from Carl's fertile imagination and it would be easy to dismiss it as being entirely make-believe. However, I was presented with many examples of documents and shown things like secret ink pens and shoulder-holsters; I observed inter-gang rivalry in the playground based around attempts to get each other's 'secrets'; and I collected many examples of other children's accounts of such activities. I certainly gathered enough data to reinforce my view that accounts such as Carl's reflected genuine activities and perspectives, despite their occasional embellishments.

Thus, one has to be careful. Such data is certainly valid in one way, in that it reflects culturally informed subjective meanings. At the same time it may be judged to have less complete validity as an account of 'objective reality' — but it is still data. The point here is that the type of questions which are asked of the data require different types and levels of validity to have been established. Thus, during the process of analysis the interpretive researcher constantly has to make decisions about the quality and nature of the data which are collected. One thing that simply cannot be done, though, is to devalue subjective data in itself merely because it comes from children. Indeed, I would argue that, provided the researcher working with children can demonstrate that he or she has maintained the necessary reflexivity or 'scepticism of himself' (Vidich, 1969) in data-gathering situations, then there is no reason to doubt the inherent validity of the data gathered any more than that collected in work with adults.

Part 2: Bridging the Gap

A key research problem for most ethnographers is that they must bridge the gaps between different types of culture. Whilst a member of one they must become thoroughly appreciative of another — for which a degree of acceptance and support from the group being studied is very often needed and asked for. In the case of work with children this is inherently problematic for several reasons. In the first place, as Holt (1975), Calvert (1975), Davies (1982) and others have argued, very important elements of child cultures are derived and maintained by the structurally-based tensions of adult-child relationships. The key factor here is the balance of power. As one recent children's joke book, aptly titled *How to Deal with Grown-Ups*, puts it in its preface:

> Frankly, adults have had their own way for too long. If kids want to do anything they have to get permission from an adult. Why? Because adults are in charge. But why are they in charge? Because they are more intelligent? No, most adults haven't got the brain of a grasshopper. The reason is that adults are
> (a) bigger
> (b) have all the money.
>
> (Aldridge and Aldridge 1985).

We may laugh, but in most situations it is true that adults are able to plan, to initiate, to define, to structure and to judge in ways which are quite unavailable to children. As a result it is left to children to watch, to respond, to imitate, to adapt and to cope as best they can. Of course, this is not all that children do, for they also engage in more creative forms of action by which they collectively generate their own perspectives, meanings, rules and interpretations of events, and it is these of course which are of particular interest to the ethnographer. It is thus the case that, in essence, adult ethnographers are asking children to describe, explain and share a culture and social world which has, in many respects, been developed as something which is exclusive and which derives much of its meaning as a defence against adults. It is a significant request and important ethical considerations and responsibilities to the children thus derive from what must be, to some extent, a deliberate attempt by the researcher to overturn conventional adult-child relationships (Fine and Glassner, 1979). However, the situation is even less clear-cut in some ways, because a researcher, especially if he or she is a teacher-researcher, also has responsibilities beyond those of the study. For instance, if teasing, bullying, fighting, theft, racism or sexism become apparent, a decision has to be taken on what to do. An ethical dilemma may have to be faced and no-one but the researcher can resolve it. In my own work I eventually found this difficulty to be less problematic than might have been expected. I think this was probably an outcome of discovering mechanisms for resolving and controlling disputes or conflicts, and for supporting each other, which existed within the children's society itself. This certainly eased some anxieties for me, but it required a certain amount of faith and patience prior to the mechanisms coming into action. Such resolutions were fortunate, because a relationship of trust which has been established with children in order to obtain accurate data is likely to be seriously damaged by an adult reverting to a more distanced and authority-based role — however principled he or she might take it to be.

An additional, if obvious, problem is that, unlike the position of researchers on some projects, no adult can possibly 'pass' as a member within children's culture in any way at all. As Glassner (1976) reported realizing ... 'I'm three feet too tall, my voice is too deep, and my energy is way too low, (1976, p. 18). Nor can an adult even present themselves to children entirely satisfactorily as a 'neutral stranger' for any adult is, by definition, 'from the other side' by virtue of their age. A teacher-ethnographer has a further problem because the fact of being an adult is compounded by the additional fact of being a teacher. This could be very significant for some children, since it has often been suggested that schools can provide a particular, and problematic, type of experience for 'pupils'. As Schostak (1982) rather graphically put it. . . .

> Being a pupil entails allowing oneself to be manipulated, losing self-responsibility, losing oneself within a web of manipulative intents and progressive submissions to the other, allowing oneself to be measured by the criteria of others, to be the material for their production goals and character moulds (1982, p. 182).

Without considerable safeguards, one would hardly expect children to trust a representative of a system which almost blindly accepts such outcomes.

A gap then, between the adult researcher and the children with their culture, has to be bridged. The trust of the children has to be won. In reflecting on my own attempts to gain this trust and to enlist the children's help and collaboration I have identified five aspects of my research at Moorside which, in retrospect, seem to have been important. I list them below as general issues of importance in research with children prior to further discussion and illustration.

1. The way in which the children perceive the researcher — his or her 'identity'.
2. The explanation which is offered to the children, the way access is sought and the ethical position which is taken up.
3. The actions and previous actions of the researcher.
4. The time that is allowed for the project to become accepted.
5. The way in which the research fits into child culture itself.

Identity

This is a tremendously important issue. Essentially the children will want to know two things — 'Who is the researcher?', and 'Can we trust her/him?'. 'Bridging the gap' in a genuine and open way so that high quality data becomes available, can, in my view, be achieved only through building up trust. Thus, whilst every ethno-graphic researcher participates and both immerses and uses his or her 'self' to some extent as a tool in the research process, the way in which they present themselves is vital. In the case of an adult researching with children, no ideal presentational role is available. As we have seen, one cannot be a real 'participant' or expect to be treated as a 'member', but one can be participatory by interaction. In other words, one can present oneself to be judged by the children 'as seen and experienced'. Stephen Ball (1985) has written about my study at Moorside Middle School and concluded that in the eyes of the children I was ... 'not a proper adult, not a proper teacher,' and I think (although I have no wish to flout my peculiarities) this is probably the essence of the case. As I explained to Ball in informal interview ...

> I think I had a reasonable identity in the school. The fact that I'd taught those kids before, that we'd had a few sets of experiences, ... and I think I measured up reasonably well on their own criteria of a teacher who is fun to be with, is liked. I'd had the advantage of doing various kinds of things which don't do one any harm if one wants to talk to kids like that. I was the one who threw custard pies at the headteacher in the school pantomime during this year. I had something of a reputation in the playground as somebody

who could play marbles, and I spent a lot of time in the playground playing games, chatting to them, talking to them. So I think I had an identity which was open and they trusted me, and particularly in a way I was being sponsored by certain of the children ... (quoted in Ball, 1985, p. 39)

I will come back to this issue of identity in various other ways below.

Explanation, Access and Ethics

A second aspect of gaining trust concerns the type of explanation of the research which is given to the children and the ethical approach which is taken up. In addition, the basis of access raises issues which are all too easy to gloss when dealing with a relatively powerless group such as children. The tendency is to talk only to the powerful gatekeepers — to the adults. However, irrespective of the views of teachers or parents, who are often consulted, it is clear that an adult researcher should obtain the consent of the children before embarking on the project, and, if it is to be ethically sound, this needs to be consent which is as informed as possible. Let me be frank too and point out that a sound ethical position is also likely to be a sound tactical position from the point of view of gathering 'backstage' data. Of course, such issues are likely to be especially important if the researcher is also a teacher, and in this case it is particularly likely that the children will act cautiously in the initial stages of the study until relationships are built up and confirmed.

In my study at Moorside I felt that the strategy of involving children themselves in the collection of data seemed particularly productive because it broke the presentational and ethical problems into two phases. The first phase consisted of explaining and nego- tiating with the relatively small group of seven fourth-year children who were to act as my initial group of research collaborators. The scale of the operation and the degree of publicity were relatively modest at this point, so that plenty of time could be taken to explore the issues which concerned the children. This took several weeks during which time the children became firmly involved, had discussions and held interviews with each other, with some other second-year children and with me. They asked about confidential- ity, about anonymity, about what 'transcribing' was, about their involvement in the analysis and about when I would write the study up so that they could see it. In my answers I attempted to make it clear that I would respect their confidences and that I was calling upon them as the 'experts' to help me. Having worked through these issues with a relatively small group meant that they could actually help me in the second phase of presenting the study to the rest of the children. Since I had deliberately attempted to involve children who I judged to have some influence with others, they were a considerable resource and handled most of the questions which were put to them without help from me — a much more sound situation than if I had been trying to establish the credentials of the study alone from my position as a teacher. Nonetheless there was still the issue of proving that what I said, I meant.

Actions

The actual behaviour of the researcher is probably the most important factor in determining the degree of trust which can be developed and the amount of help in 'bridging the gap' which the children are prepared to offer. I have no doubt at all that the children at Moorside Middle School carefully evaluated my actions when I began my research and also considered what they knew of me from the previous year when I had taught them. This was quite independent of the way in which I presented myself to them when the main study was initiated. Many children, like researchers, seem to me to know that they must deal with observable evidence as well as stated intentions and again this suggests a reason for taking some time at the initial stages of work with children. I felt that it was almost as if a stock of case-law about my actions and reactions was being accumulated and being spread among the children to form both a verified sense of my identity and a 'file' on the parameters of my likely actions.

I recall one particularly dramatic incident which probably contributed considerably to this putative 'children's file' on me. This occurred at a relatively early phase of the research when the headteacher surprised an interview session involving myself and a particularly troublesome gang. He wanted to tell them off severely and proceeded to do so. What he did not know was that we had been discussing 'getting done' the moment before, that the tape was running, and that he was fulfilling the children's expectations almost to the letter. Both the children and I were acutely aware that he was thus fulfilling the role of 'subject' at that moment far more than the role of 'authority figure', despite the fact that he was working so hard at it. So quickly had it all happened that no opportunity had arisen to tell him or warn him at that point without considerable embarrassment and I did not discuss it with him until much later. Meanwhile, the event, which had run its course, had both provided a 'good laugh' and provided evidence that I could be trusted. I am quite sure then, that as I began my research, the degree of threat and the authenticity of my new presentation was being measured and evaluated in some way, and with particular regard to my actions.

Time

Time is crucial in the development of trust for two reasons. The first and obvious reason is that it is over time that things change, that appearances alter, that good resolutions are forgotten and agreements fade. Can the researcher's or teacher's initial assurances stand this test? What will they do in new situations, perhaps when under unforeseen pressures? These are the sort of questions to which children are likely to want to know the answers. The incident described above provided a particular test of this sort for myself when working at Moorside but many other 'testing' situations occurred over the period of the research. These, though less dramatic, enabled the children to monitor my responses and to assure and reassure themselves of my position. In this, the detail of my face-to-face reactions to their opinions and revelations provided a supplementary and continuous sort of testing and was probably as important as the position taken on more major events. I did, of course, attempt to be appreciative and accepting, and in this I was spurred on by a sense of discovery and fortified by a relativistic understanding of the importance of subjectivity in its own right. This brings us then, to a second point regarding time.

Rather than being necessary for 'testing' the researcher, time can also, once the basis of trust has been established, be important to allow that trust to spread and develop. I did not realize the importance of this when I first began my research but, in retrospect, I have come to realize that what was in some ways a fairly slow rate of interviewing (I could only work at this over lunchtimes) was in some ways an asset rather than a constraint. At the time though I remember the sense of frustration which I felt, and indeed it was a lack of time to collect data which eventually resulted in my failure to gather sufficient data from a significant number of children of

Asian family origins to make a confident analysis of their perceptions. On the other hand, the lack of speed gave the children time. It
enabled them to talk extensively among themselves, to share experiences of being interviewed and of doing the interviewing. They thus
came to understand the procedures and take them for granted —
something which, I would argue, is far more advantageous than the
quick one-off strategy which might be available to larger teams of
researchers. Because of the passage of time the data was not 'forced'.
Although much of it was gathered by interview it was gathered at
what might be regarded as a naturalistic rate and I think this preserved a sense of child control.

Fitting in

A further way in which the degree of trust between children and
researcher might be affected concerns the degree to which the research process itself fits into, takes the form of, or relates to the
social processes and culture being studied. In the case of the Moorside research I was fortunate in several ways. In the first place,
lunch-time activities and clubs were common. Thus the idea of
engaging in some indoor activity with a teacher was far from strange
and in fact I took advantage of this by referring to the interviewing
activity as a club. The children coined the name of the 'Moorside
Investigations Department' for themselves. This leads into the
second respect in which the activity 'fitted in' — this time into an
aspect of child culture itself, for playing at 'secret societies' and
being 'investigators' was an established game at the time. The involvement and assistance which I hoped to gain from the children
was thus relatively meaningful to them even before I began, and, in
a sense, I had only to develop and structure an interest which was
already in existence among these particular children. What we have
here then are two examples of fortuitously being able to exploit
existing social arrangements for the purposes of the research, thus
maintaining the naturalistic character of the initiative to a greater
degree than would otherwise have been possible.

Control

I want to conclude this discussion about the development of trust
by identifying a summary issue — that of control. I would argue

that the quality of data from children will be affected most of all by the degree of control over the research process which they feel they have. If they mistrust the researcher, feel that they are being pressurized, are unclear about who will have access to data, or sense that they are being 'used', then the data is likely, in my view, to lose a considerable amount of validity. Again, in the Moorside study I must confess that I acted on this more out of intuition and a pragmatic realization that I lacked other alternatives than because I had a conscious strategic plan, but, as it turned out, I did enable the children to feel that they had a considerable degree of control over the project. They helped me to decide who was likely to be available for interview next, operated recorders, initiated discussions, labelled and catalogued the cassettes and helped me considerably by discussing my analysis as it unfolded. I offered them the role of 'experts' — which in many senses they were. What was familiar to them was relatively strange to me. I played the role of the naive adult so that whilst I was there to 'learn', they, perhaps a little flattered and entertained by my interest, agreed to 'teach'.

To summarize and generalize for a moment, there thus seem to me to be two particularly strong arguments for adopting collaborative strategies when trying to develop trust and conduct ethnographic research in suitable settings. The first is that the internal validity of the data collected is likely to be very high. The second is that the researcher may well get a considerable amount of assistance in collecting it.

I want now to move on to look at some specific examples of the interviews which the children participated in, and this forms the third part of the paper.

Part 3: Collaborative Triangulation

There are, of course, many forms of methodological triangulation, but the rationale for the strategy remains the same. This is that, because of varying strengths and weaknesses, different types of method and forms of data can offer a check on, and can illuminate, each other. As Burgess (1982) has put it ...

> The use of multiple methods, investigators, sets of data and theories in field research can provide flexibility, cross-validation of data and theoretical relevance. (1982, p. 166)

When using this strategy one might, as Bossert (1979) did, set data gathered by observation of classroom activities alongside such records as field notes on conversations with the participants and transcriptions of interviews. In my own study of the children at Moorside I used a variety of techniques. These ranged from those which required some intervention on my part, such as sociometry, interviewing and the collection of written opinions across the year-group, to the gathering of much more naturally occurring data by field notes of playground and classroom observation and the collection of documents such as the children's rough workbooks — their 'jotters'. These were all fertile sources of information and arguably contributed to my understanding as a whole far more than would otherwise have been possible. The point is that triangulated data should focus on the same substantive case and issue, thus providing more layers and depth to the understanding of that case and enabling each source and element of data to be checked against others.

There is nothing unusual about this discussion and it is typical of the reasons which are often given in favour of an analysis based on triangulation. Of course, in much ethnographic work there has been an emphasis on 'generating grounded theory' (Glaser and Strauss, 1967), so that data collection, coding and analysis have proceeded simultaneously rather than in the sequential way which is the tendency in more positivistic research. In my work at Moorside I was consciously aiming to achieve this goal of generating theory through the on-going process of data collection and analysis, but initially I was not fully aware of the way my use of children as collaborating research assistants also structured a particular type of continuous triangulation into the research design. In this retrospective analysis I have dignified this outcome with the term 'collaborative triangulation'.

Following the brief discussion in the introduction of this paper, a little more detail on the child-interviewing procedure which I adopted is necessary here before explaining collaborative triangulation further. The idea of using children as interviewers of other children was my solution to the problem of how I, as an adult and as a teacher, could gain a genuine access to children's culture and perspectives. I knew two things. First, I knew that if I just set off to interview children myself I would be likely to encounter a lot of problems and that the data would be highly questionable. Secondly, I knew that there were a lot of interesting and articulate children in the school with whom I had a good rapport and whom I trusted and respected. In working with the children I therefore tried to turn the constraint of being a full-time teacher into being an asset. I felt that it could be done because I knew the children well, having taught them previously — and of course, they knew me. It should not be forgotton though that I had very few alternatives which were viable. Over the year in which the 'Moorside Investigation Department' met, and out of the eighty children who were the focus of the main study in the year-group, the total number of children involved in MID was thirteen. About six of these were usually active at any one time and although the membership thus had a degree of turnover I always tried to involve children from a range of friendship groups. Nevertheless, there was a tendency for children from 'joker' groups to be more consistently active. They were also productive so I did not discourage them and, in the end, they made up eight of the thirteen, with two members of 'good' groups and three members of 'gang' groups also being involved. This, in fact, reflected the composition of the year-group as a whole fairly closely. However, I think that had I been more conscious at the outset of the potential for collaborative triangulation I would have tried harder to involve more good and gang group members.

I began, as part of a pilot and exploratory phase, by asking the fourth-year interviewers to interview some of the second-year children from whom I had been collecting other sorts of data over some time. At this stage the interview was intended to be semi-structured and I gave them a list of fourteen questions to draw on. As an example, one item was:

> Think of a time when you got into trouble with a teacher.
>   What happened?
>   How did you feel about it?
>   What do you think your teacher thought?
>   What do you think your friends thought?

The results were patchy, but they were also instructive. In the examples below the first is of a fourth-year joker girl interviewing a rather 'good' second-year girl in a straight and unempathic way — with limited results. In the second example two joker boys are together with a slightly more conversational delivery of the questions. This yielded rather better data.

> *Jo:* Can you think of a time when you were in trouble with a teacher?
> *Heather:* No, I don't think I can.

Jo: Not at all?

Heather: No, sorry.

Jo: Can you think of a time when you did something wrong and didn't get caught?

Heather: No, I can't.

Jo: Do you like being in your class?

Heather: Yes.

Jo: Why?

Heather: Well, I like my teacher, I have my friends.

Jo: I see. How well do you think you get on in school work?

Heather: Alright really.

*****

Philip: Can you think of a time when you got into trouble right bad?

Neil: In't first year....(whispers)....when I nicked a five-pound note from m'mummy, ... her purse.

Philip: What happened?

Neil: Well, I swopped it. I were buying stuff, ... handing money out to everybody, n' then I had one pound left and I was going to swop it for one of those flowers that you squirt and water comes out — but n' then somebody called Paul, he found out, he saw me and he went and told Mr. Smith. N' then Mr. Smith came into my class an' says, 'What have you been doing?'....and I told him, and he says, 'Where did you get it from?' I says, 'I found it in the road.' ... but I didn't, I got it from m'mum's purse.

Philip: How did you feel about it?

Neil: Me? Awful.

Philip: N' how do you think the teacher thought?

Neil: Naughty, bad.

Philip: What did your friends think?

Neil: Nothing really, they thought it were great.

Now obviously there are many possible causes for differences in the types of answer given, including variations in the perspectives and communicative competence of the children. However, I took the view, when reviewing a number of interviews, that one of the main necessities was to break down the degree of formality in the questioning so that more rapport could be established. The MID children themselves also had ideas on this and when we discussed the first round of interviews they suggested that when problems arose they did so. . . . .

> . . . .because they (second-years) respect us (fourth-years).
> . . . .because they're too shy, they haven't been in school long enough and I don't think they trust us as mcuh. Maybe with someone y'know, who've you've kept many secrets with 'em, then maybe it'd be better.

At my suggestion we thus decided to start to work with other fourth-year children instead of the second-years and to begin with friends of the MID members. I was not too worried by this change since it had been always in the back of my mind as a possibility, with work with second-years then being seen as a pilot. Nevertheless, had the work with second-years been strikingly successful it would have been possible to compare between year-groups — given enough time. Notwithstanding this, the point which is raised for collaborative research of the type that I am illustrating is that one must collaborate with individuals who are seen as being genuine members of the group being studied. By failing to realize this initially and by ignoring the important link which the children perceived between age and identity, I caused myself an immediate problem. This might have weakened the value of the collaborative procedure considerably.

I also agreed with the children to stop using interview schedules in favour of starting with a more general 'finding out about what children think about school'. It was agreed that I would be absent from the room when the interviews started but that I would join in after a few minutes, thus enabling me to regain some control over the direction of the discussions. The results of this strategy seemed rather better and immediately raised both the likelihood that the interview would take on the character of a relatively naturalistic event in itself and also the possibility that interviewers and interviewees would check and balance the contributions of each other, since they had more shared experiences on which to draw and now had a clearer opportunity to do so in a conversational situation. The example below is fairly typical.

It involved some joker group girls and shows the way in which a sense of an agreed perspective often emerged. In this case a conception of 'sensible clothes' to wear in school grew out of a difference of opinion on school uniforms (children at the local comprehensive school were required to wear uniforms). I was not present in this part of the interview. Julie was ostensibly the interviewer but the conversation had taken on its own momentum at this point. The topic of uniforms was raised by Carol.

Carol: I disagree with school uniforms.

Tessa: Well, I'll tell you why I agree with uniforms. I agree with uniforms because there could be some kids right, like they have parents who can't afford the clothes all their mates have. When their friends are up to date and they can't afford to buy the clothes and they feel left out, ... so the uniform ... they're all wearing the same ...

Julie: Yea, but them that can't afford the uniform are having to borrow money to buy it. It's ridiculous that. If they just says to 'em all wear sensible clothes then that's all right.

Tessa: .. 'N friendship-wise it's better because they're all dressed the same, I mean, there could be some two people together, somebody who's a rich kid, who's well off — the parents are well off and everything.

Julie: Them that's poor'll have a scruffy uniform probably.

Tessa: Oh no, I don't think so.

Jayne: Like my mum, she couldn't afford a navy-blue skirt you see, and all the others had a navy-blue skirt, but she had to have a light-blue skirt — not very light, not very light, but she had to. She had to wear a blue corduroy with a blazer but she didn't have....all she'd got was a new jumper and she couldn't afford it couldn't m' mum and she felt left out.

Carol: I disagree with blazers and ties and that sort of thing.

Tessa: I think they should just have the colour....just a certain colour right....and any clothes that's that colour....and that works out a lot cheaper instead of having one certain particular thing, like a certain blouse and that kind of skirt. I think we should be able to wear anything which is the colour of the uniform.

Jayne: Yea, but I think we should be able to wear striped socks. I don't see what's wrong in red, white and blue socks.

Julie: I know but they're not exactly sensible to go to school in.

Jayne: They are, they are.

Carol: I think they're a bit fancy to go to school in but I suppose really it varies.

Julie: I suppose they're O.K.

> *Carol:* I mean, some parents, they're not bothered, you can go to school in anything, ...trousers like Bay City Roller trousers ...
>
> *Jayne:* Oh no. We shouldn't come in trousers like Bay City Rollers trousers and things like that; after all school's only to learn at, not to be so smart and be a fashion show.
>
> *Carol:* I think we should go in sensible things.
>
> *Jayne:* Oh yea, that's it.
>
> *Carol:* We're not going to show what we look like ... see who looks best.
>
> *Jayne:* I haven't seen anybody this year wearing silly clothes, I've seen everybody wearing sensible clothes.
>
> *Julie:* Yea, but I know teenagers that do.
>
> *Carol:* Teenagers are the worst for that.
>
> *Tessa:* I'll tell you what's the worst.....Unit Three, the ones who cause the trouble, the ones who dress like punk rockers, I mean there's girls wearing monkey boots and trousers at half-mast.
>
> *Carol:* Yea, Unit Three's the worst for that.
>
> *Jayne:* Unit Three, they dress up as punk rockers....wear the striped socks....everybody can see 'em, y'know. But socks're there to keep your feet warm ... and uniform .....but teachers don't wear 'em. At least they wear sensible clothes.

Interviews of this type seemed to me to be productive because of the way in which children would provide immediate contrast to the views of each other, and yet some sense of shared agreement, as above, would often emerge. This was done with an authenticity which I simply could not match.

It was also particularly noticeable, and valuable in terms of understanding the children's perspectives, that contrasting interviewees and interviewers would often begin to show up boundaries of agreement and disagreement. In the example below, June, a member of the high status 'netball group' of jokers interviewed the members of a gang group of girls, Janine's Terrors, who were widely respected for their toughness. Initially all the children show that they are united in their dislike of Mr. Smith who frightens them. However, June is specific whilst the other children readily generalize to other teachers.

> *June:* Do you think maybe if Mr. Smith were like our other teachers and you weren't afraid of him like you are now, you

wouldn't be afraid to go out to him would you, you'd be able to do your work a lot better?

Janine: Yea.

Lorna: Yea.

June: I think that's what I find as well.

Margaret: Yea, 'cos ... it's them what really put y' into not working properly by saying things that ... 'you can't do it' 'n that.

Janine: Yea, they don't give you 'owt, don't give you a chance to do.

Jenny: They don't learn y' much.

Margaret: Yea, 'n they give y' another name like....they don't use y' proper name....they say ... 'Come here Charlie' instead of using y' proper name.

June then turned the issue around and further distinctions emerged between her views and the views of the group on the fairness of the strategies of some teachers and on the relevance of the curriculum.

June: What teacher do you like best, ... for the way they teach, er ... Not like Mr. Matthews y'see ... he isn't very good when you come to think of it, ...I know you have fun with him, but he doesn't, he, he doesn't really teach y'very much.

Jenny: He's good, he teaches y', he learns y' stuff.

Barbara: Yea, my best are Mr. Matthews and Mr. Brodie, 'cos Mr. Brodie never shouts at y' and Mr. Matthews don't neither.

June: But do you think that's right?

Barbara: Yea.

June: Ah, no, but, you see, that, ...I don't think that's correct really........ well, what do you think about the lessons that y' do?

Janine: Maths, we have maths too much and English too much, n' then art and handiwork and all that, well y' don't have them as much.

Lorna: And we have French three times a week now....

Jenny: ....I think we should cut R.E. out altogether. ....What do we want with that?

June: ... I know about that, but when y' go to different countries y'd like to learn about them.

Lorna: I know, (laughs) but we won't go to different countries.

June: Ah, but y'never know, y'might do, 'n you'll need it for your 'O' levels.

Lorna: Y' don't really need French.

June: You do! Y'see, if you go to another country, say France, and you don't know how to speak it, ... What would you do then?

Lorna: Well, well, general studies ... that doesn't tell you much does it? 'N science.

June: Yes, I know, but if you do map work like in general studies, and you go out on a walk, you'll have to know how to use a map or a compass, won't you? ... else you'll ... you'll get lost.

Jenny: Yea, but y' Mum can learn y' how to use them can't they ...

June: I know, but what if she's never been taught, ... and if it goes on like that ...

Margaret: You'll just have to learn y'self.

June: Yea, but how can you? You won't know, won't know how to write, read or anything if you didn't go to school.

The interview then started to break down as even clearer differences emerged.

June: Well, do you think if there wasn't a school you'd be happy or sad? Not a school at all.

Jenny: Well, I wouldn't be happy 'n I wouldn't be sad.

Margaret: I'd be in-between.

Lorna: Yea.

Barbara: Yea.

Janine: I like m'friends.

June: Would you prefer just Sunday Schools?
(silence)

June: Well, I do except in summer 'cos we go on holiday....
but you've got to pray to God in some way.
(silence)

June: 'Cos it'd be only once a week, would you like that instead?

Janine: Yea.

What we have here then, in my opinion, is a type of dynamic comparative method which I have called 'collaborative triangulation'. It has been illustrated here with regard to interviews only and in a short paper it is difficult to convey the value of transcripts of this type when set alongside other types of data. Together, they enabled me to produce a much more holistic understanding of key concepts, understandings, alliances and perspectives than would otherwise have been possible. This had a lot to do with the nature of what seemed to be very genuine debates which were structured into the interview situations themselves. Following the notion of theoretical sampling I explored many concepts and issues in this way — teacher mood, boredom, 'getting done', 'being sensible', 'having a laugh' — and eventually was able to construct an understanding of the children's social structure, culture and perspectives as a whole.

In conclusion, I would draw attention again to the fact that in many ways I was attempting to make a virtue of necessity. I muddled through, attempting as I did so to be theoretically aware and trying to be creative in obtaining the best quality data that it was possible for me to manage in my circumstances. Perhaps 'doing sociology of education' is often a little like that in practice, particularly for researchers working alone. However, I am concious, retrospectively, of the fact that it might have been possible and productive to have begun with a much more clear-cut awareness of the issues involved in the collection of this sort of data. On the other hand, in a study which developed less spontaneously and responsively, things might not have developed as productively as I think they eventually did. Indeed, I might well have squeezed out the quality of collaboration and trust which I think I did manage to develop with the children. Apart from anything else it might have been less fun.

Acknowledgement

I would like to thank Geoffrey Walford for his comments on a draft of this paper.

References

ALDRIDGE, J. and ALDRIDGE, D. (1985) *How to Handle Grown-ups*, London, Arrow.
ASHER, S.R. and GOTTMAN, J.M. (1981) *The Development of Children's Friendships*, Cambridge, Cambridge University Press.
BALL, S. (1985) 'Participant observation with pupils', in BURGESS, R.G.

(Ed.), *Strategies of Educational Research: Qualitative Methods*, Lewes, Falmer Press.

BOSSERT, S.T. (1979) *Tasks and Social Relationships in Classrooms*, Cambridge, Cambridge University Press.

BURGESS, R.G. (Ed.) (1982) *Field Research; A Sourcebook and Field Manual*, London, Allen and Unwin.

CALVERT, B. (1975) *The Role of the Pupil*, London, Routledge and Kegan Paul.

DAVIES, B. (1982) *Life in Classroom and Playground*, London, Routledge and Kegan Paul.

DEAN, J.P. and WHYTE, W.F. (1958) 'How do you know the informant is telling the truth?', *Human Organization*, 17, 2, pp. 34–38.

DONALDSON, M. (1978) *Children's Minds*, London, Fontana.

FINE, G.A. and GLASSNER, B. (1979) 'Participant observation with children: promises and problems', *Urban Life*, 8, 2, pp. 153–174.

GLASER, B.G. and STRAUSS, A.L. (1967) *The Discovery of Grounded Theory*, London, Weidenfeld and Nicolson.

GLASSNER, B. (1976) 'Kid Society', *Urban Education*, 11, pp. 5–22.

HOLT, J. (1975) *Escape From Childhood. The Needs and Rights of Children*, Harmondsworth, Penguin.

MACKAY, R. (1973) 'Conceptions of Children and Models of Socialization', in DREITZEL, H.P. (Ed.) *Childhood and Socialization*, New York, Macmillan.

McGURK, H. (Ed.) (1978) *Issues in Childhood Social Development*, London, Methuen.

POLLARD, A. (1985a) 'Opportunities and difficulties of a teacher-ethnographer; a personal account', in BURGESS, R.G. (Ed.), *Field Methods in the Study of Education; Issues and Problems*, Lewes, Falmer Press.

POLLARD, A. (1985b) *The Social World of the Primary School*, London, Holt, Rinehart and Winston.

RICHARDS, M. and LIGHT, P. (Eds) (1986) *Children of Social Worlds*, Cambridge, Polity Press.

SCHOSTACK, J.F. (1982) 'The revelation of the world of pupils', *Cambridge Journal of Education*, 12, 3, pp. 175–185.

SILVERS, R.J. (1977) 'Appearances: a videographic study of children's culture', in WOODS, P. and HAMMERSLEY, M. (Eds) *School Experience*, London, Croom Helm.

VIDICH, A.J. (1969) 'Participant observation and the collection and interpretation of data', in McCALL, G.J. and SIMMONS, J.L. (Eds) *Issues in Participant Observation*, Reading, Massachusetts, Addison-Wesley.

5   Theory and Practice in Fieldwork Research: Some Personal Observations in Perspective

Denis Gleeson and George Mardle

Background

This chapter provides an account of the research procedures adopted in a recent case study of a local Further Education College.[1] In so doing it considers both the methodological procedures adopted and the assumptions which guided the researchers in the field. The study represented an attempt to understand what it was like for craft students and their teachers to learn and teach within the FE sector. It furthermore sought to examine the relationship between the college, its local industrial environment and the broader social and economic issues affecting FE. Thus, although the study looked primarily at the day-to-day workings of one particular institution, Western College, the major objective was to reach a wider under-standing of those issues which comprise the complex relationship between FE and the world of work.

What follows in this chapter represents an attempt to explain rather than simply justify the methodological approach taken in the study. It seeks to provide the reader with some insight into the theoretical and practical problems involved in conducting case study research. We start from the premise that how researchers construct their arguments and conduct their research should be made publicly available. Only in this way, it is maintained here, can the *plausibility* and therefore *generalizability* of case study research be evaluated.

Denis Gleeson and George Mardle

Introduction

Towards the end of most empirical studies, the writer(s) usually attempt to explain the theoretical foundations of their methodological procedures. In a study of a macro-orientation, such an attempt might take the form of some pre-emptive explanation of the design and various research instruments employed during the course of the study. In a study of a micro-orientation, such an attempt might tend towards an 'apologetic' glimpse at the various sources of information, or at the particular observational theme carried out.

The basis of our process of legitimation, however, lies in the necessary justification of the initial epistemological stance *vis-à-vis* the world and the object of study. Indeed, without such a justification, it would seem to us that social science might aptly be described as mere speculative philosophy. Such a position, however, has of course been recently challenged by those either seeking a structural analysis of society or alternatively those who deny the possibility of any coherent empirical method.

The attempt to explain our methodological procedures, therefore, must take into account not only our research activities, but also those arguments which challenge their validity. The problem is that methodological pluralism or 'anarchy' as Feyerabend (1975) has recently described it, tends to give rise, in the search for public legitimation, to a kind of research purity which is totally inconsistent with its data. Indeed, as Bernstein (1972) points out:

> Every new approach becomes a social movement or sect which immediately defines the nature of the subject by redefining what is to be admitted or what is beyond the pale, so that with every new approach the subject starts almost from scratch.

In effect what Bernstein is suggesting is that so much time is spent in debating the various possible approaches, that insufficient attention is given to the object of study. To paraphrase Bernstein, one might say that it is not 'news' about 'news' which is important, but the 'condition' of news production which dominates the arguments.

What we shall argue in this chapter is that while the condition of news is undoubtedly important, it neither precedes nor follows the news itself. Thus, a static deliberation of methodological choices not only ignores the very nature of *creating* knowledge, but also ignores the nature of the social world, namely its dynamic, processional character. Producing news, therefore, involves a set of active practices that are both complex and insecure.

Because of the complex nature of any methodology, many of the arguments we shall advance will overlap and interrelate. In order to provide clarity, we shall divide our materials into a number of specific areas: first, the pre-emptive issues, or the problems related to carrying out an empirical study; second, a consideration of the way in which we developed our particular methodological course; third, the relationship of that methodology to our specific empirical situation; fourth, the problematic nature of writing up empirical data; and finally, some conclusions upon the methodological procedures adopted.

Our concern in this chapter is to highlight and provide insights into the process of doing research. We shall in no way suggest that our particular research activities represent a definitive text upon methodological procedures. What we would wish to argue is that they offer a commentary to our arguments and conclusions, which allows the reader some insight into our involvement at the empirical level. Before proceeding to the specifics of our procedures, however, some issues of prior theoretical importance would seem to require further consideration.

Pre-emptive Issues

Until quite recently it was commonly believed that any researcher entering the field had at his or her disposal a variety of tried and tested formulae to choose between. Indeed, traditions as diverse as documentary investigations, experiments and ethnographic observations provided the research with a ready-made list of viable procedures. For the most part, the choice of any method was pre-empted by two related factors: first, the nature of the object of study (populations, small groups or individuals), and second, the particular theoretical orientation espoused by the researcher (assumptions, conceptions and hypotheses). An interesting observation upon such choice is that rather than being of a positive nature, the result of logical argument about a set of assumptions related to the researcher and his or her object of study tended to be negative in character, researched by the rejection of inappropriate alternatives. Examples of this process of rejection may be found in the preambles to numerous small-scale studies of a participant-observational nature, particularly those inspired by the phenomenologically and inter-actionist-oriented sociology of the early 1970s. Many such researchers, while rejecting the scientism of the natural sciences, failed to fully articulate the logic of their own particular methodological assumptions. More importantly, the process of rejection often resulted in inconsistencies at a number of levels within the studies themselves. This in turn led to the well-founded accusation that they were merely 'speculative', and failed to contribute to the rational advancement of the social sciences.

Although the wide division between scientific and interpretative modes of analysis and its resolution has been at the heart of much recent debate upon methodology, the basic premise of that debate had undoubtedly been founded upon a general belief in the value of empirical work. Thus two important and highly divergent texts, Cicourel's (1964) *Method and Measurement in Society*, and Moser and Kalton's (1971) *Survey Methods in Social Investigation*, at least agree upon their object of interest and fundamental principles of social research, which necessitates entering the field to gain information. Disagreement occurs at a much higher epistemological level, namely the question of the validity of research observations regarding the *real* nature of the phenomena under analysis. However, with the recent resurgence of interest in Marxism within British sociology, a new variable has entered the equation. Indeed, structuralism suggests that all forms of empiricism, as a means of gathering information, are of secondary importance to the process of prior theorization. One exponent of this position, Saussure (1960), perhaps summarizes it best when he argues: 'Far from it being the object that antedates the viewpoint, it would seem that it is the viewpoint that creates the object'. In other words, theoretical deliberation must *guide* research activities, rather than issue from them. The debate about how a subject knows an object which has constituted the major point of contention within empiricism, is thereby submerged within the assertion that the object of study becomes *known* through theoretical deliberation. Although the proponents of such a view would undoubtedly disagree, this assertion clearly echoes Schutz's concern that problems of understanding the empirical world derive from pre-emptive suppositions of the researcher regarding their object of interest (Schutz, 1972).

While there exist strong arguments which affirm the similarity of those apparently opposing perspectives, certain basic epistemological differences clearly cannot be denied. Generally speaking, such differences arise from the problem of consciousness and its relation to the construction of the *Liebenswelt*. Within *verstehen* analysis, consciousness becomes the prime focus of consideration while, within more structurally oriented analysis, consciousness is merely an epi-phenomenon, determined by the underlying structural relations of the participants involved. Thus, from such apparently divergent perspectives, methodological premises may be based entirely upon *perception*, or at another level, be founded upon issues of *structure*. In the latter case, perception is considered to be determined by structural forces which constitute the real focus of investigation.

This incompatibility suggests that theoretical deliberation generates from within a clearly bounded set of assumptions. More importantly, such incompatibility requires that certain positive decisions should be carried out in order to avoid a state of methodological anomie. Clearly, one way forward might involve the adoption of a synthesis model, thereby producing some grand new methodological insight. However, such a course often represents little more than a search for the elusive pot of gold at the rainbow's end, so that what one ends up with has proceeded from such contradictory premises that it ultimately satisfies none of them.

Such courses of action, although theoretically interesting, lack one very important ingredient: they are guilty of abstracting the development of methodological procedures from the underlying processes of the research itself. So that ultimately it is of little importance what was decided before entering the field, because it is the actual activities of the researcher within the field which determine their success or failure. Thus, it is of little value to involve oneself in problems of an epistemological nature too early within the course of a study. What is of prime importance is to recognize those tensions and contradictions as they occur, so that they become part of the justificatory foundation of the study.

The compromise, therefore, is not between one theory and another, but between theory and practice. The researcher must examine as closely as possible the assumptions made about the object of analysis, how those assumptions informed his or her initial methodological stance, and how in the course of the study they became modified. One does not start, therefore, from what *should* be done, but from what *was* done. It is the relationship between the two which is vital, and it is to the consideration of that relationship, with regard to our own study, that we now turn.

Development Methodology

Our initial concern, as outlined in the introduction to this chapter, was to locate the nature and form of social relations within FE. In addition, we were concerned to highlight the possible relationship of those social relations to the industrial infra-structure. Such concerns suggested to us that it was necessary to proceed from an initial understanding of the structural relations between the participants within our object of study, Western College. Clearly, one way of examining such relations would have been to undertake a morphology of the institution, without carrying out any form of empirical investigation. But, in our view, such a course of action represented little more than an illusionary game. Indeed, this explanation is based upon the notion that the social world can be understood *totally* independently from its material practices. While such explanation might appear coherent, its definition of terms within the area of discourse ultimately represents little more than an idealized and speculative model of the social system, which in our view is over-deterministic in the extreme. What this kind of structural explanation fails to address is how the form of the structure relates to the existential activities of its members. In particular, it ignores how similar structural forces often give rise to dissimilar and sometimes contradictory formations at the empirical level.

It seemed to us that if our understanding of the structure of Western College was to mean anything, then some discussion of the material practices which characterized that structure was desirable, if not essential. In our view, the structure itself cannot be understood without some examination of the ways in which its participants relate to the material conditions of their world. Only then can the researcher develop an understanding of the ideological and potentially mystificatory nature of social reality. To construct a morphology of the institution, therefore, seemed to us to relegate those involved to mere puppets operating in a reified dynamic, and unable to transcend their own reality. Such a course of action, moreover, rests on the assumption that the understanding of the theorist is superior to that of the participant.

What we would wish to argue is that the explanation of the social world is neither dependent upon nor independent of the object of study. Rather, it is the linkage between theory and its objects which is vital and needs articulation. Thus it was necessary for us to reach a rigorous understanding of both the activities and the perceptions of the actors involved. Such perceptions, however, were not simply to be accepted as a definitive explanation of material practice, but were to be linked to the underlying 'structural dynamic' we sought to articulate. So, we proceeded to gather information about how those involved perceived the day-to-day organization of college affairs, the relationship between their work and local industry, and the material and ideological constraints imposed upon their practice. These perceptions did not represent topics in their own right, but provided a focus around which theoretical discussion and deliberation might take place.

As a result of our initial methodological course, based upon the relationship between theory and the empirical, three problems of specific importance came to light.

First, there was the question of validity. Without wishing to ignore the initial question of 'validity to whom', and a highly theoretical discussion of its specific definition, we chose to adopt a purely pragmatic approach in respect. In our view, validity can only really be assessed in terms of the particular theoretical position of the proponents. To appeal to some independent and objective principles, which deny the complex links between theory and practice, would seem to us to be simply contradictory. More importantly, such an appeal would elevate highly problematic scientific practices to a position far beyond any proven justification. In our case, and within the scope of our own particular assumptions, two types of criteria were adopted as a measure of validity. First, our structural explanations were required to be rational and coherent, and second, substantive and coherent links were seen to be an essential feature of the mediation between our descriptive and analytical categories. Very simply, at each stage of our argument, we sought to explain how our particular descriptions of social reality related to our specific theoretical frame. How, for instance, the practices of departmental members within a competitive and institutional structure bore relation to the wider demand for trained labour. We sought, moreover, not only to demonstrate that relationship, but to reduce the possibility of any alternative explanations. For the less likely the validity of any such alternative explanation, the more coherence our explanation assumed, not only in terms of our own criteria, but also in those of others.

The second problem that we confronted was that of bias. Many of the arguments we have advanced in relation to the problem of validity are also of relevance to this area. Traditionally, the question of bias has been related to the process of data selection *vis-à-vis* the argument one seeks to advance. If the researcher adopts a model based upon the premise that the social world is *independent* of its method of discovery, then the question of bias becomes highly contentious. Our particular model of social explanation rests on the assertion that the basis of such explanation resides in the vital links between theory and material practice. It is within those vital links, however, that bias may potentially occur. In our view, the major mechanism through which such bias may be avoided involves a scrupulous attendance to the criteria adopted in order to assess validity, namely that the vital links between theory and material practice should be both rational and coherent. Within our model of explanation, therefore, bias may be said to occur where the relationship between analytical and descriptive categories is insufficiently substantiated, for instance, where some aspect of classroom practice might be described as a feature of capitalism, without a thorough exemplification of that conclusion. In other words, our model seeks to avoid the simplistic choice of data to *fit* theory, and requires that the links made between theory and data should be fully substantiated.

The third immediate problem which arose on entering the field, concerned the nature of the information gathered. While we have tended to concentrate so far upon issues of a theoretical nature, it is the problematic question of the relationship between theory and practical methods which so often gives rise to the most important difficulties. A large number of methodologies contain within themselves a number of intractable propositions with regard to the collection of data. In our case, however, we experienced no such hypothetical imperative. Indeed, our major concern was to examine practice and the descriptions of practitioners in relation to the theory which sought to explain that practice. More importantly, the ontological status or validity of those descriptions did not pose for us a central issue, since our conclusions were not entirely dependent upon their truth. On the other hand, we could not ignore the fact that there are limits to what is available and what can be accepted within any social scene one seeks to understand. In particular, the sheer complexity of any institution, both hierarchical and bureaucratic, renders the collection of 'sensitive' information extremely difficult. Indeed, the complex character of any institution tends to constitute its own rationality, which must be brought to bear upon the statements of participants and their potential use. In the section which follows, we shall look more closely at such problems.

Entering the Field — or Where the 'Talking' Stops

Prior to entering any particular field of discourse for the purpose of collecting data, the researchers must act upon a number of specific decisions regarding the relationship of their theoretical position to the practical course they propose to adopt. As indicated in the previous section, we experienced no specific imperative in this respect, which many alternative methodologies undoubtedly impose. Indeed, a large number of paradigmatic persuasions share a common failing in their separate attempts to eliminate bias on the part of the observer. Thus, given our assumptions about the nature of theory, the idea of the social world as being independent of its theoretical articulation simply did not pose a problem. Our expressed purpose was not merely to observe, but rather to explore certain interests, ideas and theories. Therefore our immediate concern was to gather what might be described as 'focused information'. In other words, we sought to explore that information in terms of its relevance to the structural parameters of educational practice we were attempting to understand.

On entering the field, however, our major assumption was immediately challenged. We had expected to find at Western College a relatively close fit between its practices, both cognitive and affectual, and the workings of the immediate industrial environment it expressly sought to serve. But such a close correspondence was far from the case, and in fact very few of our observations of college practice appeared to bear immediate relation to the local industrial world. We concluded that at this stage we were seeking to *prove* a correspondence between theory and practice, rather than to examine the two as interrelated aspects of the same process. Having arrived at that initial conclusion, we then ceased to be so dogmatic about what we were looking for.

From our modified premise information had no greater significance than its face value. It might derive from a variety of sources, at many levels, and through a complex number of means. Hearsay gleaned perhaps from an informal discussion over coffee could not be attributed lesser significance than, say, a pre-meditated question asked of the principal during a formal interview, since that would be to assume a level of validity inappropriate to our model. This level of generality, with regard to what should count as data, was complicated by a number of problems associated with time, since not only does the institution change over a period of time, but also the information the researcher collects regarding the workings of that institution. For example, when we commenced our fieldwork, the development of new technical courses was being carried out, and we were able to observe to some extent the course of that development. However, our fieldwork came to an end before the college administration had modified those courses in terms of their relative success or failure after one year. That meant that we were unable to fully follow up our observations of course development with regard to these 'new' initiatives.

A second problem we immediately confronted centred upon the degree of confidence we, as researchers, were able to establish with those we sought to observe. Indeed, the level and kind of information gained from a first interview differed significantly from that acquired from subsequent ones, but to suggest that the data gained from later interviews is any nearer the truth than that acquired from initial ones is to assume that truth does *in fact* exist. Thus, we chose to view both forms of information as expressions of separate aspects of the social relations of the institution, so that the use of any account did not depend upon its degree of confidentiality, but upon the explanatory power it bore in relation to our theory.

In line with our particular assumptions, therefore, our model of data collection became no more than a process of gathering information. More specifically, the major means we adopted of acquiring that information was through verbal contact with members of the college staff. Thus we might involve ourselves in informal discussions with departmental members, or, alternatively, in more formalized interviews of an exploratory nature, or in semi-structured interviews which were to be recorded on tape. We also sought to include any written records of college activities that we were allowed access to.

We were also aware of a further important problem, which is intrinsic to a large number of research methodologies, namely that of *no* apparent information with regard to a particular aspect of the object of study. The priority of many interpretative forms of research often gives rise to the assumption that if it has not been said, then it cannot be articulated. In our view, such an assumption simply accepts the dominance of verbal access to understanding, which far exceeds its capability of describing much that is of interest in the social world. Moreover, it would seem to us that in certain areas of social life there exist a number of aspects of social relationships which are 'closed' even to the participants themselves, and which for the researcher are very difficult to gain access to. In such circumstances, the researcher can only make inference from what is available.

In the preceding sections we have attempted to set out the logic of our particular theoretical position, together with some problems related to its translation into practical formulations. Now the purely practical process of collecting data, and the further complications that this gave rise to, clearly warrants careful documentation, and in the section which follows we shall attempt to highlight some of the difficulties we confronted in the course of that fundamental task.

Collecting Data

It would not be an exaggeration to say that many people regard social scientists with considerable scepticism. Indeed, the image of the social researcher as an interfering, uncomprehending theorist is often justified, particularly when one reads certain obscure forms of analysis which have been carried out in the name of social science. Many studies of a 'macro' orientation, for example, which have utilized highly sophisticated forms of survey methodologies, can be well understood to be seen by participants as yet more statistics for the DES computer. Alternatively, it is easy to understand why many of the in-depth studies of classroom practice have been interpreted by participants as mere 'teacher-bashing' programmes. Thus, the most important initial problem that the researcher must deal with on entering the field concerns the image he or she presents to those he or she is attempting to understand. Indeed, one cannot expect to find out about the world, if one denies the world knowledge of oneself. Yet that very attempt at mutual contact involves numerous unavoidable and sometimes disagreeable consequences. Indeed, the 'presentation of self' usually determines whether or not further avenues of potential understanding will remain closed. Thus, in the initial negotiations, the researcher must take into account that the teacher who is questioned about his or her procedures of assessment, may well interpret those questions as a blatant attack upon personal practice. Moreover, the head of department, who is approached about the process of decision-making within his or her department, is usually only too well aware of the political significance of those questions. Thus a clumsy beginning can often close many doors for ever for the researcher. On the other hand, an over-indulgent attitude towards the interviewee can often make of one's research little more than an exercise in psychotherapy.

That said, establishing oneself in the research context and building a relationship with participants serves only to designate the
parameters within which a number of initial and rather pragmatic
decisions will be made, and from which the study will hopefully
develop. For example, one of our most important initial decisions
concerned which aspect of the institution was most favourable for
the observation of our interests. Here our choice was guided by two
important assumptions: first, since our major concern was to examine the relationship between FE and industry, we needed to
locate our study within a college whose major task was to prepare
students for their future industrial roles; and second, we needed to
narrow that focus to an institutional setting where little else other
than vocational courses were carried out. In other words, we
assumed that given such a 'manifest' setting, it would be easier to
explore the 'fit' between FE and industry, and to assess the validity
of our theory of that relationship in terms of our observations of
practice.

Having made those initial rather *ad hoc* decisions, we then had
to deal with the problem of access. Through a variety of informal
negotiations, it became possible for us to locate our study within a
number of colleges within the area. We finally opted for Western
College because the institution seemed the most appropriate setting
within which to examine the practical manifestation of our research
interests.

Our initial contact with the staff at Western allowed us access
to only *one* particular department, and since our research interests
were such that we needed far wider access to the processes of the
institution, we again confronted a serious obstacle. As we soon
discovered, initial access to one aspect of any institution often
impedes entry to others. In particular, our original contact felt
considerable responsibility for our actions. Thus our movements
were often restricted until we had gained official consent through
various bureaucratic channels. In the meantime, we attempted to
establish a number of informal contacts among a range of college
staff. Inevitably, however, having arranged an informal meeting with
a member of another department, which had not been officially
cleared by our original contact, we found ourselves called to a
meeting and reprimanded for not going through official channels.
This demonstrated to us the very precarious control the researcher is
able to exert over his sources of information. This limited control
was further exemplified a few weeks later, when having gained
official permission from a head of department to approach his staff,

we were presented with a list of pre-arranged interviews. This meant that we had no control over the selection and context of those interviews and it became very difficult to gain access to the views of departmental members regarding the social relations of the department, because we were so clearly identified with the authority structure of the department.

Throughout the course of our fieldwork we continually found that as a new channel of information opened, another closed: the problem being that when one is seen to be close to a particular person or group of persons, relationships with others become problematic. Indeed, we found on the one hand that simply being seen in an accidental conversation with, say, a head of department often pre-empted any further discussion with certain college staff. On the other hand, we also became aware that our research was not enhanced if we were seen to be in close relations with those members of the college staff who were identified by their colleagues as in any way 'deviant'. In addition to such problems, we had to deal with the further complication of establishing fruitful links with both students, employers and other outside agencies, so that our initial activities within the field had to be tempered with considerable discretion. Our pragmatic decision with regard to the kinds of problems outlined above was to adopt what we referred to as a 'spiral technique' of contacts. That is to say, we sought to begin our relations with the various college personnel at an informal level. We simply discussed FE in general in the hope that we would gain both their confidence and some useful perspectives upon their activities. When and if we had gained sufficient information in this way, we adopted a different course of action. For those sources who were prepared to discuss their work in greater depth, we sought to arrange more formal interviews and to tape-record any useful information. Records of other discussion were simply recorded in our field notes. We did not, however, carry out this 'spiral technique' in our dealings with the organizational hierarchy of the college. We felt that a more formal approach was more appropriate in such circumstances. Here our questions were prepared, but the situations were usually unstructured.

It is important to mention at this point that we did not rely entirely upon information gained through interviews. Two of the research team acquired some part-time teaching at the college and were thus enabled to gain more first-hand knowledge of both staff and students. We also observed numerous lessons within various college departments. Indeed, such classroom observations proved invaluable in guiding the direction of subsequent interviews with college personnel. It is as well to point out here, however, that such a form of data collection is extremely difficult to negotiate, and often antagonizes those under observation. Thus we provide few examples drawn from our observations of classroom practice.

In addition to our examination of activities within college, we considered that substantial contact should be made with those external bodies who were also concerned with the structures and processes of FE. We sought to interview a range of employers, training officers, employment officers, trade unionists and school staff, especially those engaged in link courses with the college. Again our activities had to be tempered with considerable tact, particularly when the question of limited time posed innumerable problems of technique. Our solution was to engage in guided discussions which would allow the participants to express their views on the process of FE in general.

In this section, we have attempted to elaborate the specific procedures we adopted in order to gain useful information from the participants we sought to understand. In effect, the role of the researcher is lonely, difficult and often boring. He or she spends the greater part of the time building up to 'doing' something, rather than actually doing it. Not only do contacts have to be made, re-made and sustained, but also dissolved, when the researcher wants to move on to other areas. Information must be checked and re-checked, ideas sounded out and procedures re-evaluated if procedures of adequate triangulation are to be adopted. Thus we often found at our research meetings that we had spent several hours discussing the problem with very little to show for our efforts. Very often the person we had arranged to interview had been called away, or did not turn up, or simply did not want us in his or her classroom.

Our greatest enemy was undoubtedly 'time'. We 'wasted' innumerable hours collecting information which simply did not make sense or relate in any useful way to our theoretical frame, and we were continually rejecting materials which had appeared eighteen months before to be crucial but which now with the knowledge of hindsight were totally irrelevant to our major concerns. And finally, we had to continually re-charge our initial enthusiasm since it was so easy to lose sight of our original idea, and indeed during the course of our field-work that idea often appeared irrelevant to the day-to-day practicalities of FE.

Our major means of controlling the course of our work at this time was through regular meetings of the research team, where we discussed our observations and gave some on-going impetus to the fulfilment of our initial objectives. However, those meetings provided only minimal support during a period of potential alienation. Indeed, we still faced the difficulty of condensing our materials and structuring them into a rigorous, well-founded report. In the section which follows we shall outline some of the problems associated with writing up research observations.

Writing Up

The problems discussed above in relation to data collection become infinitesimal when compared with those associated with writing up. At best the structuring of research materials can only be described as an exercise in reducing a whole range of dynamic social relations to mere words upon a page. Indeed, it is extremely difficult to avoid reproducing an artificial description of human forms. The problem is that social scientists have few tried and tested formulae to guide them. Traditional forms of research have largely relied upon the process of abstracting an argument from ever-reducing materials. But our theoretical position did not allow us to adopt such a procedure. Rather than being concerned with abstracting a theory from data, we had set ourselves the task of exemplifying our theory through the materials which were available. In other words, our methodology required that we should convince an audience that our observations of the empirical related coherently to the assumptions we had made about the nature of the structural.

Our major objective, therefore, was to construct an interpretation of practice which was more plausible than any alternative explanation. Inasmuch as we would not wish to deny the possibility of alternative interpretations, however, it is equally the case that we seek to avoid the trap of relativism. For to adopt a relativistic stance would be to support the view that reality has a transient nature, and to deny the significance of those material practices which underpin it. In our view, the validity of alternative interpretations must be assessed according to their ability to explain their own particular structural assumptions in terms of the accounts used to exemplify them.

An area of difficulty which is highly relevant to our methodology lies in the problem of empathy with regard to the accounts of participants. Since our major concern was to exemplify the structural in terms of the empirical, the practices we sought to describe could not always be treated as commonsensical accounts, and they often appeared to be extremely critical, yet it was never our intention to attack those we sought to understand. We were concerned simply to explore the conditions of practice, rather than the reactions of participants to those conditions. Those reactions, however, served as a means of gaining greater understanding of the social relations under observation. In other words, rather than concentrating upon the accounts of participants, which might well be undervalued or indeed overvalued, we focused upon the relationship between those various accounts and our specific theoretical assumptions. Our major difficulty, however, was that the relationship could never be totally and reflexively monitored, and we found ourselves involved in a process of trying and re-trying particular explanations, which changed both over the course of time and as we received new information. Consider, for example, the following comments from Terry, a third-year craft apprentice, which would appear on face value to be a plausible criticism of much technical teaching. Indeed, his remarks echo the commonsense view held by many students that teachers are out of touch with present-day industrial reality:

> The trouble with him (i.e. the teacher) is that he's been away from the job so long that he's out of touch ... things have changed since he did his apprentieship ... I know he means well ... in fact he's a good bloke ... and can teach ... but he gets us making things, using equipment and methods that must have gone out with the Ark. I know he's a craftsman ... but you see craft has changed ... blokes like him aren't needed any more.... Yet he gets us making bits and pieces of machinery, parts and the like ... the kind of machinery that either isn't used any more or that at work you simply send down to the stores for. It seems that so much of what we learn, even in the workshop, doesn't relate to what we do at work ... the blokes at work tell us not to pay too much attention.... You don't know where you are.

Clearly, from accounts such as this, the researcher might achieve considerable 'mileage' with regard to the similarity of Terry's account with the corresponding problems outlined in the recent Great Educational Debate (1976–1979), namely that of the lack of fit between education and the occupational structure. Yet we were not entirely convinced by the apparent correspondence between such remarks and much that had recently been stated in public debate. For it seemed to us too simple an explanation of our industrial problems, and implied that if teaching could be up-dated, then all would be well. Moreover, such an explanation clearly begs the whole question of how teachers themselves view their contribution to industry. When one juxtaposes Terry's account with that of his teacher, a very different version emerges, which while recognizing the lack of fit, views the teaching difficulties from a very different angle:

> Yes ... of course he's right, but it does depend on how you look at it. I'm sure apprentices don't need to know a good deal of the stuff we have to teach them ... the City and Guilds and the Professional Institutes have a lot to answer for on that one. On the other hand, just because the lads can get parts from the stores, does that mean they shouldn't know more about those parts; how they're made, what they're made from ... even how to make them? Yes, I often get my lads making things, learing manual skills and using measuring procedures that they won't use at work ... I also get them to strip machinery down, demonstrate its principles ... get them to know how it works. But just because they're never likely to do all this at work, it doesn't mean to say it's irrelevant.... He's right, people like me aren't needed any more ... technology has turned craft into a process of fitting replacements ... that sort of thing .. the skill element has largely gone. But these lads are still on craft apprenticeships and I'm not just concerned with teaching them to fit and replace spare parts as if they were robots ... they're already like that, some of them. I think they need to know what's behind the technology ... even if they aren't called on to work on it ... though they might want to get involved in that side of things one day ... but if they haven't a clue, how can they? So, if everything I teach doesn't relate to the routine humdrum of everyday work you can say that what I was doing was irrelevant. But it depends how you see things.

The comments quoted above provide an alternative to Terry's explanation of the problem of relevance. The lecturer is operating with a critical perspective of changing work patterns, and recognizes the implications of craft de-skilling for teaching and training. His account suggests that he sees his role as providing more than a simple introduction to the limited demands of work, so that he would seem to demonstrate a more comprehensive understanding of the requirements of modern technology than Terry would give him credit for. Although he recognizes that 'people like me aren't needed any more', he avoids the temptation to treat his students like robots, thus exercising some power of intervention in the process of training.

Having considered both accounts of the problem of correspondence between industry and training, we were able to reach an alternative viewpoint *vis-à-vis* that problem. For, from their different viewpoints, both accounts argue that training can be irrelevant to the work situation. Moreover, that overlapping of views suggests that participants perceived education to be to some extent autonomous of the economic base. However, what was of interest to us was that both actors, while recognizing a lack of fit, continued to support existing practice. Thus, having located that initial contradiction, we attempted to arrive at some plausible explanations of it, and in this way the process of elaboration continued. Clearly, we had no power to set limits upon empirical possibilities, only the motivation to propose limited theoretical alternatives. The process of developing links between theory and empirical reality can never be adequately realized, for it requires a continual re-negotiation of accounts at both the theoretical and empirical levels. Thus the researcher must also explore the views of participants with regard to each other's accounts, not to triangulate some assumed reality, but simply to generate alternative conceptions which will shed greater light upon his or her own theoretical elaborations.

Finally, we are aware that in articulating our methodological procedures, we are speaking to a small audience, and that a large number of that audience will be more interested in criticizing the 'conditions' of news than in examining the 'news' itself. Indeed, given our particular perspective, such a response is to be expected. Our concern, though, is not entirely with such readers, as we hold that the practical involvement of social scientists in any situation requires a high degree of empathy with those they seek to understand. We wish to make it clear, therefore, that our major purpose in this chapter has been to develop an explanation of how (in the widest sense) we constructed our argument. As social scientists, we attempt to look beyond the obvious, yet in doing so we cannot ignore the social relations we find and the world to which we speak. We hope that our readers will appreciate that our primary concern has been simply to locate and exemplify the opaqueness and contradictions of everyday life, and if we have in any way succeeded in locating those contradictions, we will have at least provided some food for thought for those who wish to gain some control over them. We have attempted to argue that methodological procedures are at best idealistic, and at worst simply *ad hoc* pragmatism. The researcher can do no more, however, than set out his or her combination of ideas and practices as they develop, so that they will provide a basis through which the study may be examined. In our view, it is not the question of methodological purity which is important, but whether we have justified our own assumptions, and arrived at some plausible explanations of the process of FE.

Clearly, one could produce a volume devoted entirely to the issue of methodology, but as the proverb suggests, 'the proof of the pudding is in the eating'. Thus we have provided minimal insight into our procedures, and leave it to the reader to judge their appropriateness. It is our contention, moreover, that the reader can only do this when the researchers have made public their specific theories, assumptions and prejudices. Methodology is, after all, only a means to an end, and not an end in itself. It is perhaps worth remembering this point at a time when the impetus is toward training researchers in the art of *technique* rather than in the art of identifying problems and in asking the right questions.

Note

1. See GLEESON, D. and MARDLE, G. (1980).

References

ALTHUSSER, L. (1969) *For Marx*, Harmondsworth, Allen Lane, The Penguin Press.

ALTHUSSER, L. (1971) 'Ideology and ideological state apparatuses', in *Lenin and Philosophy and Other Essays*, London, New Left Books.

BERNSTEIN, B. (1972) *The Sociology of Education: A Brief Account*, E282, Unit 17, Milton Keynes, The Open University.

CICOUREL, A.V. (1964) *Method and Measurement in Sociology*, New York, Free Press.

DE SAUSSURE, F. (1960) *Course in General Linguistics*, London, Duckworth.

FEYERABEND, P. (1975) 'Against science', *Radical Philosophy*, 11.

GLEESON, D. and MARDLE, G. (1980) *Further Education or Training? A Case Study in the Theory and Practice of Day Release Education* (with the assistance of John McCourt), London, Routledge and Kegan Paul.

MOSER, C.A. and KALTON, G. (1971) *Survey Methods in Social Investigation*, London, Heinemann.

SCHUTZ, A. (1972) *Phenomenology of the Social World*, London, Heinemann.

6   Issues and Dilemmas in Action Research

Judith Byrne Whyte

Introduction

The Girls Into Science and Technology (GIST) project (1979–84) was an action research programme based in ten schools in the Greater Manchester area. The twin aims of the project were: to explicate the reasons for girls dropping scientific and technical subjects as soon as they become optional in the fourth year of secondary school; and simultaneously to explore the feasibility and effectiveness of intervention strategies designed to reduce the drop-out and modify the sex stereotyping of subject choice.

At the time of writing, GIST is still the most substantial British investigation of gender differentiation at school carried out with a feminist interventionist as well as research-based approach. It addressed several pressing questions for those concerned to improve the position of girls in education. Will proposals such as eliminating sex bias in textbooks or changing teaching styles actually work? Is it a good idea to try and persuade girls to enter previously all-male occupational fields? Is single sex schooling, or the compromise of single sex classes in the mixed school more desirable? The trouble with well-meant educational innovations is that they do not always turn out as intended. Strategies like positive discrimination may well result in a reduction of opportunities for women. Janet Finch, in her book about education as social policy (Finch, 1984) has pointed out that schools may simply not be capable of producing the kind of profound social change implied in an alteration of the relations between the sexes, and that it is difficult to devise strategies of social engineering which will not in the end be counter-productive to the interests they were meant to serve.

This chapter does not discuss in detail the efficacy or otherwise of the GIST model of action research, as that is quite fully dealt with elsewhere (see Kelly, 1985; Whyte, 1986). Instead I want to focus on four research issues thrown up by GIST, and which have, I think, important implications for educational research aimed at social change. These are:

1. The occasional tensions between action and research goals.
2. The researcher-practitioner relationship and difficulties we encountered in negotiating a mutually acceptable ethical framework with the teachers.
3. The methodology we used, and whether it was appropriate to the context.
4. The way GIST has been reported and disseminated, and the implications for policy-oriented research in general.

GIST Outcomes

The activist purpose of GIST was to produce changes in teachers' and pupils' attitudes to science/technology and sex roles, in the hope that options at 13-plus would alter in the direction of less stereotyped subject choices. A number of intervention strategies were negotiated in eight 'action' schools: bringing women scientists and technologists into the classroom as role models, modifying materials and courses to make them less male-biased, observing classroom interactions and helping teachers devise ways of increasing girls' participation and motivation. In all ten schools, children's knowledge of and interest in science, their attitudes to science and other school subjects, their social backgrounds and attitudes to sex roles were investigated through a battery of tests and questionnaires administered on entry to secondary education. In the two 'control' schools, testing and attitude surveys took place, but no attempt was made to change attitudes or practices. In the pupils' third year, a second survey measured the degree to which attitudes had changed, and option choices were monitored. The analysis of this data, together with school observation over the 3–4 years of the project showed that a number of factors operate to discourage girls from pursuing studies in science or technology. These are discussed at more length elsewhere (see Kelly *et al.*, 1984; Whyte, 1986) but briefly, the 'masculinity' of science — the people who do it and the context of the way it is taught — the attitudes of pupils, teachers and parents, the lack of female role models in male-dominated occupations and differences in the treatment of male and female pupils all contribute to a process which channels girls out of science/technology and into arts and humanities. The identification of such factors as important marked a shift in the project from seeing the problem as essentially to do with girls' motivation, towards a fuller recognition of the structure of attitudes and expectations which make it difficult, if not impossible, for schoolgirls (and to some extent for schoolboys) to make a non-traditional choice.

The purpose of GIST had been to change both attitudes and behaviour. A significant difference in attitudes to science and sex roles did show up between boys and girls in the action schools compared with the control cohort. They were less stereotyped about sex roles, less likely to view science as masculine, and the girls in the action schools were more likely to mention a scientific or technical job as a possible career for them in the future.

The results of the interventions in relation to subject choice were disappointing. There was no consistent increase in girls opting for physical science or crafts. Although in four of the action schools the interventions had the effect of temporarily increasing choices of physics by girls, there were comparable increases in both the control schools! The small improvement may have been due not to the interventions, but simply to being 'one of the GIST schools'. A follow-up study by the EOC in the year after GIST ended, found that the proportion of girls opting for physics fell back in the following year to the same or a lower level than before (Clarke, 1985). The overall pattern in all ten schools is confusing, with boys' and girls' choices changing over the period, probably in relation to factors other than gender stereotyping of subjects.

1. Action-Research Tensions

The earliest proposal for GIST was drafted by the writer for the EOC in 1978 and was ambitious in terms of money and staffing: £25 000 per annum for eight years, with a research team of one full-time Research Fellow, a group of female teachers and scientists to work directly in schools, and finally an unspecified number of teacher training and psychology students to administer and score questionnaires. If that proposal had been accepted, GIST might have proceeded very differently. In fact after it had gone to the EOC, I was informally advised that a large research programme in conjunction with the Social Science Research Council was being planned, and that it was hoped I would resubmit my proposal to the joint panel.

In the intervening period, Kate Purcell, a mutual friend, introduced me to Alison Kelly, another feminist who had already carried out survey research in science education, leading her, from a different direction, to the conclusion that the next step was to undertake some action research; she was already preparing a proposal to SSRC. We therefore joined forces and agreed to work together, despite certain differences of emphasis between us about the source of the 'girls and science' problem. A few weeks later, advertisements appeared in the press inviting applications for research under a new EOC/SSRC Joint Panel, on 'women and underachievement'. The revised joint proposal laid more stress than before on exploring attitudes to science, and envisaged a much smaller research team: Alison and I would work on the project jointly, at no cost, and the remaining staffing was simply a full-time research officer with the possibility of two linked SSRC studentships at a later stage. Barbara Smail was appointed to the former post, and worked with us on the development of questionnaires and liaison with schools from the start. As a chemistry teacher with several years of experience she proved to have considerable credibility with science teachers, independently mounting a lot of curriculum work. She also registered for an M.Ed. and became expert in the analysis of GIST data. John Catton completed the team, a year or two later, when the pressing need for a craft specialist had become obvious.

Both Alison and I continued to be involved in normal teaching during the life of GIST, imposing constraints of time from the start, and even at the peak of the project team, with four people and two project secretaries, there never seemed to be time to do everything one might have wanted.

The number of GIST schools owed more to the desire to get a large sample of pupils for the attitude survey and its subsequent analysis than to an estimate of the best starting point for change, and it is now clear that the shortage of woman hours available to carry out the GIST project should have led to greater caution in the decision about the number of schools to include in our sample. With the tiny team we now composed, three or four action schools was really the maximum in terms of managing change. Instead, ten schools were selected, including two controls, because this would offer a good sample of (approximately 2000) pupils. This was the first sign of a tension between priorities for action and for research, a familiar theme in the literature, and to which the GIST project was no exception.

Action and research are both greedy activities in terms of time. Normal or traditional research can be, and often is, combined with teaching and administration. But action research requires the presence of the researcher on the site: the research is where the client, or practitioner is. The time required is often unpredictable and difficult to programme in advance, and yet all the other usual research activities of data analysis and writing up also have to be carried out. Secondly, research is, or at any rate is supposed to be committed to scientific values of objectivity, while action generally depends on values of a more controversial kind. Action research is usually about promoting some set of values in preference to another, and to some extent the goal of objectivity cannot simultaneously be held on to.

In terms of GIST, we felt acutely the pressure of, on the one hand, our feminist consciousness of the way schools treat girls as second best, and a consequent desire to change not just the pattern of option choices, but the sexist reality of the schools, and on the other an interest as researchers in the investigation of the phenomenon of girls' under-representation in science/technology and a commitment to acceptable social science methodologies to ensure that measures of the response to interventions were reliable and valid.

An existing body of research evidence about girls and science generated certain hypotheses which laid the basis for an action research programme of tests, questionnaires, observation and action/intervention. We found unsatisfactory any definition of action research as simply two parallel processes which interface from time to time, and tried rather to interweave action and research so that the research findings informed practical decisions, and the action was accommodated in a fluid research design. The tests and interventions were 'done to' the teachers and pupils. But they, as social beings, also began to form their own hypotheses about the nature of the problem. Indeed this process of hypothesis-forming was a hoped-for outcome of the programme. That is, when pupils began to regard their choices as at least partially determined by social factors, their attitudes and ultimately their choices would change; as teachers began to perceive the problem as one of professional interest, their account of what happens to channel girls out of science would lead them to changed classroom practice. The decisions then made by

Figure 6.1: A model of action research

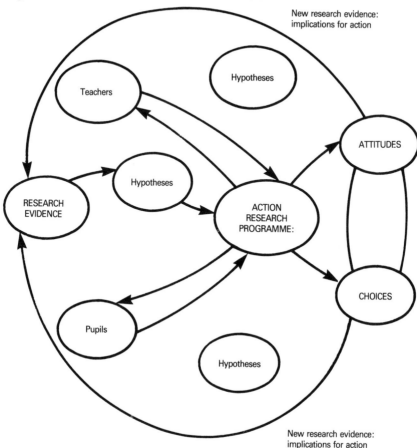

both groups were to form the basis for new research evidence about how pupils, teachers and schools may change, generating further research hypotheses (see Fig. 6.1).

This model of action research has been called 'simultaneous-integrated' (see Kelly, 1985) and was built upon an account of action research from the field of management, which we found came close to the emerging GIST model. Hult and Lennung, extending an earlier definition by Rapaport (1970) say that action research:

  i.   simultaneously assists in practical problem-solving and expands scientific knowledge, and
 ii.   enhances the competence of the respective actors;
iii.   is performed collaboratively;
 iv.   in an immediate situation;
  v.   uses data feedback in a cyclical process;

vi. is aimed at increased understanding of a given social situation;

vii. is primarily applicable for the understanding of change processes in social systems; and

viii. is undertaken within a mutually acceptable ethical framework.

(Hult & Lennung, 1980)

Although it would be preferable to see all of these processes as intertwined, in order to highlight some of the action-research tensions we encountered it is helpful to sub-divide the definition into action and research goals:

RESEARCH GOALS	ACTION GOALS
Expands scientific knowledge	Practical problem-solving
Aims at increased understanding of a given social situation	Enhanced competency
	Performed collaboratively
Contributes to understanding of change processes in social systems	In an immediate situation

which should be employed 'using data feedback in a cyclical process', to be regarded as the heart of the definition, and 'undertaken within a mutually acceptable ethical framework'. This division makes it clear that, roughly speaking, the action goals involved working directly with practitioners — the teachers, while the research goals included observation of schools and teachers as objects of investigation.

GIST research goals were not just to investigate the girls and science problem, but also to monitor and analyze attempted change; the action goals were directed through the teachers to the pupils. Just as action and research betoken different values and orientations, so we as researchers had values additional to and distinct from the practical orientation of the teachers. The relationship between us as researchers (but action researchers) and the teachers as practitioners was much more crucial than we had really recognized at the start of the project.

2. The Researcher-Practitioner Relationship

Once the principle had been established — after some long and gritty team discussions — that a survey of pupil attitudes would yield valuable data and would be the most effective way of monitoring changes, the research goals almost inexorably encroached on the time and energy available for action. The task grew mammoth: ten questionnaires in all, in the first survey, were administered to the 2000 GIST children. Each one had to be delivered to the school, given to the teachers with explanatory notes, collected some days later, coded and put on to punch cards for the computer, then analyzed.

The associated visits to schools were used by the team for initiating discussions about the aims of the project, but not unnaturally teachers continued to see the questionnaires as the central legitimate activity, and became occasionally impatient with what seemed like irrelevant conversations about girls and science. Even when a meeting of departmental staff was arranged, I can remember in one case a head of department saying to me 'You really have got a bee in your bonnet about this girls and science thing, haven't you?' He was immune to the idea that both the meeting and our conversations were as central to the project's purposes as the questionnaires. Looking back, work with the teachers was wrongfooted even in the initial workshops because of their prior understanding of what a research project was about, compunded by the difficulty we experienced in coming clean about the action aims in relation to teachers. The misunderstanding was only reinforced by the number of large brown envelopes being dropped off and retrieved from schools. This is why, I think, the evaluation report showed that the majority of teachers had no sense that the project was aimed at them as much as at the pupils (Payne *et al.*, 1983).

This element of false consciousness about the true relationship between ourselves and the teachers highlights what appears to be a recurrent feature of action research: what Cherns (1975) calls the 'inescapable suggestion of manipulation' which is especially likely to be present when action research directed towards organizational change is opposed by those who are, in a sense, the clients. A rather nice industrial parallel is reported by Barry and Webb (1976), whose intention was to introduce innovations in roles, attitudes and communications amongst managers in a small printing firm. At first the proposed changes seemed to be accepted, but when a financial crisis hit the firm, plans for growth and change were immediately abandoned, and indeed the clients actually thought that acceptance of the research group's recommendations, by increasing administrative overheads, had brought about the financial disaster. The researchers considered withdrawing altogether, but finally decided to work with the management to help them overcome the crisis, and postpone their own action research plans until the atmosphere was more propitious.

In a sense, something similar happened during the GIST programme. Teachers' past experience of research projects led them to expect a product which could be delivered to pupils in the classroom, and there was a good deal of pressure, not fully resisted by the Schools Liaison Officers, to devise new curriculum materials and approaches. The attempt to work on teacher attitudes put us on less familiar ground: one way was to observe pupils and teachers in labs and workshops, reporting back immediately on patterns of interaction. This had limited success with the few teachers who invited observation and engaged in discussion afterwards (see Whyte, 1984); it probably had more value as a source of data on what happens in school to discourage girls from taking boys' subjects.

By the time the GIST cohort had reached their third year we knew the schools, and therefore that the science and crafts staff were far from seeing GIST goals as an organizational priority. There was no observable pressure from senior management for teachers to change. Although heads expressed general support, this never led any of them to insist on proof of non-sexist attitudes or to offer real rewards for non-sexist teaching. There was a brief flurry of interest in GIST when a number of individuals were applying for senior posts during reorganization in one authority which had included equal opportunities as one of the responsibilities, but there was a sense that this was a kind of impression management on the part of the LEA and that everyone concerned would be satisfied if candidates could make the right noises.

Some teachers became very interested and committed during the course of the project, but others saw GIST as external to their interests, voiced vague sympathy, but were essentially passive in their attitudes. For instance, they would agree to receive women visitors, but sit at the back of the class marking instead of taking part, or they would put posters of women scientists up on the walls, but refuse to explain to the children why they had done so, in case that seemed too much like propaganda. A smaller number revealed some covert resistance to the perceived feminist thrust of GIST, usually expressed in a way that projected hostility on to someone else: 'I don't think I can get my colleagues to agree', or 'It's difficult in terms of the timetable', rather than 'I don't really want to make any positive efforts to encourage girls into my subject'.

The GIST research plan (as opposed to its action plan) was

originally based on a series of hypotheses about pupils, rather than teachers. The focus of the questionnaires was on the way girls — and boys — felt about science and sex roles. In retrospective self-criticism it might be said that we did not have a sufficiently well-developed theory of how and why teachers would change. On the other hand, a study of teacher attitudes to sex equality carried out in 1981, but not published until 1984, indicates that male phy-sical science teachers, and craft teachers of both sexes are likely to be the least 'progressive' of all in relation to sex equality (Pratt *et al.*, 1984). Most of the teachers we worked with taught science or crafts, and 75 per cent of them were men.

At the start of the project we had considered working only with committed feminist teachers. The idea was dropped, first be-cause it would have meant too wide a scattering of schools for the survey research, and secondly because we suspected there were not enough feminist teachers to be found in Greater Manchester in 1979, and most of them were probably women teaching English or Sociol-ogy, not male teachers of traditionally male subjects. The way we had chosen to construct the project meant it was unavoidable that we would end up with the least promising group of teachers from our point of view.

The action programme started with a series of three workshops in each school. It took some persuasion to have these all take place on school premises and within school time. The first workshop defined the GIST problem and provided evidence about the shortfall of girls in science and technology; the second began a process of 'de-stereotyping' teachers' attitudes, and the third started negotiat-ing agreement about the kind of intervention each school would undertake.

In team discussions about how to approach the workshops there were at least three theories about how teachers might change. If they are unrepentant sexists, then only a cathartic shake-up of their beliefs and practices, both personal and professional, will bring about change; this might be the 'normative-reeducative' model (see Bennis, Benne and Chin, 1961). Or perhaps teachers will only change their views about gender equality if it becomes an important issue for the management of the school, so that promotion actually hangs on your success as a non-sexist teacher, or being interested in gender equality puts you in the head's good books; this would be the 'power-coercive' strategy, an unrealistic option given the atti-tude of senior staff at the time. Alternatively again, one could assume that teachers, when confronted with the evidence of girls' potential in science, and the injustice of the way they are presently treated at school, will come to see the reasons for change: the rational enlightenment model.

No doubt the latter sounds the least convincing, yet it was the assumption that, for largely pragmatic reasons, we ended by adopting. Traumatically confronting teachers with their own sexism, though it might well have changed them, was never a feasible strategy for a team of outsiders such as we were. It was only too clear that teachers who did not want to experience disturbing revelations about their own sexism would just quietly depart and cease all contact with GIST. Our strategy by default was therefore the rational-empirical one of trying to exploit teachers' ideal professionalism, and to persuade them to change on the grounds that otherwise their sexist attitudes might have negative effects on girls' educational performance.

The notion of trying to work with, rather than against, teachers' own ideal view of their task is hardly original, and several writers (e.g. Weiner, 1984; Taylor, 1985; Adams, 1985) advocate 'feminist' education on the grounds that girl-friendly practice is also good educational practice. What is less clear is how you solve the problem of the dysfunction which is bound to emerge between professional ideals and personal beliefs about sex roles. Despite our decision to take a softly-softly approach, the evaluation report shows that some teachers still perceived us as rampant and single-minded feminists. This seems to have been because we constantly brought issues of gender to their attention, even when they would rather have talked about something else. John Catton, who worked with male craft teachers, repeatedly found them turning the conversation on to other topics, as if they found it embarrassing that a man should make so much fuss about gender equality. Several remarked to the evaluators that John seemed more reasonable than the other members of the team, a point which rather annoyed John who felt he had been operating in just the same way as the rest of us.

The tenuousness of our 'action' as opposed to our research relationship with the teachers must have been an important reason why the changes in pupil choices were relatively small. Yet the research itself seems to have been productive, and the research stance lent respectability to a project which might otherwise have been dismissed as entirely ideologically feminist.

A rather cynical analysis of the dilemma of researchers trying to please more than one audience indicates that there is inevitably a gap between the images of the project presented to the practitioner on the one hand, and the world of academia on the other (MacDonald and Walker, 1976). Negotiation with teachers has to take account of the priorities of the professional practitioner; the survival of the work itself depends on the continuation of this relationship, which might well involve considerable modification of original aims on the part of the researchers. On the other hand, the survival of the research team as academics or writers depends on a successful presentation of the research 'product', which may have to be sanitized and idealized if it is to be accepted. The research team as piggy in the middle is negotiating with two disparate worlds, and juggling distinct sets of values and assumptions.

For GIST there was a third world, and a third audience — of feminists, important to us because of the overtly feminist aims of the programme. From this group there have been criticisms — more often voiced in face to face meetings than in documentary form — that there are inherent contradictions between the kind of research stance GIST adopted and the idea of feminist activism.

3. The GIST Methodology: Did it Contain Contradictions?

The feminist criticisms of GIST have been on two linked grounds: that the adoption of positivist, natural science type methods is inconsistent with a feminist philosophy of research, and that by advocating more girls take up natural science, the project uncritically accepted the norms and paradigms of male science, rather than forging a new feminist science or science education (see Bentley and Watts, 1985, for a discussion of the latter).

The earliest substantial criticism of this kind appeared in a *New Statesman* review of *The Missing Half*, a book on girls and science education edited by Alison, and to which I had contributed a chapter. The reviewer remarked that 'a fat book written by many hands will contain salutary contradictions', defining the chief contradiction as between a feminist stance and the value stance of the book as a whole, encapsulated in Alison's leading article, described by the reviewer as: 'an acceptance of the conventional methodology of social science, as borrowed with all its powers and dangers, from the methodology of natural science'. The dangers included an allegedly blinkered moral neutrality in the face of standard scientific method and values. In particular, the review lambasted the inclusion of a chapter by Gray (1981), putting forward female biological deficiency as revealed by spatial ability differences between the sexes as the reason so few girls succeed in the natural sciences. The rather neat point was made that if natural science methods lead to the adoption of theories of female inferiority, they will hold little attraction for women.

The argument of the review reflected early debates within the team, for example about the importance or otherwise of investigating the biological theory of sex difference in intellectual performance. The question later raised in team discussion was whether as feminists we should ignore the possibility, leaving the onus on those who argued for female inferiority to prove the case, or whether as researchers we ought impartially to include the theory as one possible factor when it came to the research design. In fact, the inclusion of spatial and mechanical ability tests in the initial survey can be seen as an indirect exploration of the biological theory, and is written up in that way by Barbara Smail, who did much of the work on that aspect of the programme (Smail, 1983). Perhaps it *is* a waste of valuable feminist time to give any credence at all to biological theories. On the other hand, the reading and discussion associated with the GIST investigation of spatial competence convinced me, at any rate, that the evidence for female genetic inferiority is amazingly thin, compared with the impact it seems to have made on the minds of science teachers. As a group, they and the craft teachers were strongly inclined towards biological rather than social explanations, which has led me to wonder whether policy makers may not have a similar bias when they first consider gender issues, a point I shall return to later.

If so, then it was vital to have dealt as thoroughly as we did with the 'reactionary' biological point of view, by including a spatial ability test in the range of measures of pupils. The objectivity implied by exploring the spatial ability hypothesis, in addition to the use of statistical survey techniques, gained the project considerable respectability in the science education community, which of course is peopled by those who tend to accept scientific methodology and values. A good example of how the qualitative approach can be a handicap is mentioned by Ball (1984) writing about his study of Beachside Comprehensive. Significantly it was a head of science who questioned the scientific adequacy of his work, and dismissed a defence of the epistemological basis of ethnography as 'Honestly, absolute drivel'. No doubt we would have met with this reaction more often had GIST not been armoured in advance by so obviously employing natural science type research methods. But there was a price to pay for this accommodation to the prejudices of science teachers. A considerable proportion of the team's energies was directed towards the community of science educators and academics, possibly at the expense of developing a constructive challenge to the anti-feminist bias of their values.

I was probably the least committed individual on the team to these values. My own first foray into research, several years before GIST started, was a small investigation of gender differences in career aspirations amongst students in a college of further education in Berkshire. The students maintained in their questionnaire responses that no-one had influenced their choice of course of career, though informal discussions, interviews, and essays written by the students indicated that parents, peers, the school and the LEA careers services had all had important effects on choices at sixteen plus. This was the source of my scepticism about questionnaires and positivist methods generally. I was doubtful that paper and pencil tests could illuminate what happens in school to discourage girls from science and technology. I felt the answer lay in interactions and unspoken expectations too subtle to be uncovered by questionnaires alone. But my own attitudes to research and action have undergone something of a transformation because of GIST. While it may be valid to stress the limitations of attitude questionnaires, it is less justifiable to combine this position with the assumption that natural science methods, large-scale surveys, and certain underlying values are a package which has to be accepted altogether. No doubt we had fallen victim to the very powerful tradition in British social policy research, of what Taylor-Gooby calls 'arthritic empiricism' (Taylor-Gooby, 1981). I think it *is* wise to be suspicious of the assumptions and norms of positivist empiricism; there is too often a comfortable and naive assumption that all a researcher has to do is reveal whatever is holding back a disadvantaged group, and the policy makers will obediently step in with the appropriate remedy. As the same critique of British social administration research and practice puts it:

> To regard policy change as the triumph of evidence over dogma is to reduce the background to policy to the considerations that would influence a reasonable practical and unbiased person: to reduce history to progress and to give it an excessively tidy shape ... (Taylor-Gooby, 1981).

He goes on to argue that policy advisers can often find themselves accepting governmental solutions or panaceas for social problems, along with the idea that any newly defined social need must imply rationing of the available resources between competing groups of people. There is already an observable tendency for those on the left as much as the right to see advances in opportunities for women as something that can only be achieved at the expense of men.

All the same, the briefest examination of EOC publications shows how necessary and important it is to be able to draw on reliable statistical material if policy decisions are to reverse discrimination against women. An automatic response of suspicion about statistical methods amongst feminists is similar to that in the field of race relations, where there is still some tension about the drawbacks of collecting information, which in a racist society may be used for racist ends. But to go from that to argue that feminists have to avoid quantitative methods altogether is untenable; many field workers involved in anti-racist intiatives have already decided that policy formulation is weakened if not founded on reliable evidence.

However, the argument is less about whether statistical methods can ever be used, than about whether, for feminists, investigation of social constructs such as attitudes is better approached by quantitative or qualitative methods. My own view about GIST now is that despite the perhaps natural antipathy of feminism to positivism, some sort of quantitative measuring device is very useful indeed if you want to determine whether changes have taken place. A major value of the GIST 'before and after' attitude surveys has been to show that the children's views about science and sex roles did change significantly more in the action than in the control schools, but that this was not matched by a move towards different option choices. Without them, we would have had almost no way of demonstrating that the GIST interventions had an effect, and less of a basis for making the argument that it is not just pupil attitudes but the beliefs and attitudes of teachers and the context of schools, which inhibit non-traditional subject and career choices.

Contrast this with the evaluation report which used ethnographic methods, and which, in the view both of the evaluators and the GIST team, showed that teachers *had* changed because of the project, even if they were extremely reluctant to admit they had done so. Because of the nature of the material — summaries and transcripts of interviews — this has to be an interpretation rather than demonstrable fact. Other readers can, and have, made different interpretations; for example, an article in *The Times Educational Supplement* suggested that GIST had met with only stubborn resistance from the teachers (which was vigorously denied in the Letters column by the evaluators).

Perhaps precisely because statistical work has for so long held a dominant position in British government policy-making, there may be unforeseen difficulties in using alternative approaches:

> Simply to offer ethnographic data or other qualitative material as 'facts' without interpretation could well lead to conclusions far removed from any the researcher herself would support. (Finch, 1985, p. 120)

These considerations have shifted my views somewhat towards greater methodological eclecticism.

4. Dissemination of GIST and its Policy Impact

GIST is already a piece of educational history. At the time of writing, it is nearly two years since the project proper came to an end. Even in this time, my views on the value or otherwise of the GIST idea have undergone all sorts of changes and shifts in perspective. The project *was* a kind of drama, with central characters and crowd scenes. Perceptions of what was going on differ according not just to whether you were an actor or an onlooker, but also in relation to the amount of time that has passed since the first and final acts. Players in the GIST drama were ourselves — the project team, intensely involved during the action, and now trying to see how GIST looks from a more remote perspective; and the teachers in the schools, who mostly performed with the curtain drawn, excepting those who have written about the play (Thompson, 1982; Bowes, 1986; Slater, 1986; Ward, 1986). The GIST children mostly had walk-on rather than speaking roles, but may now or later make life decisions in some way influenced by GIST. Behind the scenes were the evaluators, who took a snapshot of the teachers while they were still on stage, an inside view, but partial and perhaps ephemeral. Onlookers include other researchers and teachers, and feminists interested in the outcome of an experiment on gender equality in schools. They did not actually observe the drama, and so have to depend on second-hand accounts: the 'crits', the team's reports of the project, the evaluation report, or coverage in the educational press.

The explanation for the widespread publicity GIST received may lie precisely in the drama of combining such disparate and apparently ideologically opposed methodologies, the action research approach making it difficult for the project to be easily characterized or simplistically treated. Action research has become a 'hurray' word in education. The concept seems to promise both rigorous investigation, because of the use of reliable research methods, and practical relevance because of the down-to-earth approach of the practitioner. It was no bad thing for a feminist, policy-oriented project to choose a mode in which research is supposed to contribute to more effective practice, and action to ensure the relevance and applicability of research. Most definitions of action research are persuasive, that is to say, they strongly imply that something worthwhile is happening. The portmanteau appeal of action research is bound to be increased in the context of education, where many writers have remarked on the failure of educational research to change, in any demonstrable way, educational practice (Nisbet and Broadfoot, 1980; Eisner, 1985). Many educational innovations, from new methods of reading, to Keith Joseph's special payments for student teachers of physics, have been introduced without prior research to establish their viability. Currently, quite a number of local authorities have announced equal opportunities policies, and some have sent guidelines to schools recommending changes in classroom practice or school organization (see Whyte *et al.*, 1985). It is not at all clear that these guidelines, if indeed they are being implemented, are based on research evidence: the intention is to reduce patterns of sex stereotyping in schools, but the means by which this is to be done are still far from clear.

GIST is, at the very least, useful for answering questions about equality policies in education. Several publications from the project, different in emphasis, but with certain points of agreement (Smail, 1984; Kelly *et al.*, 1984; Catton, 1985; Whyte 1986), may be illuminating. These are that schools and teachers, rather than girls' motivation, are central to the GIST problem; that it is easier to change attitudes than behaviour; and that some institutions are particularly impervious to change. The response of teachers in the evaluation report is interesting, because they maintained that the project had not changed their views at all, they had 'always' treated girls and boys equally, while the text of their interviews shows in many cases how they had begun to reflect on gender divisions at school in an entirely new way. It seems that individuals prefer to believe any changes of viewpoint are the result of their own unaided rise in consciousness. Those who wish to change attitudes in the future can draw the appropriate lesson. Teachers are not an undifferentiated group: factors such as sex, and subject taught, considerably affect the kind of attitudes a teacher is likely to have towards sex equality, and it might even make sense to have separate in-service provision for men and women (see Adams, 1985).

What is rather interesting in the case of GIST is that the project has acquired an image of success. Perhaps because we were aware of the high expectations of our feminist audience, our joint account of the project (Kelly *et al.*, 1984) now seems to me painfully honest and low key. It makes no grand claims for success, and indeed probably underrates the positive outcomes. Neither that nor the apparently negative conclusions of the evaluation report seem to have dented the GIST image. It continues to be quoted and referred to as if all the desired changes had already taken place, when in reality, as the many letters still received by GIST testify, they are only just beginning in schools around the country.

I see GIST now as a very small rock which stood for a time against some rather large waves, creating ripples as the water was forced to move round us, and showing only that a much larger bulwark is needed to push the water into different channels. As Janet Finch has said in relation to the apparent 'failure' of education to redress social inequalities:

> The fact that redistribution appears so far to have been a relative failure does not necessarily mean that it can never succeed. There is a case for arguing that it has not seriously been tried. (Finch, 1984, p. 136)

Whenever GIST has been referred to in the educational press, it appears as 'Girls Into Science and Technology, the best known research project in this area'. Modestly staffed and budgeted, GIST is so far unique in Britain as an action as well as research-oriented project in the field of gender differences. Other comparable affairs are the Equal Opportunities Commission's funded research into curriculum options (Pratt *et al.*, 1984), and the Sex Differentiation Project supported jointly by the EOC and the then Schools Council (Millman and Weiner, 1985). Neither of these had an action research framework; the Pratt study used traditional survey and interview methods to look simply at the status quo of curriculum differentiation by gender in schools, while the Schools Council project had a more activist, propagandistic approach, promoting equal opportunities policies, but without an underpinning of research. So far there has been no growth in major funding for similar purposes. This cannot be due to any lack of interesting research questions to explore, nor to a lack of direct policy implications. The main beneficiaries would be women and schoolgirls, but it would seem that their needs have a rather low priority in the present climate.

References

ADAMS, C. (1985) 'Teacher attitudes towards issues of sex equality', in WHYTE, J., DEEM, R., KANT, L. and CRUICKSHANK, M. (Eds) *Girl Friendly Schooling*, London, Methuen.

BALL, S.J. (1984) 'Beachside reconsidered: Reflections on a methodological apprenticeship', in BURGESS, R.G. (Ed.) *The Research Process in Educational Settings: Ten Case Studies*, Lewes, Falmer Press.

BARRY, B. and WEBB, T. (1976) 'Action research in the smaller firm: An exemplar', *Management Education Development*, 7, pp. 111–119.

BENNIS, W.G., BENNE, K. and CHIN, R. (1961) *The Dynamics of Planned Change*, New York, Holt, Rinehart and Winston.

BENTLEY, D. and WATTS, D.M. (1986) 'Courting the positive virtues: a case for feminist science', *European Journal of Science Education*, 8, 2, pp. 121–34.

BOWES, D. (1986) 'Single sex science teaching: A route to bias-free choices in science for third year pupils', in HUSTLER, D., CASSIDY, T. and CUFF, T. (Eds) *Action Research in Classrooms and Schools*, London, Allen and Unwin.

CATTON, J. (1985) *Ways and Means: The Craft, Design and Technology Education of Girls*, School Curriculum Development Committee Pamphlet, York, Longman.

CHERNS, A.B. (1975) 'Action research', in DAVIS, L.E. and CHERNS, A.B. (Eds) *The Quality of Working Life*, 2, New York, Free Press.

CLARKE, K. (1985) 'Fourth year option choices: a follow-up in the GIST schools', mimeo, Manchester, Equal Opportunities Commission.

DEEM, R. (Ed.) (1980) *Schooling for Women's Work*, London, Routledge and Kegan Paul.

EISNER, E.W. (1985) *The Art of Educational Evaluation*, Lewes, Falmer Press.

FINCH, J. (1984) *Education as Social Policy*, London, Longman.

FINCH, J. (1985) 'Social policy and education: Problems and possibilities of using qualitative research', in BURGESS, R.G. (Ed.) *Issues in Educational Research: Qualitative Research*. Lewes, Falmer Press.

GRAY, J. (1981) 'A biological basis for the sex difference in achievement in science?', in KELLY, A. (Ed.) *The Missing Half: Girls and Science Education*, Manchester, Manchester University Press.

HULT, M. and LENNUNG, S.A. (1980) 'Towards a definition of action research: A note and bibliography', *Journal of Management Studies*, 17, 2, pp. 241–50.

KELLY, A., WHYTE, J. and SMAIL, B. (1984) 'Final Report on the GIST Project', mimeo, Manchester, Manchester University Department of Sociology.

KELLY, A. (1985) 'Action research: What is it and what can it do?', in BURGESS, R.G. (Ed.) *Issues in Eductional Research*, Lewes, Falmer Press.

MACDONALD, B. and WALKER, R. (1976) *Changing the Curriculum*, London, Open Books.

MILLMAN, V. and WEINER, G. (1985) *Sex Differentiation in Schooling: Is there a Problem?*, York, Longman.

NISBET, J. and BROADFOOT, P. (1980) *The Impact of Research on Policy and Pratice in Education*, Aberdeen, University of Aberdeen Press.

PAYNE, G., CUFF, T. and HUSTLER, D. (1983) 'GIST or PIST: Teacher perceptions of the GIST Project', mimeo, Manchester, Manchester Polytechnic.

PRATT, J., BLOOMFIELD, J. and SEALE, C. (1984) *Option Choice: A Question of Equal Opportunity*, Slough, National Foundation for Educational Research.

RAPAPORT, R.N. (1970) 'Three dilemmas in action research', *Human Relations*, 23, 6, pp. 499–513.

SLATER, S. (1986) 'Curriculum innovation and evaluation', in HUSTLER, D., CASSIDY, T. and CUFF, T. (Eds) *Action Research in Classrooms and Schools*, London, Allen and Unwin.

SMAIL, B. (1983) 'Spatial visualization skills and technical crafts education' *Educational Research*, 25, 3, pp. 230–31.

SMAIL, B. (1984) *Girl Friendly Science: Avoiding Sex Bias in the Curriculum*, Schools Council Programme Pamphlet, York, Longman.

TAYLOR, H. (1985) 'Inset for equal opportunities in the London Borough of Brent', in WHYTE, J., DEEM, R., KANT, L. and CRUICKSHANK, M. (Eds) *Girl Friendly Schooling*, London, Methuen.

TAYLOR-GOOBY, P. (1981) 'The empiricist tradition in social administration', *Critical Social Policy*, 2, pp. 6–21.

THOMPSON, J. (1982) 'GIST: Girls into science and technology' *Teaching London Kids*, 19.

TOFT, P. and CATTON, J. (1983) 'More than half way there', *Times Educational Supplement*, 7 October.

WARD, G. (1986) 'Observing with GIST', in HUSTLER, D., CASSIDY, C. and CUFF, T. (Eds) *Action Research in Classrooms and Schools*, London, Allen and Unwin.

WEINER, G. (1984) *Just a Bunch of Girls*, Milton Keynes, Open University Press.

WHYTE, J. (1984) 'Observing sex stereotypes and interactions in the school laboratory and workshop', *Educational Review*, 36, 1, pp. 75–86.

WHYTE, J. (1986) *Girls into Science and Technology: the Story of a Project*, London, Routledge and Kegan Paul.

WHYTE, J. DEEM, R., KANT, L. and CRUICKSHANK, M. (1985) (Eds) *Girl Friendly Schooling*, London, Methuen.

7 After 'Teaching Styles and Pupil Progress': Issues in Dissemination and Theory Development

Neville Bennett

It is now a decade since *Teaching Styles and Pupil Progress* was published in an orgy of press and academic coverage. For some considerable time the educational air was clouded with the dust of controversy but this has long since settled, making it an appropriate time to reflect on the nature of that turbulence, and to consider the theoretical and technical developments that the study spawned or heralded. In order to achieve this the chapter is in two parts. The first concerns dissemination and particularly the role of the media in that process, whilst the second considers theoretical developments relating to the study of teaching and learning processes in classroom settings.

Dissemination

The book, published in April 1976, reported findings from a relatively small, but representative, sample of teachers in Lancashire and Cumbria. The major findings were that on standardized tests of arithmetic, English and reading children who were exposed to formal or mixed teaching showed greater gains than those exposed to informal methods, although most progress was in fact made by an informal class. The overall conclusions were that it appeared to matter how much time teachers allocated to work on reading, writing and arithmetic; how involved their pupils were; how the curriculum was structured; and that it required skills of a high level to successfully implement more informal approaches. These results were not new either in this country or elsewhere. Cane and Smithers (1971) had, for example, already reported almost identical findings in relation to reading progress in infant schools, and HMI were later to report very similar findings in their primary school survey (1978). In America, Rosenshine (1976) had, about the same time, reviewed studies which had been undertaken in the United States and reported similar outcomes.

Nevertheless, when the book was published it was accorded unprecedented publicity. *The Sunday Times* broke the press embargo and splashed it on their front page. All Monday's papers reported it, usually with an accompanying editorial. It was reported on ITV and BBC news, 'Horizon' devoted their programme to it and the report in the *Times Educational Supplement* covered five pages and contained three reviews. The educational and quality press were inundated with letters, and questions were asked in the House. The word 'Bennett' was no longer the surname of 'a mild man who talks with a quiet north country accent' as the *Times Diary* quaintly put it; instead it became a symbol to be loved or hated. At the same time *Teaching Styles and Pupil Progress* became personalized as the Bennett, or Lancaster Report.

The link between familiar findings and unprecedented publicity would be confusing only if the prevailing social and educational climate were ignored. As a lead article in the *Times Educational Supplement* aptly put it 'It is a long time since any piece of research in the social sciences has received such treatment. With respect to Dr Bennett it owes more to the present educational climate than to any profound evaluation of his work'.

There is, as Cronbach (1975) has argued, a tide in the affairs of issues, and hearings given to social evidence depend on the times. In 1976 the time was ripe for controversy. The findings challenged an educational orthodoxy — that informal methods are more appropriate for primary age children irrespective of age, ability, sex or race. This orthodoxy was at that time already under fire, fuelled mainly by the William Tyndale affair, the closure of a so-called progressive school at the instigation of governors and working class parents. Levels of public anxiety had also been heightened by claims of falling standards, claims capitalized on by one of the Black Paper Series which laid all the educational ills of the nation at the doors of progressive, or as they preferred to call them, permissive teachers. They had no evidence for this of course, but the publication of *Teaching Styles* unwittingly gave the educational right wing the research findings that they had been waiting for. As such from the day of publication we found ourselves fighting a rearguard action against the excesses of this group. Despite protestations and disclaimers our findings were constantly misrepresented, overstated or sloganized. The day after publication Rhodes Boyson exhorted parents to 'Go out to your schools and check on whether permissive rubbish is being used and if so demand a change'. Note again the change of term from 'informal' to the more emotive 'permissive' as if the two were synonymous. The Lancaster M.P., Mrs. Kellet-Bowman, was quoted as saying 'It exposes so-called progressive teaching methods for the menace they are and the educational damage they are doing to hundreds and thousands of children'. Meanwhile in Fife, education officials were accused of operating a blacklist on certain books, the main one in question being our report. The accusation came from a Tory Councillor who said, 'The Report's overall conclusion given in 107 tables, charts, figures and 163 references broadly show that the trendy methods have largely been an unmitigated disaster greatly damaging to the careers of our children'. One final example of misrepresentation emanates from a report in the journal *Education*:

> The world was given a preview of Conservative education policy, prior to the conference debate, in a policy statement *The Right Approach*, published last week. In it the Conservatives dwell on the two main strands of their educational bow: standards and choice. On standards the Conservative document acclaims the research by Lancaster University's Neville Bennett....

Some of our protestations did get reported although occasionally with an innuendo. The *TES*, for example, published a story under the headline 'Dr. Bennett shrugs off Black Paper Connection'. Further headlines such as 'Bennetts Bullets for Boysons Blunderbuss' indicate just how thoroughly politicized the debate was at that stage. Shipman (1976) was clearly correct when he argued that the cautions of the researcher and the conditions and contents originally circumscribing the evidence are often ignored by the public and media. Researchers are frequently misunderstood and may suffer as their work is used selectively to support political positions that they personally reject! The same phenomenon can be seen in the report by Ford (1976). It is in such ways that researchers occasionally become inappropriately branded by their data.

The politicization of the debate served to exacerbate the disparate reactions to the findings. In the main, however, these were predictable either as a confirmation of common sense or manifestly absurd, i.e., they merely prove what we think we know, or, failing to confirm our prejudices, must be rejected.

Politicians and the media are mutually parasitic. However it would be unfair to criticize journalists for having a vested interest in highlighting controversial issues and for not always being paragons of virtue. The media make mistakes, distort and present biased views because they are, like the rest of society, run by human beings. Nevertheless, the media cannot abdicate their responsibilities for, for example, the use of clichè which degrades communication to propaganda, or to the printing of libellous material. Much of popular press coverage is cliché-ridden, of course, and the findings of *Teaching Styles* were used and abused in this way. A typical example was the editorial in the *Daily Express* which was headed 'a trendy flop' in which it heralded the end of the 'fun revolution'. Such clichés are part of the taken-for-granted aspects of popular press coverage, but much more serious are published articles containing libellous material. Fortunately only one such article appeared and it was not in the popular dailies but surprisingly in the normally august *Times Educational Supplement*, written as a consequence of what came to be wrongly regarded as a complete re-analysis of the *Teaching Styles* data.

The most persistent criticism of the study concerned the statistical analysis of change scores, an easy target since statisticians themselves disagree both about the techniques and their underlying assumptions. At that time most quasi-experimental studies used analysis of covariance as the most appropriate model, and after discussing the issue with measurement specialists in the United Kingdom and the United States, this was the model adopted, in the knowledge that no statistical technique available was by any means perfect. The statistical analysis was therefore fair game as indeed it was for the later controversial study *Fifteen Thousand Hours* by Michael Rutter and his colleagues (1979). Improvements were only possible with more powerful computer programmes than were available at the time and with the help of specialists in statistical techniques who had an interest in educational data. This became possible when a Professorial Fellow in Statistics was appointed at Lancaster. Subsequently a project was established, funded by SSRC, to consider the statistical analysis of complex classroom data bases.

This project was very successful in developing new statistical techniques by creating a cluster analysis programme based on sound statistical theory, and through the use of multi-level analysis of change data. Parts of the *Teaching Styles* data were utilized to test out these new techniques (*cf* Aitken, *et al.*, 1981).

Long after the completion of this project, and without any

discussion or prior warning, the *TES* published an article by the former research assistant claiming I had lost some of the *Teaching Styles* data. This little gem, buried in the middle of the article, was suitably embellished and distorted by the assistant editor such that a page 1 trailer included my photograph and carried the question 'Should Neville Bennett have thrown away his data?' In the article itself were larger photographs with similar nudge and wink questions, giving the clear impression that I had found it necessary to salt away certain data sub-sets. At no time did the *TES* contact me prior to publication to ascertain the facts of the matter. The facts were that we had been meticulous in keeping all the data and had in fact deposited a complete data set in the ESRC data bank eighteen months before the article was published. What is more astonishing is that the same research assistant actually deposited it.

Here is not the place to consider the motives of the actors in this little drama, simply to make the point that the prospect of a good story can lead to unpredictable behaviour in the most respectable of outlets. Where accountability is poor editorial discretion is not always commensurate with truth, common sense or equity. An example of the latter occurred when the journal *Educational Research* published the major criticism of the study (Gray and Satterly, 1976) but denied us the opportunity to reply for eight months (Bennett and Entwistle, 1977).

In this inevitably brief consideration of dissemination issues it seems clear that researchers who tackle controversial issues can and do come under fire. The attendant publicity both distorts and over-simplifies and often appears to harden rather than modify established attitudes and beliefs. Yet the analysis and explication of educational issues is surely the *raison d'être* of educational research, and it is to be hoped that researchers will not allow themselves to be deflected from this course by that prospect. Indeed it may not be too pessimistic to predict that this situation could worsen as education becomes more centralized and politicized, and as the political extremes become more strident, more violent and more dismissive of freedom of speech and action. In these circumstances it is even more crucial that independent voices be heard.

It is perhaps significant in this context that the central figures in SSRC and DES funding at the time of publication of *Teaching Styles* dismissed distortion and over-simplification as minor irritations which should not detract from communicating to a wider audience. In commenting on the reaction of *Teaching Styles*, Wrigley (1976) wrote: 'Their report has been criticized both fairly and unfairly and their conclusions distorted in shortened accounts of their work. Yet one would not wish for their conclusions to have had less publicity, nor has one the slightest regret in their choice of topic'. He went on to call for bolder approaches from researchers who should be prepared to take more risks and also for publications to achieve maximum effect on the various audiences. Kay (1977), in similar vein, concluded 'the publicity that may follow such wider dissemination of research findings carries risks since it often distorts in an attempt to simplify. Nevertheless the risks must be taken if the general public is either to recognise the potential importance of educational research, or to be influenced by it'.

Theoretical Developments

The advances in statistical analysis directly spawned by the *Teaching Styles* study have already been alluded to. Here the focus is on developments in theory relating to teaching-learning processes in classroom settings.

As its name implies the study was part of a strand of research on teaching which adopted a teaching styles approach. These began in the early 1970s and continued through that decade. They were characterized by the collection of data on teacher behaviours on which were based classifications or typologies of teachers. The resultant teacher types or styles were then related to changes in pupil achievement. The labels attached to these styles reflected the theoretical perspective underpinning the study and choice of variables. Two perspective were commonly used, one emanating from prescriptive theory and the other from interaction models.

The prescriptive theory was provided by the Plowden Report which posited what was essentially a two-box theory of teaching, i.e. that teachers can be broadly categorized as either progressive or traditional. The teacher activities and behaviours on which these categorizations were based were broad features of classroom and curriculum organization, such as the type of pupil groupings, extent of testing, modes of motivation and the degree to which subject matter was compartmentalized or integrated. This broad focus precluded specific attention to the type or extent of instructional or social interactions.

Research utilizing this perspective ranged from Barker-Lunn's study of streaming in the primary school (1970), the Cane and Smithers (1971) study of reading in infant schools, and the HMI survey of primary schools in England (1978), where, in a representative sample of over 500 schools they found that children taught by didactic or mixed styles were significantly better than those taught by exploratory styles on standardized tests of maths and language. In the United States the same approach resulted in a plethora of studies grouped under the heading 'open education'.

The ideological basis of the Plowden theory, aligned as it was to a particular set of political beliefs about the nature of man and society, meant that the results of studies on teaching styles tended to generate more political heat than pedagogical light. Nevertheless most contemporary reviewers in Britain and the United States are agreed that formal or traditional teaching does appear related to increased learning gains in mathematics and language but that there may be gains in the affective area from open or informal teaching (Gray and Satterly, 1981; Anthony, 1982; Giaconia and Hedges, 1983).

The second perspective informing teaching style studies emanated from interaction analysis, the systematic observation of pre-specified behaviours hypothetically related to the dependent variables. Typical examples of these include Eggleston *et al.*'s (1976) study of teaching styles in science, and the more recent ORACLE study. The latter identified six styles based on types of teacher-pupil interaction and class management and organization. In this study the style relating most clearly to pupil achievement on standardized tests was the 'classroom enquirer'. This style comprised teachers who devoted more time than other styles to whole class teaching and emphasized questions stressing factual knowledge, relating to the tasks set (Galton and Simon, 1980).

Despite the fact that teaching style approaches followed two distinct theoretical perspectives they shared common conceptions and assumptions about the nature of teaching and learning, and their relationship. Learning was conceptualized on behaviourist principles and as such the teacher was perceived as a source or store of knowledge and skills who so organizes the classroom in order best to deliver that knowledge. As such it was equally assumed that a direct relationship exists between teacher behaviours and student achievement, implicit in which is a denial of the influence of pupils themselves on their own learning.

In addition to sharing assumptions they also shared difficulties, both of a technical and substantive nature. Since teaching styles are composed of a number of teacher behaviours the differential impact of individual behaviours within the style is impossible to ascertain.

Thus, for example, it was not possible to identify the specific behaviour or behaviours within a formal style which maximized
achievement or those within an informal style which appeared to
engender improved motivation. As such the findings were of little
value in seeking improvements in teaching. Secondly, examination
of this literature indicates that within-style differences in achievement were often as large as between-style differences, indicating that
style itself is insufficient to explain differences in outcomes. Seeking
improvements through studies of teaching styles was thus unlikely
to be successful. It was a theoretical cul-de-sac.

New models and new directions were needed and the clue for
our own future work on, for example, open plan schools (Bennett
et al., 1980), emanated from close analysis of the observational data
in the teaching styles study. Two findings were seminal. The first
was that formal teachers spent more time on language, reading and
mathematics, and the second was that pupils in formal classrooms
exhibited more involvement in their work, this being particularly
noticeable among the highest and lowest achievers. These two
aspects of time — time allowed for the study of given content, and
time spent on task, linked in well with notions being simultaneously
considered by researchers in the United States based on a neglected
model of school learning put forward over a decade earlier by
Carroll (1963).

The 'time' or 'opportunity to learn' approach assumes no direct
relationship between teacher behaviours and pupil achievement,
arguing that all effects of teaching on learning are mediated by pupil
activities. In particular the amount of time a pupil spends actively
engaged on a particular topic is seen as the most important determi-
nant of achievement on that topic. In this model the pupil is the
central focus, with the teacher seen as the manager of the attention
and time of the pupils in relation to the educational ends of the
classroom.

Examination of the literature in this field led to the development of a summary model designed to synthesize the evidence
around a coherent framework (Bennett 1978; 1982). This is presented as Figure 7.1. The focus in the model is on pupil achievement
and the factors delineated by empirical studies which relate to that.
The broadest definition of 'opportunity to learn' is the amount of
interaction children have with school — the extent to which they are
exposed to schooling. Quantity of schooling relates to the total
amount of time the school is open for its stated purpose and is
defined by the length of school day and school year. Length of

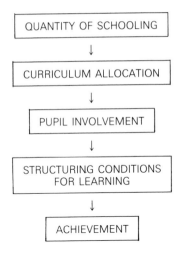

Figure 7.1 A model of teaching-learning processes

school day has, for example, been found to vary as much as six hours per week in Britain even in the same geographical locality. At the level of the individual pupil, exposure to schooling varies in relation to the extent of pupil absence, and to school-based policies regarding the amount of homework presented. There are indications that length of school day, the amount of student absence and homework are all related to pupil achievement.

The time available for schooling is allocated to various curriculum activities, and in Britain, where there is no central or local control of curriculum, the curriculum emphasis or balance achieved varies markedly from school to school and, at primary school level, from class to class in the same school. In our national enquiry into open plan schools, for example, we found the average amount of curriculum time allocated to primary school mathematics was 4.5 hours but varied from two to seven hours. In language the average was 7.5 hours per week but varied from four to twelve hours (bennett, *et al.*, 1980). What is clear from this and other studies is that children receive quite different educational diets depending on the school they happen to go to, and as in other areas of human functioning, diet appears to relate to growth. The evidence would indicate that different curriculum balances result in different patterns of knowledge acquisition (Berliner and Rosenshine, 1976; Fisher, *et al.*, 1978).

If curriculum allocation is conceived as the opportunity provided for pupils to interact with given curriculum content, then pupil involvement or engagement can be conceived as the use that pupils make of that opportunity. Many studies have provided descriptions of the extent of pupil involvement across all school ages and, although the working definitions of pupil involvement are not always completely compatible, there appears to be a 'law of two-thirds' emerging. On average, pupils appear to be involved about two-thirds of the time, but this varies markedly from class to class, and from pupil to pupil in the same class.

The extent of pupil involvement has also been studied within the framework of instructional and social interactions between pupils in the immediate social context of learning, which, in British primary schools, is the classroom group. In Britain such research has been limited to descriptive observational surveys of existing classroom practice, in direct contrast to that in the United States where, since the use of such groups is not typical, research has been directed toward linking theory and practice by implementing experimental programmes with the aim of changing, rather than describing, practice (Slavin, 1983; Bennett, 1985).

Research relating pupil involvement to achievement has reported positive relationships of widely varying strength. In general however, the data would seem to lend some support to William James's argument of 1902, that 'whether the attention comes by grace of genius or by dint of will, the longer one does attend to a topic the more mastery of it one has'.

Nevertheless, the amount of time pupils interact with their task is by no means a complete explanation of achievement. Time has been likened to an empty box (Gage, 1978) which requires filling with comprehensible and worthwhile content. The element in the model entitled 'Structuring Conditions for Learning' reflects this. The cluster of variables which have been of concern here include: the presentation of the task; the sequence, level and pacing of content; teachers' levels of expectations of their pupils, and types of feedback from teacher to child, including those with behavioural and those with academic intentions.

The outcomes of research studies within the 'opportunity to learn' paradigm have been relatively consistent and have been used as the basis for hortatory pleas for teachers to increase time on task (Denham and Lieberman, 1980), for the development of prescriptive models of teaching (Berliner and Rosenshine, 1976), and to develop experimental intervention programmes for teachers, either to increase pupil achievement or to improve classroom management

(Emmer *et al.*, 1981; Gage and Colardarci, 1980; Good and Grouws, 1979). Such efforts are likely to be only partially successful however, because of limitations in the opportunity to learn model itself and in its associated research.

It has been shown that there is little to be gained from high pupil involvement on tasks that are not either comprehensible or worthwhile. Time is thus a necessary, but not sufficient, condition for learning. As was argued earlier, time is an empty vessel but the research within the opportunity to learn approach has generally restricted itself to delineating and quantifying the dimensions of the vessel rather than attending to the quality of its content. Exhortations to increase curriculum allocation or to improve levels of pupil involvement are of no avail if the quality of the task set is poor or not related to pupils' intellectual capabilities. The teaching styles and opportunity to learn approaches have provided abundant evidence on the relationship between teacher and pupil behaviours and long term, norm-referenced, achievement measures. But what have been neglected are the mediation processes by which teaching and learning influence each other, together with an almost total neglect of the learning process itself. Such limitations throw into sharp relief issues central to the explanation of teaching and learning. Activities of the learner on assigned classroom tasks may be seen as crucial mediators in converting teacher behaviours into learning behaviours but the models so far considered offer little comment on how these processes operate in practice. There is little description, analysis or explanation of how classroom tasks are assigned or worked under normal classroom conditions and constraints, despite the fact that most intended school learning is embedded in the tasks teachers assign to pupils. The opportunity to learn model had therefore been productive but limited. Further development was necessary.

Classroom Tasks

Most recently there has been a shift from the process-product, to the process-process or mediating-process, paradigm (Doyle, 1979, 1983; Evertson, 1980), representing a move from time, to task, utilizing insights provided by cognitive psychology. From this perspective the tasks which pupils engage in structure to a large extent what information is selected from the environment and how it is processed. Tasks organize experience and researchers wishing to study and understand that experience, and the process of acquisition, must therefore first understand the tasks on which pupils engage.

An acceptance of this perspective requires a shift in the conceptions of the learner from a behaviourist to a constructivist position, i.e. from a portrayal of the learner as an objective, passive recipient of sensory experience who can learn anything if provided with enough practice, to a learner actively making use of cognitive strategies and previous knowledge to deal with cognitive limitations. In this conception learners are active, constructivist and interpretive, and learning is a covert, intellectual process providing the development and restructuring of existing conceptual schemes.

Nevertheless, reliance on a cognitive psychological perspective is insufficient to explain classroom phenomena. Constructivist models of the child contain no serious treatment of the nature of the social environment in which learning takes place. Thus any study which seeks to explain the dynamics between teaching and learning also requires a model of classrooms as complex social settings.

The notions of children as constructivist learners operating within complex social settings underpinned our recent research published under the title *The Quality of Pupil Learning Experiences* (Bennett *et al.*, 1984). In this study, of 6 and 7-year-old children, data were gathered on teacher intentions, task specifications, pupil performance on their tasks, their understanding or misconceptions of tasks, children's cognitive and social interactions and teacher diagnoses of completed tasks, to characterize the intellectual demands of the tasks set and whether these demands were appropriate to the pupils' capabilities.

Although the numbers of studies using the task model is yet limited, their findings have raised a number of fundamental issues relating to a wide range of enduring classroom issues. These include teacher task planning, task appropriateness, classroom management, the role of pupil discourse, teacher explanation and diagnosis and the role of teacher knowledge systems in classroom practice. These are rich new veins and it seems that the task model holds out great promise for the future improvement of teaching and learning.

Summary

In considering the period following the publication of *Teaching Styles and Pupil Progress* this article has focused on aspects of the dissemination process and the development of new theoretical perspectives on teaching-learning processes.

Many calls have been made in the last decade to improve the dissemination of research findings. Indeed, some have argued that until we, as a research community, do improve it 'educational research will remain an exercise in futility' (Burdin, 1976). However, this over-simplifies the issues raised both for the producers and consumers of research evidence. School and classroom processes are exceedingly complex requiring labour intensive research methods to acquire relevant, reliable data. As such samples tend to be small, unrepresentative and ungeneralizable. Most researchers are cognisant of this and are suitably cautious in their inferences, but such caution is to no avail if the findings are perceived to be controversial. At worst they will be distorted and oversimplified by the media, politicians and, let's face it, academics with differing political or ideological leanings. This was clearly apparent in some of the reactions to our study, and to the Rutter study on secondary schools, and reached its horrific peak in response to Jensen's celebrated article on IQ and race (Jensen, 1969). His subsequent experiences are recorded in a sixty-eight-page preface to his book *Genetics and Education* (1972) and amply support Cronbach's view that 'One cannot assume that scholars collectively will bring a debate to a sober finale'. Given this situation it appears somewhat naive of writers like Jacobs and Eccles (1985) to claim that 'ultimately it is the responsibility of the researcher to recognize the possible impact of social forces ... and to insist that media reports do not contain unwarranted.....conclusions'.

No panacea is offered here. It is crucial that evidence relating to the improvement of teaching and learning be made available to the relevant audiences in a form which they can understand. Thus, in the short term researchers must learn to live with possible distortion and oversimplifications. In the longer term the ideal solution might be to free audiences from reliance on the media by, for example, ensuring that teachers are trained in the relevant techniques to adequately evaluate research evidence in primary source form.

Theories, like human beings, outlive their usefulness and are superseded by more vigorous offspring. In viewing the recent history of research on teaching-learning processes it is clear that three distinct trends are discernible, each characterized by a unique set of theoretical premises, assumptions, variables and methods. The broad categorization of teachers into types or styles was too gross and the empirical evidence too equivocal to inform the improvement of teaching. In accepting the assumption of a direct relationship between teaching and learning, pupils were inevitably neglected as mediators in their own learning. Models embodying variables relating to opportunity to learn redressed the balance and directed attention to time allocations in schooling, curriculum and tasks. However, quantifications of time on task totally emphasized time and consequently neglected task. And, in common with the styles approach, it neglected the process of learning itself.

Until recently research on learning has tended to ignore the processes of teaching, and research on teaching has largely ignored the processes of learning. However, the recent focus on task structures has heralded an attempted reconciliation whereby concepts and models developed by cognitive psychologists are being brought to bear on problems specified with increasing precision by researchers on teaching. Thus time or involvement is now viewed as a necessary but not sufficient condition for learning, and the focus has shifted to study the interactions of teachers, pupils and tasks within complex social settings. The last decade of research on teaching and learning in classroom settings can therefore be characterized as one of shifting paradigms and significant progress in achieving better understandings of classroom phenomena. The theory underpinning the *Teaching Styles* study is dead, but from its dying embers have been fanned the flames of technical and theoretical advance.

References

AITKIN, M., BENNETT, S.N., HESKETH, J. (1981) 'Teaching styles and pupil progress: A re-analysis', *British Journal of Educational Psychology*, 51, pp. 170–186.

ANTHONY, W.S. (1982) 'Research on progressive teaching', *British Journal of Educational Psychology*, 52, pp. 381–85.

BARKER-LUNN, J. (1970) *Streaming in the Primary School*, Slough, NFER.

BENNETT, S.N. (1976) *Teaching Styles and Pupil Progress*, London, Open Books.

BENNETT, S.N., and ENTWISTLE, N.J. (1977) 'Rite and wrong', *Educational Research*, 19, pp. 217–22.

BENNETT, S.N. (1978) 'Recent research on teaching: A dream, a belief and a model', *British Journal of Educational Psychology*, 48, pp. 127–147.

BENNETT, S.N., ANDREAE, J., HEGARTY, P. and WADE, B. (1980) *Open Plan Schools: Teaching, Curriculum and Design*, Windsor, NFER.

BENNETT, S.N. (1982). 'Time to teach: Teaching-learning processes in primary schools', *Aspects of Education*, 27, pp. 52–70.

BENNETT, S.N., DESFORGES, C.W., COCKBURN, A., WILKINSON, B. (1984) *The Quality of Pupil Learning Experiences*, London, Erlbaum.

BENNETT, S.N. (1985) 'Interaction and achievement in classroom groups' in BENNETT, S.N. and DESFORGES, C.W. (Eds) *Recent Advances in Classroom Research*, Edinburgh, Scottish Academic Press.

BERLINER, D. and ROSENSHINE, B. (1976) 'The acquisition of knowledge in the classroom', *Tech. Rep. IV–I, Beginning Teacher Evaluation Study*, San Francisco, Far West Lab.

BURDIN, J.L. (1976) 'Realism in research objectives for educational personnel and citizens'. *Journal of Teacher Education*, 27, pp. 1–2.

CANE, B., and SMITHERS, J. (1971) *The Roots of Reading*, Slough, NFER.

CARROLL, J.B. (1963) 'A model of school learning', *Teachers College Record*, 64, pp. 723–33

CRONBACH, L. (1975) 'Five decades of public controversy over mental testing', *American Psychologist*, 30, pp. 1–14.

DENHAM, G. and LIEBERMAN, A. (Eds) (1980) *Time to Learn*, Washington D.C., National Institute of Education.

DOYLE, W. (1979) 'Classroom tasks and student abilities' in PETERSON, P.L. and WALKERG, H.L. (Eds) *Research on Teaching: Concepts, findings and implications*, Berkeley, McCutcheon.

DOYLE, W. (1983) 'Academic work', *Review of Educational Research*, 53, pp. 159–200.

EGGLESTON, J.F., GALTON, M., and JONES, M.E. (1976) *Processes and Products of Science Teaching*, London, Macmillan.

EMMER, E.T., SANFORD, J.P., EVERTSON, C.M., CLEMENTS, B.S. and MARTIN, J. (1981) *The Classroom Management Improvement Study*, Research and Development Centre for Teacher Education, University of Texas at Austin.

EVERTSON, G.M. (1980) 'In search of what outcomes mean for an ecological theory', in *Schooling Outcomes: Five Multidisciplinary Perspectives*, San Francisco, Far West Lab.

FISHER, C.W., FILBY, N.N., MARLIANE, R., CAHEN, L.S., DISHAW, M.M., MOORE, J.E. and BERLINER, D. (1978) *Teaching behaviours, academic learning time, and student achievement*, Final Report, Beginning Teaching Evaluation Study, San Francisco, Far West Lab.

FORD, J. (1976) 'Facts, evidence and rumour: a rational reconstruction of "Social Class and the Comprehensive School"', in SHIPMAN, M. (1976) (Ed.) *The Organization and Impact of Social Research*, London, Routledge and Kegan Paul.

GAGE, N.L. (1978) *The Scientific Basis of the Art of Teaching*, New York, Teachers College Press.

GAGE, N.L. and COLADARCI, T.C. (1980) 'Replication of an experiment with a research based in-service teacher education programme', Program on Teacher Effectiveness, School of Education, Stanford.

GALTON, M., and SIMON, B. (Eds) (1980) *Progress and Performance in the*

Primary Classroom, London, Routledge and Kegan Paul.

GIACONIA, R.M. and HEDGES, L.V. (1983) 'Identifying features of effective open education', *Review of Educational Research*, 52, pp. 579–602.

GOOD, T.L. and GROUWS, D.A. (1979) 'The Missiouri Mathematics effectiveness project: an experimental study of fourth grade classrooms'. *Journal of Educational Psychology*, 71, pp. 355–62.

GRAY, J. and SATTERLEY, D. (1976) 'A chapter of errors', *Educational Research*, 19, pp. 45–56

GRAY, J. and SATTERLEY, D. (1981) 'Formal or Informal? A reassessment of the British evidence', *British Journal of Educational Psychology*, 51, pp. 187–96.

HMI (1978) *Primary Education in England*, London, HMSO.

JACOBS, J.E. and ECCLES, J. (1985) 'Gender differences in maths ability: the impact of media reports on parents', *Educational Researcher*, 14, 3, pp. 20–25.

JENSEN, A.R. (1969) 'How much can we boost IQ and scholastic achievement?' *Harvard Educational Review*, 39, pp. 1–123.

JENSEN, A.R. (1972) *Genetics and Education*, London, Methuen.

KAY, B. (1977) Letter introducing DES policy on research funding.

ROSENSHINE, B. (1976) 'Classroom Instruction', in GAGE, N.L. (Ed.) *The Psychology of Teaching Methods*, 75th NSSE Yearbook, Chicago, University of Chicago Press.

RUTTER, M., MAUGHAN, B., MORTIMORE, P., OUSTON J. (1979) *Fifteen Thousand Hours*, London, Open Books.

SLAVIN, R.E. (1983) *Cooperative Learning*, New York, Longman.

SHIPMAN, M. (1976) (Ed.) *The Organization and Impact of Social Research*, London, Routledge and Kegan Paul.

WRIGLEY, J. (1976) 'The impact of educational research', *SSRC Newsletter*, 32, pp. 3–4.

8 Longitudinal Survey Research into Progress in Secondary Schools, Based on the National Child Development Study

Jane Steedman

Introduction

In a certain kind of empirical educational research, most of the work is done before you know what the results will show. That is why you do it. Once the research is written up, however, it is not easy to remember what it was like before you knew the results. Looking back on the piece of research with which this chapter is concerned, a study carried out at the National Children's Bureau (NCB) between 1977 and 1983, is not too difficult. Explaining how we did it or, rather, where you should turn if you want to know in detail what we did is straightforward. Trying to go beyond the basic methodology, however (a methodology fully explained in the various publications referred to later which have arisen from the study), in order to disentangle something hitherto unpublished about why we did the research in the way we did, is a less obvious task. More challenging still is to draw out the implications for research work of this type, that is, studies requiring analysis of statistics from large numbers of school pupils with some relevance to educational policy.

The study in question was set up at the NCB and funded by the Department of Education and Science (DES), to 'evaluate aspects of educational progress in selective and nonselective secondary schools in England'. Initially, the funding was for a six-month feasibility study in 1977, on the basis of which it appeared that there were just enough school pupils in our sample to permit the study to be done. On the strength of that, we were given the funding for a three-year investigation of the progress in comprehensive and selective secondary schools of a national sample of children, based on the National Child Development Study (NCDS). In 1980, the NCB published the results (Steedman, 1980). A further three years' work was then funded, again by the DES, to consider the same children's progress in their comprehensive or selective schools, this time measuring it by their examination results (Steedman, 1983).

Some readers may be reminded of the study we are going to consider, by recalling the publicity that greeted the 1980 publication. The report of the first three years' work, three hundred pages of detailed research methodology and statistics, was basically the final report to sponsors and hardly calculated to grab headlines. Even the condensed, thirty-page summary which accompanied the publication (Steedman and Fogelman, 1980) had the circumspect style of research based on weighing up statistical evidence. Yet the London *Evening Standard* that day devoted its front page to the research results, under the banner headline, 'Excellent report for the comprehensives'. *The Times* next morning gave the story a page lead, and an accurate report with the headline, 'Clever children do as well in comprehensives as in grammar schools, study shows'. 'Report explodes comprehensives myth', was *The Guardian*'s version.

A more sober account would be that the sample on which we based our findings showed no clear overall advantage or disadvantage to selective or comprehensive schooling, on tests of attainment in mathematics and reading, and no consistent pattern of selective/comprehensive differences in student's plans for the future, attitudes to school or ratings of their own abilities in school subjects. There were large and important differences between grammars and secondary moderns and between comprehensives and secondary moderns, which might have received more attention, but we did not find consistent or sizeable differences between selective (grammar-and-secondary modern) and comprehensive groups. The examination results published in 1983 confirmed the previous stage of the study 'almost an anti-climax', as Professor Lacey has said (Lacey, 1984). Yet in 1980 not only were our findings seen as newsworthy, but also they prompted a vitriolic attack from an acknowledged Tory 'think-tank'.

Why did our research receive such attention? Partly, of course, because the debate over comprehensive and selective schooling is always with us, however we might wish to leave it behind. The response to our findings could have been due simply to their illustrating that comprehensive pupils did not, on average, do worse, as measured by progress in tested mathematics and reading, than pupils in selective (grammar and secondary modern) schools. The observation was 'newsworthy', and perhaps particularly so in the context of statistics already in public use which did not allow for intake differences in schools and which therefore suggested that something to do with comprehensives was to blame for some of their pupils having lower exam grades than many grammar school pupils. We were thus not unhappy to have our, better quality, research given attention.

But the reception in 1980 of the first report of the project came long after the initial stage of curiosity and excitement of designing the research study, and after the painstaking years of its execution. I explain first in this chapter something of those earlier stages, starting with what prompted the study. I shall explore both the factors that made it seem a study worth funding — work which needed doing — and, in so far as these can be distinguished, the considerations that made us researchers want to do the particular study in question. Then I shall go on to a more detailed sketch of why this investigation took the precise form it did, the decisions and even compromises that made up the design and execution of the study.

Not all of the sequence of events that formed this work is appropriate to the present chapter. All the detailed discussion of methodology and consideration of alternatives is in the two major reports that were published arising from the study (Steedman 1980, 1983). A great deal of worthwhile discussion of the research has been contributed in reviews and in journals since, including Lacey (1984), Heath (1984), Goldstein (1984) and others, some of which are detailed in the reference section here. Later in this chapter there is a brief, further discussion of the publications arising from this project, of the influences that operated to make the reports take the form they did, and of the reception of the findings of the study. Finally, there is a place for some general remarks on the experience of doing empirical research in policy-related fields.

What Prompted the Study?

It is worth looking at why the study was judged important enough in 1976 to be funded by the DES, to understand the atmosphere in which we embarked on the project. An overall motive for commissioning the study was, presumably, that it offered the opportunity to monitor the reorganization along comprehensive lines of Britain's schools. It had been seen as important for many years to compare the progress of students in comprehensive and in selective schools. Comprehensive schools were, during the 1960s and 1970s, replacing the bipartite grammar-and-secondary modern system (or tripartite grammar-technical-secondary modern schools). To monitor the progress of children in order to see how they were affected by a major change in educational provision was essential. Educational and theoretical claims for selective and for comprehensive schools seemed to need testing, and empirical answers concerning the relative merits of the two systems might save a considerable amount of ideological time-wasting. It would have been irresponsible, as at any stage in the history of education, not to try and see how children were faring. It looked as if the attempt was worth making, moreover, given the existence of a suitable, up-to-date source of data, the NCDS.

Another strong argument in favour of commissioning the NCB to do the work was that the timing of NCDS was right. The stage of comprehensivization captured by NCDS data was one at which sufficient numbers of pupils existed, nationally speaking, in the comprehensive schools, in secondary moderns and in grammars, to make the study possible. Our study, then, has the major advantage over earlier and subsequent work of focusing on a uniquely revealing period in the piecemeal reorganization along comprehensive lines of the British educational system. By 1974, when students in our sample were aged 16, there were already enough people who had gone through comprehensives to count, while there yet remained enough pupils who had been at grammar and secondary modern schools with which to compare them. The year in which NCDS measured school-leavers, 1974, was therefore arguably a good stage at which to investigate the state of the system. But the continued existence of grammar schools meant that no school was exactly comprehensive. It was acknowledged in 1977, when we began the study, that, even where Local Education Authorities (LEAs) were nominally fully comprehensive, there were either very few schools at all or the LEA was still at a transitional stage, with selection affecting the older pupils, if not the intakes, of secondary schools. Where grammar schools still operated, they would continue to draw off 'academic' children from schools elsewhere, even from schools in other LEAs. NCDS data, given this, would allow the only reasonable assessment of pupils' progress, because they could establish how the coexistence of selective and non-selective schools affected school intakes.

NCDS: A National Longitudinal Sample

The chief strength of a study based on NCDS data lies in the fact that the NCDS is a longitudinal data set. For every pupil we studied when they were 16 years old, we could say what they had been like before the start of secondary school, at age 11. The assumption behind the funding of the study, a point made in our 1980 publication, was that *progress* in secondary school is the important indicator of what secondary schools may do. It is not measuring results of secondary schools to measure 16-year-olds and fail to take into account the characteristics of those pupils which existed before secondary school. By using NCDS data, we could take these characteristics into account whereas even some of the better recent publications on the issue (e.g., Gray *et al.*, 1983) have been unable to use a longitudinal approach.

It is necessary here to describe the special nature of the NCDS more fully, in order to describe its peculiar value for this investigation and also to explain how it determined some of our research approaches. Originally a national survey to study perinatal mortality rates, the NCDS started as a survey of every one of the 16 000 children in Great Britain born in the week of 3–9 March, 1958. NCB was subsequently funded to trace the subjects afresh at 7 years old, in 1965, which established the NCDS, and then at 11 years old (1969) and at 16 years old (1974). At each stage, information was collected on the health, the home circumstances and background, and the education and performance of the children. There existed at NCB, therefore, a wealth of information on a cross-section of Britain's 16-year-olds, all of which could be linked to their home circumstances and to their attainments before secondary school. The main strength of our study, unique among contemporary research, was in its ability to use longitudinal data in multivariate analysis in order to take into account extraneous factors in assessing the role of secondary schools.

Previous research had been too early to conduct the selective/comprehensive comparison (Douglas, 1968) or unable to take into account characteristics of children on entry to secondary school. We knew in advance that we needed longitudinal data to compare like with like, since the intakes of grammars and comprehensives, by definition, differed. Our study could cope with that. What made it essential to do so for a selective/comprehensive comparison, we were able to discover from our data, was that in fact the intakes of comprehensives in England at that time differed not just from the intakes of grammar schools but also from the intakes of the selective combination of grammar and secondary modern schools. Comprehensive pupils, on average, were starting secondary school with lower levels of skill in reading and maths, and lower test scores for general ability, than the average for the selective combination. In social class terms, the comprehensive pupils were slightly less advantaged than secondary modern pupils, at the start of secondary school. Detailed figures are in the first reports of the project (Steedman, 1980; Steedman and Fogelman, 1980). As well as demonstrating these differences in intakes which showed that comprehensive pupils started off at a disadvantage relative to selective pupils at 11, we could also, in a statistically precise fashion, take account of the differences when evaluating the end results of schooling. The longitudinal approach is what makes our results valuable and interesting.

Another essential requirement of such a study was that it should be based on a national sample, and NCDS offered that. Our study concerned the evidence, in so far as it existed, on implementation of national education policies. Given how schools vary, it is important not to extrapolate from one or two examples but to claim implications for characteristics of schools or categories of pupils only if one has a large national sample, as in this study. We saw our investigation as implicitly concerned with the national picture, and the value of NCDS as its ability to provide information at a national level. The advantage of a national picture based on national averages (or averages of a national sample) is that it offers the chance of generalizations about types of school.

This national quality can be a drawback, too. It may be of less interest to educationalists to read of national average characteristics of categories of school pupils than to look at more detailed characteristics of particular schools or authorities. The latter tend to offer more scope for educational explanations, hypotheses and even prescriptions for action. National figures tend to interest policy makers and politicians more than educationalists. An audience of policy makers was interested in national questions such as, 'Are comprehensives producing worse or better results?' Statistical information on national averages is what such questions need. To make statements about 'comprehensive' or 'selective' schools requires information from a sample like the one we worked with, drawn from the entire population (for instance, pupils in English comprehensives) which one is considering.

Although as educational researchers we were interested in more detailed questions about schools, we happened to be working with a study particularly suited to national generalizations, with necessarily limited sensitivity to the variety between and within schools and to changes in schools over time. NCDS was, by virtue of its size and complexity, slow-moving compared to schools; educationalists' interests and school practices, local or more widespread, can change very fast. Gathering data on thousands of instances and finding patterns in those data takes time. There is a trade-off, then, between sensitivity to variety, on the one hand, and generalizability on the other hand, and this will be apparent in the discussion later in this chapter of the type of measures of student progress or 'outcomes' of schooling that were chosen as appropriate for this national study.

The context for the commissioning of this research, then, was chiefly the need for empirical research on the changeover to comprehensives at that precise stage of the reorganization, based on a high quality, national sample which, most importantly, had a longitudinal base. Our own motivations as researchers were not dissimilar; they were largely to do with the existence of a suitably longitudinal data-base for comparison of comprehensive and other pupils. The comparison could never be wholly satisfactorily done, nor was it thought of as the only way to judge comprehensives or secondary schools. But this was the proper data set for such a study and we were curious, as researchers have to be, about what it would yield. We also had some technical interests in applying techniques of multivariate analysis in order to assess school progress.

An additional stimulus was earlier work in this area. Several important studies of selection and educational opportunity had predated and informed the move to comprehensive schooling (Floud (Ed.) *et al.*, 1956; Husén, 1960; Halsey, 1961; Douglas, 1968). Some contributors to research in this field had helped to define the educational arguments for and against different types of school. The intention of the bipartite system, it will be remembered, was to offer a separate channel for those judged most able academically at 11, while the majority of children (about four-fifths) went to secondary moderns. During the 1950s, research had shown that this did not necessarily guarantee access to the grammar school channel even for those academically suited. Educational opportunity was not distributed efficiently, in that sense (Floud (Ed.) *et al.*, 1956). But research has also suggested that the mere act of channelling pupils into overtly 'academically successful' and 'academically unsuccessful' paths might contribute to their performance (Newsom Report, 1963; Hargreaves, 1967). In the case where the majority were 'not passing' the selection exam, it could be inferred, the majority could be adversely affected. Both strands of research suggested hypotheses on which our study might contribute relevant evidence.

An additional motive was that we had the resources to explore the conclusions of some earlier studies which had not the advantage of a sample drawn from the whole country. A feature of some research in this area (even more recent attempts, for example, Cox *et al.*, 1983) is that evidence is drawn from a non-representative sub-sample of local education authorities (LEAs), for instance, rather than from all LEAs. At the time we started our project, a great deal of prominence had been given to the conclusion of Ford (1969) that comprehensives had failed to offset class bias in educational attainment, a conclusion based on three specific schools. Would a national picture confirm her view?

Our motivation to explore the question of comprehensive and selective school progress was curiosity about education. The relative merits of comprehensive and selective schools, however, still make up 'an issue which divides people along party political lines' (Booth, 1983). Politics enter into the relation between educational provision, educational opportunity and educational outcomes, and, when research explores national averages, it can be mixed up with issues of national policy which divide politicians of one political complexion from those of another. Because education often becomes political in Britain, there was a risk that, whatever empirical research showed about the schools of Britain, it would provoke political reactions. Social scientists, however, cannot be deterred from trying to find things out, nor from using and revealing the best possible evidence, by the fact that their work may overlap with political beliefs.

The political nature of this apparently empirical question had led in addition to some particularly poor quality answers to the question of whether children in comprehensives fared worse or better than they would have done under selection. As researchers, we wanted to improve the quality of research in this area. Notably inadequate had been the observations of the Black Papers (Cox and Dyson (Eds) 1969(a), 1969(b), 1970; Cox and Boyson, 1975). These had been based on very poor standards of research, research which had made uncritical use of examination measures, had compared comprehensive schools with grammars rather than with the grammar-and-secondary modern combination, and had failed to allow in any way for intake (Wright, 1977).

By professional research standards, that kind of research seemed 'parti-pris'; it appeared to take as a starting point the myth that 'education had all gone wrong' since comprehensivization. The Black

Papers appeared to promulgate a dramatic anti-comprehensive view, rather than to look at evidence. Our study was not particularly addressed to politically-motivated writers in this area. The essential limits to any such empirical study, namely that one is attempting to interpret the world as it really is, rather than to evaluate the merits of various ideals, had positive appeal. But our work would confront the Black Papers by offering an authoritative, national picture, based on research of a quality that surpassed theirs and challenged their right to base claims on inferior figures. Whether or not our findings would be politically challenging, however, and if so to whom, would depend on how the results turned out.

We undertook the work with a number of questions to be tackled and with open minds as to possible results. It was not advocacy of any one way of organizing schooling that prompted our investigation. It may be necessary to say that now, but the climate in 1977 was one in which research to see how the educational system was working was accepted as important, and not regarded as politically threatening. If there were inadequacies in parts of the system, it was necessary to reveal them. Of course, the implications of results would not be obvious. If progress had turned out to be worse, for example, in comprehensives than in selectives, this could have pointed to inequalities in provision for comprehensives rather than defects inherent in comprehensives. Furthermore, we wanted to explore many questions other than simply asking 'Are comprehensives better or worse?' As social scientists, we were exploring what was going on, in so far as that was amenable to empirical scrutiny, rather than what ought to be. It was not a foregone conclusion what the research would show and it was impossible to predict what it would be seen as showing.

Determinants of the Detailed Shape of the Study

The overall limits of the study were set before we started by the influences outlined in the previous section. The scope and detailed form of the project, though, were determined by a host of factors, of which examples are given below. Details are published already elsewhere; here we should highlight points with general implications for researchers. An important general point which this section will illustrate is that empirical studies of educational provision have to approximate a best fit in two ways. Firstly, they have to find a fit between the empirically verifiable world and various ideal worlds of educational theory. Secondly, they have to find the best possible fit between the data of the real world and the set of data available to them. Many of the factors contributing to our research strategies can be classified, accordingly, into one of two groups. The first group is a definitional, analytical set of questions which were nonetheless required of us by the contingencies of the empirical world we were studying. This group of decisions was indeed created by the lack of exact fit between the theoretical world of questions of educational policy and the actual practice and provision of education. We were exploring data from the real world, rather than from theoretical models of educational systems. The second group of influences on the shape of the research was similarly forced upon us by the availability (or lack) of appropriate data, but might be called the more practical considerations. Into this group fall certain limits both in the data at our disposal and in the techniques appropriate for investigating such data. (Some additional influences on the research existed which fall into neither of the above groups to do with presentation of findings and 'consumers', that is, the audience for publications. These are also to be discussed here, and in the subsequent section). So our thinking on design and methodology reflected educational, analytical, theoretical factors, and technical and practical considerations. After the main research was done, we also allowed 'consumer factors' to enter into our decisions, but for now will discuss the reasons behind our design and methodology.

There were a great many questions the study could tackle. Our publications show that we were able to look at, among other things, the average progress of children in different schools, as measured by attainments, something of their own opinions on school and on their own progress, their own self-image and values. We could explore whether patterns held for all the pupils in a school category or whether pupils of particular levels of skill before secondary school, say, differed from the rest. This was important, for example, because a pervasive view of the comprehensive, common school — a result perhaps of contrast with the aims of selection — was that comprehensives would cater for children of average ability at the expense of those who would have gone to grammar schools. Schools which contained the full range of abilities, some people held, could not produce attainments among the most academic children to match those fostered by a selective school. Since the tripartite system differentiated according to test performance at age 11, it was significant that NCDS data included each child's test scores at age 11, and that the assumptions of these theories could be tested.

There were aspects of the educational aims of comprehensive and selective schools which we could not explore with a national sample. We had only limited ways of looking within schools, to uncover data, for example, which might inform the theory that a selective system was inherently socially divisive and fostered competition, while a comprehensive system might be taken to imply a greater emphasis on collaboration and cooperation. It is a shortcoming of much research measurement that it is unable to reflect some sensitive but maybe observable developments in schools. Anne Jones has drawn attention to this problem:

> Anyone who works closely with young people will realize that many of them no longer share the assumptions upon which most schools and research into schools are based ... in an age when academic achievement, individual success and paid 'work' as a means of gaining status and self-esteem are gradually being supplemented or replaced by a new ethic which places more stress on cooperation, caring and coping. ... we still appear to judge both our pupils and our schools on the criteria of the past (Jones, 1985, p. 206).

Conscious of this sort of bias, we had from the start combed the data for potentially enlightening sources on aspects of 16-year-olds other than academic progress, exploring whether pupils valued 'helping other people', for example. Though there was a little data available to shed light on students' ethics, 'in the debate on selection performance measures easily become paramount' (Wright, 1977). It must always be recognized, though, that empirical research is constrained by the real world. Educational reforms imply that something currently exists that can be changed, and research looks at what currently exists. So there is a time-lag for testing changes.

Analytical, Theoretical Questions

We have pointed out the gap between the 'is' of empirical work and the 'ought' of theory which has to be resolved in research design. The commonplace usage of terms like 'comprehensive', for example, is inadequate in a study which starts by finding out that, even after we had excluded from the study pupils who changed school, over half of the 16-year-old pupils in schools called comprehensive in 1974, were in schools which had changed from selective grammars or secondary moderns into comprehensives while they were there.

Who should count as a 'comprehensive' pupil, who as a 'selective' pupil? The actual data highlighted the gap between apparently educationally significant questions and the availability of empirical evidence. The artificial selective/comprehensive distinction is an example. For one thing, while comparing the relative progress of children in comprehensives with that of their counterparts in the selective system, we were not able to compare 'what a fully comprehensive system would be like' with 'what a comparable selective system was like'. There never has been the pattern of educational provision which would offer appropriate data; for the purpose of our research, we would have liked a line drawn from Bognor Regis to Berwick-on-Tweed with a fully comprehensive system on one side and a fully selective system on the other. We had to recognize that, at the time children in NCDS were at school, a fully comprehensive system had never existed in this country and even 'comprehensive' LEAs contained pupils who had experienced selection. Certainly, our sample as a whole contained an immense variety of school experience.

The study was at pains to clarify its definitions of 'comprehensive' and 'selective' schools by careful description of who went to what school, in order, in part, to inform any debate on the subject. One of the crucial stages in the study was, therefore, to define our terms very carefully and justify our definitions.

Our analytical stage included careful delineation of which members of the sample were to count as going to which type of school. I do not know of other research studies which have been able to be as strict as we were in ensuring that pupils in their samples really did receive their entire secondary schooling in the specified type of school. (Details are in the first publication from the project.) Yet it seemed an obvious precaution, in advance of any knowledge of the results, to restrict the grammar, secondary modern and comprehensive samples to pupils known to have attended those schools and not others. Contingencies in the questions asked in 1974, which might not have played such a part if data had been gathered for the specific investigation of comprehensive and other schools, meant that in order to know the type of school attended we had to limit our sample to those who had remained in one school throughout. This was an artificial restriction but one which allowed of easier interpretation.

We also looked separately at those children who, although in comprehensives at 16, had started at a grammar or secondary modern which had then become comprehensive ('transitional'). It did not seem correct to call them comprehensive pupils in quite the same way as those who had been in a comprehensive throughout — even though the majority of those who were in one school and in comprehensives at 16 had been in a school which was redesignated comprehensive during the time they were there.

These were all discoveries made at the analytical, preliminary stage of the project which constituted some of the most important insights the study had to offer. It was a fairly rigid definition of comprehensives which included schools which were new and in which populations were relatively unstable. We did our best to make our terms meaningful, however, by limiting our 'comprehensive' sample to those whose school was at least called 'comprehensive' in the year they entered the school, and to those who stayed at the same school for the normal number of years (from 11 when the school started at 11, from 12 where schools started at 12 and from 13 where schools started at 13). The same restrictions applied to the selective sample.

It has been a very clear defect of some naive comparisons in this field that the average for grammar pupils is compared with the average for comprehensive pupils. The appropriate comparison if one is evaluating possible alternatives is that between the comprehensive average and the combined average for grammars and secondary moderns together. Only in that way are two comparable groups, even in theory, being studied. Some sociologists would want to argue that it is quite reasonable to compare grammars with comprehensives, as long as it is the comparison you wish to make. But if you want to illuminate the relative merits of selective and comprehensive schools, you have to take into account logical necessities of which you are aware, namely that schools that take 20 per cent of the population (grammar schools) cannot exist without having schools for the other 80 per cent (secondary moderns) (assuming universal secondary education). You cannot legitimately compare pupils of grammars with pupils in comprehensives without also looking at how the pupils of secondary moderns fared. In fact, as our findings on the intakes of the schools showed, the average of comprehensive pupils' attainments at 11 was well below that for the grammar-and-secondary-modern combination, before the start of secondary school. This was partly because a proportion of the fully comprehensive range was 'creamed off' to grammar schools and partly to do with the constitution of those LEAs which had gone comprehensive. The intakes of the comprehensives at that time were closer to those of the secondary moderns, on average, than to the grammar-and-secondary modern combination. The intakes of schools are interdependent.

We did initially consider it important for a realistic assessment of comprehensives to study longer-established comprehensives. Some of the comprehensives were very new schools. Unfortunately, we could not find sufficient examples of long-established comprehensives. Few comprehensives, even by 1969, when our NCDS students were 11, had been going for many years as comprehensives. In order to explore whether we could detect any effect of age of comprehensives, we separated very new comprehensives (set up 1966–69) from the ones which had been set up for four years or more by the time our sample pupils were 11 (relatively well-established). As it turned out, results for the latter were not systematically better than for more recent (1966–1969) comprehensives. One difficulty in interpreting that finding was the fact that, as well as having intakes with lower attainments on average than recently-set-up comprehensives, the 1965-or-earlier comprehensives were set up in slightly different circumstances, with other factors influencing what schools remained in their areas to compete for intakes.

We started with the view that we should include in our design the investigation of a question that is of obvious importance on a local level, namely the influence on intake and morale of fairly newly-formed comprehensives of the reputation based on the schools from which they were formed; many of our comprehensives were formed from one selective school. We therefore compared comprehensives formed from grammars with those formed from a secondary modern, and with other comprehensives. By the time we had classified our comprehensive pupils according to whether they were in ex-grammars, ex-secondary moderns, amalgamations of two or more schools or purpose-built schools, we had fairly small samples. It seems reasonable to suggest that the categories of amalgamations and purpose-built schools, looked at nationally, embrace such a variety of circumstances that we were not able to detect systematic patterns in their results. We saw from NCDS data that schools called 'comprehensive' did not have representative, comprehensive, intakes, many pupils being 'creamed off' to grammar, direct grant or independent schools. We were operating with analytical definitions; the names of schools only put them into the selective or comprehensive 'camp'. What can be clearly stated is that, by allowing for intake, with a longitudinal approach, we were taking the only reasonable approach. Since the educational system did not present a controlled comparison, we had to use statistical controls instead.

The artificiality of the selective/comprehensive comparison is an example of several similar problems where 'unreal' variables were created to address questions of educational significance to which answers are empirically unobtainable.

Another variable which was of educational significance but could not in the end be used in the study was the proportion of pupils in a Local Authority (LEA) in comprehensives. We wanted to distinguish 'comprehensive' pupils in LEAs where 20 per cent were in grammars from pupils of comprehensives in fully-comprehensive LEAs. The real world made this impossible, however. The proportions officially in comprehensives varied during a child's school career. This is likely to affect schools' intakes but the proportion fluctuated within and between LEAs during the secondary school years in question and no suitable variable could represent this.

Although NCDS data are from the whole of Great Britain, we deliberately excluded Scottish pupils from the comparison of selective and comprehensive schools because comprehensive schooling South of the Border has a different history and definition from that in Scotland. For that reason the simultaneous study of Scottish Educational Data Archive (Gray *et al.*, 1983) is an interesting comparative study of a different set of comprehensives (and is, although not longitudinal, a study which respects the need to allow for intake).

Ways in which some research decisions can be altered by events in the public domain may interest some readers. As an example of the sort of thing that can happen (though it seemed at the time merely the slightest of bureaucratic nuisances), an external factor entered into the decision to base analyses on England rather than England and Wales. This was to do with the division of responsibilities for Welsh schools to the Welsh Office. As it happened, the decision to base the study on England alone rather than England and Wales was taken after we had started the study, so some early tables were based on England-and-Wales. (Later analyses including Welsh data bore out our earlier conclusions that no average consistent difference existed between comprehensive and selective pupils.)

Practical Decisions or Constraints

Some of the influences on research practices are to do with mundane limits to the data available. For example, if you work with a study which has taken many years to build up a longitudinal data base, you inevitably find your design shaped, in part, by what is possible and available. Your study cannot be precisely tailor-made. It is worth mentioning that relatively little of the funding for the three major longitudinal national surveys instigated since the end of the Second World War has been longitudinal; this must have detracted in some measure from their usefulness if not their potential. The point of mentioning this is that the team of researcher, statistician and data-processors who worked on this study had no hand in the data collection for the first stage of this study. It is also to emphasize that the data already existed before the project was envisaged, so that we were working on data collected by a variety of people over many years for many (mostly unspecified) purposes. This could be seen as a source of strength in the research, in that it entails detachment at the data-collection stage from the issues explored by our study. It also put some constraints on the questions we could address. Although there was a wealth of data on which to draw, the questions asked in 1974 were not infinite, and our choice of measures had to be made from among the variety of possibilities available. There were, accordingly, necessarily comparisons we could not make; we could not go back and include extra items on questionnaires administered in 1974. Some information we would have liked was not there because the question had not been asked. Some data were not there, did not exist, because the educational world did not offer examples (such as many instances of mixed ability teaching). Some did not exist because NCDS members were not born until 1958. With data on people who were in their 20s by the date of publication we would have liked to look at longer-term outcomes of schooling such as jobs and attitudes to continuing education, but we were at that stage operating with an age limit — school age. When we started the project, the NCDS members were not yet in their 20s; the 'fourth sweep' of the study was yet to be funded. Some data were not there although they existed and efforts had been made to gather them. The information on the social composition of each child's school is an example. NCDS did not offer adequate school-based data on the social class composition or the ability mix of each child's school. The 'social mix' measure exemplifies problems of 'missing data' common to quantitative research. It could not be used here because not all headteachers answered this question and we were not confident of the basis for the answers there were. Because of this, while we recognized the interdependence of school intakes from the start, we lacked one possible means of handling its implication that intakes of schools in the same category will differ.

But there were plenty of usable indicators of 16-year-olds' progress, and we were able to design a full and detailed set of analyses to shed light on many aspects of schools. What determined our choices of 'outcome' measures?

The first stage of the study deliberately used a variety of measures of 16-year-olds (more than many studies of secondary schools) in an attempt to do justice to the variety of endeavours schools and 16-year-olds engage in. One aspect of the progress of 16-year-olds, as far as we were concerned, was to do with academic attainments. For that part of the study, it was of exceptional value to have at our disposal not only pupils' own views on their attainments, but also the scores on a maths and a reading test obtained at 16 years old by every member of the sample. We were quite fortunate; these test score indicators are far superior to examination results for the sort of generalizations about the attainments of aggregations of pupils which we were engaged in. It seemed to us unnecessarily limited to explore only attainment measures, in looking at influences of schools. The NCDS data offered scope for far more, and in the end we explored nineteen aspects of educational progress in the first stage of the project.

One factor determining our choice of 'outcome' variables was that measures had to apply to all the pupils in the sample, in all areas of England. We needed to find common ground, therefore, in the aims of selective and comprehensive schools in order to use measures of school success which any school might hope to achieve. Indicators of attitudes to jobs might be accepted as reflecting something schools saw themselves as affecting. Whether students liked school or not would be something of concern to any school. (We did explore these variables, though some of the interpretation of results was difficult when responses did not reflect all social class groups or both sexes, for instance.) The attainment tests administered to every member of the sample at age 11 and at 16 were the clearest example of measures that applied to all the pupils. Some other measures were less satisfactory; for example, the proportions 'truanting' were so low that results have to be treated with circumspection. But our focus at the initial stage on measures other than exams was unusually revealing.

In 1977, it seemed an advance on existing research that we did not have to rely on exam results as indicators of progress. The study was originally undertaken, it should be clear, with no intention (of mine, anyway) of analyzing examination results. In 1977, it was too early to gather examination results in any case; some cohort members were still taking their 'A' levels. Furthermore, examination results are a notable example of measures which would not apply to the whole sample. Any measure you can devise as an indicator of examination performance is too weak for such a study. An examination measures only those who are put in for it and reveals nothing of the academic attainment of pupils who did other exams or anything else. The grades of examinations, moreover, are not distributed over a national sample in a fashion suitable for these analyses; they are not designed for 'number-crunching'. Aggregation of examination results nationally would be unsatisfactory, creating measures that would be hard to interpret.

There are, of course, educational arguments against emphasizing exam results. It was not until later that John Gray issued as a warning to educational researchers what had been a familiar caveat among teachers and educationalists:

> There is a distinct danger that by emphasizing the primacy of examination qualification, we produce models of effective schools which are inadequate to the needs of a substantial minority of pupils and their teachers. (Gray, 1981)

While this was an important consideration, our objections to examination results as measures were more mundane, research-based and technical; they would not do as tools for the job of comparing the children in our study.

Yet advisors to the project argued that our original study lacked examination results and should be extended to include investigation of examination performance. Funding was forthcoming to collect examination results from 1978, and in 1979 funding was agreed for the comparison of selective and non-selective schools using examination results. In some ways, this seemed a retrograde step in our research methodology, a compromise with non-research considerations. The compromise was tolerable because we were able to design the second stage of the study to explore a considerable range of different indicators of examination performance and to devote large sections of the book of the study to pointing out inconsistencies between measures and discussing their worth in detail. There was, too, a strong research-based motive for looking at examination results, which was the wish to compare our results with those of other researchers. We adopted one particular indicator of examination performance, for example, because it had been used in the National Survey of Health and Development (NSHD; Douglas, 1968), the longitudinal study (1946 cohort) which was the forerunner of NCDS. Thus we compared two populations of school children a dozen years apart. We also wanted to be able to compare our own cohort's examination results with their performance on tests at the same age. When starting the examination results study in 1979 we had an incentive, therefore, to follow the first stage of our study.

Technical Influences

By repeating our analysis design in the second stage of the study, we allowed a reasonable comparison between two measures of the same people at the same age, measures which might be supposed to measure some of the same things. This was valuable, but should not be interpreted as a sign that we felt our analysis design could not be improved. That design was a function, in part, of what was possible with the techniques of computing, data handling and multivariate statistical analysis then available. The NCDS then was enormously cumbersome to work with. As researcher, I knew about the trials of handling this longitudinal data set only at second hand; Bob Wellburn and other colleagues at NCB were faced with the real problems of computing data amounting to millions of facts, gathered in different ways at intervals years apart, over a period of sixteen years during which vast changes in techniques of data storage had occurred. Simply gaining access to data was then a big undertaking; what looked to be simple enough requests for tables from researchers took time to fulfil. Since those days, it has become customary to extract a working file of the data needed for a particular study, so that researchers can handle data directly. The large scale of analyses and the difficulties with the data set, during the time of this project, precluded researchers' control of data analysis.

It may not be appreciated how lengthy a process it can be, too, to manipulate complex data from thousands of children into a form suitable for analysis. Our experience of collecting examination results data from 1979 to 1980 serves as an illustration. A formidable task involving thousands of letters and forms, hours of clerical and coding work and painstaking attention to detail, the collection of 'raw' examination data was only the beginning. Of course, there are researchers' tasks, such as defining the form in which data should be supplied and stored, but these are the tip of an iceberg of computer programming necessary to ensure that researchers' designs for indicators of examination performance are implemented. The merging of newly-assembled data with the data from earlier stages of the study, so that each of the 16 000 individuals has their own exam results and not someone else's, attached to information on their housing at age 7, for example, is another massive task. Fortunately, some of these operations are made easier by technical advances as years pass.

The magnitude of the data set, combined with limits to the complexity of multivariate analysis then technically possible, influenced the eventual shape of the investigation. The computer programs for doing this kind of longitudinal analysis permitted only a limited number of variables to enter the calculations. We therefore had to specify only a limited set of 'background' factors to be allowed for in the statistical estimation of 'progress' attributable to secondary school. Any reader who wishes to know the details of the statistical techniques should turn to the Statistical Appendix written by Dougal Hutchison, then Principal Statistician at NCB, for the first report of the project (Steedman, 1980). Subsequent developments in our thinking on techniques of analysis contributed to a later study of NCDS data on mixed and single-sex schooling (Steedman, 1985).

Our original model, for both the first stage and the later, examination results study, took into account in every comparison between pupil groups: the social class of a pupil's parents and the interest they were said to show in their child's schooling; the sex of the pupil; and their attainments and tested 'ability' at 11 years old. These were variables established as important by earlier research. Further variables, though, which could influence progress independently of secondary school, were not included for two main reasons. We could estimate from colleagues' work on NCDS data some of the likely importance of factors like family size or primary school attendance, though the evidence was tangential and, with more time, we would have liked to explore more rigorously the potential contribution of such additional variables. Our other reason for excluding some background variables from analysis was technical, to do with limits to the number of background variables we could build into analyses. The restrictions also determined the number of school variables we could explore. We operated within those constraints in the belief that additional background variables would not have been likely to alter our explanations.

Our choice of 'outcome' measures indicating school progress, too, was determined in part by technical limits. The complications in analyzing longitudinal data, allowing for several 'home background' factors, mean that 'outcome' variables are frequently most convenient in dichotomous form, such as, 'Do you plan to stay on at school after the age of 16, yes or no?'. These 'all-or-none' measures may be insensitive to underlying reasons.

The complicated analyses are expensive and only possible with the use of a large computer. When we began, it was highly complicated to do analyses. Some of the flexibility needed for scientific discovery was thereby denied to us. Researchers were unable to investigate what happened with a given model, modify the design in light of the results and reanalyze. We would make a best first design, based partly on the work of other researchers and partly on our own work. Variables in NCDS known to be unreliable or not to add much to the explanation were discarded. But the choice of variables had to be a best first guess. We could design many analyses but there was no possibility of seeing what variables contributed to explaining results and then changing the design. The cost and the time analyses took prevented that, despite the length of time and money available. So the learning from results that is a normal part of research was not as extensive as it can be, and modifications of a scientific nature to the procedures were precluded.

From the preceding section some of the factors which form such a study can be drawn out. A mixture of educational issues of importance and of the existing research literature generate research questions. The data available then have to be considered. Some data will offer unprecedented opportunities to explore questions no-one has been able to tackle properly before. But some questions cannot be explored, either because the educational world has not yet put into practice the theory that prompts the question, or because the data are not in the data set you are using (the question was not asked, the answers are unreliable, or the question was not answered). Technical developments then facilitate or hinder what you do. Beyond the initial design stage of this study, then, there was not unlimited freedom to interpret and explore the data. This may be a way of preserving neutrality and detachment from findings, but it was largely a function of lack of time to interpret findings, let alone reanalyze in the light of them. There was therefore relatively little interaction between the researchers and their data. Efforts to obtain additional funding for time to write about the study were un-successful, so the researcher moved on to become fully occupied with subsequent projects by the time each stage of the study was reported to sponsors. This has a bearing on the following section, on issues of the publication, presentation and reception of our reports.

In the Public Arena

It may now be clear how painstaking and long-drawn-out this large-scale, longitudinal research can be. The length and detail of the final reports to sponsors reflect this, and reflect the little time left for analysis and interpretation. Despite this, it was considered important to make findings available as swiftly as possible once the report had been sent to the Secretary of State. In the absence of funds for publishing from either the DES or a commercial publisher, NCB apparently found £1000 to print a few hundred copies which were sold at a relatively high price (£13). Unlike some significant publications in the field, then, ours did not have the assistance of a publisher's promotion. In the event, its reception meant a small reprint, but the report was never easily obtained, let alone part of any 'hard sell'.

Before the 1980 publication, though, news of the findings was 'leaked' and, by March 1980, Secretary of State, Mark Carlisle, was denying that he had held up publication. The focus of the 'leak' foreshadowed later press interest; *The Times* of 19 March described 'a report which shows that bright children do not suffer academically in comprehensive schools'. The newsworthiness of this depended both on the commonly-held assumption that alternative systems must be opposed to the concerns of the system they replace and on the ability of poorer quality research to feed that assumption. The attention which our work got was largely a product, more immediately, of the introduction by the new Conservative government of the Assisted Places Scheme, designed to remove 'bright' children from comprehensive schools.

The publicity in March 1980 alerted us as to the eventual reception of the report. We were therefore at pains to point out other aspects of the findings when, in July, the study was published. Press reports did focus on test results at the expense of other measures of 16-year-olds. But the tests were reasonable measures and results were relevant to a topical debate. That topicality was of course undreamt-of in our research design; it just happened that our discoveries on the progress of 'able' children were such as to question assumptions of selection and to challenge a policy of the government of the day. The change of government as we were completing our initial investigation had a significant effect on the reception of our study. On the whole, though, the serious newspapers made us feel the findings would get a fair hearing and the research would be taken seriously. Perhaps we should not have been surprised that, a few months later, our work led to a strong reaction. Nevertheless, the attack which came in September, 1980, was unexpected as well as astonishing in its vitriol. A pamphlet by people *The Times* described as 'contributors to the Black Papers' was published from the Centre for Policy Studies (CPS), which we learnt was a right-wing Tory 'think-tank' set up by Sir Keith Joseph and Margaret Thatcher. The nature of this pamphlet and our response to it are well-documented and there is no space for the story here (Cox and Marks, 1980; Steedman *et al.*, 1980). Some implications, though, with hindsight, may be of use to other researchers, because this political attack was directed not simply at our findings but at standards of educational research.

We saw that the essence of this study was its ability to evaluate the progress of pupils during secondary school by allowing for performance before secondary school. This was vital to any comparison of selective and comprehensive schools, because the intakes of selective schools differed from the intakes of comprehensive schools, on average. We had for some years been operating on the assumption that our figures, allowing for the stage reached by 11 years old, would be more interesting as genuine approximations to estimates of progress in secondary school than simple averages which were not longitudinally related to earlier attainments. There already were any number of sources of figures on average performance in selective and comprehensive schools which did not allow for initial attainment before secondary school (not least, the DES's own published *Statistics of Education*). It therefore seemed highly inappropriate for the CPS subsequently to call for our 'raw data', as they put it. (By the latter term they meant not raw data but averages for comprehensive and selective pupils which did not take account of attainments before secondary school.) It was a criticism of a most unsophisticated kind. The attack was not as laughable as it at first appeared, however, since its presentation ensured extensive press attention. Its suggestion that we had somehow fiddled the figures, in carrying out conventional statistical corrections to allow for children's attainments at 11, seemed ignorant to professional researchers. We knew that the correct statistical term for this —

'adjustment' — did not mean 'fiddling'; we knew that we were unaware in advance of what results would show; we knew that
unadjusted figures would not be informative here, that our up-to-
date research techniques would be an advance on crude, unadjusted
comparisons (let alone on 'raw data'). But readers of newspaper
articles did not necessarily have our advantage, and it may have been
an effect of the CPS's cry for 'raw data' that pressure was exerted on
us later to include in the eventual report on examination results of
the same children the averages for comprehensive and selective
pupils without the necessary adjustments or corrections for earlier
attainments. We argued that unadjusted figures, being simpler to
understand, could be given more credence than the more helpful
corrected figures. Having been persuaded to provide, for that later
book, unadjusted averages as well as results of more sophisticated
analyses, we were dispirited to see that the only figures to reach the
front page of the *Times Educational Supplement* (in an otherwise
fair report) were unadjusted; the 'news' seemed to be the 'fact' that
'an average, grammar school pupils got just over five 'O' levels
while comprehensive pupils got just over one-and-a-half' (*TES*, 20
May 1983).

The CPS attack in 1980 accused us of biased research, particularly irksome given our lack of motive for bias and the lack of
opportunity for bias in our distanced relationship with our cumbersome data. Our lack of funding for publication meant it was galling
to have greater media attention given to people with the backing and
political funding of the Centre for Policy Studies. Cox and Marks
had time and energy for publicity; they had not got their eyes down
for the next research project as many other researchers would have
done — indeed, had. It was hard for the National Children's Bureau
to respond, too, given the evidence on progress in comprehensives,
without entering into unwelcome confrontation with the government of the day, even though what was at stake was research
standards as a whole.

The question for researchers today is, would this be likely to
happen with any piece of research? There are reasons for thinking it
would not. For one thing, the content of the study was closely
linked to policy. Secondly, the finding could be interpreted as
countering a fairly widespread prejudice. Thirdly, the study happened to coincide with a change of government and a highly ideological shift of education policy with an innovation — the Assisted
Places scheme — at odds with the ongoing move to a comprehensive
system. The publication of the later, examination results stage, in

May, 1983, attracted much less press reaction. This may have been because of the 1983 General Election, though educationalists' attention is always on education, even when there's politicking going on. It may have been because our results did not come out as quickly as we had hoped; by 1983 our data were 9 years old. Nevertheless, there was an aftermath, in that Cox and Marks followed our study with a book published by the National Council for Educational Standards (NCES) which appeared in September and provoked very public arguments over their methodology (Marks *et al.*, 1983). As Professor Goldstein pointed out,

> The NCES study has had considerable publicity; more so than the technically superior NCB study. In part this may be due to the NCB study appearing in the middle of the 1983 general election campaign and largely being overlooked. In part it may be due to more efficient publicity by the NCES and in part it may be that the NCES conclusions are more acceptable to the majority of the media than those of the NCB (Goldstein, 1984).

If the last is true, a change seemed to have taken place since the response of education journalists to our original findings back in 1980. Another noticeable change from the climate in which we had begun our study in 1977 was that, by 1983, examination results were given great prominence in judging schools, as local authorities were first required by law to publish them.

So there were factors in the timing of the study and the nature of its conclusions that meant it was uniquely exposed. Nevertheless, there are dangers highlighted by the public reception of our work which have implications for research as a whole. We have seen the influence of the reaction to the 1980 publication on the presentation of findings in 1983. Yet we remained relatively ill-equipped to provide journalists with short, 'newsy', sentences, compared to our politically motivated adversaries. There were more profound effects, on us as researchers, some of which were touched on in an article by Professor Wragg (Wragg, 1981). The main threat to researchers in the public domain is that, in order to retain what we tend to take for granted — research standards and integrity — we may have to engage with people who have no real interest in adding to our knowledge of the evidence and no real wish to help the education system by informed evaluation of what there is. Such people can, by skilled use of the media, make more impact with inferior numbers than is made by authoritative evidence based on the best data and techniques available. We have to be clear, as Professor Lacey has explained, that there are 'two distinctly different research styles or traditions', and one is at odds with the other (Lacey, 1984).

Conclusions

This has been an attempt to draw out some of the characteristic features of a piece of longitudinal, national survey research and to look back at the experience of carrying it out, in the hope of assisting research of this kind. A powerful influence on the study was its link with educational policy. Policy-related research may be doing well if it manages to steer a middle path between prejudice and expert opinion. Research that is directed to policy questions is often a modest attempt to provide the best possible information on the workings of a policy, recognizing the limitations of the evidence. Its results are not always intended to inform those who know a lot about the area already because research, however well done, often has limited sensitivity and takes a long time. A researcher often addresses a problem from outside, has to look at out-of-date data, or is required to generalize. Research may be trying to answer some fairly ill-informed questions, because these answers help to generate better questions. One may therefore be more dedicated to countering prejudice and ignorance than to advising experts.

Part of doing sociology of education (or psychology or statistics of education) is taking on the sweeping generalizations of policy and doing all you can to examine their assumptions. If people claim that one kind of school is a better idea than another, they must have evidence. But empirical researchers start not knowing what the evidence will show. The report of our study has justly been described as atheoretical (Lacey, 1984). This lack of opinion stems in part from contingencies in the circumstances of its writing, in part from an empirical bias, sacrificing theoretical analysis in the later stages of the project to ensuring technical accuracy of statistical analysis. The limited theoretical discussion stems too from an appreciation of the wealth of educational theory on the subject and an assumption that readers will draw on that. In the questions implied by its investigations, though, the study contained an approach to a number of the issues of selection, and such answers as it yielded were based on evidence of a quality that exceeds that in many theoretical studies. The policy statements to which the study was targeted were fairly crude simplifications; we aimed to inform the debate over those statements.

Policy-oriented research is often constrained to artificial problems and compromises with reality. In this work, for example, we knew that the idea of a 'comprehensive pupil' was elusive. We tied it down to a purist definition, different from that used by other researchers like colleagues at the Centre for Educational Sociology (Gray *et al.*, 1983). Nevertheless, we knew we should work with this fabrication in order to address the issue to which some would-be policy makers felt they had an answer. Such research as had been done hitherto was inadequate to answer the question, 'Do pupils fare worse or better in comprehensives than in selective arrangements?' In the attempt we made to improve the standard of information relevant to that question, and the questions that should be explored, we were conscious of the limits of empirical answers to such a sweeping national generalization of a question. The concluding section of our 1980 report is an attempt to point out the danger of equating an artificial comparison of real data with an answer to a theoretical, non-empirical question. Partly because of the history of research and debate on comprehensives, our research tackled the question of selection/non-selection on a particular level, comparing comprehensive with selective pupils as a whole. The variety of school factors we could look at was limited, and this was not wholly a function of the research being related to overall, national policy considerations. Although some limits were to do with the need to summarize a national picture and generalize in a way that would have implications for all schools, we were also restricted by the relatively few detailed variables revealing the internal workings of schools that you can obtain from a national survey. We were tied, moreover, to the state of education provision represented by our data, which meant that few instances of now-topical educational developments, like mixed-ability teaching, existed for us to measure. We had to operate, as well, within the confines of certain technical limits to the complexity of analyses. These factors helped to narrow the focus of our study and to determine its scope, over and above the constraints of policy-related research.

Of course, ours was not the only way of defining 'selective' and 'non-selective' pupils, nor, importantly, was it the only comparison we made. Certainly, we did not explore many levels of selection that operate in education (between and within comprehensives, for instance), as Professor Lacey points out. Though of enormous interest in the 1980s, these questions were not best tackled with a national data set spanning the early 1970s, before most children went to comprehensives. Reviewers who have argued that we should have paid more attention to school factors are not forced, as we were, to narrow down their interests in the cause of using data from a national survey in an authoritative, generalizable, longitudinal way. These reviewers will of course be aware that it is in the nature of this kind of empirical, quantitative research that the kind of factors discussed above restrict options.

Partly because we had relatively few school-level variables, the research results are not likely to be altered by the kind of multi-level analysis favoured for school studies lately (Aitkin and Longford, 1983). The variety of approaches and educational questions we studied were not at a variety of levels of the system, so much as a range of differences between pupils and between different aspects of pupils. But more essentially, the study was to do with pupils, as distinct from schools, so that the number of pupils in any one school in the study (and so the statistical contribution of 'school-level' variance) is presumably very small.

It has been hard to reconstruct the main stages of the study, when we were doing educational research, before knowing the results, even though it is in the nature of such work that its whole course is run in order to find out the results. It is harder, though, to understand how the writings of people who draw on inferior data to make polemical points should receive more attention. The CPS attacks were alien to the spirit of inquiry in which genuine research flourishes. In an open inquiry, researchers often address a great mixture of questions. They explore, as we did, what data are available as well as how to get the most reliable answers, at the same time as investigating the answers to a host of substantive, educational questions. It is not always clear to the researchers themselves why their studies have had the particular focus they have, and it is certainly not clear what will come out of it. Interpretations depend on the results. That is part of the spirit of the kind of research we were engaged in, the kind of thing researchers enjoy. The politically-motivated attack on our research, by contrast, was less open in its scope, narrow in its motives and fundamentally incurious about the evidence, the antithesis of doing empirical educational research.

References

BENN, C. and SIMON, B. (1972) *Half Way There*, 2nd edn., Harmondsworth, Penguin.

BOOTH, T. (1983) in BOOTH, T. and POTTS, P. (Eds), *Integrating Special Education*, Oxford, Blackwell.

COX, C.B. and DYSON, A.E. (Eds) (1969) *Fight for Education: A Black Paper*, London, Critical Quarterly Society.

COX, C.B. and DYSON, A.E. (Eds) (1969) *Black Paper Two: The Crisis in Education*, London, Critical Quarterly Society.

COX, C.B. and DYSON, A.E. (Eds) (1970) *Black Paper Three: Goodbye, Mr. Short*, London, Critical Quarterly Society.

COX, C.B. and BOYSON, R. (Eds) (1975) *Black Paper 1975*, London, J.M. Dent.

COX, C. and MARKS, J. (1980) *Real Concern*, London, Centre for Policy Studies.

DOUGLAS, J.W.B. *et al.*, (1968) *All Our Future*, London, Peter Davies.

FLOUD, J. (Ed.) (1956) *Social Class and Educational Opportunity*, London, Heinemann.

FORD, J. (1969) *Social Class and the Comprehensive School*, London, Routledge and Kegan Paul.

GOLDSTEIN, H. (1984) 'Standards of research', *Forum*, 26, 2, Spring, pp. 41–2.

GRAY, J. (1981) 'A competitive edge: examination results and the probable limits of school effectiveness', *Educational Review*, 33, 1, pp. 20–35.

GRAY, J., MacPHERSON, A.F. and RAFFE, D. (1983) *Reconstructions of Secondary Education — Theory, Myth and Practice Since the War*, London, Routledge and Kegan Paul.

HARGREAVES, D.H. (1967) *Social Relations in a Secondary School*, London, Routledge and Kegan Paul.

HEATH, A. (1984) 'In Defence of Comprehensive Schools', *Oxford Review of Education*, 10, 1, pp. 115–123

HMSO (1963) *Half Our Future*, A Report of the Central Advisory Council for Education (England) (Newsom Report), London, HMSO.

HUSÉN, T. (1960) 'Loss of talent in selective school systems', *Comparative Educational Review*, 48, 2, pp. 70–4.

JONES, A. (1985) 'Studying school effectiveness: A postscript' in REYNOLDS, D. (Ed.) *Studying School Effectiveness*, Lewes, Falmer Press.

LACEY, C. (1984) 'Selective and non-selective schooling: real or mythical comparisons?' *Oxford Review of Education*, 10, 1, pp. 75–84.

MARKS, J., COX, C. and POMIAN-SRZEDNICKI, M. (1983) *Standards in English Schools*, London, National Council for Educational Standards.

REYNOLDS, D. (Ed.) (1985) *Studying School Effectiveness*, Lewes, Falmer Press.

STEEDMAN, J. (1980) *Progress in Secondary Schools*, London, National

Children's Bureau.

STEEDMAN, J., FOGELMAN, K. and HUTCHISON, D. (1980) *Real Research*, London, National Children's Bureau.

STEEDMAN, J. (1983) *Examination Results in Selective and Nonselective Secondary Schools*, London, National Children's Bureau.

STEEDMAN, J. (1984) *Examination Results in Mixed and Single Sex Secondary Schools*, Manchester, Equal Opportunities Commission.

STEEDMAN, J. (1985) 'Boys' and girls' examination results in mixed and single sex schools' (Proceedings of BERA Annual Conference School Differences Symposium, 1983), in REYNOLDS, D. (Ed.), *op. cit.*

STEEDMAN, J. and FOGELMAN, K. (1980) 'Secondary schooling', *Concern*, July.

WRAGG, E. (1981) 'Educational research and the media', in *Children's Progress in Secondary Schools*, Perspectives 6, School of Education, University of Exeter, June, pp. 32–9.

WRIGHT, N. (1977) *Progress in Education*, Beckenham, Croom Helm.

9 Constructing a Public Account of an Education System

Peter Burnhill, Andrew McPherson,
David Raffe and Nils Tomes

Here are some statements about the world that share several things in common.

The rise in school-leaver unemployment since 1977 is primarily a consequence of the recession, and not of structural change specifically affecting the school-leaver labour market (Raffe, 1984a; Shelly, 1986).

Within large cities the employment chances of school leavers with comparable educational and family backgrounds do not depend on the area of the city in which they live (Garner, Main and Raffe, in press).

Young women who were on the Youth Opportunities Programme in October 1980 increased their employment chances the following spring by about 8 percentage points relative to unemployed young women not on YOP; the male advantage was about 4 percentage points (Main, 1985).

In the year after the university cuts of 1981, the probability that a school leaver with minimum or better qualifications for higher education would enter university fell by almost a quarter when compared to the years before the cuts (Burnhill, 1985).

The achievement of qualifications for entry to higher education is better predicted by the socio-economic status of the father when the child has reached the age of 16 than by the father's status sixteen years earlier (Bibby and Garner, 1986).

Between 1971 and 1981 the educational, occupational and marital aspirations of well-qualified female school leavers converged with those of their male counterparts (Burnhill and McPherson, 1984).

At a time of rising youth unemployment rates of serious truancy from school have fallen; and they have tended to be slightly lower in areas of high youth unemployment (Raffe, 1986).

Pupils of nationally average socio-economic status have tended to attain higher in schools having a higher average pupil socio-economic status (McPherson and Willms, 1986).

What these statements share in common is that they can all be made empirically on the basis of data that are publicly available for reanalysis; that they have been made about Scotland; and that no empirical statements of this order can be made about England at the national level, and few at the local level.

Of themselves such statements do not constitute anything like a full public account of education. But they have become possible by virtue of the existence in Scotland of one pre-requisite for the construction of such an account, namely a regular sampling frame of leavers from all secondary schools that is available to educational and social research, as well as to government. This facility emerged in Scotland in the mid-1970s from embryonic arrangements established in 1971. What may develop into a comparable arrangement for England and Wales first appeared a decade later in 1985, influenced in part by the Scottish model. Prior to this, the differing survey arrangements north and south of the border influenced what could be said on the basis of research about education and labour-market issues. For example, when the Department of Education and Science wanted to project the future demand for higher education in England and Wales, it was obliged to use Scottish data on social-class-specific qualification rates, there being at the time no comparable data for England and Wales (DES, 1984).

One purpose of this chapter is to describe the development of the Scottish survey series and the recent emergence of similar arrangements for England and Wales. We focus in particular on the relationship between the aims of government and the technical means required by researchers, and we develop an argument about the role that social research might play in improving the public account. This argument addresses two key issues: the resources that are required for social research; and the means by which the validity of its descriptions and explanations are established. We also touch on the ways in which survey research is designed and reported, that is, who it describes, who it involves and who it is for. Some of the developments in the Scottish survey arose from an action-research programme of 'collaborative' research that the Centre for Educational Sociology (CES) undertook with SSRC support between 1975 and 1982. This SSRC programme was itself an attempt to place more of the performance of social research in the public domain in the hope that we could thereby reduce the gap between the formal research methodology, and the practicalities of politics and resources.

Some Theoretical Issues

The CES began survey-based research that involved cooperation with government in the early 1970s. At about this time some social researchers were beginning to abjure quantitative methods in general, and survey research in conjunction with government in particular. Central to their critique were three propositions. First, it was argued that such research tended to take government's problems as given, and therefore to disregard other problems. Essentially this is part of the problem of values in social research. Second, survey research was criticized on the grounds that it must always elicit its data in ways that abuse or incompletely represent the understandings of its 'subjects'. Essentially, this concerns the problem of knowledge, validity, and human interests. Third, there was the view that the explanations and models constructed from such data have always to rely on assumptions and methods that are ultimately arbitrary, one of these assumptions being that researcher and subject inhabit separate, non-interacting, worlds. Overall, the view was that survey research, *sui generis*, was pathological, and could only serve the interests of the powerful.

If there were a corporate CES view in the mid-1970s it was that one should accept much of the force of these three criticisms, but not all of it. After all, it was not clear that these problems were unique to survey research in the social sciences, or to quantitative research, or even to social science itself. Nor was it clear that the acknowledged bias of much survey research towards the interests of the powerful, and especially towards those of government, was an inevitable bias, rather than a contingency of politics and history.

In our programme of collaborative research we set out to decentralize control of a national survey in order to see whether at least some sources of this bias might be contingent and open to change. We tried to widen the circle of involvement in the choice of problems, framing of questions, analysis of data, and dissemination of results. Among those who became involved were teachers, careers officers, pupils, and officials and advisors from local government. There was little success in reaching parents, and, to be honest, little effort in this direction. The main public documents to emerge from the action were the ten issues of the *Collaborative Research Newsletter* published between 1977 and 1982. There were also a variety of academic papers, and several books, principally *Fourteen to Eighteen* (Raffe, 1984b), and *Reconstructions of Secondary Education* (Gray, McPherson and Raffe, 1983).

Reconstructions offers an empirical evaluation of the public account of education that guided Scottish policy and practice in the thirty years after 1945. It shows how this account was both biased and injurious, mainly because it treated 'non-academic' pupils as individuals of no account. In *Tell Them From Me* (Gow and McPherson, 1980), pupils who had been defined in this way gave their own account of their schooling. In some ways this acted as a corrective to the more optimistic public account from which non-academic pupils were at the time excluded.

Reconstructions also argued, however, that the very concepts through which data on 'academic' pupils were expressed themselves constituted a further source of bias towards optimism in the public account. The book locates the source of this bias in the tension between knowledge and civil authority. Government suffers from one unique disadvantage in doing adequate social research, and that is its need, and responsibility, to maintain authority. To put it crudely, this requires that government appear to know what it is doing, and that it appear to be doing the right thing. It must either avoid criticism, or at the very least manage and control it. Its repertoire of controls includes the selective way in which it represents, by means of verbal and statistical description, the world of education, and the other social worlds for which it is responsible. Hence the tension that is sometimes apparent between policy-maker and professional or researcher, both inside and outside government. Yet the public practice of scepticism is part of the scientific method. In maintaining its authority, government puts at risk its capacity to conduct research or to generate knowledge of comparable logical status.

The particulars of government's account of education can be more easily engaged if potential critics have access to the same raw data as government, and to the same means of generating alternative data. This facility is rarely conceded. Moreover, the concepts through which government represents the world of education are not easily shifted by data, because they are deeply rooted in its daily exercise of authority and judgments of value. Later studies have shown, for example, how the values and beliefs that underpinned government's account of the Scottish education system also formed the basis of recruitment to the Schools Inspectorate, and of the appointment of eminent teachers to public bodies. A structure of authority and practice was based on shared definitions of 'good' teaching, and these definitions in turn were sustained by shared, but highly biased, explanatory beliefs about the 'reality' of the Scottish education system (McPherson, 1983; McPherson and Raab, in press).

We shall show how the coverage of the Scottish survey series, and its attendant biases, have been influenced by these considerations, thereby sustaining a public account that is more 'optimistic' than would otherwise be the case. We shall also show how a decentralizing and critical social science can reduce the effects of bias. We do not, however, argue that government should therefore forswear involvement in research. In the longer term the authority required to command the resources needed for the regular sampling of a population for the purposes of research can only, and ought only, to be invested in an accountable and public authority. Here we are talking not only about financial resources but about human and other resources as well. One of the greatest resources available to social research is the informed consent and cooperation of persons who understand the pre-conditions and purposes of the enquiry such that they may interpret and promote it, whether as sponsors, gate-keepers, agents for the sampling frame or, indeed, as the respondents themselves. In the final chapter of *Reconstructions* we argued that this resource is the key that simultaneously unlocks the problem of authority and knowledge stated above.

Developments in the Scottish School Leavers Survey, 1966–1983

We now describe the changing structure of the SSLS series up to the early 1980s, and some of the events that precipitated change.

Surveys of Scottish school leavers were first conducted by the Scottish Education Department (SED) in 1966 and by the CES in 1971 (Figure 9.1). Several features of the SSLS have remained unchanged since its inception. The SED has always conducted the first phase of each survey by constructing the sampling frame. Also, the survey has always used a questionnaire administered postally to young people in the year after the academic session in which they left school. This feature immediately distinguishes the Scottish sur-

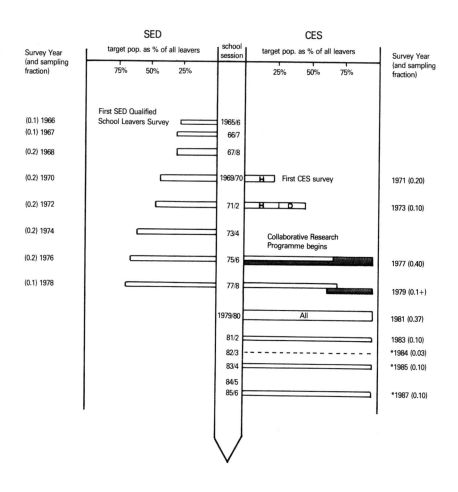

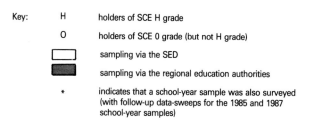

Figure 9.1   *School leavers surveys in Scotland: incidence, target population and sampling fraction*

vey from the leavers' survey conducted by the Department of Education and Science (DES). The DES procedure has been to ask the headteacher to complete a questionnaire for each sample member. This has two consequences for the DES survey: no data have been collected directly from ex-pupils; and few data have been available on the experiences of the sample members as they progress to post-school education or to the labour market. The Department of Employment (DE) has also carried out surveys of labour-market entrants but these surveys have not usually contacted the young people themselves, and few education data have been collected. Two distinguishing characteristics of the SSLS are that the data describe school leavers' own accounts of their experiences, and not what teachers or careers officers believe about them; and also that the education data may be analyzed in the light of data on the school leavers' transitions to the labour market or to post-school education, and *vice versa*. The national cohort studies recently launched by the Manpower Services Commission (MSC), the DES, and the DE are now beginning to supply some of the data deficiencies in England and Wales (see below).

Other features of the Scottish survey have changed. The early surveys of Scottish school leavers were conducted solely by the SED, and largely to supply government intelligence for in-house use. Between 1971 and 1979, however, there were additional surveys, with an academic research function, conducted by the CES. This arrangement was achieved by two data-sweeps of the same sample, the first conducted by the SED in the autumn, and the second by the CES in the following spring, about nine months after the majority of the sample had left school. The SED questionnaires contained a brief description of the subsequent CES survey and gave respondents the opportunity to contract out of it if they wished. Only the names and addresses of those who had not contracted out were passed on to the CES (Jones and McPherson, 1972).

A further change has been the expansion of the target population. The survey originated in a concern with the flow of qualified young people from school. Until the mid-1970s the target population was restricted to school leavers who held qualifications in examinations conducted by what is now called the Scottish Examination Board, plus the small number holding GCE 'A' levels. In the CES surveys of 1977 and 1979 the target population was extended to include all school leavers (other than 2 per cent from special schools), whether or not they had achieved awards in public examinations. Meanwhile the SED's own surveys were still directed at qualified leavers only, and the sampling frame for unqualified leavers in the CES sample had to be obtained through the regional education authorities.

With the expanding population definition came a changed emphasis in the topics covered by the survey. School leavers were still asked, as appropriate, for the objective record of their curriculum and attainment in the middle and upper stages of secondary school, for details of the transition to further and higher education, for accounts of perceptions, aspirations, decision-making and attitudes, and for details of home background. The surveys now also included more questions on the transition to the labour market, employment and unemployment and special programmes for the unemployed.

In the 1981 survey there were two further changes. First, the SED again constructed a sampling frame, but this time the target population was all school leavers whether or not they had been presented for public examinations. The extensions of the target populations in the CES surveys of 1977 and 1979 were thereby incorporated in government practice. Second, the SED decided not to conduct its own survey of leavers, qualified or unqualified, in 1981 or in the foreseeable future. Instead it would use the data from the CES surveys. The SED would continue to provide the sampling frame and to influence the content of the questionnaire, but only the CES would actually collect questionnaire data. These two arrangements continued to apply in the surveys of 1983, 1985 and 1987. The contracting-out procedure, whereby potential sample members had a prior opportunity to contract out of the CES survey, was retained in the 1981 survey. This was therefore the first survey in which the SED itself suffered from the attrition that the contracting-out procedure entailed, for the SED was now itself a user of the CES survey data. Such attrition, of course, reduces the reliability of the resultant estimates, and may also increase their bias. The 1983 survey and subsequent ones have dispensed with the contracting-out option in the construction of the sampling frame.

The sampling fractions for several of the early surveys were either 10 or 20 per cent, based on the day of birth. But in 1977 the fraction was a shade under 40 per cent; and in 1981 it was 37 per cent, giving an achieved sample size of about 25 000 school leavers. A feature of the CES surveys since 1977 has been the use of different but interlocking questionnaire versions, randomized across equivalent sub-samples. Some questions are asked only in a limited number of questionnaire versions; some questions are common to all versions. A larger number of questions can thereby be posed without placing an undue burden on individual respondents.

How did these changes come about? Credit should go to the SED for first suggesting around 1970 that it was failing to exploit the full potential of its survey, and that the sample members might be asked further questions for research purposes. But the SED did not want too close a public association with the research. The contracting-out arrangement in the early surveys enabled the SED to dissociate itself from the research activities of the CES. We called the early surveys 'Pilate' surveys, because the civil authority, like Pontius Pilate, could wash its hands of us should the need arise.

One catalyst of change was the collaborative research programme. The large sampling fractions in 1977 and 1981, and the continuing structure of interlocking questionnaires, arose from the attempt to decentralize participation in the survey. If local education authorities or, indeed, any potential user concerned with small-domain estimation were to use the data, he or she would need sub-samples of a size sufficient for reliable analysis. Also, if we were to widen participation in the survey to the point where people were not only analyzing its data but also determining its data, we had to find some way of reducing the pressure on us to arbitrate between a large number of questions competing for a small amount of questionnaire space.

The collaborative research programme also brought us into conflict with the SED, as we explain below. For the 1977 survey the SED passed us a sample of qualified leavers in what, by then, was the usual way. But we ourselves supplemented this sample by approaching the regional education authorities and, through them, all 440 or so of Scotland's maintained secondary schools. We thereby drew a different and additional sample, also by date of birth. Unlike the sample coming through the SED Pilate procedure, members of this 'regions' sample, as we shall call it, had not first answered an SED questionnaire. Nor had they been offered an opportunity to contract out of the survey.

The regions sample supplemented the SED sample in two ways. First, through the regional education authorities, we sampled for the first time non-certificate school leavers, who had not sat public examinations while at school. In the mid 1970s these young people constituted about one third of the age group. Second, we also supplemented the sample of qualified school leavers passed to us by the SED, in an attempt to increase the sample size. These two additions to the 1977 CES survey are shown by the crossed areas in Figure 9.1.

The SED had not itself been willing to supplement the sample, nor to be associated with our approach to the twelve regional education authorities. Some opinion within the SED opposed the collaborative research programme, and attempts were made to influence SSRC support (McPherson, 1984). Once funded by SSRC for the collaborative (non-SED) elements of the 1977 survey, we then spent over a year establishing our credentials with the regional education authorities. The story was one in which suspicion, intrigue, frustration and conflict figured alongside genuine and generous cooperation. In approaching 440 schools we had to work through established channels of authority and communication. A small research team could do no other. Inevitably we became embroiled in the tensions and disputes that flowed along these channels. Inevitably also, our own requirements also elicited opposition. Our wish for a larger sampling fraction appeared to duplicate the SED's own requirements. Nevertheless, administrators in several of the larger authorities were intrigued at the prospect of access to local data-bases, and intrigued also at the prospect of aggregating up these local data-bases to provide an alternative account of the national system to that provided by the SED survey. They carried many of their colleagues in other local education departments. Where they could not, influences from outside education, from policy-planning for example, were brought to bear. Even so, we ourselves had finally to go into some fifteen or twenty schools to collect names and addresses for the sampling frame.

Changes in the means of sample collection and the extension of the sample definition both had effects on the coverage of the survey. Coverage has several components. First, there may be deficiencies in the sampling frame in that the achieved frame may not map directly onto the population being surveyed, and may undercount people in particular subgroups. Figures 9.2 and 9.3 give estimates of sampling-frame deficiency for the 1977 survey sampling frame collected via the regional education authorities, compared to the SED-constructed frame. Also, the SED has recently found that first-term leavers (who are, on average, less qualified than other leavers) are under-represented in the sampling frame, and it is currently revising procedures to improve coverage in this respect.

Secondly, the sampling frames up until 1981 were constructed with a contracting-out clause, allowing sample members to opt out

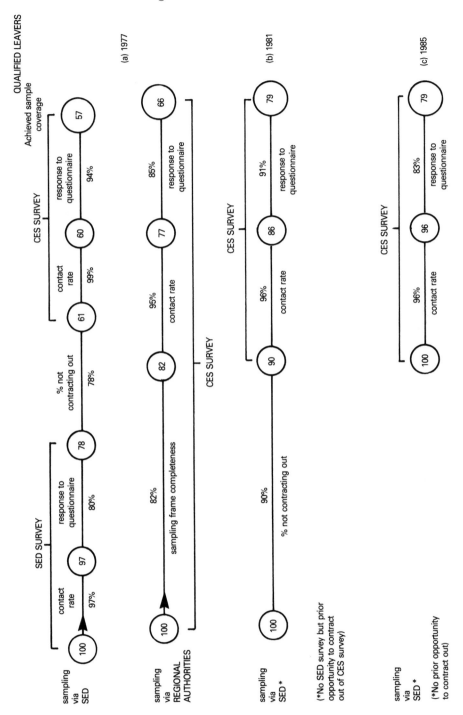

Figure 9.2 Attrition of target sample by source of sample in 1977, 1981 and 1985: qualified leavers only

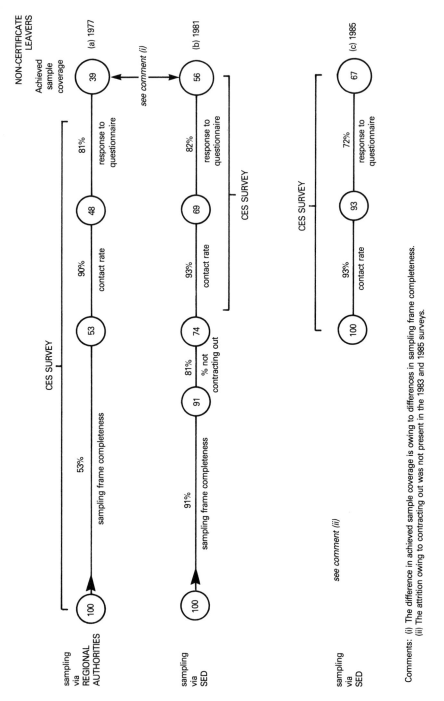

Figure 9.3 Attrition of target sample by source of sample in 1977, 1981 and 1985: non-certificate leavers only

of the CES survey. There was therefore an attrition component related to cooperation. Third, not all of the sample members' addresses are either accurate or current, causing a loss of coverage due to non-contact. In many cases, the non-contact rate can be reduced by the updating of addresses through the original contact address, through an intermediary or through an agency. Excluding errors of processing, the remaining non-coverage is due to the response to the questionnaire itself, either as a whole or to particular items within a questionnaire. Response to questionnaires is boosted by readministration and reminders appropriate to the target population for each type of questionnaire. Final coverage takes all of these elements into account and is calculated as a percentage of valid returns over the original target sample. Each of these coverage elements may vary independently in response to external or design factors, and the final achieved sample coverage varies with the composite elements. For example, the final achieved sample coverage may rise, despite a fall in the response-to-questionnaire rate, because the sampling frame is more complete; it is because more of the people likely to be non-respondents or non-contacts are included that the response rate falls.

In Figure 9.2 we compare the coverage of the target sample achieved by the SED with that achieved by the CES when sampling via the regional authorities. The figure is restricted to the subset of qualified leavers. In 1977 the SED achieved better coverage of its target sample (78 per cent) than did the CES with its regional sample (66 per cent). Nevertheless, sampling via the regional authorities gave us better sample coverage (at 66 per cent) than the 57 per cent we achieved through the part of the CES survey based on the SED Pilate procedure. Sampling-frame deficiencies accounted for the major part of the total non-coverage in the CES regional sample. We collected only 82 per cent of the sample of qualified leavers that we should have collected from the regions.

In 1981, using a sampling frame constructed by the SED, the CES survey coverage was increased to 79 per cent, a figure comparable to the 78 per cent achieved by the SED in 1977 in its own survey. Both the 1977 and 1981 surveys gave sample members the opportunity to contract out when the sampling frame was constructed. This was not the case in 1985, but there was no corresponding benefit to the coverage rate which was again 79 per cent, mainly because the response-to-questionnaire rate was lower (83 per cent compared to 91 per cent).

We drew three lessons from our experience of the 1977 survey.

The first was that we could not construct a sampling frame as effectively as the SED. The quality of the SED's sampling frame is achieved partly through the repeated checking with schools of sample members' details using other information available to central government (such as the record of examination presentations). The schools, of course, find this checking time-consuming and somewhat alienating, and it tends, therefore, to exhaust much of the goodwill that might otherwise be available to non-government researchers. Plurality of criticism based on a plurality of separately derived samples taken from the same institutions, has a high perceived cost. A second lesson was that we were able to exploit differences of interest between central and local government in establishing our access to the additional sample. At the same time, if the wear and tear that we suffered were to be experienced in subsequent exercises, only a tattered survey series could ever emerge, if any at all. A third lesson was that the exercise would never have got under way without financial and other support from the SSRC.

As well as these three lessons, however, the conflicts over the funding of the 1977 survey, and over the construction of the sampling frame, also left us with an enigma. A major innovation of the 1977 survey was the extension of the target population to include non-certificate leavers. But when we embarked on the SSRC programme in 1975 we had neither intended this change, nor thought it possible. The enigma concerns the fact that we were forced in this direction by the very regional authority that most vigorously opposed our access to its schools, and resisted our claim to be the final arbiter of the questions that were asked. The experience raised some interesting and uncomfortable questions about the accountability of the social researcher, and it forced us to think seriously about the process through which groups of people and categories of experience can be left out of the public record.

The Politics and Practice of Bias

There are, of course, good reasons for not restricting a school leavers' survey to those leavers who have passed public examinations. Apart from the obvious descriptive limitations, there are also considerations relating to the explanatory potential of the data. A survey of a target population that is something less than an integral population cannot describe the crucial processes by which members are selected into a sub-population of interest, in this case 'qualified' school leavers. The reason why this did not matter much in the past was that the DES and SED surveys were more concerned with what happened to qualified pupils on leaving school than they were with the process of becoming qualified. This in turn helps explain why the schools and the local education authorities did not always feel well served by the qualified leavers surveys.

One reason why we ourselves had accepted the restriction to qualified leavers in the surveys of 1971 and 1973 was convenience. It was nice to have one's sample passed to one. But we also felt we had sound methodological reasons for accepting the *status quo*. In earlier surveys, the response rates among those with lower qualifications had been poor, and this was also the case in 1971 (Jones and McPherson, 1972). This seemed to confirm the survey-methodology orthodoxy that response rates decline with declining levels of educational attainment. Thus, when the recalcitrant regional education authority, mentioned above, insisted that the price of its cooperation in sampling was that we include the non-certificate leavers in our survey, we were happy to comply. We anticipated that we would pilot the survey of non-certificate leavers and get questionnaire response rates of something under half. We expected that the local authority would then accept that this reflected the limits of our honest endeavour, and clearly indicated that only a survey of qualified leavers was possible. In the event, we were thrown into considerable financial, organizational and intellectual disarray, when our first two pilots produced response rates of over 80 per cent of the non-certificate leavers whom we contacted. Actual response-to-questionnaire rates were of this order in 1977 and 1981 (Figure 9.3).

One result of the extension of the target population in 1977 has been that about one-third of young people in the leaving group, persons who had previously been of 'no account' in the sense that their cases did not figure in numerically evidenced public discussion, have become at least of some account in the subsequent surveys. But the bias towards optimism in the surveys before 1977 did not result simply from the selected nature of the target population. We have already shown that the point of greatest attrition in the CES surveys of 1977 and 1981 was the construction of the sampling frame. In those schools that we ourselves visited in order to construct the frame, we found that the individual record tended to be most deficient for those school leavers who had not attempted public examinations. Not only had such young people been excluded hitherto from the official account, they had also tended to figure less frequently in school records. They could often not be found in the official record, and, if found, the details were often inadequate. Pupils who were to be entered for public examination tended to be more adequately recorded in the school record, the school being required to intimate to the Scottish Examination Board the correct details of an intending candidate. This was not the case for the one-third of the year group who were not entered for public examinations, the 'forgotten children' as one such described them (Gow and McPherson, 1980). In this sense they were persons of no account, and in a second sense too, in that their absence from the record reflected their lower status within the school. By this we mean that Scottish schools have tended to value pupils primarily for their potential for success in public examinations.

We may draw attention here to two consequences of this situation. In Figure 9.3 one can see that the final coverage of the sample achieved in the 1977 survey of non-certificate leavers was as low as 39 per cent. Most of this shortfall resulted from the incompleteness of the sampling frame supplied by the schools via the regional authorities. With sampling through the SED in 1981 the coverage was raised to 56 per cent. The 1981 shortfall again derived partly from the incompleteness of the sampling frame. But the major cause was the SED's Pilate procedure: only 81 per cent of the non-certificate leavers who were approached when the sampling frame was being constructed agreed to cooperate with the CES survey. One may contrast this 81 per cent with the 90 per cent cooperation rate among the qualified in the 1981 survey (Figure 9.2). By 1985 the contracting-out procedure had been dropped, and the final coverage for the non-certificate leavers was raised to 67 per cent. But this was still well below the comparable figure for qualified leavers of 79 per cent (Figure 9.2), mainly because of a lower response-to-questionnaire rate (of 72 per cent compared with 83 per cent).

Thus the bias against non-certificate leavers has arisen both from deficiencies in the school record and from the alienation of the young people themselves. With considerable empirical support (Gow and McPherson, 1980) we conjecture that both these factors owed something to the way in which non-certificate leavers had been treated at school. The irony is that a public account constructed from such data cannot reveal the full extent of such treatment. Moreover, the alienation of such pupils also touches their teachers, and the officials who administer their schools. The greater the difficulties that teachers were having with pupils, or that officials were having with school teachers, the less likely they were to be sympathetic to the survey and to promote the arrangements for sampling in their own domain. It is not difficult to see how such responses also help to sustain an over-optimistic account of the school system.

The effects of non-coverage can be mitigated in analysis by weighting the data according to known population parameters. The SED supplies the CES with population weights for each survey, stratified by sex and level of school attainment. But such weighting only reduces bias in estimation to the extent that the parameters in question correlate with the variables that are estimated in the analysis. For the qualified leavers in the 1977 survey we were able to compare weighted population estimates derived from the regions and the SED samples. The extent of the bias varied according to the level of school qualification, but among leavers with only SCE O-grade qualifications, the 'bias towards optimism' in estimates from the SED sample was quite marked. The following examples are illustrative: 4.5 per cent of the SED sample were unemployed on 31 January 1977, compared with 6.7 per cent of the regions sample; 7.3 per cent of the SED sample admitted to prolonged truanting, compared with 9.6 per cent of the regions sample; 40.1 per cent of the SED sample achieved three or more SCE O-grade awards at A, B or C grade, compared with 35.6 per cent of the regions sample; and 71.3 per cent of the SED sample enjoyed their last year at school, compared with 65.2 per cent of the regions sample. Both the SED and the regions samples will have produced biased estimates, the coverage rates being only 57 per cent and 66 per cent respectively for qualified leavers (Figure 9.2). But the CES Pilate sample, having the lower coverage, produced the more optimistic estimates.

A second illustration comes from a survey in 1986 of a national cohort of young Scots, first surveyed in 1985, in the year after they had completed the compulsory stage of their schooling. The 1986 survey was sent not only to respondents to the 1985 survey, but also to non-respondents (some 20 per cent of the target sample). Two findings are apposite. First, some 35 per cent of the 1985 non-respondents responded in 1986. Second, the non-respondent subset was highly atypical of the original sample, being almost half as likely to be in full-time education as were the first sweep respondents and twice as likely to be unemployed. 60 per cent of them had no qualifications on leaving school.

These findings reinforce two points. First, even with high coverage rates significant biases towards optimism remain in the captured data. Second, the alienation of young people from a survey on schooling, and other topics, may well be a function of their alienation from schooling itself.

Recent Developments in England
and Wales and in Scotland

Since 1983 two major developments have occurred. First, the survey has spread to England and Wales. Second, a longitudinal element has been added to the design.

In 1985 some 12500 members of a school year group of young people from across England and Wales were surveyed in the first data-sweep of the national cohort (or Pathways) survey conducted by Social and Community Planning Research and Sheffield University (Clough and Gray, 1986). This followed a successful pilot in Bradford and Sheffield in 1984. The Scottish example influenced the Bradford and Sheffield pilot, and the subsequent national study, in three ways. First, the CES helped to set up the Bradford and Sheffield study, bringing together the MSC, the LEAs and others involved, and encouraging a collaborative model with the full involvement of the two LEAs. Officials of both authorities had earlier attended courses run by CES under its collaborative research programme, and discussed the collaborative model of LEA involvement (Harrison 1978). Two had also been involved in an attempt to interest the DES in a collaborative venture on Scottish lines. The CES was able to activate these existing links. Second, John Gray at Sheffield University played a leading role both in the Sheffield and Bradford study and in the national Pathways survey. A former member of the CES, he had been involved both in the setting up of collaborative research in Scotland and in the development of the SSLS, and he was able to draw on this background in the English studies. Third, the materials and experience of the SSLS in areas ranging from sample construction to questionnaire design, were drawn on both in the initial planning of the Pathways survey and in its subsequent implementation. Much of the CES's own thinking about the new survey, and its ideas about how it might be run on a collaborative basis, were spelt out in its own, unsuccessful, tender for the England and Wales cohort study (CES, 1984).

In the event, the collaborative model which characterized the Bradford and Sheffield studies, through the close involvement of the LEAs, was not preserved in the Pathways survey, although it is intended that the data will be made public. Although sample numbers are larger than the Scottish surveys, the population is also considerably larger, and sampling fractions are much smaller. Without resort to cluster sampling, analyses at an LEA level therefore pose problems of reliability. The target population in England and Wales comprises, not school leavers, but young people who were in the fifth year (equivalent to the Scottish S4) in the previous school session. Under present plans fresh cohorts are being contacted in 1985, 1986 and 1987 and each cohort is being contacted three times at yearly intervals. The year-group design enables the survey to follow young people through the different routes they may take after compulsory schooling, in school, college, the Youth Training Scheme (YTS), employment or unemployment: and the longitudinal component enables the consequences to be assessed over a longer period. On the other hand, the lack of a school-leaver sample in England and Wales has meant that much information, for example, on school-leaving qualifications, is delayed until the cohort ages. It also means that the displacement effects of young people leaving from different school years and impacting simultaneously on the labour market or on post-school education, cannot be observed from a single survey. A complex merging of data from two or three successive surveys is required.

The main impetus to the development of the Pathways study in England and Wales was the advent of YTS in 1983. In Scotland too, change was stimulated by YTS, and by the SED's own *Action Plan* reforms of non-advanced further education introduced in 1984. The Scottish survey changed in two main ways. First, the sample design was adapted to include a school-year group of former fourth-year (S4) pupils, equivalent to the former fifth-year pupils surveyed in England and Wales. The year-group sample supplemented the leaver sample but did not replace it. In fact, the target population now comprised two overlapping groups, respectively of young people who had been in fourth year in the previous school session, and of young people who had left school, from whatever year, in the previous session. This 'L-shaped' design shared the advantages of the school-year-group design used in England and Wales but it avoided the disadvantages described above. By retaining the school-leaver arm of the sample it gave the capacity to analyze those topics, such as entry to higher education or the labour market, for which a leaver perspective remained appropriate, and also permitted comparison with the earlier Scottish surveys. By the mid-1980s the SSLS had become a unique source of data on trends in education and the youth labour market since the mid-1970s or earlier, a period of substantial and far-reaching change. The new L-shaped design was successfully piloted in 1984 (Bryant *et al.*, 1985).

The second major change to the Scottish survey was to extend it longitudinally. The 1983/84 S4 cohort, first surveyed in 1985, is being followed up in 1986 and again in 1987. Fresh S4 year groups will be contacted biennially, and it is likely that each year group will be followed at least to a point more than three years after most of its members were first eligible to leave school. Later data-sweeps, at age 21 or even 25, are under discussion.

These changes are radical in terms of the design of the survey and its capacity to generate knowledge about the 16-plus age group, but most of the underlying features of the SSLS that had evolved since the early 1970s remain unchanged. In particular, the relations between the CES and government, and the sampling arrangements remain, in broad terms, the same. The CES also retains a commitment to the principles of collaborative research, although a lack of resources limits what it can do in practical terms. The ESRC's (formerly SSRC) recognition of the CES as a Designated Research Centre with effect from 1987 may help in this respect.

Beyond this, it is probably too early to assess the wider implications of these later changes for the themes of this paper. Will, for example, the attrition generally associated with longitudinal surveys increase the 'bias towards optimism' we have described above? We would like to believe that the success and extension of the SSLS provides at least some confirmation for the technical and, underlying that, the social and political model of research outlined in this chapter. It may reflect other things, too. For example, policy changes in education, the development of MSC activities and, underlying these, economic transformation, youth unemployment and the fear of social breakdown, may all have led to a stronger public and government interest in the erstwhile 'forgotten children'. The changed sample design also reflects, in part, a threatened breakdown of the categories formerly used to define the survey populations. The concept of a 'school leaver' is becoming increasingly problematic as more young people leave school only to re-enter it, and as the boundaries between school and college and between school and unemployment become increasingly blurred. The definition of a school-year group appears less problematic, for the time being at least. This flux also threatens the generation of good data. Postal surveys have always relied upon the assumption that researchers and respondents can share understandings of the world and the terms in which to describe it. The new modular courses of further education in Scotland, and the lack of an agreed vocabulary to describe them, pose problems that we have still not wholly overcome. Similarly, the plurality of meanings which young people attach to the term 'training' and the plurality of forms that training itself can take, inhibit the generation of good data on the topic.

These problems provide another illustration of how the technical quality of survey research is interdependent with the authority of government. In this case, it is precisely because government, be it the MSC or the SED, is itself actively challenging accepted categories that research is hampered in the attempt to describe and evaluate its actions. Yet there is, in this case, no lack of will on the part of government for the description and the evaluation to take place. Our account has, we hope, illustrated the inadequacy of the critique of government-research relations that we discussed earlier. Although there have been confrontations, a simplistic confrontational view of these relations does not fit well with our experience. We do not attempt here to offer a final verdict on collaborative research. It is not for us alone to say whether and to what extent we have (for example) taken the problems of government and served the interests of the powerful. We do, however, claim to have shown that some of the assumptions embedded in the critique of survey research are contingent, not inevitable, and we have demonstrated some ways by which they may be changed.

Note

Earlier versions of this paper were read to the Edinburgh local group of the Royal Statistical Society, November 1978, and to the Social Statistics Section of the Royal Statistical Society in London in November 1983. The views expressed here are those of the authors, and do not necessarily reflect the views of the sponsors of the surveys. The research has been supported at various times by the Economic and Social Research Council (formerly the Social Science Research Council), the Scottish Education Department, the Manpower Services Commission and several other departments of central and local government.

References

Bibby, J. and Garner, G. (1986) 'When should social class be measured? A comparison of birth-certificate and school-leaver data as predictors of educational achievement', Phase 1 Report of the Demand for Higher Education Project, Centre for Educational Sociology, University of Edinburgh.

BRYANT, I., BURNHILL, P.M., LAMB, J.M. and RAFFE, D. (1985) *Report on the 1984 Pilot of the Scottish Young People's Survey*, Centre for Educational Sociology, University of Edinburgh.

BURNHILL, P.M. (1985) 'A contribution to the Royal Statistical Society meeting on Projections of Student Numbers in Higher Education', paper read to the Royal Statistical Society, November 1984 and published in *Journal of The Royal Statistical Society* (A) 148(3).

BURNHILL, P.M. and MCPHERSON A.F. (1984) 'Careers and gender: the expectations of able Scottish school leavers in 1971 and 1981' in ACKER, S. and WARREN PIPER, D. (Eds) *Is Higher Education Fair to Women?* London, Society for Research in Higher Education.

CLOUGH, E. and GRAY, J. (1986) 'Pathways 16–19: National Youth Cohort Study (England and Wales) 1985–1990', unpublished paper, Division of Education, University of Sheffield.

DEPARTMENT OF EDUCATION AND SCIENCE (DES) (1984) Technical Appendix to *DES Report on Education Number 100*, Department of Education and Science.

GARNER, C.G.L., MAIN, B.G.M. and RAFFE D. (in press) 'Local Variations in School-Leaver Unemployment within a Large City', *British Journal of Education and Work*, 1.

GOW, L. and MCPHERSON, A.F. (1980) *Tell Them From Me: Scottish School Leavers Write about School and Life Afterwards*, Aberdeen, Aberdeen University Press.

GRAY, J.M., MCPHERSON, A.F. and RAFFE, D. (1983) *Reconstructions of Secondary Education: Theory, Myth and Practice since the War*, London, Routledge and Kegan Paul.

HARRISON, M. (1978) 'The Scottish Education Data Archive and Local Authorities: England' *Collaborative Research Newsletter*, no. 4, November, Centre for Educational Sociology, University of Edinburgh.

JONES, C.L. and MCPHERSON, A.F. (1972) 'Implications of non-response to postal surveys for the development of nationally based data on flows out of educational systems', *Scottish Educational Studies*, 4, 1, pp. 28–38.

MCPHERSON, A.F. (1983) 'An angle on the Geist: persistence and change in the Scottish educational tradition' in HUMES, W. and PATERSON, H. (Eds). *Scottish Culture and Scottish Education 1800–1980*, Edinburgh, John Donald.

MCPHERSON, A.F. (1984) 'An episode in the control of research' in DOCKRELL, B. (Ed.), *An Attitude of Mind; Twenty-Five Years of Educational Research in Scotland*, Edinburgh, Scottish Council for Research in Education.

McPHERSON, A.F. and RAAB, C.D. (in press) *Governing Education: A Sociology of Policy since 1945*, Edinburgh, The University Press.

McPHERSON, A.F. and WILLMS, J.D. (1986) 'Certification, class conflict, religion and community: a socio-historical explanation of the effectiveness of contemporary schools' in KERCKHOFF, A.C. (Ed.), *Research in Sociology of Education and Socialization* (*vol. 6*), Greenwich, Connecticut, JAI Press.

MAIN, B.G.M. (1985) 'School-leaver unemployment and the Youth Opportunities Programme in Scotland', *Oxford Economic Papers*, no. 37, pp. 426–447.

RAFFE, D. (1984a) 'The transition from school to work and the recession: evidence from the Scottish School Leavers Surveys, 1977–1983', *British Journal of Sociology of Education*, 5, 3.

RAFFE, D. (Ed.) (1986) *Fourteen to Eighteen: The Changing Pattern of Schooling in Scotland*, Aberdeen, Aberdeen University Press.

RAFFE, D. (1984c) 'Unemployment and school motivation: the case of truancy', *Educational Review*, 38, 1.

SHELLY, M. (1986) 'The decline and fall of Scottish school leavers' employment, 1977–1983', unpublished working paper, Centre for Educational Sociology, University of Edinburgh.

10 No Best Method — *Qualitative* and *Quantitative Research in the Sociology of Education*

Ronald King

My experience of research in the sociology of education spans a period of over twenty years. Apart from the substantive area of the research, from technical colleges to infants' classrooms, each project varied in many other ways. Their scale covered the range from seventy-two secondary schools and over 7000 pupils, to three infants' schools focusing on thirty-eight teachers. The social relations of the research include being a part-time research student, a lone academic researcher, and being the director of a small team including research assistants. The relations with my research subjects varied from an exchange of correspondence, to days being the only other adult, to the teacher in a classroom. My research data has always been both qualitative and quantitative, but with an emphasis on one or the other. With extensive quantified data, statistical and computer analyses have been used. My methods have been mixed: observations, interviews, questionnaires and document analysis, but with one or two predominating. Some of the projects were externally funded.

Five projects have been completed (a sixth has been started of junior schools).

1.   *Values and Involvement in a Grammar School* (1969); my PhD case study of the school where I had been a pupil and was, at the time, a teacher. The main method was the use of questionnaires, and the data were mainly quantified.
2.   *School Organisation and Pupil Involvement* (1973); a large-scale funded project with research assistants, quantified data and computer analysis.
3.   *School and College: Studies of Post-Sixteen Education*

(1976a); a study, slightly marginal to the sociology of education, with a mixed set of interests, including local authority policies, and students' experience of different kinds of post-sixteen education. This was a funded, team project with quantified data.

4. *All Things Bright and Beautiful? A Sociological Study of Infants' Classrooms* (1978); lone research using mainly qualitative data through direct observations.

5. *Curriculum and Organizational Change in Secondary Schools* (1981a, 1981b, 1982a, 1982b); a partial replication of the School Organisation study.

Each of the projects has brought different satisfactions and different problems, both ethical and methodological. I hope to show how the different dimensions of each piece of research were related to one another, and to put each into the contexts of the recent history of the sociology of education and of my own career, going beyond the limitations of the published accounts. (Further details of the infants' school research appear in King, 1984).

Values and Involvement in a Grammar School

I did not obtain a job at the school, where it happened I had been a pupil, in order to do research there. In 1962 I approached my teacher in the sociology of education, Jean Floud, with a research proposal which she gently and quite properly turned down. It was to follow up a group of junior school children into their different secondary schools: grammar and modern. It was not that it was a poor idea, but that I could not easily do it; why didn't I use the school I taught in? There were few models of school case studies available then; I only came across Gordon's (1957) study some years later. This was the period when the only British textbook in the sociology of education was Ottaway (1960), and apart from Jean Floud's own study (1956) of Middlesborough and S.W. Hertfordshire, our major research literature was the Early Leaving Report (1954) and the second volume of the Crowther Report (1960). Her suggestion was that I did a Crowther report on my school, but in addition she directed my attention to a book by Philip Jacob (1957), which had caused a stir in America, concerned with the values of college students.

At the beginning of 1963 Jean Floud left the London Institute of Education for Nuffield College, and her headship of the Department of Sociology of Education was taken by Basil Bernstein, who also took over, rather reluctantly I felt at the time, as my research supervisor. I fairly soon felt I knew what my research was to be about: the social values of boys (using Jacob as the model) taking into account their social origins (Crowther and Floud the principal models) and their school status, principally their stream status. There were some psychological studies of streaming but this predates the Manchester studies, (Hargreaves, 1967; Lacey, 1970).

Following Jacob and a rather neglected study by Miller (1961), I went to the pro-grammar school literature as a source of putative values, and constructed my first questionnaire, completed by my staff colleagues. Some researchers teach in a school in order to do their research (e.g., Hargreaves, 1967, and Lacey, 1970), I was teaching to earn a living, but my position was advantageous for my research, indeed, made it possible. My colleagues and other staff were generally co-operative, most completing the questionnaire and helping in other ways. I took care in my relationships with them, especially not to become associated with any of the semi-permanent cliques of the staff room, which may have jeopardized the co-operation of non-members. Their general attitude was of sceptical interest with either a slight amusement or bafflement. I took care only to talk about the project when asked, which was not often, but I did not want to be a research bore.

One of Bernstein's reservations about taking over my supervision was, I learnt later, that he thought I was doing social psychology. This was true to the extent that I used the techniques of attitude measurement in the teachers' questionnaire (and in the pupils' too). However, in relating the values so measured to social structure (school and home background), I felt, and still feel, I was doing sociology. I completed the analysis of the teacher's questionnaires and sent each a short resumé of the results, partly out of politeness and gratitude for their help, but also to introduce the idea of a survey of the pupils. In all my research, I have tried to provide some feedback to those who have helped (although I have done so with pupils only in my current research).

Constructing the pupils' questionnaire was a lengthy business. That I should use a questionnaire was never doubted. At that time it was *the* instrument of the survey method. I did carry out loosely structured interviews with groups of pupils, but the transcripts were not regarded as usable data, but sources for question construction. The qualitative was quantified. The final version of the questionnaire contained more than 150 questions and was completed by 274 pupils. With the cooperation of colleagues I administered the questionnaire in teaching groups on two days, separated by six weeks, so that in a matter of hours I had more than 40 000 data items. I would never have been able to gain such data through interviews on my own.

I had the headteacher's generous permission to conduct the pupils' questionnaire, and had modified a question at his suggestion (I also included some questions at Bernstein's request). For the survey of pupils' parents I also had to gain the permission of the chief education officer, who laid down certain conditions, mainly about avoiding personal questions, which I could easily comply with, the parents' questionnaire being a version of the teachers'. This was sent home with the end of term report, with an introductory letter from the head, and returned with the report acknowledgement slip; this was good use of existing administrative arrangements and prevailing authority relationships. The success of the parents' survey was particularly important to me. I was originally registered for a Master's degree; the survey was a condition of my re-registering for a doctorate, a rare permission for a part-time student.

I can remember Basil Bernstein saying that your first piece of research is about discovering yourself. There is something in the general point, but it was almost literally true for me when I analyzed the school records, for as an ex-pupil my school career was there on paper. The lesson of that analysis for me (it took the best part of a summer 'holiday') was that every table of results is a summary of some aspect of the lives of people. In the published account of the research (King, 1969), table 1, the 50.5 per cent of the intake of 1945 who were manual workers' sons includes me and many of my friends of the time, whose names I could be prompted to remember. Some of them and I are part of the 20.7 per cent of manual workers' sons of that intake who went into higher education.

With the three surveys completed I set about the statistical analysis. I must have done thousands of chi-square calculations, with the aid of nothing more than a set of mathematical tables and a four-figure spiral slide rule. This was the grind of the research, but what joy when something came up statistically significant. Fortunately, this was a job that could be done whenever even a little time was available, in my life as a teacher and a father of small children.

Writing a thesis has its difficulties, but at least there is a kind of formula to follow, and you know who you are writing it for — your supervisor and the external examiner, (John Eggleston, as it turned out). Being a research student is a lonely experience particularly when you get to the point of feeling only you know what you are doing. There were times when I found my supervisor supportive, encouraging and generous with his time, with many a Sunday morning spent going over drafts on his living room floor. At other times he was inaccessible and sometimes queried the worth of the whole exercise, so it was with some relief to me that the thesis was accepted in 1967.

That research was of its time; what became known later as the orthodox sociology of education. The book version of the thesis had some currency, and it is a source of satisfaction that its analysis of grammar school values anticipates Bourdieu's (1974) idea of cultural capital, he being one of the key authors of the new sociology of education.

School Organisation and Pupil Involvement

The idea of approaching the newly-formed Schools Council to support a research project concerned with the organization of secondary schools existed before my lectureship appointment at the (then) Institute of Education of Exeter University. The Institute's Director, Robin Pedley, invited me to join a group discussing the idea, and in consequence I wrote a major section of the proposal that was accepted by the Council. I became research director of a project funded from 1967–70. A former student, Joan Fry, was research assistant from the start, joined by Gary Easthope for the second two years.

I had a free hand in the design of the research, but had few precedents to draw on. There was my own recently completed thesis, the research of Hilde Himmelweit (1963, 1966), two essays by Basil Bernstein (1966), and, perhaps most importantly, the work of the Industrial Administration Research Unit at the University of Aston (Pugh *et al.*, 1963). From them I took the view that organizational analysis was best pursued by operationalizing measurable variables. Since their starting point was Weber's (1948) concept of bureaucracy, this also marked the start of my own neo-Weberian approach to the sociology of education. The basic design was to gather data on the organization of secondary schools which could be operationalized into scales. In addition, an investigation would be made of the pupils' subjective experience of being organized, using the concept of involvement, mainly derived from Etzioni (1961).

In the first year of the project, we constructed all the major research instruments. These all started as qualitative data and were processed into quantifiable data. Pupils' experiences of school were gathered through group interviews and samples of commissioned written work. These formed the basis of the items in a questionnaire where each response could be assigned a score for involvement on the basis of judgments made by a sample of teachers. Three major instruments were constructed for the measurement of organization: a questionnaire, an observation schedule and an interview schedule for the headteacher and senior staff. These were based upon pilot observations in schools and interviews with headteachers and teachers.

In the first term of the second year, most of the seventy-two schools were surveyed. There were anxious times as we waited for responses to our requests for help, ticking off the list on the wall and looking for alternatives where a refusal was received. Joan and Gary bore the burden of this exercise with thousands of miles of driving, and overnight stays in modest accommodation. In the second term the survey of 7500 pupils in a sub-sample of thirty schools was completed. This involved taking the questionnaire to the school on the day of administration. The logistics of these exercises were complicated, and depended very much on the cooperation of the staff. A few times this was not forthcoming, despite the previous assurances of the headteacher, who had obviously not discussed the matter satisfactorily before our arrival, so that we were met with reluctant and disgruntled staff, who sometimes only agreed to help after an explanatory meeting with me. Sometimes we were a stick for the staff to beat the head with. When all went well it was possible to take away several hundred questionnaires, all completed in one school period.

The satisfaction of this kind of research is in looking at the piles of completed questionnaires and other schedules, the result of a carefully planned exercise akin, I always feel, to a bank robbery. All this research capital had to be processed. The pupils' questionnaire was pre-coded but the organizational data had to be put on to coding sheets, with over a thousand items, which could be processed into scales, a task requiring more than a slide rule.

These were the early days of the university computer, and the prevailing philosophy was that lecturers should learn how to program their own analyses. We did not have time to do this for such a big job, so the Schools Council agreed to our using the Atlas Computing Service of the University of London. Atlas gave us an estimate of the cost of the analysis we required, but once they had started revised this four-fold — well beyond our budget. After several meetings a pruned schedule was agreed at double the original estimate. At this time I was literally dreaming nightly about this problem, but the nightmares were not over. When computer print-our began to arrive we found (apart from silly mistakes like counts of the number of girls in a boys' school), serious errors, shown by internal inconsistences in the results. This meant that every batch had to be checked and the incorrect print-out returned. There seemed to be much job mobility among the programmers at Atlas, and we had to deal with a new one every few months. We had the vision of each new appointment being assigned to the notorious Exeter job, only to be beaten by it and to hand in his notice. We did not obtain what we felt were a full set of correct calculations until six months after the official end of the project. It is not always possible to create tables of results straight off a computer print-out, and secondary calculations were often necessary, using a slow noisy Facit electro-mechanical calculator, where there was time to whistle a tune while it did a long division sum.

Throughout the research, our link with the Schools Council was through their Research Officers, who paid us visits every few months and received our six-monthly reports, and seemed generally approving of what we were doing. With them I developed an understanding that I would write a full account of the research for the Council. By the winter following the official end of the project, we had enough reliable data for me to begin writing. I did so against two deadlines; the first meeting of a pipeline of meetings in the Council, and for my turn to come up on a surgical waiting list. Less than well, I wrote for long hours, feeding the material to my wife for typing. (She was familiar with my handwriting and our regular typist was ill in the early stages of pregnancy.) I sent off the report two days before the deadline, knowing that my operation would be the following week. Six weeks later, as I still convalesced, I heard that the report had not proceeded through all the required meetings, because of an unexpected amount of business. However, I was assured that, a few points aside, it had been well-received and would probably reach the final committee and approval in the next round in three months time. It eventually did reach this stage, but I was informed that the committee would like the report re-written, putting the tables, theory and methods in appendixes. This I did, but three months later I was told that the committee did not want to use the report for publication. At no time was I allowed to attend committees or communicate directly with the Council, other than through the research officers. Since that time I have had intimations of what happened. My report was part of a move by the research officers to maintain the sponsorship of pure research against the growing tendency to back only curriculum development projects. They, and I, lost. Some years later, I did get an oblique informal, shamefaced, oral apology for 'the way the Council treated you'. I had not been seconded to the project and did not receive an honorarium for my work, which I undertook in addition to my university responsibilities. When the rejected report was sent back to me, a rather snooty accompanying letter gave me permission to 'try to seek publication elsewhere'. It was a great pleasure to reply to that letter within a few weeks, to say that the original version of the report had been accepted for publication by Routledge's new International Library of Sociology.

I do not look back on this research with much pleasure. It was, perhaps, too ambitious and too often things seemed out of my control. The project was started in the era of the orthodox sociology of education and ended at the beginning of the new, when its positivistic methods were being eschewed. The book (1973) has received some recognition, as authors have dipped into particular sections. However, it remains, as Olive Banks (1982) has recently acknowledged, the only study of its kind.

School and College — Studies of Post-Sixteen Education

This project actually overlapped the Schools Council research. It started adventitiously and its final form was adventitious. In the late 60s two areas in the South West were proposing to introduce the first tertiary colleges as part of the secondary reorganization. It seemed a research opportunity worth taking. In the time before the Schools Council project ended, and when the flow of reliable computer print-out was slow, we had the research capacity to take an interest in these reorganization proposals. We were allowed to attend and make notes of meetings, to have access to documents and interview administrators. I applied to the Schools Council for a supporting grant to allow us to follow the process of reorganization. However, this was unsuccessful because, it was said, technical colleges were involved and they were outside the brief of the Council. Fortunately the Social Science Research Council made a grant which enabled me to retain Joan and Gary (and, after Gary left, Bonnie

Lucas) as assistants. They actually worked on the reorganization project in Schools Council time, and, because of the computer delays, worked on the Council project in SSRC time; but it was all public money.

Our original plan was to follow up the organizational changes in the two technical colleges which were planned to become tertiary colleges, and the college principals were both initially encouragingly cooperative. But hardly had we started than one principal, we infer, apprehensive that our research activities would exacerbate a sensitive political situation, withdrew his support. In addition, the material for an examination of staff mobility in relation to reorganization was proving too scanty for the task. So we had some spare research capacity. Very quickly, we reformulated the design to compare different kinds of post-sixteen provision: integrated sixth forms, sixth form centres, sixth form colleges, technical colleges and the one putative tertiary college we were able to gain access to.

This involved surveys of a dozen institutions, involving some observations, but mainly interviews with students and staff, and a questionnaire for students. Most of the arrangements for this were made by Joan Fry, most capably. The three of us had worked together long enough for me to outline processes and for Joan and Gary to fill in the details. Apart from the occasion when Gary left a box of completed questionnaires on the train going to Penzance, and a two-month postal strike, things went fairly smoothly, allowing me to recover slowly from my operation and get on with re-writing the Schools Council report. Fortunately, the policy for the use of the university computer had been changed so that professional pro-grammers of the Data Processing Unit were available, and they did an excellent job of the analysis we required.

The main published report of the research (1976) is something of a rag-bag (hence the sub-title). Much of the material we gathered could not be reported. This included details of meetings which could not be cloaked in anonymity. As it was, even the rather cautious reports that were made caused some offence that lingers to this day.

All Things Bright and Beautiful? A Sociological Study of Infants' Classrooms

One of the areas where a tertiary college was being introduced as part of secondary reorganization, was also reorganizing the primary schools from infant and junior to first and middle. We had enough research capacity to survey the schools, with brief observations, interviews with heads of staff and a questionnaire. I applied to the SSRC for a grant to extend this kind of survey, but I was not disappointed when the application was refused for not being big enough. By that time all my research assistants had new jobs and so I no longer felt obliged to help them. In addition, I was getting tired of the kind of research that was increasingly impersonal (to me), and heavily administrative. I sought refreshment in, to use the phrase of the time, doing my own thing; an open-ended, mainly observational study of infants' classrooms.

With funded, large-scale, quantified research, its plan must be made in advance of the actual data collection (even if, as in the SSRC project, circumstances may lead to alterations). My main motive in studying infants' schools was curiosity. There had been no socio-logical studies at the time I started, 1972, and there was a gap to be filled in the literature. The methods I used followed from this ignorance. Not knowing what the qualities of infants' classrooms were, the best way to find out was to make direct observations — non-participant observations (sometimes from inside the Wendy house), since participation led to the children treating me as a teacher surrogate, which prevented my observing and recording. Although it was possible to interview teachers (loosely structured, close to conversations), I had great difficulty in trying to inter-view the children. Most lacked the degree of reflexivity required to be an interviewee. Their levels of literacy precluded the use of questionnaires, although I did analyze samples of their written work.

The only quantification that led to figure results was made on school records, but in a loose sense all the qualitative data, mainly half a million words of notes of 600 hours of observations, were quantified. In their analysis, all the recorded examples of a particular activity, for example, teachers' use of sex-differences to control children's behaviour, were collated. If a particular activity had been observed in all or most of the thirty-eight classrooms, then it could be regarded as typical. Any that were particular to one of the three schools, or to a sub-group of teachers, required a different explana-tion. Any observation data that is used beyond straight descriptions, is, in this sense, being quantified, even if no figures are actually calculated. This could have happened had I structured my later observations more to record limited, specific activities.

The satisfactions of paper-instrument, data-calculated research is in accumulating the data and finding patterns in the results. In direct observations, in my experience, there was satisfaction in the actual doing of the research, not only because of the amenable people I was studying, but also because the act of research was also the first stage of the analysis. Patterns of behaviour can be seen, sometimes anticipated, and immediately compared with previous observations. Relationships with research subjects in quantitative research are limited and partial; letters, phone-calls, please fill in the questionnaire. Qualitative research takes the observer closer to the subjects and more often; whole days with one class with everything to be seen, in close proximity, to the extent of not being able to politely refuse a child's request to sit on my lap. It is not too fanciful to say, I was living my research.

With research for a thesis, someone else decides when you have done enough. With funded research, time is a pre-arranged, limited commodity. My infants' school research was open-ended, which meant that when the teacher I had originally intended to follow up over an extended period of time left to have a baby, I could switch my plan and use other teachers, and when my second school turned out to be less middle class in composition than I thought, I could remain there without regret, knowing I would have to seek access to a third school with a more middle class social composition. Theses are written to a kind of formula to satisfy a limited number of people. Reports of funded research have to satisfy a remote set of people. I wrote the account of my infants' school research (1978) as a pleasure to myself, aiming to reach a wide readership, aware that its sociological credibility might be impaired.

The more detailed a study is, the more likely it is that some readers may make imputations about the origins of the reported observations, despite the use of pseudonyms. Someone thought they recognized themselves in the book, and thought they had been misrepresented. There were many months of anxiety, with the threat of legal action, before the matter was resolved. With quantified data, the information about individuals is tucked up in the tables, safe from identification and hurt pride.

The research was done not only as a response to my own situation, but also to the new sociology of education. Not that I embraced the symbolic interaction/phenomenological version that was current in the early 70s, or the neo-Marxist version that appeared soon after. I tried to develop the neo-Weberian approach (King 1980) that I had started in the Schools Council project, although I can even see elements in my thesis.

Ronald King

Curriculum and Organisation Change in Secondary Schools (King 1981, 1982)

Despite the unrewarding experience of Schools Council project, even as it was completed I had the vague idea of repeating something like it in the future. Two large filing cabinets and many boxes of material, questionnaires, coding sheets, computer print-outs, were lugged from one storage place to another, and as the tenth anniversary of the original survey (1968–69) drew closer the prospect of some kind of follow-up, whilst not attractive, seemed almost unavoidable; at least I might regret not having tried.

Even as we analyzed the original data I thought we could use it to test some of Bernstein's propositions about the sociology of the school and curriculum. I sent a draft article based upon a secondary analysis to Professor Bernstein (published, 1976b). It took nearly a year before I received a rather non-committal reply (the results were not very supportive of the theories). A repeat survey of the schools could provide data to test these theories further. I made an application to the Social Science Research Council for a grant, but my main argument was for the value of what would be a unique follow-up study of change in secondary schools; the Bernstein analysis was presented as a possible bonus. The application was rejected, but I was invited to re-apply making the Bernstein testing the principal objective. The SSRC received applications three times a year, and I had a short time (most of my Christmas 'break') to re-write. This too was rejected, because, and I still do not understand their reasoning, they said I could not do a replication study and test Bernstein. But the replication study would provide the material for the testing. However, I submitted a third application making no reference to the value of the replication exercise, which was accepted.

Gail Tucker and Martin Bloomer were appointed research assistants in 1978, for two years. The survey of the forty-five surviving schools of the original seventy-two used only slightly modified versions of the original instruments, and used similar coding procedures and analysis, excellently computerized by the university data processing unit. Gail and Martin did most of the field work, (the extension of motorways cut the expenses from 1968–69; over-night stays were less often required). Ever since my first internal promotion, I had been (unwillingly) accumulating more administrative responsibilities, so it was fortunate that I could confine myself to the final stage analyses and to writing up. I now have several hundredweights of research material, some nearly twenty years old, but I cannot think about the approach of 1988–89 . . .

Doing Sociology of Education — No Best Method

The sociology of education is the study of the social structure of education, that is, the patterns of relationships between the participants, mainly, teachers and taught. The sociologist has to make some kind of relationship with those whose relationships he or she wants to study. In any kind of action approach (neo-Weberian in my case), some elements of the consciousness of the subjects, as they relate to one another, must become part of that of the researcher. No matter the scale of the research, that is, how many relationships are investigated, the two elements are always there: the structural and the subjective. The only structures that people directly experience are micro-structures, such as those of classrooms and playgrounds, and these are the only scale of structures that researchers can directly encounter (King, 1985). No one directly experiences a whole school, much less an educational system.

Direct observations yielding qualitative data are the closest a researcher can get to the educational process, so close that the subjective meanings of the observed can often be inferred, but these are usually confirmed through interviews — social structures created for research purposes. Sociological theory consists of attempts to explain what has been empirically shown to happen, and, as Julienne Ford (1975) puts it, 'Explaining is generalizing. Generalizing is theorizing'. Small-scale direct observations, what is usually called ethnography, allow us to generalize about a lot of things a few people did. It would be foolish if we were to limit ourselves to a method that prevented our generalizing on a wider scale. Larger samples, using questionnaires, provide information on a few things about a lot of people, and so enable generalizations about a range of micro-structures. Quantitative methods are sometimes rejected as positivist, but, as Brian Davies (1982) points out, 'All sociologies . . . are empirical and positivist if they collect and generalize about data'.

All methods have their limitations. There is no best method in the sociology of education, only suitable and feasible methods, so we should try to use as many as possible. My current research, in junior schools, is intended to complement that in infants' schools, but, although direct observation has been the main method, I've found that, unlike younger children, 8-year-olds can be interviewed and 10-year-olds can complete a simple questionnaire. The educational experience of children provides many of them with the skills of discussion, of reading and writing. We would be foolish if, with suitable care, we did not use these for our research purposes.

No research is easy, but the effort is all the more important with the recent neo-Marxists' incursion into the sociology of education, some of whom, as Olive Banks (1982) points out, eschew research, because as Brian Davies (1982) puts it, they 'regard it as a wasted notion as they know the story already'. The sociologist's special contribution to the professional and political dialogue about the nature of education should be to deliver what Basil Bernstein (1972) calls the 'sociological news'; that is, empirically realized interpretations of what has been shown to happen, rather than what is supposed or is desired to happen.

References

BANKS, O. (1982) 'Sociology of education', in COHEN, L. and THOMAS, L. (Eds) *Educational Research and Development 1970–1980*, Windsor, NFER-Nelson.

BERNSTEIN, B. (1966) 'Sources of consensus and disaffection in education', *Journal of the Association of Assistant Mistresses*, 17.

BERNSTEIN, B. (1972) 'Sociology and the sociology of education', in *Eighteen Plus*, Milton Keynes, Open University Press.

BERNSTEIN, B., ELVIN, H.L. and PETERS, R.S. (1966) 'Ritual in education', *Philosophical Transactions of the Royal Society of London* Series B, 251, 772.

BOURDIEU, P. (1974) 'The school as a conservative force', in EGGELSTON, J. (Ed.) *Contemporary Research in the Sociology of Education*, London, Methuen.

CENTRAL ADVISORY COUNCIL FOR EDUCATION REPORTS (1954) *Early Leaving* (Gurney-Dixon) London, HMSO.

CENTRAL ADVISORY COUNCIL FOR EDUCATION REPORTS (1960) *15 to 18* (Crowther) Vol. 2, London, HMSO.

DAVIES, B. (1982) 'Sociology and the sociology of education', in HARTNETT, A. (Ed.) *The Social Sciences in Educational Studies*, London, Heinemann.

ETZIONI, A. (1961) *Comparative Analysis of Complex Organizations*, Glencoe, Free Press.

FLOUD, J.E. (Ed.), HALSEY, A.H. and MARTIN, F.M. (1956) *Social Class and Educational Opportunity*, London, Heinemann.

FORD, J. (1975) *Paradigms and Fairy Tales*, London, Routledge and Kegan Paul.

GORDON, W.C. (1957) *The Social System of the American High School*, Glencoe, Free Press.

JACOB, P.E. (1957) *Changing Values in College*, New York, Harper.

HARGREAVES, D.H. (1967) *Social Relations in a Secondary School*, London, Routledge and Kegan Paul.

HIMMELWEIT, H.T. (1963) 'Socio-economic background and personality', in HOLLANDER, E.P. and HUNT, R.G. (Eds) *Current Problems in Social Psychology*, Oxford, Oxford University Press.

HIMMELWEIT, H.T. (1966) 'Social background, intelligence and school structure, an interaction analysis' in MEADE, J. and PARKES, A.S. (Eds) *Genetic and Environmental Factors in Human Ability*, Edinburgh, Oliver and Boyd.

KING, R.A. (1969) *Values and Involvement in a Grammar School*, London, Routledge and Kegan Paul.

KING, R.A. (1973) *School Organisation and Pupil Involvement*, London, Routledge and Kegan Paul.

KING, R.A. (1976a) *School and College: Studies of Post-Sixteen Education*, London, Routledge and Kegan Paul.

KING, R.A. (1976b) 'Bernstein's sociology of the school: some propositions tested', *British Journal of Sociology*, 27, 4, pp. 430–43.

KING, R.A. (1978) *All Things Bright and Beautiful? A Sociological Study of Infants' Classrooms*, Chichester, Wiley.

KING, R.A. (1980) 'Weberian perspectives and the study of education', *British Journal of the Sociology of Education*, 1, 1, pp. 7–23.

KING, R.A. (1981a) 'Bernstein's sociology of the school: a further testing', *British Journal of Sociology*, 32, 2, pp. 259–65.

KING, R.A. (1981b) 'Secondary schools: some changes of a decade', *Educational Research*, 23, 3.

KING, R.A. (1982a) 'Sex composition of staff, authority and collegiality in secondary schools', *Research in Education*, 26.

KING, R.A. (1982b) 'Organizational change in secondary schools: an action approach', *British Journal of Sociology of Education*, 3, 1, pp. 3–18.

KING, R.A. (1984) 'The man in the Wendy house: studying infants' schools', in BURGESS, R.G. (Ed.) *The Research Process in Educational Settings: Ten Case Studies*, Lewes, Falmer.

KING, R.A. (1985) 'On the "relative autonomy" of education: micro-and-macro structures', in BARTON, L. and WALKER, S. (Eds) *Social Change and Education*, London, Croom Helm.

LACEY, C. (1970) *Hightown Grammar*, Manchester, Manchester University Press.

MILLER, T.W.G. (1961) *Values in the Comprehensive School*, Edinburgh, Oliver and Boyd.

OTTAWAY, A.K.C. (1960) *Education and Society*, London, Routledge and Kegan Paul.

PUGH, D.S., HICKSON, D.J., HININGS, C.K., TURNER, C. and LUPTON, T. (1963) 'A conceptual scheme for organizational analysis', *Administrative Science Quarterly*, 8.

WEBER, M. (1948) *From Max Weber: Essays in Sociology*, GERTH, H. and MILLS, G.W. (Eds), London, Routledge and Kegan Paul.

11 Developing Theory in the Sociology of Music Education

Graham Vulliamy

Introduction

Writers develop theory through a combination of their own experiences and ideas and a reaction to the theorizing of others. For truly original thinkers, I suspect, the main influence is their own ideas; for lesser mortals, and certainly for myself, the writing of others has been the major impetus. This chapter charts the main influences on my development of a sociological perspective on music education. It shows how such a perspective was originally framed by the 'new sociology of education' of the early 1970s and how it later changed under the influence of shifting concerns in the sociology of education thereafter. The chapter illustrates the impetus to theory formation which the writings of others gives. For me this impetus has taken two main forms. First, it has involved a critique of current orthodoxies, which helps then to refine an alternative view, and, second, it has involved a search for theorizing in related areas, which shows an affinity with my own work. However, since the theme of my work and the manner in which the theory has proceeded were both heavily influenced by aspects of my own biography, it is with such aspects that I begin.

Biography

As a teenager in the late 1950s and early 1960s, the contemporary mode of rebellion was the culture of the Beat Generation. In my own case the term 'rebellion' is far too strong; I was a rather conventional schoolboy. However, what 'anti-establishment' tendencies I did possess enabled me to get caught up in a schoolboy culture in which one read Kerouac instead of Dickens and listened to Charlie Parker instead of Bach. Modern jazz is frequently described as 'difficult' music — unpleasant and/or incomprehensible on initial hearings. The same is said of much classical music[1], providing an obvious justification for the kind of listening and tuition to which we were subjected in our school music appreciation lessons. In both cases, developing a deep appreciation for such music takes time — unlike the instant appeal that much 'pop' music contains. As sociologists have recently re-discovered, students spend far more time immersed in the informal culture of their friends than in the classroom. Not surprisingly, therefore, I left school with a passionate interest and appreciation of jazz, together with the black American culture that had produced it. My knowledge of classical music was restricted to the fact that I knew I *ought* to like it. However, I simply had not had the time or inclination to listen to much of it — the only composers that I had shown more than a passing interest in were those, like Stravinsky, who had themselves expressed an interest in jazz or who had been named by jazz musicians as their favourite classical composers.

I left school, then, with a great interest in music, but with a sense of frustration that I had never learned how to make music. My parents had given me the opportunity of piano lessons at school, but the tunes I was taught, together with the whole apparatus of trying to learn to sight-read, were so far removed from my experience of Thelonious Monk, or even of the more classically-influenced Dave Brubeck, that I soon gave up. Later, thanks to a jazz drummer I met during a nine-month period in America prior to going to university, I discovered what seemed to be the only instrument which I could begin by playing the music I loved. My previous barriers to music-making — notation, formal tuition, melodies and rhythms completely unrelated to my musical interests — no longer applied. After some basic instruction from my friend, all I needed was a makeshift drum set together with a record player, allowing me to accompany my favourite jazz musicians. This very process gave me the inklings of what later proved to be an essential component of the theoretical view of music I adopted. The idea that a relatively untutored violinist could 'accompany' a recording by a symphony orchestra is laughable. For some who knew nothing of jazz, the answer was that classical music is difficult, whereas jazz must be very simple technically. I instinctively knew otherwise — how could the improvizations of geniuses such as Parker or Coltrane possibly be described as simple? The ease, however, with which a novice drummer could accompany such geniuses demonstrated two points. First, the basic structure within which jazz musicians work, and especially its rhythmical nature, is a simple one. The complexity and the musical interest is developed *within* this structure, whereas classical music involves the elaborate development of the structure itself (sonata form, the symphony and so on). Most modern jazz at that time was in 4/4 time (four beats to the bar). At the simplest level, all a drummer needs to do is tap these four beats on a cymbal — just as in an African drum ensemble one drummer will be used to lay down the basic pulse. The rhythmic complexity comes from the use of elaborate cross-rhythms against this pulse. A jazz drummer achieves this through the ability to play independent rhythms with both feet and hands. The fact that I could not do this did not prevent me from playing in time with the basic pulse of the jazz records I accompanied.

The second point that my self-tuition on the drums demonstrated is that, unlike classical music, there is no requirement for a knowledge of musical notation as an intermediary to the musical experience itself. This again, as the reader will see later, formed a crucial platform for the development of my later theoretical perspectives on music and on music education.

My musical interests continued into my teaching career. They also broadened. My interest in jazz led backwards to its origins in early Afro-American music, and the ensuing interests in blues and gospel led forwards to the contemporary styles of 'popular' music that were becoming increasingly influenced by black American music — the R and B boom of the 1960s and later developments in progressive rock music. Having shared as a teenager all the jazz buff's disdain for pop, I found that by the later 1960s the popular music of the 'flower power' era was not only very different from preceding commercial hit parade material, but also that it drew its major influences from a black tradition of music. This in turn led to a personal re-education about the varieties of pop that had followed the birth of rock 'n' roll in the mid-1950s — so much of that too (soul, Motown, the early Beatles) was Afro-American music in disguise.

I spent two years teaching sociology and liberal studies at a technical college. Liberal studies teaching at that time, the late 1960s, was polarized between two philosophies. Some saw it as a means of introducing craft apprentice students to the literary and artistic traditions of 'high culture', that had been denied them in their previous experiences of schooling. Others argued that such teaching must engage with the life experiences and culture of the students themselves. In caricature, our department was split between those carrying around multiple copies of D.H. Lawrence's novels about the working classes and those mounting courses on 'sex, drugs and rock 'n' roll', where print was out (except extracts from the writing of Marshall McLuhan) and the tape recorder was in. I was instinctively drawn to the second of these approaches, not only because I was a sociologist, rather than an English specialist, but also because I shared with many of my students an involvement with 'youth' music. Since such music echoed key concerns of youth culture, one could develop liberal studies courses that introduced various sociological themes, but using music as the main medium for such teaching — an approach which led to my first published writing on the subject of music (Vulliamy, 1971).

In 1971 I went to the London Institute of Education to study full-time for their Masters Degree in the Sociology of Education. This was the year which saw the publication of Michael Young's edited collection *Knowledge and Control: New Directions for the Sociology of Education*. The impact of this book, together with the adoption of its approach in the Open University's first Sociology of Education course *School and Society* (E282), was such that it was heralded as creating a Kuhnian paradigm shift in the sociology of education (Gorbutt, 1972). This begs a number of questions related both to the over-simplicity of the 'new sociology of education' label itself and to whether Kuhn's (1962) analysis of science can validly be applied in this case. However, notwithstanding such reservations, it certainly was the case that the early 1970s witnessed a marked change of emphasis in sociological perspectives on education.

The New Sociology of Education

Since the new sociology of education became a springboard for my early work on the sociology of music education, it is worth high-lighting the main dimensions of the supposed paradigm shift. First, there was an application of the sociology of knowledge to the school curriculum. Traditional approaches to the sociology of education in Britain had viewed the school curriculum as relatively unproble-matic, whereas the new sociology of education incorporated a critical analysis of what counts as educational knowledge. Secondly, the adoption of symbolic interactionist and phenomenological approaches led to a focus upon classroom interaction and school processes — a marked change in both theory and methodology from the survey analysis characterizing much previous work. Thirdly, a combination of this phenomenological approach and reference to anthropological studies led to a questioning of commonly accepted educational categories, such as ability.

The upshot of these new approaches was to question more traditional explanations of school failure, which had emphasized the deficient home background of those who failed, and to focus instead on the social nature of what they failed at. Thus, theories of linguistic and cultural deprivation underpinning compensatory education programmes were denounced as myths, and instead both the curricula and the processes of schooling were held responsible for helping reproduce the social and cultural hegemony of the middle classes.

This was the intellectual backcloth, taught by Michael Young, against which I had to decide what to write my Masters dissertation on. It seemed natural to look critically at the school curriculum, and the new sociology of education appeared to provide a fruitful way of interpreting aspects of my own experiences with reference to music. I had begun playing the drums in jazz groups at university, and then in the last year of my period teaching in the technical college I was playing in, and managing, a rock band that later went professional. From the moment I had begun playing jazz or rock music, I had continually come across very talented musicians who had nevertheless been defined as musically inept at school. The diagnosis of 'failure' that was emerging in the new sociology of education seemed to echo this experience. With music, the problem appeared to lie with the school curriculum, because school students were demonstrably very interested in music, but not *school* music. Young's (1971) concept of the 'stratification of knowledge' — the idea that different types of knowledge have different degrees of status — could be used to analyze the rigid distinction between subject-based high status knowledge ('serious' music) and everyday low status knowledge ('pop' music). The attitude of music teachers, and of many adults in general, was that the musical culture of students was a 'deprived' one, but it was clear to me that such attitudes required viewing this culture in a totally distorted and ideological way.

It was therefore agreed that my dissertation should look sociologically at the teaching of music. A detailed examination was made of the 'subject perspective' (Esland, 1971) of music teachers, by an analysis of current texts on music teaching and historical accounts of the development of music as a school subject. At the beginning of the present century the teaching of music in all schools (other than the public schools) was confined to class singing. Since then the scope of school music teaching has widened enormously (Vulliamy, 1977a, p. 203–206). The most influential developments have been the music appreciation movement of the 1920s and 1930s, which established music as a classroom subject with its own syllabus and examinations; the enormous growth in instrumental tuition, especially in extra-curricular activities; and the challenge of the 'creative' music educators. The latter approach, which was later developed in the work of John Paynter and the Schools Council 'Music in the Secondary School Curriculum' Project (Paynter, 1983), played down the emphasis upon traditional classical music and notation and developed the use of techniques that contemporary avant-garde composers use. It also stressed the importance of the active exploration of sounds by *all* students as a part of their general education.

I was not surprised to find that a consideration of Afro-American music did not figure at all in the subject perspective of music teaching. It also did not surprise me to find the vehemence with which some music teachers castigated the influence and effects of pop music. What did surprise me, however, was the number of writers who failed to distinguish in their attacks between jazz and pop, let alone between different varieties of popular music. It was as if anything that was not 'serious' music was a load of garbage — a point made quite explicitly by some.

It is possible that, without the publication of another book which had a profound influence on me, my views on music teaching would have remained those of a defensive critic justifying his own musical prejudices against the overwhelming odds of the learned musical establishment. This book was *Serious Music and All That Jazz* by Henry Pleasants. Pleasants argued that this century will be seen by future historians as dominated by Afro-American music — a product of the fusion of African and European musical traditions amongst black people in America — in the same sense that one might associate the Romantic period in music with Germany or the Baroque with Italy:

> In each case, or epoch, we have the music and the musicians
> of a single nation or culture proving to be so irresistibly
> attractive to other nations and other cultures as to determine

the musical physiognomy of an entire civilization or age. (1969, p. 91)

Very significantly for me, Pleasants was himself a classical music critic. As such, I saw for the first time reading his work how the kinds of intuitions I had developed concerning different musical styles could be explicated using the kinds of accepted musical terminology and understanding promoted by a conventional musical education. Speaking, as it were, from within the music establishment itself, Pleasants made some poignant comments on the main debate that had been raging within the music establishment during the course of this century. This debate concerned the exhaustion of possibilities of further development within the traditional framework of tonality and the responses of serious composers to this situation, ranging from the twelve-tone and serialist developments of Schoenberg to aleatoric music and electronic music. The terms of the debate, as discussed by serious musicians, had been such that the future of music could only be thought of in terms of serious music in the tonal idiom or music in an atonal idiom. Pleasants suggested, however, that serious musicians had been led to such a view only because they had been blinkered by their own terms:

> Historians, critics and composers have made the mistake of thinking of the main stream of musical evolution solely in terms of serious music, as if there were *a* serious music and *a* popular music instead of simply various qualities of music. (1955, p. 167)

The important change of this century was not to be seen, Pleasants argued, as the move from a tonal to an atonal language, but rather as the change from a music based on theme and harmony to one based on melody and rhythm. The latter change had, however, gone unobserved by the musical establishment because it had taken place in an area of music (jazz and popular) which had not, until quite recently, normally been recognized as music at all.

Pleasants' thesis was attractive because not only did it provide substance to my musical prejudices, but it was also commensurate with the style of theorizing being developed in the new sociology of education. Like phenomenologists, Pleasants was questioning everyday assumptions; he was looking at the social origins and consequences of commonly accepted categories; and, as in Michael Young's work, Pleasants refused to 'take' the music establishment's problems, but instead 'made' new problems by questioning their most basic assumptions.

It was Pleasants' book which prompted me to look back at historical records to see how and why it was that the music establishment came to react so violently against this new musical revolution that is almost came to the point of viewing it as not music at all — and certainly not music worthy of encouragement in education (Vulliamy, 1976c, p. 20–22). The reaction to the growth of jazz in America from the 1920s onwards suggested that there were two main reasons, each of which then led to further developments of the kind of theorizing I was pursuing. First, the music was resisted because of its identification with black people, a low status group in society, and because of further identifications with crime, vice and greater sexual freedom. Second, traditionally trained classical musicians opposed the new music because it seemed to violate both classical musical standards (with blue notes, impure tones and so on) and classical cultural standards (being played in neither concert halls nor churches). Rock 'n' roll in the mid 1950s, and later developments of rock music, were generally greeted with a similar moral outrage by members of the musical establishment. Such reactions led to a central tenet of the subject perspective of music teachers being an assumed dichotomy between 'serious' music and 'popular' music, where all varieties of Afro-American music are grouped under the latter label.

The first of the reasons why Afro-American music had been resisted suggested that the legitimacy of artistic or cultural products was strongly influenced by the status of the groups associated with such products. This tied in neatly with the kind of approach developed by Bourdieu in his chapter on 'Intellectual field and creative project' in Young's *Knowledge and Control*. He argued that dominant groups in a society are in a position to impose their social constructions or meanings (concerning cultural values, the production of art works and so on) on others in a form of *'violence symbolique'*. With music, the result has been a prevalent establishment ideology concerning the nature of pop music. Part of my work then involved an elucidation, followed by a critique, of the assumptions underpinning this ideology (see, for example, Vulliamy, 1976a, p. 40–46; 1976b, p. 59–60).

Since many criticisms of pop music made by the music establishment were shared by critics of mass culture, I decided to review the literature on the mass culture critique. Condemnations of jazz and popular music came, as one might expect, from conservatives who saw moves towards political democracy and social and economic equality as threatening the preservation of elitist high culture. More surprisingly, however, I found that radical theorists, especially from the Frankfurt school, shared many of these worries, albeit for different reasons. In doing so, it seemed to me, they also demonstrated the kind of lack of understanding of the nature of Afro-American music that characterized the music establishment ideology.

This brings me to the second reason why Afro-American music was resisted — because it did not conform to classical music standards. The limited dabbling into musicology that I could manage indicated that, however valid the approaches of music aestheticians might be with reference to classical music, the assumptions they made about jazz and popular music were demonstrably misguided. With the notable exceptions of the rare theorists, such as Schuller (1968), who had practical experience of Afro-American musical styles, musicologists failed to recognize the existence of alternative musical criteria derived from an African tradition of music. Instead, standards of judgment appropriate to composed music concerned primarily with harmonic exploitation were imposed on an improvised music, which incorporates complex rhythmic and melodic inflections. Thus, I argued that Meyer's well-known attempt to discover what it is that 'makes music great' (Meyer, 1959) involves a reification of classical music criteria and a basic misunderstanding of styles of music which are not located in the European serious tradition. In like manner, Adorno's critique of jazz and popular music in terms of their submission to the phenomenon of 'standardization' depends upon a concept of standardization that reifies musical criteria derived from the serious music tradition, where the main stress is on the harmonic structure and form of music (Vulliamy, 1977b, p. 184). Here I found that an increasing clarification of my own perspective was developed as a result of pinpointing those aspects of the writings of other theorists which did not accord with my own ideas or experience.

Following the work of jazz musicologists such as Keil (1966) and writers on popular music such as Chester (1970), the way forward seemed to be to develop alternative criteria for the understanding of musical styles, such as Afro-American ones, which were based upon very different principles than composed classical music. My lack of knowledge of musicology, however, meant that little progress could be made along this path until I had the opportunity much later to co-author a book with two musicologists with similar views to my own (Shepherd *et al.*, 1977). The long discussions we had together facilitated a process whereby I could 'get inside' the kind of socio-musical perspective they had developed, in a manner which would have proved impossible had I simply read their material without the opportunity for verbal probing and clarification.

A Case Study

The final input to my early analysis of the sociology of music education came from a piece of empirical work. Young had written in his introduction to *Knowledge and Control* that we have very few studies of 'how contemporary definitions of culture have consequences for the organization of knowledge in the school system' (1971, p. 10). This, together with Keddie's chapter 'Classroom Knowledge' in the same book, which looked at the social assumptions under-pinning teachers' definitions of knowledge and ability in the context of interaction in the classroom, prompted me to carry out a similar participant observation study in a school music department.

At the outset I had no idea how or where I was going to conduct such a study. In a proposal to my tutor before the study, I simply said that, having looked at the assumptions of music educators through literary sources, I would like to examine them in practice. Following Keddie's (1971) work, this might involve seeing how teachers perceive knowledge ('music') in the classroom context and how they perceive their students. In addition, having read so much about the 'aims of music education', I thought I could ask teachers the same question in the course of their work. The only practical experience of this type of study that I had was the fact that during the first term of my Masters course, I had spent about one day a week in the music department of a technical college, where a jazz musician friend of mine was teaching. This was a very unusual music teaching context (see Vulliamy, 1976c, p. 27–28), in which all varieties of music were equally acceptable. Criteria of musical ability were very different from those that had been revealed from reading about school music teaching. To give one example: all the school music examination syllabuses, from the high status 'A' level to the lower status CSE, stressed the importance of musical notation and knowledge of classical music. At the technical college, however, many of the department's keenest and most talented musicians were rock musicians who could not read a note of music. Moreover, in music appreciation lessons, timetabled as a liberal studies option, the head of music played and discussed music spanning an enormous spectrum from classical, through folk and jazz, to rock and pop.

My fear was that conducting a more detailed study in a school music department would simply reinforce all my pre-existing prejudices about the irrelevance of traditional approaches to music teaching. It was clear from the music education literature what the assumptions of music teachers were likely to be. It was also clear from my own experience that such teaching would only be effective for a small minority of students with a prior interest in classical music. The craft apprentice students whom I had taught at technical college had been scathing in their criticisms of school music lessons. That they were not atypical was confirmed by the finding of the Schools Council *Enquiry 1: Young School Leavers* (HMSO, 1968) that, out of fourteen subject areas, music was perceived by students as the most boring and least useful.

In retrospect, the choice of the school in which I conducted the case study could not have been a better one for my purposes, since it embodied a wide range of music, including jazz, and the hypotheses which were later developed from the study concerned the relationships between varieties of 'what counts as music' and teachers' assumptions about students. However, I ended up at this school more through luck than design, because before I began the fieldwork I was not clear as to what the purposes of such a case-study were to be, other than in the most general terms of observing the practice of music teaching.

My access to a school was facilitated by a lecturer in the music department at the Institute, who had a wide knowledge of London schools through the teaching practice circuit. I told him that I wanted to go to a school music department with a very high reputation — given my prior views on music teaching, and the evidence of surveys such as the Schools Council one, there seemed no possibility that my own assumptions could be challenged, and hence my ideas refined, in a run-of-the-mill department. A school whose music department had a high reputation was selected for me and I made a preliminary visit. Although I was only there for a day, it confirmed my initial worries. A further problem was that there appeared to be a strong conflict between the two members of the music department staff. One was an adherent of what I called (Vulliamy, 1977a) the 'traditional' paradigm of music teaching and the other a convert to what I called the 'avant-garde' paradigm, stressing creative music-making approaches. I decided that were I to research there, the main focus might well end up as the personal conflict between these two teachers.

A second possible school was suggested. On making a preliminary visit, I was amazed to find that the school had a large dance band, playing jazz/swing styles of music, in addition to military bands, choirs and orchestras. Very large numbers of students appeared to be involved in playing musical instruments and, in addition to three full-time music teachers, there was a range of peripatetic music teachers visiting the school, including a teacher of the drums. Quite by accident, I had stumbled on what turned out to be one of the very few schools in London at that time with such an orientation. I immediately knew that, whatever else, I would find a term in such a music department both interesting and enjoyable. Moreover, I was made very welcome by the head of music, who was understandably self-confident about the achievements of his department, and the department's use of jazz connected with my own interests (although, to preserve greater validity of my data pertaining to teachers' attitudes to jazz and pop, I did not reveal this to the staff until a feedback session after the research had been completed).

The details of the study are available elsewhere (Vulliamy, 1977a, p. 208–21). The school proved very fruitful in generating hypotheses, both because of its unusually wide definition of 'what counts as music' and because of its achievements in motivating large numbers of students to become involved in music. Their success highlighted the boundaries of such success in a manner which would have been impossible in a school whose music department was following the predictable path of alienating the vast majority of its students. The boundaries at my case-study school were such that their wide definition of 'what counts as music' was accommodated within the more traditional legitimate concerns of music teaching. Thus the main emphasis of the music department was to produce good all-round instrumentalists with a thorough grounding in the 'discipline' of music. This definition of 'what counts as music' (backed up by classroom music lessons on musical notation, history and appreciation, and traditional theory) both made music approximate to other academic disciplines and excluded any style of music (such as rock or pop) that did not fit these criteria.

This definition of 'what counts as music' had consequences for the delineation of the boundaries concerning which students would be viewed as the most musical. Choices had to be made as to which students could make use of the very large, but necessarily limited, supply of instruments the school had built up over the years. The approximation of their definition of 'what counts as music' to an academic discipline seemed to be associated with the fact that the teachers tended to assume that those students (in the upper streams) who were good at other academic subjects might also be good at the discipline of music, whilst those students who had failed at other academic subjects would also fail at music. In addition, to succeed in classroom music, just as in Keddie's (1971) study, appeared to require that students took over the teachers' definition of the situation (or at least pretend they did), which involved, amongst other things, an acceptance of the kind of dichotomy between serious music and popular music that I had found in the music education literature.

The suggested relationship at this school between 'what counts as music' and teachers' perceptions relating to intelligence, family background and musical ability had been a surprise and only became further refined when I examined the assumptions of other music educators with very different notions of 'what counts as music'. Adherents of the avant-garde paradigm of music teaching, for example, held a more open-ended view of what constitutes valid music and also tended to believe that all students had the potential for musical creativity (see Vulliamy, 1976c, p. 26–27).

Further Developments of the Theory

The strategy I had adopted for my dissertation was that promoted by Young (1971) at the outset of the new sociology of education. An original focus for the study was the music teacher's widely expressed 'problem' of the hostility that many teenagers show towards music education in schools. Rather than take this problem for granted, by making 'what counts as music' in schools problematic, I had attempted to show some of the assumptions implicit in its formulation. The central conclusion — that, with music, prevailing conceptions of educational knowledge play a significant role in maintaining traditional patterns of educational success and failure — confirmed one of the basic insights of the new sociology of education.

However, from the outset, the new sociology of education was subjected to a number of strident criticisms. Given that my sociological view of music education was so dependent upon the new sociology of education, such criticisms provoked me to ask whether, if valid, they challenged the theory I had developed or whether the theory could in some way accommodate them. It was therefore a response to such criticisms that led to further refinements of my views.

Philosophers such as Pring (1972) and Flew (1976) argued that Young's application of a sociology of knowledge perspective to educational knowledge is in places highly suspect epistemologically, in its celebration of what is seen as an extreme form of relativism. In the absence of alternative truth criteria for alternative knowledge structures, philosophers can persuasively argue that high status knowledge is as it is simply because it is better. The corresponding viewpoint in music education is that our emphasis on classical music reflects the fact that such music is better and more highly developed than other styles of music, like jazz or pop, coexisting in our society. In countering this, I was able to move beyond my earlier arguments about alternative musical languages, thanks to collaboration with the work of Shepherd (1977) on the sociology of music and on music aesthetics. Shepherd's critique of the objectively conceived aesthetic of writers such as Langer (1960) and Meyer (1956) provided a more sustained argument that a valid social theory of music must be based on an acceptance of the relativity of aesthetic judgment across different musical traditions (Vulliamy, 1978, p. 116–18).

A second criticism of the new sociology of education was that phenomenologically-based participant observation studies, such as that by Keddie (1971), were a-historical and put too much emphasis on the ability of participants actively to construct or change their realities (Sharp and Green, 1975, p. 15–35). Where the focus is on teachers, this can lead to an over-simplistic 'blame the teacher' view. Such a criticism led me to build in a historical approach which attempts to locate current attitudes as part of an ongoing historical process (Vulliamy, 1978, p. 119) and also to stress the power of external forces in constraining the activities of teachers (Vulliamy, 1977a, p. 227).

The final criticism, and in my view the most powerful one, to be addressed was the contention that the new sociology of education was over-optimistic about the possibilities of radical educational change and that it lacked an adequate theory as to how such change could be brought about (Whitty, 1974). Following Whitty's argument that radical social studies teachers are constrained in their efforts to promote change by a widespread 'culture of positivism', I viewed progressive music teachers as being equally constrained by the force of the dominant music establishment ideology of a dichotomy between serious music and popular music, with its accompanying ideological assumptions.

Following the publication of Bowles and Gintis' book *Schooling in Capitalist America* in 1976, sociological accounts of schooling in Britain became increasingly dominated by neo-Marxist perspectives on the hidden curriculum and on the role of schooling in social and cultural reproduction. This, together with the influence of the work of Shepherd (1977) and Wishart (1977) in the sociology of music, led to further modifications of theory. In collaboration with Shepherd, it was argued that the processes of school music teaching contribute not only to the legitimation of a dominant *musical* ideology but also, more speculatively, to much more pervasive ideological assumptions underpinning capitalist societies (Shepherd and Vulliamy, 1983).

Such conclusions arose from a comparison of school music teaching in England and Ontario and were developed while we taught together a course on the sociology of music in Canada. In a participant observation study designed to replicate my own work, Shepherd (1983) found that, unlike in England, no overt culture clash was found in Ontario schools between 'school' music and 'students'' music. This was for two main reasons. First, music curricula in North America tend to be based largely on big band, dance band, show and light classical music. While this music has enough in common with the criteria of 'what counts as good music' to satisfy parents and school boards on the one hand, it frequently alludes suffiently to the inflectional, improvisatory and timbral qualities of the students' own subcultures on the other to mollify, although not eradicate, possible opposition to classroom music. Second, unlike in most English schools, music is not a compulsory subject in Canada.

However, Shepherd had been struck by the number of classroom examples he had come across whereby a notational filter had been used unconsciously by teachers to defuse the essential Afro-American musical characteristics of pop and rock music, when students were either playing or listening to such music in the classroom (Shepherd and Vulliamy, 1983, p. 7–8). This was analogous to the emphasis I had placed on how notation had proved a major constraint on attempts to reform school music teaching in England (Vulliamy, 1978, p. 123–124). We therefore argued that, by focusing on the deep structure of the pedagogical process, as opposed to surface features of classroom interaction, despite the differences in social context between Ontario and England, particular ideologies of the dominant musical culture are transmitted in very similar ways.

Finally, drawing further upon the work of Wishart (1977) and Shepherd (1982), we argued that the dominance of a notated conception of music has a much more deep-seated ideological significance than might at first be apparent, because it helps socialize students into fundamental epistemological assumptions underpinning industrial, capitalist society (Shepherd and Vulliamy, 1983, p. 10).

The above modifications to the original theory arose from criticisms made by sociologists of the new sociology of education perspective. The other principal critique of my work has come from Keith Swanwick, Britain's first Professor of Music Education (Swanwick, 1984a and b). This led in turn to clarification of our differences concerning the aesthetics and social nature of music (Vulliamy and Shepherd, 1984b and 1985). We also attempted to relate certain observations that Swanwick made concerning the processes of schooling to wider sociological theories of schooling that helped make sense of the kinds of constraints that Swanwick had correctly identified. The final impetus from his work was perhaps the most important. Swanwick argued that, in our general theoretical defence of a relativistic approach to different musical languages, we were evading the practical implications of our position for the reform of school music teaching and evading also the issue of the relative worth of different styles of music. To make our position more explicit on these points required the adoption of the kinds of theoretical frameworks developed in recent ethnomusicological analysis, together with an assessment of the implications of these for the practice of music teaching (Vulliamy and Shepherd, 1984a, p. 257–64 and 1984b, p. 71–74).

Conclusion: The Circumscribed Nature of Theory

What lessons can be learned from this attempt to chart the major influences on the development of my theoretical perspective on the sociology of music education? In the concluding part of this chapter, I want to argue that, in my case at least, the development of theory has been crucially affected by biographical factors and by the kinds of intellectual influences to which I have been exposed. A consequence is that the theory has been inevitably limited by such factors, presenting only one of many possible sociological perspectives on music education.

First, the impetus for my work was originally derived from the sociology of education, rather than from either music education or music, or indeed from mainstream sociology itself, and its scope has shifted according to changing intellectual fashions in the sociology of education. These shifting fashions have been closely paralleled by those in other sub-disciplines of sociology. For example, the development of the sociology of medicine over the last two decades has been a response to very similar influences. In the 1950s and 1960s the dominance of a structural-functionalist perspective meant that the concept of health itself was rarely made problematic (consider, for example, the notion of the 'sick role' in Parsons, 1951), just as in the traditional sociology of education the concept of education was seldom questioned. However, in the same year as the publication of Young's *Knowledge and Control*, Dreitzel was arguing that 'there is no "objective" definition of illness; instead it is necessary to ask in whose interest and with what purpose in mind illness is socially defined by different people' (1971, p. vi). As with the new sociology of education, this was followed by a range of studies from both interactionist and phenomenological perspectives. What counts as health was relativized and interest shifted from macro issues to micro studies of the processes of doctor-patient interaction (Dingwall, 1976; Wadsworth and Robinson, 1976). The critique of the new sociology of education implied in Bowles and Gintis' neo-Marxist position was also mirrored by Navarro's (1976) analysis of the way in which health care systems help reproduce the economic and social bases of a capitalist society. Much ensuing research in both the sociology of education and the sociology of medicine can be seen as exhibiting a lively tension between the phenomenological and structural poles of a continuum on which sociologists have critically analyzed the role of educational and health care systems in capitalist society (for education, see the units and course readers for the Open University *Society, Education and the State* (E353) course (1981); for health, see Stacey *et al.*, 1977; Dingwall *et al.*, 1977; Doyal and Pennell, 1979).

Without having conducted similar such analyses, I nevertheless suspect that many sub-disciplines of sociology have shown a parallel drift in intellectual concerns. By accommodating itself to such a drift, the sociology of music education perspective I adopted has therefore to some extent kept in touch with mainstream sociology — a process that indicates also the ways in which theoretical developments in one area are mirrored in others. However, its location within the sociology of education has clearly been limiting in important ways. The focus has been upon the ways in which the teaching of music has exemplified, or even contributed to, the reproduction of social class relations in capitalist society through both its overt and hidden curricula. As such there tends to have been a concentration on social class at the expense of other variables such as age, sex/gender and race/ethnicity[2]. For example, Frith and McRobbie (1978) initiated a debate on the relationship between rock music and sexuality, when they argued that teenagers learn to identify with and internalize adult sex and gender roles through their orientation to different sex-linked styles of rock music. Dominant ideologies of masculinity and femininity are conveyed through the machismo of 'cock rock' on the one hand and the romanticism of 'teeny bop rock' on the other. The implications of such sociological research on education or socialization *through* music for a sociology *of* music education have yet to be explored.

If a location within a sociology of education paradigm has been one limitation of this sociological view of music education, another equally important one has been the restricted interest in Afro-American and related popular music styles. As argued earlier, such an emphasis is a product of biographical factors — namely my background as a rock musician with no formal training in classical music. As a consequence, I have not pursued the kinds of issues addressed by Wright (1975) in what, to my knowledge, is the only other research programme in the sociology of music education to have been carried out in Britain (excepting a few unpublished undergraduate dissertations and graduate theses).

A further limitation of the sociological view of music education discussed in this chapter is its emphasis on *school* music teaching, which has led to a neglect of the kinds of 'socialization into musicianship' studies (whether rock or classical) to be found in the United States. Nor has there been the collection of empirical data pertaining to both classical music and mass media institutions that has characterized the collaboration of sociologists and music educators in MEDIACULT (the International Institute for Audio-Visual Communication and Cultural Development) in Europe.

The creation of theory, then, emerges as a very personal enterprise, in which developments are highly circumscribed by disciplinary, institutional and biographical factors. I have shown how the adoption of a sociology of knowledge framework to the school subject of music, in conjunction with my own idiosyncratic musical experiences, has produced a particular view of the sociology of music education. I have also shown how a combination of different personal interests and different intellectual stimuli would almost certainly have produced theoretical developments with a markedly different emphasis.

Acknowledgement

I am very grateful to Rosemary Webb for her helpful comments on an earlier draft of this chapter.

Notes

1. Throughout this chapter the term 'classical' music is used in a loose sense to refer to that part of the music of Western Europe from the Middle Ages to the present which forms the basis of conservatory training. For definitions of the other musical styles referred to in this chapter, see VULLIAMY and LEE (1976, p. 4).
2. This point is further developed in VULLIAMY (1984) — an article that also contains some sections reproduced in this chapter.

References

BOWLES, S. and GINTIS, H. (1976) *Schooling in Capitalist America: Educational Reform and the Contradictions of Economic Life*, London, Routledge and Kegan Paul.

CHESTER, A. (1970) 'Second thoughts on a rock aesthetic: The Band', in *New Left Review*, 62, pp. 75–82.

DINGWALL, R. (1976) *Aspects of Illness*, London, Martin Robertson.

DINGWALL, R. *et al.* (Eds) (1977) *Health Care and Health Knowledge*, London, Croom Helm.

DOYAL, L. and PENNELL, I. (1979) *The Political Economy of Health*, London, Pluto Press.

DREITZEL, H.P. (Ed.) (1971) *The Social Organization of Health*, London, Macmillan.

ESLAND, G. (1971) 'Teaching and learning as the organization of knowledge', in YOUNG, M.F.D. (Ed.) (1971) *Knowledge and Control: New Directions for the Sociology of Education*, London, Collier Macmillan, pp. 70–115.

FLEW, A. (1976) *Sociology, Equality and Education*, London, Macmillan.

FRITH, S. and McROBBIE, A. (1978) 'Rock and sexuality', in *Screen Education*, 29, pp. 3–19.

GORBUTT, D. (1972) 'The new sociology of education', in *Education for*

Teaching, Autumn, pp. 3–11.

KEDDIE, N. (1971) 'Classroom knowledge', in YOUNG, M.F.D. (Ed.) *Knowledge and Control: New Directions for the Sociology of Education*, London, Collier Macmillan.

KEIL, C. (1966) 'Motion and feeling through music', in *Journal of Aesthetics and Art Criticism*, 24, pp. 337–349.

KUHN, T. (1962) *The Structure of Scientific Revolutions*, Chicago, University of Chicago Press.

LANGER, S.K. (1960) *Philosophy in a New Key*, Cambridge, Harvard University Press.

MEYER, L.B. (1956) *Emotion and Meaning in Music*, Chicago, University of Chicago Press.

MEYER, L.B. (1959) 'Some remarks on value and greatness in music', in *Journal of Aesthetics and Art Criticism*, 17, pp. 486–500.

NAVARRO, V. (1976) *Medicine Under Capitalism*, London, Croom Helm.

PARSONS, T. (1951) *The Social System*, New York, Free Press.

PAYNTER, J. (1983) *Music in the Secondary School Curriculum*, London, Cambridge University Press.

PLEASANTS, H. (1955) *The Agony of Modern Music*, New York, Simon and Schuster.

PLEASANTS, H. (1969) *Serious Music and All That Jazz*, London, Gollancz.

PRING, R. (1972) 'Knowledge out of control', *Education for Teaching*, Autumn, pp. 19–28.

SCHULLER, G. (1968) *Early Jazz*, Oxford, Oxford University Press.

SHARP, R. and GREEN, A. (1975) *Education and Social Control: A Study in Progressive Primary Education*, London, Routledge and Kegan Paul.

SHEPHERD, J. (1977) Chapters 1–3 of SHEPHERD, J., VIRDEN, P., VULLIAMY, G. and WISHART, T. (1977) *Whose Music? A Sociology of Musical Languages*, London, Latimer, pp. 7–124.

SHEPHERD, J. (1982) 'A theoretical model for the sociomusicological analysis of popular music', *Popular Music 2*, London, Cambridge University Press, pp. 145–177.

SHEPHERD, J. (1983) 'Conflict in patterns of socialization: the role of the classroom music teacher', *The Canadian Review of Sociology and Anthropology*, 20, pp. 22–43.

SHEPHERD, J., VIRDEN, P., VULLIAMY, G. and WISHART, T. (1977) *Whose Music? A Sociology of Musical Languages*, London, Latimer.

SHEPHERD, J. and VULLIAMY, G. (1983) 'A comparative sociology of school knowledge', *British Journal of Sociology of Education*, 4, pp. 3–18.

STACEY, M. *et al.* (Eds) (1977) *Health and the Division of Labour*, London, Croom Helm.

SWANWICK, K. (1984a) 'Problems of a sociological approach to pop music in schools', *British Journal of Sociology of Education*, 5, pp. 49–56.

SWANWICK, K. (1984b) 'A further note on sociology of music education',

British Journal of Sociology of Education, 5, pp. 303–307.

VULLIAMY, G. (1971) 'Black music and liberal arts', *The Times Educational Supplement*, 16 April.

VULLIAMY, G. (1976a) 'Definitions of serious music' in VULLIAMY, G. and LEE, E. (Eds) *Pop Music in School*, London, Cambridge University Press, pp. 33–48.

VULLIAMY, G. (1976b) 'Pupil-centred music teaching' in VULLIAMY, G. and LEE, E. (Eds) *Pop Music in School*, London, Cambridge University Press, pp. 49–61.

VULLIAMY, G. (1976c) 'What counts as school music?' in WHITTY, G. and YOUNG, M. (Eds) *Explorations in the Politics of School Knowledge*, Driffield, Nafferton Books, pp. 19–34.

VULLIAMY, G. (1977a) 'Music as a case study in the new sociology of education', in SHEPHERD, J., VIRDEN, P., VULLIAMY, G. and WISHART, T. *Whose Music? A Sociology of Musical Languages*, London, Latimer, pp. 201–232.

VULLIAMY, G. (1977b) 'Music and the mass culture debate', in SHEPHERD, J., VIRDEN, P., VULLIAMY, G. and WISHART, T. *Whose Music? A Sociology of Musical Languages*, London, Latimer, pp. 179–200.

VULLIAMY, G. (1978) 'Culture clash and school music: a sociological analysis' in BARTON, L. and MEIGHAN, R. (Eds) *Sociological Interpretations of Schooling and Classrooms: A Reappraisal*, Driffield, Nafferton Books, pp. 115–127.

VULLIAMY, G. (1984) 'A sociological view of music education: an essay in the sociology of knowledge', *Canadian University Music Review*, 5, pp. 17–37.

VULLIAMY, G. and LEE, E. (Eds) (1976) *Pop Music in School*, London, Cambridge University Press.

VULLIAMY, G. and SHEPHERD, J. (1984a) 'The application of a critical sociology to music education', *British Journal of Music Education*, 1, pp. 247–266.

VULLIAMY, G. and SHEPHERD, J. (1984b) 'Sociology and music education: A response to Swanwick', *British Journal of Sociology of Education*, 5, 57–76.

VULLIAMY, G. and SHEPHERD, J. (1985) 'Sociology and music education: A further response to Swanwick', *British Journal of Sociology of Education*, 6, 225–229.

WADSWORTH, M. and ROBINSON, D. (Eds) (1976) *Studies in Everyday Medical Life*, London, Martin Robertson.

WHITTY, G. (1974) 'Sociology and the problem of radical educational change', in FLUDE, M. and AHIER, J. (Eds) *Educability, Schools and Ideology*, London, Croom Helm, pp. 112–137.

WISHART, T. (1977) 'Musical writing, musical speaking', in SHEPHERD, J., VIRDEN, P., VULLIAMY, G. and WISHART, T. (1977) *Whose Music? A*

Sociology of Musical Languages, London, Latimer, pp. 125–153.

WRIGHT, D.F. (1975) 'Musical meaning and its social determinants', *Sociology*, 9, pp. 419–435.

YOUNG, M.F.D. (Ed.) (1971) *Knowledge and Control: New Directions for the Sociology of Education*, London, Collier-Macmillan.

12 On Becoming a Feminist in the Sociology of Education

Miriam E. David

Over the last 20 years I have been involved more or less continuously in the sociology of education. During this period of time my perspective, research ideas and methods have all changed dramatically. In this chapter, I would like to try to account for this radical change of emphasis. I want to argue that the reasons I have moved from doing statistical and empirical research to more policy-oriented and theoretical work are not only a growing 'maturity' but also broader 'political' reasons. The changes came about, first, as I moved from a research-based academic position to a teaching post in an academic social policy setting; second, with a growing commitment to academic women's studies and explicitly feminist research; third, as a result of previous research experiences and a gradual disillusionment with quantitative methods; and fourth, 'senescence', (the theory that old age brings with it conservative political views) although I now feel ready to return to more empirical research, albeit from a feminist perspective.

Tracing the reasons for my shift of focus has led me to examine afresh not only all the stages in the research endeavour from initial conception, through design and execution, to analysis and interpretation, but also to the nature of the biases often hidden within those stages. This has reaffirmed an earlier conclusion of mine that research in both the social sciences generally and in the sociology of education is, at present, sexist. That is, 'it is informed and shaped by a male viewpoint resulting in a distorted picture of social reality' (Eichler, 1986, p. 38). Of course this conclusion is neither startlingly new nor especially original. Increasingly over the last couple of decades feminist scholars have been developing this critique both in the social sciences and in the sociology of education. On the whole, however, such critiques have been of the nature of the research endeavour, uncovering the apparently hidden biases. There has been much less work on developing an alternative approach and, where there has, little agreement on what it might consist of. This is partly because of the lack of consensus on the objectives of the exercise. It is also because of lack of agreement on what constitutes research.

An early and important feminist critique and alternative contribution to feminist research was made by Alison Kelly. She argued that sexism could only intrude on two of the three elements of the research process:

   (i)   choosing the research topic and formulating hypotheses;
  (ii)   carrying out the research and obtaining results;
 (iii)   interpreting results (Kelly, 1978, p. 227).

She argued that feminism can and must enter the first and third stages, but not the second. Indeed, she saw research methods as objective and not susceptible to influence or bias. In other words, feminism could influence only the choice of topic and the analysis and interpretation of results. In the initial stages of developing a feminst critique, this approach was certainly central. However, others have argued against this 'liberal feminist' approach and for an alternative feminist methodology. For example, Ann Oakley has argued for a more explicitly feminist interviewing procedure. She argues for a relationship between interviewer and interviewee which is non-hierarchical and in which the interviewer is prepared to invest his or her own personal identity in the relationship. 'No intimacy without reciprocity' (Oakley, 1981, p. 41). Yet others have argued for even more dramatic solutions. Dorothy Smith (1974) argues that we should take the everyday world in which we are located physically and socially as the problematic and look from the standpoint of women at those social and organizational processes. These differing feminist solutions start from different premises about the research endeavour. They share a common goal of trying to go beyond sexist social science.

This goal of developing an alternative approach to sexist social science is not shared by many, other than committed feminists. Despite the volume of feminist scholarship on research in the last couple of decades, there has been little impact on what might, using a Kuhnian approach, be called normal social science (Eichler, 1986; Kuhn, 1970). As a committed feminist, too, I see the problem of sexism in the social sciences as of such importance that it needs to be solved before we can proceed with the endeavour traditionally known as research in the social sciences. Moreover, if we are to convince others of the urgency and importance of the problem we have not only to continue to demonstrate the ways in which sexism intrudes in the research process at every stage (however these stages may be defined, depending on one's approach) but also to present a viable alternative. Otherwise other researchers can with impunity argue that the problem of sexism may now be severe but that it is unavoidable.

It can be argued that feminists have begun to develop two differing alternative approaches to sexism in the social sciences. One of these approaches, however, may not be seen as generalizable as it attempts to redress the balance of the male bias by substituting a female bias. In other words, this is what may be called the 'woman-centred' approach, or women's studies as a form of what Spender has called 'men's studies modified' or feminist studies (1982). In essence, this involves research on, by and about women. A second approach is what Eichler has called 'non-sexist'. This approach attempts to eliminate all biases on the basis of sex, whether male or female, and develop a solution to research which, whilst being sensitive to the problems of sexism, is, in essence, sex-neutral. It would attempt to present a picture of social reality, incorporating both male and female perspectives.

Reassessing the ways in which I have engaged in research is one way in which I can begin to develop a model of what is possible or not possible as far as feminist or non-sexist research is concerned, at the same time as reinterpreting the impact that sexism has had on the general research process and my research approach in particular. In the conclusion to this paper, I shall try to develop a way of doing research in the sociology of education which goes beyond both the sexist bias and the feminist attempt to alter that bias by developing a woman-centred approach. It is, therefore, an attempt to develop a more universalistic, non-sexist approach to the sociology of education, incorporating both male and female perspectives.

In tracing my own personal development, I will draw heavily on a model proposed by Eichler for understanding the stages of social science research and feminist efforts to eliminate sexism. Eichler draws on Kuhn's paradigm for scientific revolutions to argue that 'normal social science' has been relatively unaffected by 'the impressive amount of work done by feminist scholars in a very short time'. She argues that 'normal social science' remains sexist, untouched by what 'may at best constitute a bit of unrest that is taking place at the distant margins of their respective fields, just barely at the periphery of their field of vision, and therefore at most dimly perceived' (1986, p. 42). She argues that this constitutes the 'business as usual approach'. A second approach is that in which the claims of sexism have been acknowledged and incorporated into the conventional research endeavour. She argues that this is the 'liberal' approach, and that it

> results in studies that show that one's own theoretical framework — Marxism, phenomenology, ethnomethodology, demography, symbolic interactionism, role theory, etc. — are in fact admirably fitted to incorporate women. It results in publications which have, typically, one chapter or one section on women, often connected by an 'and', namely whatever the topic is 'and' women (1986, p. 43).

Eichler's third and fourth alternatives to the problems of sexism in research in the social sciences are those that I have already mentioned as the 'woman-centred' or 'non-sexist' approaches. Both of these argue that women cannot simply be 'added-on' to conventional research strategies, but that alternatives need to be developed. She then looks at the relationship between these two latter approaches.

Eichler's model of solutions to sexism in research in the social sciences seems admirably suited to understanding my own personal development. I shall now attempt to account for my changing approach by showing how I have moved through these four solutions as a result of a number of external influences on my sociological research career.

Business as Usual

As an undergraduate at Leeds University in the mid-1960s, I was trained in what we would now call 'the business as usual' approach to sociology. This was despite the best efforts of my teachers to develop a 'new' sociology, which was to be a radical or Marxian approach, sometimes then referred to as 'Rexian' sociology. It drew on John Rex's newly published *Key Problems in Sociological Theory* and, later, one of my tutors developed the themes in a now classic article 'The Two Sociologies' (Dawe, 1970). This innovative approach eschewed all reference to sexual divisions. It was an attempt to operationalize a new theoretical perspective. The model chosen for this empirical method was Neal Gross's *Explorations in Role Analysis*, a study of the conflicting expectations of the role of the school superintendent. This engrossing study indeed captured my imagination and I became determined to replicate the study for another role in the British educational system. Such an aim remained with me until I eventually went to the USA six years later to the Centre for Educational Policy Research at Harvard University, in 1972. Neal Gross had left the Harvard Graduate School of Education a few years previously and his study was no longer seen as a model for educational research. I was finally rudely disabused of his, and his research methodology's, eminence.

But I run ahead of my research development. Neal Gross' model for research not only influenced my interest in research topic and overarching methodology. It was also influential in that it involved large-scale survey methods of investigation and statistical analysis. Arguably, too, it was not pure empiricism because it was an attempt to test hypotheses drawn from a rigorous theoretical framework. It therefore confirmed me and, I believe, some of my fellow students in the necessity and efficacy of large-scale social research, utilizing complex social statistics. I had, in any event, a penchant for such statistical methods as I had not only studied elementary statistics at school but also followed optional courses in statistical theory and demography at Leeds University. I prided myself on my numeracy and interest in statistical methods.

When I graduated the climate of opinion amongst sociology students was that it was morally reprehensible to take up any career in industry and so serve capitalism. Our choices of career were therefore strictly circumscribed. We could either become social re-searchers, academics or teachers or some combination of research degree and part-time teaching. Indeed, teaching at secondary, fur-ther or higher education level was seen very much as our mission and a way of changing the world. It also absolved us of any respon-sibility for maintaining the capitalist system or so we rather naively believed. I decided against doing a research degree and part-time teaching, although I harboured a desire to do a role analysis of school-teachers.

Instead, in part persuaded by my parents that a career in statis-tics and computing would be more secure than in teaching, I took a post as a statistical research assistant. I was also put off a career in teaching by my mother who had herself been a full-time teacher and a married woman returner when I started secondary school. She did not want any of her three daughters to teach. Ironically, we are all now teachers. My two sisters teach in further and secondary educa-tion and I in higher education. But again I run ahead. This is just to argue that my involvement in the sociology of education as a specialty was delayed by the influences of my mother, and the technological focus of my father, who was a professional engineer.

My job as a statistical research assistant was at the London University postgraduate Institute of Psychiatry on a US-funded study of cross-cultural comparisons of mental illness. I was immediately thrown into a large-scale survey of mental patients at hospitals in London and New York. My tasks were various, but I was not at all involved in the design of the study. That was the preserve of the psychiatrists who had proposed it. I was both an administrator of data collection and low-level analyst of the data. At first my tasks were those of a clerk: filing, coding and classifying the two sets of interview schedules. One was called a 'present-state' examination; the other a history of the patient. I also had to transfer the data from the interview schedules to punch cards. I was also expected to devise ways of analyzing the data on the computer. However, at that time (1966) there was considerable ambivalence about the use of computers and the computers themselves were not very sophisticated, relying on punch cards and paper-tapes for the programs. The chief statistician at the Institute continued to do all his analyses, even factor analysis, on a manual desk calculator! A computer programmer had been appointed recently to the Institute and I was given a crash course in Fortran, computer programming. I was then expected to write programmes to analyze both parametric and non-parametric statistics. Having written the program, I also had to punch it on to paper-tape and run the data on to the computer. It took me a very long time to test the program as I was a very bad, or rather inaccurate, typist and found it impossible to get the program correctly on to the paper-tape without several efforts at splicing together bits of paper-tape. This whole operation was both extremely time-consuming and tedious. It also seemed to be very removed from the stuff of the social analysis — the mental patients, themselves.

During this time, I also toyed with the idea of doing a higher degree, looking at some other aspect of the patients than their 'mental state' or family history of mental illness. I became interested in the precipitating factors leading to the admission to hospital. I planned to look at the conflicting pressures on patients leading to their desire to be in hospital or the necessity of hospitalization: a variant of role analysis. In the event I did not undertake such a study because some of the literature becoming available then criticized this whole approach to mental illness. Both Laing (1960) and

Szasz (1961) presented alternative, more humanistic, approaches to the study of mental illness.

I was also finding this kind of job more difficult and unrewarding than I had anticipated. I took a three-month leave of absence and lived in Israel, during which time I did some interviewing of American settlers, for the Israeli Institute of Social Research. This was infinitely more satisfying than managing data collection and data analysis. It reawakened my interest in social research. I returned to the Diagnostic Project only to find that my job now was more thoroughly computer-based data analysis.

Being a lone statistical research assistant on a project staffed by male psychiatrists of some professional standing is a hazardous, lonely business. It requires some strength of character to withstand their innuendoes that, being a young single woman, I was only marking time until I could find the right marriage partner. Unable then to understand my social situation fully (and probably half-agreeing with them), I became very depressed. I spent much of my time weeping alone in one of the offices converted from an ECT room. The three psychiatrists, one of whom specialized in women's depression, never noticed! I found another research post and left! I was not yet fully disillusioned with this kind of work and the job prospects it offers research assistants.

My second research post was in the Department of Social Administration at the London School of Economics. It was on a large-scale study of the incidence of gambling. The two lecturer-directors and two research assistants had already decided on the design of the sample and had appointed a woman to select and train the proposed market research interviewers and manage the process of coding, classifying and punching the data on to tape. The plan was to carry out three area surveys, each one relying on hired interviewers, managed by one of the three research assistants. It remained for us all to design the questionnaire. This was our first task. Given the people on the project — two male lecturers in the Social Administration Department and two other sociologists, one a male contemporary of the lecturers and one a woman contemporary of mine — this process promised to be much more stimulating and rewarding. Indeed, the design of the questionnaire was an interesting task. It also involved consideration of data analysis which would be appropriate to the questions asked. One of the two lecturers who was a high-powered statistician insisted on designing some of the tables of analysis prior to designing the questions. He argued that one should know what one wished to argue before going into the field. Certainly it forced us all to consider why we wanted to ask the questions we did. It also helped with the piloting of the questionnaire. On the other hand, it forced us only to ask questions suitable for such tabular analysis.

Studying gambling as a social activity also forced me to examine its social context. It is perhaps here, most of all, that sexism entered the study. We were interested in looking at the relationship between gambling and other activities and, from a study of the literature, concluded that it was most closely connected with work and leisure. We took a particularly male perspective. Although we were very influenced by the recent fatherhood of all three of the men and their current obsession with early child-care we only drafted questions about child-care as a part of leisure. We did not focus on child-care and housework as women's *work*, albeit unpaid. I now feel somewhat embarrassed that I felt irritated with my three male colleagues for their focus on such family activities in this way. My gradual awareness of women's issues, then, was a desire not to have children and be involved in such women's work. I wanted to be 'liberated' and saw independence achieved only by paid employment and non-parenthood.

We also ignored the differences in the social contexts of men and women. Our only worry was how to elicit private family information from the interviewees. We particularly needed to know family or household income and its relationship to the pattern of spending on gambling and other activities. Accepting the conventional wisdom that women in particular either do not know or do not want to divulge such confidential information we carefully designed a way of eliciting the income levels separately from the other questions. This elaborate procedure took no account of the issues of sex and the relationships between interviewees and interviewers. In the event most of our interviewers were women and about half the sample were.

The administration of the questionnaires, whilst bearing some similarity to the previous project, was far less 'sexist'. I did not feel myself a 'servant' of the interviewers, as I had with the three psychiatrists. Indeed, my relationship was different. The interviewers were nearly all married women doing a small part-time job in market research and administering a questionnaire not designed by themselves. I was 'in charge' of ensuring their training and their adequacy as interviewers. Here as in the previous study, though, we ignored the whole question of the sex of the interviewer in relationship to the sex of the interviewee, unlike Ann Oakley (1981) or Carol Smart (1984).

The more difficult part of the study was the data analysis. Although computers were becoming slightly more sophisticated the methods of analysis remained crude. In particular, there were as yet no survey statistical packages. For the most part, we had to write our own programs. However, we now had help from a number of statisticians and computer programmers more well-versed in social survey analysis. Nevertheless the problems of using computers remained large and we frequently had to resort to the private hire of Imperial College's computer at the weekend, often a Saturday night, to try to get the data analyzed. Despite the expense and the external help we failed in this period to get the data analyzed adequately. Mechanical and technical failures beset the whole process. Finally I was forced to look for another job as funds had run out before the project was written up.

During the course of the project I had taken on some part-time teaching for London University's Extra-Mural Department for the Diploma in Sociology. I found this work, mainly with mature women students, extremely enjoyable. However, although I now had a choice between a job teaching sociology in a polytechnic or being a researcher in a university Economics Department, I chose to stay in full-time research. I continued to teach part-time for the Diploma in Sociology and developed a new course on sociological theory. I also was offered some part-time teaching on statistics and political sociology in the department. This decision to remain a researcher on 'soft' money had far-reaching consequences. It involved me centrally in educational research yet at the same time confirmed me in my marginal and female academic status as researcher. Only two other members of the combined economics and politics department were women: all the rest were men and all were lecturers or in senior positions. On the other hand, I had only a vaguely defined research project which I could shape, design and develop as I wished. Professor Maurice Peston had obtained funds for a three-year research project on decision-making in local education authorities (LEAs) from the DES. I was appointed to develop and carry out the study.

I did not, of course, have complete license to design the study: the parameters had been clearly set by Professor Peston and the DES. Nevertheless, Professor Peston did not really want day-to-day involvement and I had considerable freedom within that context to do a more sociological than economic analysis of LEA decision-making. I designed a two-part study. I would look at the decision-makers in LEAs and analyze their roles, relying again on a modified version of Gross' role analysis. I would also do case studies of how certain decisions were made, looking back at issues after the event. Here the majority of the decisions investigated were of the reorganization of secondary education on comprehensive lines. I also looked at the reorganization of higher education and the setting up of North-East London Polytechnic and at the internal reorganization of two LEA education departments. The focus was on administrative and professional decision-making rather than the more overtly political aspects of the decisions.

In this design I avoided a statistical approach, although I planned a lot of interviews with education officers. I had come to believe that statistical methods were not the only or most appropriate way of analyzing social questions and were fraught with technical complications. Since the sample of LEAs was to be small, because of the costs of travel built into the research funds, I decided that semi-structured interviews with the professional staff of education offices would yield the necessary data for a study of professional organization: about fifty interviews in all. This would also provide the basis for the case studies of an actual decision taken, although these would be followed by study of the archival and administrative material on file. Analysis would be a form of content analysis and manual analysis of the interview schedules. This plan meant that I avoided having to use the computer, about which I was heartily relieved.

I had not anticipated, however, some of the pitfalls involved in the interviewing of an almost entirely male population and in spending long hours absorbed in archival data. In particular, my own job interview had made me absolutely determined to complete the study satisfactorily, since I had been cautioned not to leave on the grounds of marriage before the study was completed. However, this became a 'double-bind' situation for my determination led me into a number of what might be considered compromising situations. I was subject to a lot of what would now be called 'sexual harassment', although I did not realize it at the time or give that name. I had patronizing comments made, paternalistic ones and directly sexual comments. On the whole, however, I was treated as a rather naive young girl who was doing a rather trivial study. On the other hand, I posed no personal or professional threat to the status of the interviewees and so was given an enormous amount of 'secret' or 'confidential' information on professional rivalries that had no relevance to the study and no meaning to me. I kept the filing cabinet full of such interview schedules for fifteen years before I felt able to have them shredded. I certainly had no way, at that time, of making sense of this kind of sexism in research procedures, nor did I find or was I given guidance on such matters in the literature on research methodology. I ignored it in my research reports and publications (David, 1971, 1972, 1973, 1975 and 1977; Peston and David, 1973).

Towards the end of the study, I was encouraged to develop another research project to enable me to continue to work in the Department. Initially, I started to plan a study of chief education officers alone, hoping to interview all 144. But I was becoming very disillusioned with this kind of lonely social research, despite having appointed a research assistant for two of the three years of the DES study. I felt that working in the USA might reinvigorate me. So instead of doing an entirely British study I planned a comparison of chief education officers with school superintendents in the USA. Miraculously, the SSRC agreed to fund such a study for two years, allowing me to appoint another research assistant to do the English part of the study, whilst I did the American. I was offered a base in the Centre for Educational Policy Research (CEPR) at the Harvard Graduate School of Education. Having written up a first draft of the DES study, I set off for the USA in the summer of 1972.

Although I had managed to read an enormous amount of the literature on educational politics, administration and decision-making before I designed the study I had not anticipated the nuances of the differences in educational and social research in the USA. The study I had planned was completely out of fashion and did not accord with the social and political realities. CEPR had just completed a major study of inequality and were much more interested in either a quantitative or a more political study (Jencks, *et al.*, 1972). I still did not want to return to a statistical study so I planned a study of educational decision-making which would focus on both the political and administrative aspects. I was particularly influenced by some of the other social researchers at CEPR, especially its director. I therefore did a study of the budgetary process in four school districts (smaller equivalents of LEAs). I carefully selected four districts, to compare and contrast social and class composition and style of government. This was very different from the planned study but in several trans-Atlantic discussions it was agreed that the two studies could stand in their own right.

Again, I did not predict the difficulties of doing this kind of qualitative research on a largely, although not entirely, male population. I chose to study two localities which were governed by means of direct democracy; that is, they held town meetings to vote on and finalize the annual budget. One was to be very wealthy; the other rather more middle class. I also planned to find two more 'inner city', lower middle class or working class areas which were governed by means of the more usual system of representative democracy. These two latter areas proved very difficult to find. I did not have a car of my own and therefore needed to find areas in reach of Cambridge, Mass. by means of public transport. I therefore decided on Cambridge itself as one of the areas. I had been advised not to choose the adjacent locality — Somerville — as it was riven by political strife. Cambridge was seen to be only marginally less so. Despite it containing the most exclusive and prestigious university in the USA, it was a rather ethnically mixed, working class school district. It contained large ethnic minorities of black and Portuguese. It had recently made an imaginative new appointment of a school superintendent. I approached him, having approached three others in other localities, for permission to do the study. I was rather taken aback by his bargaining procedure. He wanted some form of payment for permission to interview his staff and the school board members and to sit in on the public meetings. (By this stage, I had spent 'three years attending such meetings in England without the penalty of payment). Naively I assumed he wanted me to do some work in the office and I volunteered my services. I then realized that the services requested were probably sexual, so I quickly withdrew my research request. I found another school district instead — which was at the other end of the subway line, namely Quincy.

I was deeply disturbed by this incident. I had, for some time, come to see this kind of research as rather parasitical. I did believe that I should be able to offer some kind of exchange for the time afforded by interviewees. In the earlier English study I had felt that my work might contribute to 'better' decision-making and that the interviewees 'benefitted' in the sense of having an interviewer give them time and attention. Indeed, my filing cabinet already bore testimony to that.

Aware now that the other school districts and/or their superintendents might request similar favours to the Cambridge man, I offered my comparative report for their approval before publication. This, too, proved to be an enormous error. Having carried out interviews with all the school board members (about thirty in all for the four districts) and attended the relevant cycle of meetings in all four districts for the budgetary process, I wrote a thirty-page paper summarizing my findings and sent it to the four superintendents. By this stage I knew them all quite well and had been subject to milder forms of sexual harassment from them in varying degrees. In fact, as in England, I found their offers of drinks and meals too difficult to refuse and my own budget was at a minimum during the course of the fieldwork. I still harbour guilt and regret at not having been firm enough to refuse these social niceties. I comfort myself with the fact that the quality of my data is the richer for having been pleasantly obliging to these men. It does raise the important general question of where 'professional' research ends and personal life begins: issues that have subsequently been explored as sexual harassment at work (Backhouse and Cohen, 1978).

In my report, I tried to be objective and compare and contrast different styles of budgetary decision-making. One of the four districts had developed a modern method of budgeting drawn from the US Federal system — PPBS. The others maintained more traditional styles. Personally I was not very impressed with PPBS, since it had been developed by the Pentagon for the war in Vietnam. However I did not include that in my report. The reactions of the four superintendents and their staffs to my brief report took me completely by surprise. Three of them were pleased to receive it and did not offer detailed comments, although one printed a small comment on it in the local newspaper. The fourth, Quincy, wrote a sixty-page commentary which indicated that they were deeply offended. They presumed I preferred Wellesley's PPBS style and defended their own old-fashioned methods. Their comments were both abusive and tantamount to libellous, seeing me as an incompetent social researcher. I still smart to think of their comments. I suspect that they felt exposed as the most working class and poorest of the four districts. However, I had liked them the best and been most impressed with and attracted to their democratic style of government, despite the fact that they could not constitutionally hold town meetings.

This kind of evaluative and qualitative research was a salutory lesson to me. I rewrote and extended the report into a monograph which was published later in the USA, and I wrote a lengthy paper which was published in the *Journal of Social Policy* (David, 1973b, 1975b and 1976). I determined not to do this kind of fieldwork for a long time. I also rewrote the DES study and submitted some of that for a Ph.D. which was awarded. The study was also published by the National Foundation for Educational Research (David, 1977). The rest of the SSRC study was left to the research assistant to complete and publish on his own (Neve, 1978).

I had had my fill of social research. I applied for other jobs and, although offered a prestigious job as deputy director of a large LEA research and statistics department, eventually turned it down in favour of an academic teaching post in the Department of Social Administration at Bristol University.

The 'Liberal' Approach

During my time as a full-time researcher, I had become involved in the women's liberation movement. However, I had seen it as a political campaign, separate from my academic work. Embarking on a 'new' career as a university teacher rather than researcher opened up all sorts of possibilities. In particular, the context of being in a university with several other women with interests in women's studies allowed for more collaborative and focused work, and teaching. For example, three of us devised an optional course for second and third-year undergraduates, which was called 'Family and Social Policy'. It was a way of including women in conventional studies — 'adding-on'.

I was not engaged in any new research at this stage. I completed the DES and SSRC studies and then was approached by one of the two former directors of the gambling project to help write up the study. I agonized about the decision, not wanting to return to this kind of research but disliking incompleteness. I recognized that it would delay the development of my own research. However, I agreed to it and managed to rework some of the data so that we were able to demonstrate differences between men and women in their involvement in gambling and leisure (Downes, Davies, David and Stone, 1976). Again, this essentially constituted 'adding-on'.

I then embarked upon a study of the political confrontation at the William Tyndale primary school. It seemed to be a way of developing from my gender-blind studies of the politics of education to making sexual divisions more explicit. However, the situation was extremely complex and was not easily amenable to that kind of analysis. In fact, the parents — mothers — were arguably the more conservative in the events, although there were obvious reasons for their strategies. (David, 1978).

Given the nature of my work situation in a conventional

academic department, although increasingly drawn to women's studies as an exclusive activity, I did not feel able to embark on such research to the exclusion of more 'normal' social policy. I chose instead to do a historical, and secondary sources, study of educational policy and the assumptions about women's position in the family, school and employment (David, 1980). It was essentially an attempt to make explicit deeply embedded assumptions about the relations between men and women, and their implications for educational policy and practice. This study arose out of my teaching on the family and social policy course and was directly related to my course lectures and material. I did not explicitly consider methodology, although my theoretical framework was Marxian and I relied on the historical method and the traditional approaches to the analysis of official documents used in the study of social administration. I was determined now to avoid both fieldwork and quantitative methods. The view was shared by my closest colleague and friend, with whom I taught the course, Hilary Land. We both felt the need to revise official histories in social policy, rather than doing more empirical research (see, for example, Land, 1976; David and Land, 1983). The study of social policy traditionally lent itself to a variant of our approach.

The Woman-Centred Approach

During this time in Bristol, we developed a more structured approach to academic women's studies. I was particularly fortunate to have several stimulating feminist colleagues and friends. We also became part of a wider national network of academic feminists. Gradually we all began to develop our political interests as academic concerns. In particular, I became involved with a group of feminists interested in the sociology of education. Sandra Acker was instrumental in setting up a Centre for the Study of Women and Education in the Bristol School of Education and I became closely involved in that as an ongoing research activity.

Although I did not feel able to teach women's studies as a separate and independent subject to undergraduate or postgraduate diploma students, I felt able to supervise higher degrees by research which focused on women. I eventually had three students who completed research in this area (Trustram, 1984), although only one was in the sociology of education. This latter study utilized similar methods to my own; historical case studies but of further education for girls and women (Blunden, 1983). Such research supervision contained problems of its own, rather different from research supervision generally. In particular, feminist politics expected more personal and non-hierarchical relationships between women than is conventional in academic departments, with assumptions about styles of professionalism. It was extremely difficult to develop non-hierarchical relationships in a situation which relied for its essence on relations of dominance and submission. Staff-student relations are not of equality. Since they involve, whether at undergraduate or postgraduate level, assessment and judgment of student performance they cannot be entirely egalitarian. Finding ways of modifying and personalizing these relationships became extremely fraught. It was further complicated by the fact that I had more than one student. Interpersonal relationships and rivalries inevitably played a part. I found myself in a matronage, rather than patronage, role and although motherliness is more caring than paternalism it carries with it fewer external perks. Since I felt myself subordinate in the wider academic institution, I was unable to confer adequate rewards on my female postgraduates.

The subordination and sexism was most keenly felt when I had to confront an almost entirely male Faculty Board and justify the use of the term 'feminist study' in the title of one of the three studies. It was conventional for Faculty Board to ratify thesis titles and I could not recall any previous objections. A philosophy lecturer argued that since there was no such enterprise as feminist methodology, the term was redundant in the title and should be removed. Eventually the title was accepted on the grounds that there were different methodologies and if a Marxist study were acceptable as a title, then so too should a feminist study. Of course these little incidents affect the course of one's own research development.

I decided to pursue women's studies at arm's length from the institution. I had been involved in teaching courses for the Extra-Mural Department and a group of us came together in what became known as the Bristol Women's Studies Group to prepare a textbook for courses in women's studies (BWSG, 1979). This involved a lot of research, especially into hidden areas and of ephemera, to produce material on women's experiences throughout the life-cycle. We included a lot of material on both formal education and child-rearing and socialization. This collective research was extremely enjoyable since we were all, by now, passionately involved in the issues. Although most of us were sociologists we were extremely eclectic in our approach and methods, relying on history, literature, poetry, biography, autobiography and ephemera such as political campaigning newsletters. The book has gained an international reputation of which we are proud, although it may not be treated as a serious research document within British academic institutions. This study led on to further forms of feminist research collaboration, although it was not our only activity within the institution. We always felt constrained by its male bias not to pursue only women-centred activities. Nevertheless in terms of research, our networks became increasingly feminist ones. This was consolidated by a growing national group of feminist researchers, especially in the sociology of education. It was also facilitated by the start of the Westhill International Sociology of Education conferences. It became possible for us to meet together regularly and share interests and concerns. This network has been particularly crucial to my academic and research development, providing support and enrichment, especially at the times when the going has been more difficult. It also helped to sustain my interests in education studies and feminism when my academic workplace was at some distance from them.

The Non-Sexist Approach

Doing research on women had fired my imagination but I still felt constrained by my institution and the department I was in to have a wider perspective than women only. I chose for my next research topic the study of the history and contemporary practice of child-rearing, taking an explicitly feminist perspecitve. Although the study was to be of women's roles as mothers and carers, it also required study of the development of the sexual division of labour and institutional arrangements for child-care and education. It seemed to be an obvious combination of my twin interests in women's studies and in education and social policies. It also allowed me to continue with qualitative and documentary research, rather than quantitative and computer-based studies. I still did not see the importance of doing interview studies of women's experiences, although this does now seem to be a possibility. This approach also invited another aspect of feminist methodology, which we had practised in the Bristol Women's Studies Group — that of collective or collaborative research. Indeed, my collaborator on this study, Caroline New, pushed me beyond my traditional confines of official policy studies, to explore social structures and processes that influence the development of official policies and practices. She had trained as a philosopher and sociologist and, being an independent social researcher, was less hidebound and constrained by academic institutional practices than I. It was refreshing to consider such possibilities, although it was not without its costs in an institution as sexist as Bristol University. Such research, crossing disciplinary boundaries and essentially on the topic of women, remains low status and also subordinate to quantitative research. I did not feel valued as a 'normal' social researcher and indeed my research was not considered of sufficient merit for the purposes of promotion to reader or senior lecturer. Moreover, such critical research is not likely to endear one to one's colleagues, whether male or female. I have been accused of libel and publicly vilified in a newspaper attack on the work of sociologists. In these circumstances it is hard to remain immune from sensitivity.

Developing a collaborative approach to the study proved very difficult. Despite our desire to go beyond traditional individualistic research practices, we had been thoroughly socialized and found it hard to escape them. Both doing the documentary and literature research and writing it up together was never easy. We tried a variety of methods: doing it separately and together. As we wrote in the foreword to the book:

> Some chapters we wrote and rewrote separately, some together: one, after lots of wine, into a dictaphone, punctuated with 'ers' and giggles. We eventually decided — on our last chapter — that the best method was to agree an outline, then for each to write a complete draft, and then amalgamate them jointly. Sometimes we were forced to work separately. Caroline had only twelve child-free hours a week during 1983 and Miki had the usual teaching and administrative responsibilities of her university post. She was given study leave for the summer term to work on the book ... (New and David, 1985, p. 9).

Our choice of topic derived very much from our personal experiences. We were by this time both mothers, and had had to search for personal and practical solutions to the question of child-care. This also compelled us to look for theoretical answers to the question of child-care. But there are dilemmas about this because of the intense emotions.

> Certainly we became painfully aware of these dilemmas in the process of writing the book. We were both mothers when we came to write it, inspired both by common cir-

cumstances and divergent 'choices'. Caroline had not estab-lished a career to be sacrificed and had uneasily accepted the traditional place in the family, working part-time in a series of temporary jobs. Miki had a well-established career, and worried about sacrificing career or baby or both. Although both our partners were committed to fatherhood — both of them coming from loving Jewish family backgrounds — it was we who made whatever choices were to be made about the kinds and combinations of work and care we would create.... It is no accident that it was we, the women, who came together to write this book, rather than the men we live with. (New and David, 1985, p. 17–18).

However, although it was 'inevitable' that we as women chose this topic to research, we tried to develop a non-sexist analysis and solution to the issue. Our aim was not just to redress the balance in favour of women. Again as we argued:

Most feminist work is about the relationships between men and women. One simple reason for this is that women's subordination and male dominance are two sides of the same coin. So much is written about the ways in which this relationship operates: through marriage and sexual relations; through violence, as well as the gentle side of heterosexual relationships; through law and economic and social policies.... But all these questions are simpler in a way than the ones we have chosen to tackle. They do not force the writer and reader to ask 'How can women, men and children cooperate and live together'? As soon as you think about children and their care, this question becomes urgent and obvious.... Children are not yet the men and women who dominate and are dominated. There must be a way of shap-ing our society that stops children ever becoming the rigid men and women we so often see. (*ibid*, p. 20–21).

Our project was therefore to investigate how our society came to be as 'sexist' as it is and how we could develop ways of overcoming that sexism and making social arrangements in the interests of men, women and children. We therefore investigated not only historical arrangements and contemporary policies but also some projects that challenged conventional arrangements. We were firmly of the belief that a feminist perspective led us to a non-sexist approach to these fundamental issues. We proposed changes in the relationships between work, child-care and parenthood, inevitably also influencing the institution of education. (David, 1984, 1985 and 1986).

The quiet reception that our book has received has confirmed us in the belief that these issues remain marginal to the enterprise of social science. It has only been acknowledged as a publication, not deemed of sufficient interest to sociologists to merit a review, by *Network*, the bulletin of the British Sociological Association, the latest issue of which was published six months after our book appeared in a sociology series. Moreover, the study of children, in terms of both care and education, remains low status and combined with a feminist perspective and methodology is at best marginal and at worst ignored. Yet if we are to develop a non-sexist approach to research in the social sciences, which I believe is fundamentally important, we have to begin to expose these issues.

Conclusions

Which one of the four strategies for research now appears to be the most useful for understanding sexual divisions and going beyond both the sexist and feminist biases in research on the sociology of education? I would now want to argue strongly for the non-sexist approach to both methodology and analysis. However, I would want research questions to be chosen with sensitivity to issues of sex and sexism in all stages of the research process. In other words, choice of research study must be drawn from a theoretical perspective which includes feminism. The woman-centred approach whilst uncovering the hidden dimension of women's lives allows for feminist research to remain marginal to the central preoccupations of social science and the sociology of education. If the concern of the sociology of education is to contribute to the understanding of how our lives might be improved or even transformed then we need to consider the full ramifications of the relations between men, women and children. We need to do this in the ways in which we formulate research questions, conduct our inquiries and investigations, and in the conclusions and implications which we draw. Such heightened awareness of the ways in which sexism intrudes at every stage of the research process would help us to develop methodologies which are sensitive to gender and sexual divisions. For example, interviewing techniques need to take account of the conventionally structured power relations between men and women and the implications that these may have for the quality of data collected. Moreover, we need to be clear on the reasons for, and value of, the research to those who become our research subjects. There is an element of exchange hidden in the research process which needs to be made explicit. It may, of course, be that the exchange for research subjects lies in the fact of being given attention and respect during the process of research. But this is not self-evident and research designs need to take account of these questions of reciprocity. In woman-centred research, as Ann Oakley and others have argued, such exchanges are easier to negotiate given the objectives of this kind of research of uncovering hidden social and sexual processes.

Nevertheless, it is possible to imbue conventional research methodologies with such ideas, making explicit the range of hidden and structured social and sexual processes. Until we do this feminists at very least will remain sceptical of the value of such research, seeing it as full of male bias. Hester Eisenstein, reviewing the history of feminist thought from 1970, has argued that there are three strategies available to women to change their political and social position. Such strategies for political action match the research strategies that have been mapped in this essay. She too rejects both the liberal or equal opportunities option, and the woman-centred one which, she argues, creates 'an otherworld of female retreat'. She therefore opts for an approach which combines what she calls 'womanly values' with conventional liberal strategies. She writes that the most hopeful feminist project is

> associating feminism with the liberating traditions of West-
> ern thought ... tending in the direction of greater equality
> ... but transforming ... them with woman-centred values
> of nurturance and intimacy, as necessary and legitimate goals
> of political life. (1984, pp. 144–5).

This remains a useful strategy for not only political organization but also research. It means going beyond either male or female bias to create a strategy which will attend to sexism and create the knowledge on which we might begin to understand how these deeply embedded processes can be transformed.

Acknowledgements

I should like to thank Sandra Acker and Ann Woodhouse for their extremely supportive and useful comments on an earlier draft of this essay. I also wish to acknowledge my indebtedness to Margrit Eichler for her inspiration and approach.

References

BACKHOUSE, C. and COHEN, L. (1978) *The Secret Oppression: Sexual Harrassment at Work*, London, MacMillan.

BLUNDEN, G. (1983) 'Typing in the Tech: domesticity, ideology and women's place in further education', in GLEESON, D. (Ed.) *Youth Training and the Search for Work*, London, Routledge and Kegan Paul.

BRISTOL WOMEN'S STUDIES GROUP (1979) *Half the Sky: an Introduction to Women's Studies*, London, Virago; republished with an annotated and revised bibliography, 1984.

DAVID, M.E. (1971) 'CEOs — pioneer or prisoner?', *Education*, 137, 13, pp. 272–274.

DAVID, M.E. (1972) 'Management styles in LEAs', *Education*, special supplement, 138, 8, pp. 3–5.

DAVID, M.E. (1973a) 'Approaches to organizational change in LEAs', research report, *Educational Administration Bulletin*, 1, 2, pp. 24–34.

DAVID, M.E. (1973b) 'The citizen's voice in education', *New Society*, 25, 569, 30, August, pp. 513–4.

David, M.E. (1975a) 'Approaches to organizational change in LEAs', *Durham Research Review*, VII, 35, pp. 1047–1057.

DAVID, M.E. (1975b) *School rule in the USA*, Ballinger Publishing Co.

DAVID, M.E. (1976) 'Professionalism and participation in school budgeting in the USA', *Journal of School Policy*, 5, 2, pp. 151–166.

DAVID, M.E. (1977) *Reform, Reaction and Resources: The 3Rs of Educational Planning*, Windsor NFER Publishing Co.

DAVID, M.E. (1978) 'The family-education couple: towards an analysis of the William Tyndale's dispute', in LITTLEJOHN, G. *et al.* (Eds) *Power and the State*, Beckenham, BSA with Croom Helm.

DAVID, M.E. (1980) *The State, the Family and Education*, London, Routledge and Kegan Paul.

DAVID, M.E. (1984) 'Women, family and education', in ACKER, S. *et al.* (Eds) *The Yearbook of Education 1984: Women and Education*, London, Kogan Page.

DAVID, M.E. (1985) 'Motherhood and social policy: A matter for education?', *Critical Social Policy*, 12, pp. 28–43.

DAVID, M.E. (1986) 'Teaching family matters', *British Journal of Sociology of Education*, 7, 1, pp. 35–57.

DAVID, M.E. and LAND, H. (1983) 'Sex and social policy', in GLENNERSTER, H. (Ed.) *The Future of the Welfare State*, London, Heinemann.

DAWE, A. (1970) 'The two sociologies', *British Journal of Sociology*.

DOWNES, D.M., DAVIES, B.P., DAVID, M.E. and STONE, P. (1976) *Gambling, Work and Leisure*, London, Routledge and Kegan Paul.

EICHLER, M. (1986) 'The relationship between sexist, non-sexist, woman-centred and feminist research', paper delivered at the annual meeting of the American Sociological Association in Detroit, August 1983. Reprinted in McCORMACK, T. (Ed.) *Studies in Communications*, Vol. 3, JAI Press.

EISENSTEIN, H. (1984) *Contemporary Feminist Thought*, London, Allen and Unwin.

GROSS, N. *et al.* (1958) *Explorations in Role Analysis*, Chichester, Wiley and Co.

JENCKS, C. *et al.* (1972) *Inequality: A Reassessment of Family and Schooling in America*, New York, Basic Books.

KELLY, A. (1978) 'Feminism and research', in *Women's Studies International Quarterly*, 1, 3, pp. 225–232.

KUHN, T. (1970) *The Structure of Scientific Revolutions*, Chicago, University of Chicago Press.

LAING, R.D. (1960) *The Divided Self*, Harmondsworth, Penguin.

LAND, H. (1976) 'Women: supporters or supported?', in BARKER, D.L. and ALLEN, S. (Eds) *Women: Sexual Divisions and Society*, London, Longmans.

NEW, C. and DAVID, M. (1985) *For the Children's Sake: Making Child Care More than Women's Business*, Harmondsworth, Penguin.

NEVE, B. (1977) 'Bureaucracy and politics in local government: The role of the local authority education officers', *Public Administration*, Autumn.

OAKLEY, A. (1981) 'Interviewing women: A contradiction in terms', in ROBERTS, H. (Ed.) *Doing Feminist Research*, London, Routledge and Kegan Paul.

PESTON, M. and DAVID, M. (1973) 'Planning in LEAs', in *Local Government Studies*, 2, pp. 39–46.

REX, J. (1966) *Key Problems in Sociological Theory*, London, Routledge and Kegan Paul.

SCHEFF, T. (1966) *Being Mentally Ill*, London, Weidenfeld and Nicolson.

SMART, C. (1984) *The Ties that Bind*, London, Routledge and Kegan Paul.

SMITH, D.E. (1974) 'Women's perspective as a radical critique of sociology', *Sociological Inquiry*, 4, pp. 7–13.

SPENDER, D. (1982) (Ed.) *Men's Studies Modified*, Oxford, Pergamon Press.

SZASZ, T. (1961) *The Myth of Mental Illness*, London, Hoeber-Harper.

TRUSTRAM, M. (1984) *Women of the Regiment*, Cambridge, Cambridge University Press.

13 Theory and Practice in Sociology of Education

Patricia Broadfoot

Preamble

Academic navel-contemplation is hard to justify. Like the early omphalopsychics, we are likely to find that too much self-reflection leads to an obsessive absorption with the minutiae of individual academic struggles whilst the over-arching disciplinary quest is neglected. At a time when the ideological climate is firmly rooted in technological rationality on the one hand and hedonism on the other, we cannot afford to become preoccupied with the pursuit of sociological niceties. At the same time however, it is the very nature of the prevailing climate for academic research that makes the need for an understanding of the relationship between the discipline and its context particularly pressing. The role enjoyed by sociology in the late 50s and 60s as a major informant of various branches of social policy has evolved in more recent decades into one where the very legitimacy of its voice as an independent subject is being challenged. The failure of the policies it helped to inform, along with its inherent radicalism, makes sociology a ready scapegoat for the conservative backlash that the current combination of economic and social problems have combined to produce. In no area of social policy is this more apparent than in education, in which not only research, but even the perceived relevance of the traditional sociological input into initial training, is under attack.

Faced with the spectre of increasing marginalization, if not direct opposition, sociologists of all persuasions are being forced to come to terms with the prevailing climate by a more careful formulation of their role. In broad terms the options are relatively simple: retreat into the apparent security of an increasingly rarified academic discourse; adoption of an explicitly political commitment to changing the status quo; or trying to steer some kind of uneasy compromise between research, policy and practice. The aim of this last strategy is the generation of change through the establishment of a reflexive relationship between the three different areas. This role is arguably the most difficult to play of the three, since it requires a high degree of epistemological flexibility and political adroitness. It is certainly not for the purists since it requires many theoretical compromises to be made in the interest of achieving piecemeal changes in practice. However, as this book demonstrates, it is an approach which for many of those 'doing sociology of education' is the preferred option. That is to say, sociologists of education are involving themselves more and more in policy and practice issues at all levels of the educational enterprise. To add to the long-established tradition of the grand survey and the theoretical *tour de force* is a much newer, applied sociology of education pursued along-side, and indeed with, teachers, administrators, policy makers and developers. It takes its protagonists into the muddy areas of evalua-tion, state-funded policy research and even action-research in part-nership with the practitioners themselves.

But these new, more applied paradigms pose their own dilem-mas. Among the most significant of these is the relationship between these diverse research concerns and the application and generation of theory in the parent discipline. In part this is an issue which reflects the most fundamental dilemmas in sociology itself — be-tween system and action, positivism and interpretism, macro and micro perspectives. In any one area of substantive interest, projects which may be using a variety of theoretical perspectives and re-search methodology must nevertheless cohere sufficiently to sustain a common language for the description of that educational practice if they are to be of any use.

In addition to these problems associated with differences within the sociological community itself are other, more ethical issues about what role sociologists of education should be seeking to play in the interface between policy and practice. In particular, the ques-tion arises about the extent to which sociological theory *about* education is, or ought to be, related to sociological theory *in* educa-tion. The issue may be put another way as that between the pursuit of a *passive* as against an *active* sociology of education, in which sociologists are responding to and informing policy questions. In the broadest terms, the question concerns the kind of theories which it is appropriate for sociologists of education to pursue and how these are to be generated and used.

In this abstract form the arguments I have been making may seem arid and tendentious, their point far from clear. In what follows I shall set out to show their significance in the course of one particular research biography. By so doing, I hope to justify my initial assertion that there is a role for academic navel-contemplation if by so doing we become more highly sensitized to at least some of the theoretical issues inherent in 'doing sociology of education', and in particular the relationship between the generation of sociological theory and its use in practice.

Stage 1: Pragmatism

The story I want to tell begins in 1973 with the setting up within the Scottish Council for Research in Education of a now very well known project aimed at providing the then rapidly-increasing population of uncertificated Scottish 16-year-old school-leavers with some alternative testament to their abilities and achievements. A sociology graduate and trained teacher with some overseas experience, I was appointed to be research assistant on the project. The research was being directed by Dr W.B. Dockrell, a psychologist, and also director of the Research Council. He was in turn answerable to a working party of the Headteachers Association of Scotland which had been set up to address problems of school assessment. The development work was to be managed by this working party which, like many steering committees, was comprised of representatives from a wide range of potentially interested parties — employers, training officers, representatives of further and higher education, as well as headteachers and Her Majesty's Inspectorate. The researchers were responsible for implementing the decisions of the working party and for evaluating their impact. Their work was supported by a grant from the Scottish Education Department Research and Intelligence Unit.

Over the course of the next four years, a series of prototypes for the new 'profile' assessment procedure was developed and evaluated. A number of schools were asked to try out the procedure in field trials and their experiences and reactions were monitored by means of questionnaires, discussions and statistical analysis of the validity, reliability and discrimination of the assessments made. The approach adopted was very much that being widely used at the time for curriculum development and evaluation projects. The design of the development was informed by the professional expertise and judgment of the working party, its theoretical basis essentially educational and not reflecting the insights of any particular social science discipline. Rather the professional training of the researchers was to be used in identifying evaluation dimensions and in devising the necessary instruments to address these.

The distinction between the value judgments about desirable practice inherent in the development work and the supposed objectivity of the professional evaluation was, however, not easy to maintain. Persuading schools and teachers to undertake the field trials, explaining the procedure and the need for it to numerous gatherings of parents, teachers and employers, involved all concerned with 'selling' the project. Anyone who was not convinced of the need for the initiative and of the merits of the scheme being developed could not easily have continued with the project. Given that the 'theory' behind the initiative was essentially experiential and policy-oriented, the evaluation was couched in similar terms, namely what were the scheme's merits, its problems, its resource implications, and its desirability for outside users. Could teachers use the procedure in the way intended?

The results of the four-year development project were subsequently published in a book entitled *Pupils in Profile* (SCRE, 1977). The book explained the rationale for the project, the conduct of the field trials, the results of the evaluation and recommendations for action in the light of these findings. As in the development and evaluation work itself, it was very hard to avoid bias in the reporting of the results. The case of Sir Cyril Burt is a telling example of how easy it is for the integrity of the professional researcher to be seduced by a value commitment to the desirability of a particular initiative. Even researchers well aware of these dangers may be quite unaware of the impact of their own subjectivity in the conduct and dissemination of an evaluation. At the very least, the project is open to criticism for only being evaluated in its own terms; that is, whether it fulfilled the aims it set out to achieve. The main emphasis was on practicability and consumer reaction. The research design precluded any more long-term study of the possible impact of the scheme on pupil attitudes and motivation or of other questions more removed from the immediate issues of implementation. There was also relatively little attempt made to incorporate into the work more sustained theoretical arguments drawing on relevant bodies of social science literature.

The research and development approach which I have described here is arguably typical of work in educational evaluation. The last ten to fifteen years have seen an enormous refinement of evaluation approaches — in particular, they have seen the development of a whole range of qualitative techniques. These in turn have prompted a much greater awareness of value issues in the generation and interpretation of data. As evaluation has become more and more prominent on the policy-making agenda, so evaluators have refined their ethical codes, acknowledged their subjectivity and sought to 'triangulate' their accounts by contrasting different perspectives on the same events. But while increasing methodological sophistication has been a feature of recent years, the gulf between such applied educational research and the disciplines themselves tends to persist.

The difficulties faced by those charged with studying substantive practical or policy initiatives in education who wish to interpret their findings in relation to some larger theory is well illustrated by the 'profiles' movement that sprang from this early Scottish study. Taken up with enthusiasm by teachers and other educationalists, 'profiling' has developed rapidly as a grass-roots movement. The little evaluation work that has so far been conducted — for example, by the Schools Council, the Further Education Unit, the City and Guilds of London Institute and a small army of higher degree students — has typically been aimed essentially at uncovering problems of design and implementation. With its incorporation as official government policy for England and Wales (DES, 1984), profiles — now called 'records of achievement' — are being subject to much more widespread evaluation. Nevertheless, this evaluation is likely to be overwhelmingly in terms of the policy intentions already laid down. The data generated will be couched in the professional epistemology of problems and impact; resources and organization; training and attitudes. Its theory will be of itself — 'profiling theory' — and although a number of existing disciplines — notably sociology and psychology — will have considerable potential relevance to the interpretation of the findings and for the progressive refinement of the questions being asked, they are not likely to be prominent in the accounts produced. Rather, more theoretical discussions of, for example, the relationship between profiling and social control; or gender issues; or pupil stereotyping and social class; are likely to take place in a different arena, using a different epistemology and reaching a different audience.

The foregoing arguments suggest that there are possibly two different kinds, or levels, of theory being generated by sociologists of education. On the one hand there is that emanating from, and in turn extending, sociological questions about the nature of social life as evinced in the educational process. On the other there is the theory which seeks to apply social scientific methods to a specific initiative or problem, in which any theory generated is defined and specific to the particular topic in question. Whether this is indeed the case may be usefully illuminated by further pursuit of the theoretical story upon the telling of which this chapter has already embarked.

Stage 2: The Beginnings of Theory

Assessment is a particularly interesting area to use as a vehicle for studying the role of theory in 'doing sociology of education', since it has been such a relatively neglected area. In comparison to the long tradition and rich literature of the psychometric interest in the assessment of individual differences, sociologists have been content to use educational credentials as a useful variable without evincing much curiosity about why they exist or what role they play in education and society. For my own part, the experience of the 'Pupils in Profile' project and the inequalities and anti-educational effects of much formal assessment that it revealed had made me interested in pursuing the whole topic in an explicitly sociological way.

The first manifestation of this interest was an M.Ed dissertation on pupil self-assessment as a way of improving pupil motivation. Some very general reading in the field of pupils' perspectives, organization theory and motivation confirmed my intuitive analysis that pupil self-assessment should help to recognize pupils as equal partners in the learning process. I hypothesized that this testimony of respect, combined with better feedback to teachers and the necessity for pupils to understand the course aims better if they were to engage in assessment of it themselves, would combine to improve motivation. The results of the rudimentary experiment I constructed to test out this hypothesis seemed to support my initial supposition (Broadfoot, 1977).

Faced with more and more evidence that the means of improving the educational process, at least through the provision of alternative, more constructive assessment procedures such as diagnostic profiles and pupil self-assessment, were available to be implemented and yet were not being so, the sociologist necessarily begins to look for explanations in the *social*, rather than the *educa-*

tional realm. The first major milestone in this quest was a book entitled *Assessment, Schools and Society* (Broadfoot, 1979), which attempted to analyze patterns in educational assessement procedures and to set them in their historical and international context. In attempting to sketch in the scope for a 'sociology of educational assessment', the book used three different modes of sociological analysis — interactionist perspectives, 'grand' theories of reproduction and political economy, and middle-range 'policy studies' theory based on comparing educational systems. The aim was more to demonstrate the extent of the terrain than to pursue any one of the analyses in great depth.

Despite its eclectic theoretical basis, the underlying theme of the book was a consistent one, namely that educational assessment has four major social functions that it performs — the attestation of *competence*, the regulation of *competition*, the reinforcement of particular definitions of educational *content*, and the imposition of social *control* at both the individual and systemic levels. Whilst no single conspiracy theory was adduced, it was nevertheless consistently argued that educational assessment was a major vehicle for the incorporation of dominant cultural norms and hence for reinforcing inequality. Despite the historical origins of educational assessment in the desire to make more rational, efficient, and therefore just, the award of specific credentials and the selection for specific occupational roles, any analysis of its effects must necessarily conclude that they had in fact been very largely to continue the reproduction of existing social inequality. It is only in the conclusion to *Assessment, Schools and Society* that any very direct reference is made to policy and practice implications. Here it is argued that education should be relieved of its selection function — at least up to 16-plus level where formal assessment is now an anachronism in developed societies, and allowed to pursue a much more democratic, 'praxical' approach to both curriculum and assessment, in which pupils take a much greater responsibility for the conduct and evaluation of their own learning.

It is significant that this academic analysis of educational assessment was produced at a time when I had ceased to be employed as a full-time researcher and had instead become a lecturer in the sociology of education at a college of higher education. Removed from the pragmatic needs and constraints of actual institutions which had governed my previous, very practical, work, I was at liberty to read, discuss and generally explore sociological interpretations of my, by now firmly established, area of concern. Indeed it was my job to do so. By the same token other commitments would have made it very hard to continue major developmental work in schools.

Herein lies the most obvious explanation for the continuing gulf between academic disciplines and the development and evaluation of specific practical projects discussed above. The way in which researchers are able to pursue their general field of interest will be much conditioned by the cultural norms, resources and expectations of their occupational milieu. In particular, 'doing sociology of education' is likely to be affected by the institutional mediation of the discipline itself, in that where sociology of education is taught as an explicit subject, the work done is likely to have a more direct link to mainstream sociological theory than if the sociology is incorporated into various topic contexts such as social divisions, or deviance in schools. This latter approach invites a much more pragmatic relationship to theory in which, like 'patch' studies in school history, the ad hoc use of a variety of disciplines relevant to a particular topic trains both student and teacher in a problem-centred, substantive approach. This way of studying a topic is likely to be reinforced by the prevailing pragmatism and associated hostility towards the social sciences expressed not least in the uneasy history of the erstwhile Social Science Research Council over the last few years which has survived by virtue of a change of emphasis and name to become the Economic and Social Research Council.

The net effect of this theoretical fragmentation is likely to be a mushrooming of substantive theory areas — of assessment, for example, or profiling, or deviance — which draw on several disciplines or none, as the topic and its context of interest dictate.

Stage 3: The Search for Cohesion

The implications of this more interdisciplinary approach to theory are well illustrated by the development that I want to turn to next. In 1980 the then SSRC announced a special interdisciplinary research initiative in the field of accountability in which there was then considerable public and political interest. My analysis of the role of assessment in the control of educational systems which had been set out in *Assessment, Schools and Society* had provided one way of interpreting theoretically the notion of accountability. It argued that the more *other* kinds of system control were eroded —

such as public examinations, budgetary constraints or inspection — the more explicit moves to impose formal accountability procedures through various monitoring and evaluation exercises would be apparent. I proposd to the SSRC that this hypothesis might usefully be studied by the comparison of two very differently organized, but otherwise comparable, education systems — the French and the English.

The study they agreed to support — 'Constants and Contexts in Educational Accountability — a Comparative Study' — was a very different research initiative from the Pupil Profiles project some years before. As well as substantial fieldwork based on interviews, observations and documents at every level of each of the two education systems under study, a substantial literature survey was undertaken in the search for existing theoretical approaches that might be relevant. The end product was a series of papers and book chapters which have been published in and for the academic community, with little or no direct implications for practice.

Like '*Assessment, Schools and Society*' before it, this project embraced a number of theoretical perspectives including educational systems theory; organization theory; cultural studies; social policy theory; and exchange theory. None of these perspectives proved at all adequate to provide a single theoretical basis for the analysis of the data gathered. Social policy theory, as found for example in the work of Maurice Kogan, perhaps came nearest — largely because, I suspect, it is one of the most broadly conceived theoretical areas. One remains with the inescapable conclusion — to which Kogan's own definitive study on educational accountability (Kogan, 1986), also part of the same SSRC initiative, provides further testimony — that a substantive concern cannot be directly equated with any one theoretical approach. That is to say, 'doing sociology of education' is not — at least in theoretical terms — the same as 'doing sociology'. Rather, in my own experience, as soon as 'doing sociology of education' involves topics which are essentially educational in their definition rather than sociologcial — accountability rather than bureaucracy, for example, or assessment rather than phenomenonology — the theoretical apparatus of the discipline needs to be supplemented by those of other disciplines.

Alternatively, it may be possible to dispense with disciplines entirely, except as the *modus vivendi* of research method, and to generate substantive theories 'grounded' in a particular topic just like any other 'grounded theory' exercise. The problem with this interdisciplinary approach, as the accountability exercise was to illustrate, is that the studies conducted in a particular subject area may be so diverse theoretically and methodologically that they cannot easily be integrated into a coherent body of knowledge; that whilst this very richness may provide maximum illumination from a practical point of view, the theory itself may be a cul-de-sac not capable of producing the higher-order generalizations which must be the quest of any social science.

And yet this did not prove to be the case. The sustained study of the role of assessment procedures in the control of educational systems that the SSRC accountability project had allowed proved to be a key step towards a much more sophisticated sociology of educational assessment and this became my next project. Starting from the relatively general insights of *Assessment, Schools and Society*, I attempted to trace the different institutional patterns of educational assessment in the two countries I had studied — England and France. The starting point was policy studies and the basic theoretical model that I had developed for the accountability project. This theory maintained that there are common characteristics and therefore social imperatives that all industrialized and industrializing societies share but that these will find institutional expression according to the ideological traditions of a particular society since these determine the acceptability of specific policy initiatives at any one time. This basic theme of 'constants' and 'contexts' was carried through into this new theoretical phase and linked to the earlier conceptual framework devised in *Assessment, Schools and Society* of 'competence', 'content', 'competition' and 'control'. The overall aim was to show the different institutionalization of these same themes in two systemic contexts and from this to build some more general understanding of the role of educational assessment in industrial societies.

Despite the fact that the initial theoretical model was still grounded in the topic itself and owed little to mainstream sociological theory, I was concerned that without such a linkage, there would be relatively little long-term value in my attempt to define a sociology of educational assessment. Without being closely tied to practical issues of direct relevance on the one hand, nor contributing to the more general development of sociology of education on the other, it would be, in effect, a theoretical ghetto. Either some way had to be found of applying the more refined conceptualizations which I had teased out for the direct benefit of policy or practice in education; or they had to be translated into a broader theoretical framework. In the event I pursued both.

Stage 4: A Dash of Pure Theory

A deeper study of the 'founding fathers' of sociology — notably Marx, Durkheim and Weber — together with some more recent theorists such as Michel Foucault and Basil Bernstein, allowed me to begin to translate the social institutions I had been studying into their more generic, underlying concepts. Thus notions of competence and competition, for example, became reformulated in terms of the more generic distinctions between the collectivism of pre-industrial society and the individualism of industrial society. The picture of 'modern' society painted in the writings of Tönnies, Weber and Durkheim among many others, is of a social order in which relations are particularistic, hierarchical and rational; the individual rather than the group being the basic unit of society. It follows from this that the means to determine rationally the competence, characteristics or even needs of the individual in order to provide a rational basis for the organization of bureaucratic structures will not be long in evolving. In the same way, what Durkheim termed the 'organic solidarity' of such societies requires individuals not only to be sorted into different social roles but to compete for them. The novel problems of social control produced by such a shift from more traditional forms of society also prove to be better solved by the 'rational-empirical' science of individual differences to legitimize differential opportunity than by wasteful 'power-coercive' strategies (Bennis, Benne and Chin, 1978).

Thus educational assessment can be interpreted in more general sociological terms using the key concepts of individualism and rationality, bureaucracy and the division of labour, surveillance and control. Generating a conceptual framework for understanding *why* educational assessment evolved in industrial society must be, initially at least, an historial project. It is not merely an academic exercise, however, for using the theoretical framework so developed, it is possible to trace current changes in the nature of industrial society itself as they are affecting education. The most profound of these changes are embodied in the growing strength of the ideology of technological rationality and of associated styles of social organization such as corporate management. Thus, for example, in my paper 'Changing Patterns of Educational Accountability in England and France' (Broadfoot, 1985), I explore the way in which computer-based administration and a technicist approach to educational provision is allowing what are essentially issues concerned with competing educational values to become redefined simply as technical problems of implementation. Thus questions about 'how it may be best done' come to replace and indeed remove from the agenda of debate questions about 'what should be done'. As both phenomeno-logists and structuralists have made us aware, the embodiment of particular ways of conceiving reality in dominant modes of social discourse are the key to social power and social control. At the present time, the paper suggests, fundamental questions about the nature of the 'good life' and hence about educational values are being effectively replaced by political assumptions that greater technological efficiency and economic progress are an obvious *raison d'être* for education. Assessment has a most critical role to play in this respect, since in choosing to assess particular qualities and achievements, a society legitimates a hierarchy of skills and knowledge which gives a clear picture of elite values and, in turn, helps to reproduce these.

Stage 5: Theory into Action

It is at this point that 'grand theory' becomes linked with educational policy and practice again. The pressure for this to happen came almost entirely from the major upheavals in assessment policy of the early 1980s, and in particular from the rapidly growing significance of the profiling movement. Not only did these developments hold enormous fascination for the small, but growing, number of sociologists interested in the particular area of educational assessment, they also raised serious educational concerns for those whose interests crossed the discipline-practice divide. Testimony to this growing interest is in an edited collection of papers which was published in 1984 under the title of *Selection, Certification and Control*. The depth and breadth of analyses that this volume contains suggests that the theoretical ground is now sufficiently well prepared for mainstream sociological perspectives to be applied to specific policy aspects of assessment such as the common system of examining at 16-plus, new graded assessment and modular courses, the rampant growth of technical and vocational qualifications and, perhaps most significant of all, profiles and records of achievement.

It is possible to address these new developments from a number of perspectives. Structurally one may consider the changing power bases being incorporated into the new assessment procedures through new techniques and new organizational machinery; equally, there is the question of the status, potential clientele and content of the new sorts of qualification and the implications of these in terms of the well-worn sociological problem of educational inequality. Likewise, one may consider from an interactionist point of view the impact at classroom level of the differential impact of more personalized, comprehensive assessment procedures, in terms of pupils' race, sex and class. This too is likely to have implications for educational opportunity and social discrimination (see, for example, Broadfoot, 1986b).

Stage 6: The Enduring Dilemma

My own work reflects the current fascination of assessment policy for a sociologist. But the desire to provide some sort of theoretical explanation for contemporary developments is matched by an eductional concern about their potential impact in practice. As I have set out in this account, both of these concerns have existed in my own work since the earliest days of the Scottish pupil profiles initiative, though one or other has taken prominence at any one time. During the years in which my work centred on developing a more refined theoretical understanding of educational assessment, I continued to work on the dissemination of profiling ideas. As an educationalist I was convinced of the need to challenge the stranglehold of palpably unnecessary external examinations and to promote in their place the more equal and constructive assessment dialogue embodied in the notion of profiling.

But, whilst the rationale of profiling is liberationist, the more sustained theoretical analyses which are now beginning to be initiated to complement the mass of development work are raising serious concerns (see, for example, Baumgart, 1986; Nuttall and Goldstein, 1986; Hargreaves, 1986; Fenner and Broadfoot, 1985). Academics are just beginning to rehearse the dangers of stereotyping and labelling, racial discrimination and sexual differentiation in a procedure that relies so heavily on pupils' ability to set goals for themselves and to be able to benefit from opportunities for self-development. At the same time, the growing number of evaluation studies now being conducted are still focused on pragmatic issues, on evaluating schemes within their own terms. In most cases this means aspects such as school organization, resources, curriculum issues and in-service training implications.

The gulf between the educationalist perspective and its attendant disciplines appears to remain. One of the reasons for this is certainly structural, in that who commissions the evaluation, who carries it out, and who is perceived to be the audience exerts a major influence on the form any particular study takes. In recent years, partly, I suspect, as a result of the demise of the Schools Council, there has been an increasing tendency for government to charge local authorities with the responsibility for conducting major curriculum and development work and then to commission more or less independent, local and/or national evaluators to report on the outcomes. Theoretically this trend provides unprecedented opportunities for the gulf between theory and practice, disciplines and experience to be bridged. In my own case I have become more and more aware of the uneasy cognitive dissonance of the last decade. There has been a 'left brain, right brain' operation in which the serious doubts raised as a result of my theoretical work about the potential effects of current attempts at educational assessment reform have not been allowed to diminish my commitment to the need for such a change as an educational principle. Now that there are growing opportunities for academics to undertake specific evaluations of such policy initiatives, the task of reconciling these two perspectives is very much more feasible than it has been in the past. It is also very much more urgent if 'doing sociology of education' is not to renege on its potential role of providing insights which can be used to *improve* policy making rather than simply analyzing its effects after the event.

But is such an 'active' sociology of education possible in practice? In my own case, my appointment in 1985 as co-director of the national evaluation of the DES-funded record of achievement schemes PRAISE project provides a golden opportunity to bring theory and practice together, and thus to answer this question. It should be possible to use the understanding generated over recent years to raise searching questions about the *implications* of profiling in the long term as well as the more obvious problems of implementation in the short term. There are many factors which continue to make such a combination of perspectives problematic, however. In my own case, the remit of the evaluation team is to provide the data which the Records of Achievement National Steering Committee (RANSC) will use to draw up draft guidelines for a national scheme. Thus the evaluators must work *within* a policy commitment; unlike the Scottish 'pupil profile' project described at the beginning of this chapter, it is no longer an open question *whether* such records are desirable at all.

Perhaps more significant still is the fact that this evaluation is being conducted in the discrete area of records of achievement. No equivalent studies are being conducted of GCSE or graded assessment schemes. And yet it is the context of the continued existence of *other* kinds of certification which, theoretical analysis suggests, is likely to prove one of the most significant influences on the eventual impact of profiling. It will be for government policy makers — ministers and officials — to bring to bear the more global perspective required, but they will have to do this without a professional background in education or its base disciplines, on the basis of fragmentary evaluative evidence.

Nevertheless, it is encouraging that academics and educationists, administrators and politicians, are now working closely together in much of the current assessment development work. Not only does sociology of education have a voice at the level of evaluation, it is also involved in the in-service courses to which many of the teachers involved in the development work itself are being seconded. Thus the increasingly systematic reflexivity between theory and practice, which is more and more characteristic of my own work, is likely to be an experience shared by many in this field. We may be moving into an era when once again, sociology of education operates in close partnership with policy-making. But it will be a changed sociology of education in which the methodological upheavals of recent years will have been matched by the development of not simply new *kinds* of theory but rather new ways of *making* theory.

At the present time, major changes are taking place in the way in which both pre- and in-service training courses in education are offered. In the latter case these changes are the result of central government's desire to make such provision more relevant to local needs by giving local education authorities more direct control of the budget. At the pre-service level, it has long been recognized that students perceive a good deal of educational theory as irrelevant to their concerns. The prevailing emphasis on 'teaching quality' and practical skills is likely to hasten the demise of sociology of education in its current form. Academics are already finding themselves increasingly likely to be tied to substantive topic areas in their job descriptions rather than to the base disciplines. The experience of the natural sciences provides clear illustration of the way in which a mature discipline not only expands its field of vision but is also secure enough to change its orientation into that of the topic itself.

The academic autobiography I have sketched here is probably far from typical, though I suspect the impact of successive factors of chance such as job changes, research grants awarded and policy developments would be a feature of all such accounts. But individual careers necessarily evolve within a broader social context that provides a common mediation of the idiosyncratic effects of chance. By the same token, the evolution of the subject itself is dependent on the aggregation of the results of these mediations of chance. In my own case this evolution has been one in which an initially clear-cut separation between discipline and subject, sociological perspective and educational problem has become progressively reduced. The causes of this rapprochement have been partly personal — in the desire to reconcile two important intellectual areas of interest — but largely structural, as the nature and subject of policy-making has itself changed. The advent of more qualitative theory and method has helped to demonstrate the value of small-scale studies of process where in the past, grand designs have proved unsuitable for informing policy. 'Applied' research — in the form of evaluation — has found a market where 'pure' research could not, in its willingness to address issues in the progenitor's own frame of reference.

As the well-documented hiatus between research, policy and practice (see, for example, Nisbet and Broadfoot, 1980) has slowly been breaking down, so policy — in some areas, at least — has become increasingly dynamic. Major changes in the political and economic climate, and hence in the social context, have prompted qualitatively different educational policy initiatives on an almost unrivalled scale. Certainly there is no era in assessment policy that can rival the first few years of this decade in the United Kingdom in this respect. Thus, sociologists, like other social scientists, have been presented with both a novel and highly significant set of educational issues for study. Those who did not choose to adopt either of the more extreme options outlined at the beginning of this chapter — of retreat into the interstices of the discipline, or revolutionary politics — but chose rather to work at improving practice from the inside, have found themselves 'doing sociology of education' in relation to policy initiatives as varied as microcomputers in the classroom, anti-smoking education, or curricula for low-achieving pupils. In my own case, the area has been assessment — a topic that itself has many facets ranging, as I have shown in this account, from accountability procedures in different educational systems at one level to the formalization of symbolic interaction at the other.

Thus there are grounds for believing that the changing relationship between practice and theory that I have described in my own work is one that will have been experienced by many concerned with 'doing sociology of education'. To the extent that this is the case it suggests that my own experience of a changing focus and role for the discipline will be a common one, that the more applied, 'active' theory currently being generated, which is integrally connected in both its generation and purpose with practice itself, will be the pattern for the next stage of the discipline's evolution. It may be that the hostility surrounding sociology of education in recent years will prove with hindsight to have been the Promethean fire; that out of the ashes of the old approaches, the phoenix of a new sociology of education is already rising.

References

BAUMGART, N. (1986) 'An outsider's view of profiles in Britain', in BROADFOOT, P. (Ed.), *Profiles and Records of Achievement*, Eastbourne, Holt Saunders.

BENNIS, W.G., BENNE, K.D., CHIN, R. and COVEY, K.E. (1978) *The Planning of Change*, Holt, Rinehart & Winston, London.

BROADFOOT, P. (1977) *The role of assessment in motivation*, MEd dissertation, University of Edinburgh.

BROADFOOT, P. (1979) *Assessment, Schools and Society*, London, Methuen.

BROADFOOT, P. (1984) (Ed.) *Selection, Certification and Control*, Lewes, Falmer Press.

BROADFOOT, P. (1985) 'Changing patterns of educational accountability in England and France', *Comparative Education*, 21, 3, pp. 273–286.

BROADFOOT, P. (1986a) 'Assessment of policy and sociology of inequality', *British Journal of Education* 7, pp. 205–224.

BROADFOOT, P. (1986b) 'Records of achievement at national level: Development and evaluation issues', in FEU, *Profiles in Context*, London, Further Education Unit.

DEPARTMENT OF EDUCATION AND SCIENCE (1984) Records of Achievement. A Statement of Policy, London, HMS.

FENNER, R. and BROADFOOT, P. (1985) 'Profiles: the promise and the peril', *New Era*, 66, 2.

HARGREAVES, A. (1986) 'Record breakers?' in BROADFOOT, P. (Ed.) *Profiles and Records of Achievement*, Eastbourne, Holt Saunders.

KOGAN, M. (1986) *Educational Accountability*, London, Hutchinson.

NISBET, J. and BROADFOOT, P. (1980) *The Impact of Research on Policy and Practice in Education*, Aberdeen University Press.

NUTTALL, D. and GOLDSTEIN, H. (1986) 'Profiles and graded tests: The technical issues', in BROADFOOT, P. (Ed.) *Profiles and Records of Achievement*, Eastborne, Holt Saunders.

A Guide to Further Reading

The following guide to further reading is of necessity extremely selective. It is in two parts. In the first, an indication is given of the major books and articles associated with the empirical or theoretical research discussed in each of the chapters in the book. In some cases, especially with the quantitative research of the Scottish Educational Data Archive and the National Child Development Study, the items listed represent no more than a small fraction of the work published. In the second part, a list is given of some of the major reflexive accounts of the conduct of research in sociology, social anthropology and sociology of education. No attempt is made to include traditional text books on research methods.

Major Published Studies Associated with each Chapter

Chapter 1

HARGREAVES, A. (1986) *Two Cultures of Schooling*, Lewes, Falmer Press. The major account of the author's historical and ethnographically-based research on middle schools.

HARGREAVES, A. (1978) 'The significance of classroom coping strategies' in BARTON, L. and MEIGHAN, R, (Eds) *Sociological Interpretations of Schooling and Classrooms: A reappraisal*, Driffield, Nafferton Books. An early, but important paper which discusses the concept of coping strategy in the context of ethnographic work conducted in two middle schools.

HARGREAVES, A. (1983) 'The case of middle schools', Unit 19, E305, *Conflict and Change in Education*, Milton Keynes, Open University. An early account of some of the results of the research.

Chapter 2

WALFORD, G. (1986), *Life in Public Schools*, London, Methuen. This ethnographic study is based on fieldwork in two of the major British independent boarding schools. It mainly describes the social world and experiences of boys and schoolmasters, but also deals with the recent introduction of girl pupils and the experiences of female teachers and schoolmasters' wives.

WALFORD, G. (1984) 'The changing professionalism of public school teachers' in WALFORD, G. (Ed.) *British Public Schools: Policy and Practice*, Lewes, Falmer Press. Based on interviews and ethnographic data, this article traces the similarities and discontinuities of experience between public school teachers and the majority of teachers working in the maintained system of schooling.

WALFORD, G. (1986) 'Ruling-class classification and framing' *British Educational Research Journal*, 12, 2, pp. 183–195. Looks at the changing relationship between the public schools and higher education and employment using Basil Bernstein's concepts of classification and framing.

Chapter 3

BURGESS, R.G. (1983) *Experiencing Comprehensive Education: A Study of Bishop McGregor School*, London, Methuen. An ethnographic study conducted in a co-educational Roman Catholic comprehensive school. The first part looks at the head and teachers concerned with pastoral and academic work. The second looks at the process of becoming a teacher of the 'less able'.

BURGESS, R.G. (1984) *In the Field: An Introduction to Field Research*, London, Allen and Unwin. This is a textbook on qualitative research methods, but has many examples from the Bishop McGregor study and presents some new data.

BURGESS, R.G. (1984) 'It's not a proper subject: It's just Newsom', in GOODSON, I.F. and BALL, S.J. (Eds) *Defining the Curriculum: Histories and Ethnographies*, Lewes, Falmer Press. This paper discusses the attitudes and response of pupils to Newsom courses for the 'less able'. It describes the low status of the Newsom Department in the eyes of both pupils and teachers.

BURGESS, R.G. (1984) 'Headship: Freedom or constraint?' in BALL, S.J. (Ed.) *Comprehensive Schooling: A Reader*, Lewes, Falmer Press. Contains a section on the way the head of Bishop McGregor School conceived of headship and the way in which he defined his role within the school.

Chapter 4

POLLARD, A. (1982) 'A model of coping strategies', *British Journal of Sociology of Education*, 3, 1, pp. 19–37. Puts forward a theoretical model of classroom coping strategies for teachers which takes social context and individual teacher biography into account.

POLLARD, A. (1984) 'Coping strategies and the multiplication of differentiation in infant classrooms', *British Educational Research Journal* 10, 1, pp. 33–48.

POLLARD, A. (1985) *The Social World of the Primary School*, Eastbourne, Holt, Rinehart and Winston. This ethnographic study is based on periods of participant observation, interviewing and collection of documentary data whilst the author was teaching in primary and middle schools.

Chapter 5

GLEESON, D. and MARDLE, G. (1980) *Further Education or Training? A Case Study in the Theory and Practice of Day Release Education* (with the assistance of John McCourt), London, Routledge and Kegan Paul. Based on interviews and participant observation, this study examines a college of further education and its relationship with the local industrial environment. It looks in particular at the ways in which apprentices, teachers and employers perceive the 'functions' of further education.

GLEESON, D. (1980) 'Streaming at work and college', *Sociological Review* 28, 4, pp. 745–761. Explores the growth and influence of technical education upon apprentice relations, and examines the underlying factors which affect the social differentiation of craft and technician apprentices within further education.

GLEESON, D. (1981) 'Communality and conservatism in technical education: The role of the technical teacher in further education', *British Journal of Sociology of Education* 2, 3, pp. 265–273. Examines the role of the technical teacher in further education, and indicates how the technical teacher perceives the role of teacher as secondary to his occupational status within his former trade.

GLEESON, D. (1983) 'Further education, tripartism and the labour market' in GLEESON, D. (Ed.) *Youth Training and the Search for Work*, London, Routledge and Kegan Paul. This paper further examines the recent shift in emphasis away from traditional apprentice training to more formal patterns of further education and vocational training. The tripartism of further education is discussed.

Chapter 6

KELLY, A., WHYTE, J. and SMAIL, B. (1984) *Girls into Science and Technology: Final Report*, Department of Sociology, University of Manchester. This is the final report of a three-year action research project designed to understand girls' under-achievement in physical science and technical subjects and simultaneously to explore methods to improve that performance. About 2000 children from ten schools in Greater Manchester were involved from entry to secondary school until they made their option choices at the end of the third year.

KELLY, A. (1985) 'The construction of masculine science', *British Journal of Sociology of Education*, 6, 2, pp. 133–54. Looks at masculinity of science as a topic in the cultural reproduction of gender. Drawing on the GIST project, the paper describes the ways in which science comes to be seen as a masculine subject area.

WHYTE, J. (1985) 'Girl friendly science and the girl friendly school' in WHYTE, J., DEEM, R., KANT, L. and CRUICKSHANK, M. (Eds) *Girl Friendly Schooling*, London, Methuen. Describes methods used in the GIST project to attempt to change the nature of school science. Clarifies the concept of 'girl friendly' science.

WHYTE, J. (1986) *Girls Into Science and Technology*, London, Routledge and Kegan Paul. This is the major report of the GIST action research project.

Chapter 7

BENNETT, N. (1976) (with JORDAN, J., LONG, G. and WADE, B.) *Teaching Styles and Pupil Progress*, London, Open Books. This study is based on a sample of 871 primary schools in Lancashire and Cumbria. A typology of teaching styles is developed (formal, mixed and informal) and the prevalence of each and their effects on children's progress assessed. It is argued that progressive teaching is likely to be less effective, particularly with brighter children and anxious ones.

AITKIN, M., BENNETT, S.N. and HESKETH, J. (1981) 'Teaching Styles and Pupil Progress: A re-assessment', *British Journal of Educational Psychology* 51, pp. 170–186. A re-assessment of the data used for *Teaching Styles and Pupil Progress* in the light of criticism.

BENNETT, S.N., DESFORGES, C.W., COCKBURN, A. and WILKINSON, B. (1984) *The Quality of Pupil Learning Experience*, London, Erlbaum. A study of 6 and 7-year-old pupils which looks at pupils as constructivist learners.

Chapter 8

BUTLER, N.R. and BONHAM, D.G. (1963) *Perinatal Mortality*, London, Livingston. This is the first major report of what became the National Child Development Study longitudinal survey. All babies born in England, Scotland and Wales in the week 3rd-9th March 1958 were included in the study. Information at this stage was obtained through medical records and interviews with mothers.

DAVIE, R., BUTLER, N.R. and GOLDSTEIN, H. (1972) *From Birth to Seven*, London, Longman. This report resulted from the first follow-up conducted by the National Children's Bureau when the children were aged 7.

STEEDMAN, J. (1980) *Progress in Secondary Schools. Findings from the National Child Development Study*, London, National Children's Bureau. Data from the third follow-up study when the children were 16 in 1974.

STEEDMAN, J. (1983) *Examination Results in Mixed and Single Sex Schools: Findings from the National Child Development Study*, Manchester, Equal Opportunities Commission. A study using the 1974 study, using examination results.

FOGELMAN, K. (Ed.) (1983) *Growing Up In Great Britain*, London, Macmillan. A collection concerned mainly with the 1974 survey.

FOGELMAN, K. (Ed.) (1985) *After School. The Education and Training Experiences of the 1958 Cohort*, London, Further Education Unit. A report based on the fourth follow-up interviews of the cohort, conducted in 1981/82 when the members were aged 23.

Chapter 9

GOW, L. and MCPHERSON, A.F. (1980), *Tell Them From Me: Scottish school leavers write about school and life afterwards*, Aberdeen, Aberdeen University Press. Contains accounts of schooling written mainly by non-certificate school leavers in the 1977 and 1979 National School Leavers Surveys.

GRAY, J.M., MCPHERSON, A.F. and RAFFE, D. (1983) *Reconstruction of Secondary Education: Theory, Myth and Practice since the War*, London, Routledge and Kegan Paul. Based on the Scottish Educational Data Archive's series of national surveys of school leavers in Scotland from the early 1960s onwards. Looks at trends in curriculum, attainment, class inequality, school effectiveness, truancy and pupils' reactions to school, described in the context of an historical account of the spread of certification, comprehensive reorganization and the Scottish 'myth' of egalitarian education.

RAFFE, D. (Ed.) (1984) *Fourteen to Eighteen: The Changing Pattern of Schooling in Scotland*, Aberdeen, Aberdeen University Press. A collection of articles on various aspects of schooling in the context of recent developments and current policy proposals. Draws on findings from the 1981 Scottish School Leavers Survey.

HUGHES, J.M. (Ed.) (1985) *The Best Years? Reflections of School Leavers in the 1980s*, Aberdeen, Aberdeen University Press. Gives a selection of views on the schooling and employment prospects of school leavers from the 1981 National School Leavers Survey. Arranged according to theme and by cross-section.

Chapter 10

KING, R.A. (1969) *Values and Involvement in a Grammar School*, London, Routledge and Kegan Paul. A case study of a single grammar school, mainly using questionnaires to staff, pupils and parents and subsequent quantitative analysis.

KING, R.A. (1973) *School Organisation and Pupil Involvement*, London, Routledge and Kegan Paul. A large-scale study of seventy-two secondary schools and 7500 pupils, based on questionnaires, observation and interviews.

KING, R.A. (1978) *All things Bright and Beautiful? A Sociological Study of Infants' Classrooms*, Chichester, Wiley. An ethnographic study of tertiary colleges as part of secondary re-organization and compares the various kinds of post-sixteen provision. Interviews, observation and questionnaires were used in twelve institutions.

KING, R.A. (1978) *All things Bright and Beautiful? A Sociological Study of Infants' Classrooms*, Chichester, Wiley. An ethnographic study of teachers and pupils in three infants' schools' classrooms.

Chapter 11

VULLIAMY, G. (1976) 'What counts as school music?' in WHITTY, G. and YOUNG, M. (Eds) *Explorations in the Politics of School Knowledge*, Driffield, Nafferton Books. A brief statement of the application of the ideas of the 'new' sociology of education to music education.

VULLIAMY, G. and LEE, E. (Eds) (1976) *Pop Music in School*, Cambridge, Cambridge University Press, (new edition, 1980). Contains a version of the paper above, along with other interesting articles.

SHEPHERD, J., VIRDEN, P., VULLIAMY, G. and WISHART, T. (1977) *Whose Music? A Sociology of Musical Languages*, London, Latimer. Develops some of the ideas presented in earlier papers.

SHEPHERD, J. and VULLIAMY, G. (1983) 'A comparative sociology of school knowledge', *British Journal of Sociology of Education*, 4, 1, pp. 3–18. Reports empirical data from Britain and North America on school music. Although no overt culture clash was found in Ontario schools between 'school' music and 'students' music, it is argued that particular ideologies of the dominant musical culture are transmitted in very similar ways in both contexts. This is then linked with ideological assumptions underpinning capitalist societies.

Chapter 12

DAVID, M.E. (1975) *School Rule in the USA*, New York, Ballinger. A study of educational decision-making in four school districts in the north east of USA, concentrating on the budgetary processes.

DAVID, M.E. (1977) *Reform, Reaction and Resources: The 3Rs of Educational Planning*, Windsor, NFER. A sociological study of educational decision-making in ten local education authorities, based on interviews with the professional staff of education offices. Looks in particular at the decision-making processes involved in reorganization of secondary education.

DAVID, M.E. (1980) *The State, the Family and Education*, London, Routledge and Kegan Paul. An historical study which looks at educational policy and the assumptions embedded in that policy about women's position in the family, school and employment.

NEW, C. and DAVID, M.E. (1985) *For the Children's Sake*, Harmondsworth, Penguin. Analyzes the historical and social background to women's role as having the responsibility for childcare and their accompanying separation from social, economic and political power. Discusses feminist and socialist attitudes to childcare and argues for a fundamental change in the way childcare is organized.

Chapter 13

BROADFOOT, P. (1979) *Assessment, Schools and Society*, London, Methuen. Looks at patterns in educational assessment procedures and sets them in their historical and international context. Argues that assessment is a major vehicle for the incorporation of dominant cultural norms and hence for reinforcing inequality.

BROADFOOT, P. (1984) 'From public examination to profile assessment: The French experience'. In BROADFOOT, P. (Ed.) *Selection, Certification and Control*, Lewes, Falmer Press. A paper drawn from the SSRC accountability project 'Constants and contexts in educational accountability — a comparative study'.

BROADFOOT, P. (1983) 'Assessment constraints on curriculum practice: a comparative study.' In HAMMERSLEY, M. and HARGREAVES, A. (Eds) *Curriculum Practice*, Lewes, Falmer Press. Looks at the issue of the trend towards centralization or decentralization. France and England are often taken as classic cases of centralized and decentralized educational systems respectively, but it is argued that the degree of control over teachers' activities is similar in both systems.

BROADFOOT, P. (1985) 'Towards conformity: educational control and the growth of corporate management in England and France' in LAUGLO, J. and McLEAN, M. (Eds) *The Control of Education*, London, Heinemann. Extends the analysis of the previous paper.

BROADFOOT, P. (1985) 'Changing patterns of educational accountability in England and France', *Comparative Education* 21, 3, pp. 273–286. Explores the way in which computer-based administration and a technicist approach to educational provision is allowing issues of educational values to become redefined as merely technical problems.

Reflexive Accounts of Doing Research

AGAR, M. (1981) *The Professional Stranger: An Informal Ethnography*, New York, Academic Press. An introductory textbook on ethnography, but included here as it contains substantial comment on the author's own research.

BELL, C. and ENCEL, S. (Eds) (1978) *Inside the Whale*, Rushcutters Bay, New South Wales, Pergamon Press. A collection in which Australia-based sociologists reflect on their work. Contains an article by a feminist collective on researching female academics, and one by Bottomley on postgraduate research.

BELL, C. and NEWBY, H. (Eds) (1977) *Doing Sociological Research*, London, Allen and Unwin. A well-used and somewhat controversial collection of accounts in which sociologists reflect on their research.

BELL, C. and ROBERTS, H. (Eds) (1984) *Social Researching: Politics, Problems, Practice*, London, Routledge and Kegan Paul. A collection of essays giving accounts of sociological research. Has chapters by Jenkins on his Belfant-based study *Lads, Citizens and Ordinary Kids*, and by Scott on being a postgraduate research student in sociology.

BOGDAN, R. and TAYLOR, S.J. (1975) *Introduction to Qualitative Research Methods*, New York, John Wiley. Although designed as an introduction this includes many comments on the authors' own work. A classic.

BOWEN, E.S. (Laura Bohannan) (1964) *Return to Laughter*, Garden City, New York, Doubleday Anchor Books. A personal account of anthropological research. Originally written in the form of a novel under a pseudonym.

BURGESS, R.G. (Ed.) (1984) *The Research Process in Educational Settings: Ten Case Studies*, Lewes, Falmer Press. Ten accounts of the educational research process by Delamont, Hammersley, Ball, King, Atkinson, Rudduck, Stenhouse and others, followed by an essay by Burgess on the nature and usefulness of such autobiographical accounts.

BURGESS, R.G. (1984) *In the Field: An Introduction to Field Research*, London, Allen and Unwin. An introductory text on field research, but included here as the author includes many examples relating to his Bishop McGregor School study.

BURGESS, R.G. (Ed.) (1985) *Field Methods in the Study of Education*, Lewes, Falmer Press. Includes essays on the problems, processes and procedures involved in doing field research in education.

BURGESS, R.G. (Ed.) (1985) *Issues in Educational Research: Qualitative Methods*, Lewes, Falmer Press. A collection concerned with current issues in qualitative research. Contains interesting articles by Scott on feminist research, and Woods on the process of writing up research.

BURGESS, R.G. (Ed.) (1985) *Strategies of Educational Research. Qualitative Methods*, Lewes, Falmer Press. An interesting collection containing essays by Ball on participant observation with pupils, Measor on interviewing, and Burgess on key informants.

COTTLE, T.J. (1977) *Private Lives and Public Accounts*, New York, New Viewpoints. A personal account of the development of the art of conversation as a research strategy.

DOUGLAS, J.D. (1976) *Investigative Social Research*, Beverly Hills, California, Sage. Uses many personal examples from his own work in proposing his strategy of social research.

EVANS-PRITCHARD, E.E. (1973) 'Some reminiscences and reflections on fieldwork' *Journal of Anthropological Society of Oxford*, 4, 1, pp. 1–12. Contains the well-quoted passage in which Evants-Pritchard recounts the advice on fieldwork given to him by other eminent researchers.

FLETCHER, C. (1974) *Beneath the Surface. An account of three styles of sociological research*, London, Routledge and Kegan Paul. Describes and discusses the author's work in qualitative and quantitative empirical sociology and in critical sociology.

FRANKENBERG, R. (Ed.) (1982) *Custom and Conflict in British Society*, Manchester, Manchester University Press. A collection mainly concerned with aspects of ethnographic research pioneered by the Manchester School of Sociology and Social Anthropology. Contains an essay by Lacey on his *Hightown Grammar*.

FREILICH, M. (Ed.) (1977) *Marginal Natives at Work: Anthropologists in the Field* (2nd edition), New York, Wiley. A collection of essays concerned with anthropological fieldwork.

GANS, H.J. (1968) 'The participant observer as a human being: Observations on the personal aspects of fieldwork' in BECKER, H.S. *et al.* (Eds)

Institutions and the Person: Papers Presented to Everett C. Hughes, Chicago, Aldine. Includes reflections on the fieldwork for the classic studies *The Urban Villagers* and *The Levittowners*.

GLUCKMAN, M. (Ed.) (1964) *Closed Systems and Open Minds: The Limits of Naivete in Social Anthropology*, Edinburgh, Oliver and Boyd. Includes some reflexive accounts by British social anthropologists.

GOLDE, P. (Ed.) (1970) *Women in the Field; Anthropological Experiences*, Chicago, Aldine. A collection which concentrates on the special problems of being a female anthropologist.

HABENSTEIN, R.W. (Ed.) (1970) *Pathways to Date*, Chicago, Aldine. A collection of essays on ethnographic research. The chapter by Geer looks at research in higher education.

HAMMERSLEY, M. (Ed.) (1983) *The Ethnography of Schooling*, Driffield, Nafferton. This collection includes a chapter by Beynon on the problems of access, and by Hitchcock on his work in a primary school.

HAMMERSLEY, M. and ATKINSON, P. (1983) *Ethnography: Principles in Practice*, London, Tavistock. This is an introductory textbook on ethnographic research. It is included here because it contains reflexive accounts of research undertaken in schools and higher education by both of the authors.

HAMMOND, P.E. (Ed.) (1964) *Sociologists at Work*, New York, Basic Books. One of the first collections to try to uncover the research process in sociology. Includes articles by Blau, Dalton, Lipset, Coleman and Geer.

JOHNSON, J.M. (1975) *Doing Field Research*, New York, Free Press. An introductory volume, but includes very open descriptions of some of the author's research experiences.

PLATT, J. (1976) *Realities of Social Research*, London, Chatto and Windus. An empirically based sociological study of the ways in which sociologists conduct their research.

PLATT, J. (1981) 'On interviewing one's peers', *British Journal of Sociology*, 32, 1, pp. 75–91. An account of problems encountered in interviewing other academics for *Realities of Social Research*.

PUNCH, M. (1985) *The Politics and Ethics of Fieldwork, Muddy Boots and Grubby Hands*, Beverley Hills, Sage. Contains an account of the author's research at Dartington Hall School, a progressive independent school in Devon.

RABINOW, P. (1977) *Reflections on Fieldwork in Morocco*, Berkeley, University of California Press. A reflective account by a major anthropologist.

REINHARZ, S. (1979) *On Becoming a Social Scientist*, New York, Jossey-Bass (and Transaction Books, 1984). An account providing considerable depth of insight into the personal experience of research.

ROBERTS, H. (Eds) (1981) *Doing Feminist Research*, London, Routledge and Kegan Paul. A selection of articles presenting a feminist critique of sociological research.

RYNKIEWICH, M. and SPRADLEY, J. (Eds) (1976) *Ethics and Anthropology: Dilemmas in Fieldwork*, New York, Wiley. A collection of essays which concentrate on the ethical dimension of practical anthropological research.

SHAFFIR, W.B., STEBBINS, R.A. and TUROWETZ, A. (Eds) (1986) *Fieldwork Experience: Qualitative Approaches to Social Research*, New York, St. Martins Press. Accounts on a wide range of ethnographic research including crime, deviance, media and elite group research. Contains good chapters by Humphreys, Hoffman, Karp and Bogdan.

SHIPMAN, M. (Ed.) (1976) *The Organization and Impact of Social Research*, London, Routledge and Kegan Paul. Includes an essay by Lacey on *Hightown Grammar*, Ford on *Social Class and the Comprehensive School*, and J.W.N. Douglas on national cohort studies.

SJOBERG, G. (Ed.) (1967) *Ethics, Politics and Social Research*, Cambridge, Massachusetts, Schenkman Publishing. Contains a range of essays including Sjoberg's brief account of Project Camelot.

SMETHERHAM, D. (Ed.) (1981) *Practising Evaluation*, Driffield, Nafferton. Contains an interesting account of a qualitative evaluation which failed by Baron *et al.*

SPINDLER, G.D. (Ed.) (1970) *Being an Anthropologist: Fieldwork in Eleven Cultures*, New York, Holt, Rinehart and Winston. Personal accounts of fieldwork.

SPINDLER, G.D. (Ed.) (1982) *Doing the Ethnography of Schooling: Educational Anthropology in Action*, New York, Holt, Rinehart and Winston. Although this collection is more concerned with the presentation of new substantive research, it also discusses methods and the research process.

SRINIVAS, M.N., SHAH, A.M. and RAMASWAMY, E.A. (Eds) (1979) *The Fieldworker and the Field: Problems and Challenges in Sociological Investigation*, Delhi, Oxford University Press. A collection by Indian sociologists.

VIDICH, A.R., BENSMAN, J. and STEIN, M. (Eds) (1964) *Reflection on Community Studies*, New York, Harper and Row. Contains essays on a range of community studies, including one by Whyte on the fieldwork for *Street Corner Society*.

WAX, R. (1971) *Doing Fieldwork: Warnings and Advice*, Chicago, University of Chicago Press. The 'warnings and advice' are set in the context of the author's account of his own various fieldwork experiences.

WEINBERG, I. (1968) 'Some methodological and field problems of social research in elite secondary schools'. *Sociology of Education*, 41, pp. 141–155. A consideration of problems encountered whilst researching British public schools.

WHYTE, W.F. (1984) *Learning from the Field*, Beverley Hills, Sage. Contains much information from Whyte's many studies.

Notes on Contributors

Neville Bennett was until 1985 Professor and Head of the Department of Educational Research at the University of Lancaster. He is now Professor of Primary Education at the University of Exeter. His major interest is in the study of teaching-learning processes in classroom settings. His most recent publications include *The Quality of Pupil Learning Experiences* (1984) and *Recent Advances in Classroom Research* (1985). His current research includes studies on the integration of children with special education needs into ordinary schools, classroom group processes, and children's interactions with microcomputers.

Patricia Broadfoot is Lecturer in Education (Overseas) in the School of Education, University of Bristol. She has for many years been concerned with both practical and social aspects of educational assessment and is the author of *Assessment, Schools and Society* (1979), *Introducing Profiling* (1987) and, with Harry Black, *Keeping Track of Teaching* (1982). She is editor of *Selection, Certification and Control* (1984) and *Profiler and Records of Achievement* (1986).

Robert G. Burgess is a Senior Lecturer in Sociology at the University of Warwick where he teaches courses on social research methodology and the sociology of education to undergraduate and postgraduate students. He is especially interested in the ethnography of schooling, the uses of qualitative research and its application to the study of educational settings. He is author of *Experiencing Comprehensive Education* (1983), *In the Field* (1984), *Education, Schools and Schooling* (1985), *Sociology, Education and Schools: An Introduction to the Sociology of Education* (1986) and the editor of *Teaching Research Methodology to Postgraduates* (1979), *Field Research: A Sourcebook and Field Manual* (1982), *Exploring Society*

(1982, 2nd revised edition 1986), *The Research Process in Education-al Settings* (1984), *Field Methods in the Study of Education* (1985), *Strategies of Educational Research* (1985), *Issues in Educational Research* (1985) and *Key Variables in Social Investigation* (1986).

Peter Burnhill was the Scottish Education Department Research Fellow at the Centre for Educational Sociology, University of Edinburgh from 1979 to 1984 and was responsible for the design and operational direction of the 1981 and 1983 Scottish School Leavers Surveys and of the 1984 pilot for the Scottish Young People's Survey. He also served on the MSC planning body, Training Information Framework Youth Working Group, which designed and arranged the surveys in England and Wales. Currently manager of the University of Edinburgh's Data Library and principal consultant at the Centre for Applications Software and Technology, he continues to research through the CES focusing upon transitions through secondary school and the demand for higher education. He has written on schooling, survey methods and on secondary analysis.

Miriam David is the Head of the Department of Social Sciences at South Bank Polytechnic. She was previously Lecturer in Social Administration at Bristol University, a post she held for over twelve years. Her main teaching and research interests are in the areas of the sociology of education, education and social policy and women's studies. On becoming a mother eight years ago her academic interest in children's education was transformed into a more pressing interest in their wider care and nurturance. This led to a collaboration with Caroline New, and their joint publication of *For the Children's Sake: Making Child Care More than Women's Business* (Penguin, 1985). She has also published widely in the area of education and social policy.

Denis Gleeson lectures in the Sociology of Education at the University of Keele and is also responsible for social science teaching methods at the pre- and in-service levels. In collaboration with his co-author in this volume, George Mardle, he teaches on a Masters degree in Research Methods and also runs the 'In and Out of School' project, a day school for young people, in conjunction with Staffordshire LEA. Denis Gleeson has published a number of books: *Developments in Social Studies Teaching* (1976) (with Geoff Whitty), *Further Education or Training?* (1980) (with George Mardle) and *Youth Training and the Search for Work* (1983). He has also contributed articles on the 'new' vocationalism in schools and FE, to a range of books and journals including the University of Keele's *Sociological Review*. Currently he is working on a local evaluation of the MSC's Pilot TVEI project in Staffordshire schools and colleges.

Andy Hargreaves is Associate Professor at the Ontario Institute for Studies in Education, Toronto, Canada. He has been a lecturer at the Open University, the University of Oxford and the University of Warwick. He is author of *Two Cultures of Schooling: the case of middle schools* (1986), from which this research biography is drawn, and co-author of *Approaches to Personal and Social Education* (forthcoming). He is also co-editor of *Middle Schools: Origins, Ideology and Practice* (1980) (with Les Tickle), *Curriculum Practice: Some Sociological Case Studies* (1983) (with Martyn Hammersley) and *Classrooms and Staffrooms* (1984) (with Peter Woods).

Ronald King is Reader in Education at the University of Exeter, where he has taught the sociology of education since 1966, and is currently Dean of Education.

Andrew McPherson is Reader in Sociology and Director of the Centre for Educational Sociology at the University of Edinburgh where he has worked since 1968. He is co-author of *The Scottish Sixth* (1976), *Tell Them From Me* (1980), *Reconstructions of Secondary Education* (1983), and *Governing Education: A Sociology of Policy since 1945* (to appear shortly).

George Mardle. Lecturer in Sociology of Education at Keele University. Started teaching in 1967 in south-east England and studied part-time at Goldsmiths' College, London from 1969 for a sociology degree, then full-time at the Institute of Education in London. Has published work in the area of teacher education, further education and the relationship of education, work and leisure. Joint author (with Denis Gleeson) of *Further Education or Training?* (1980). Currently working on the Keele Youth Study, a longitudinal study of the life experience and expectations of a cohort of 16-year-olds in the north and west Midlands region.

Andrew Pollard is Reader in Primary Education at Bristol Polytechnic. He has taught throughout the primary school age range and his first book, *The Social World of the Primary School*, was published in 1985 by Holt, Rinehart and Winston.

David Raffe is Reader in Education and Deputy Director of the Centre for Educational Sociology at Edinburgh University, where he has worked since 1975. During that time he has played a leading role in the conduct and analysis of the Scottish School Leavers Survey, now the Scottish Young People's Survey. He is co-author of *Reconstructions of Secondary Education* (1983), editor of *Fourteen to Eighteen: The changing pattern of schooling in Scotland* (1984), and author of numerous articles and chapters on the youth labour market, education and training.

Jane Steedman is an educational researcher who has worked with a variety of qualitative, quantitative and mixed empirical research approaches, initially as a cognitive psychologist and then (1973–6) as a Research Fellow at the Cente for Television Research at Leeds University, investigating schoolchildren's perceptions of television programmes. In 1977, she was appointed Research Officer at the National Children's Bureau, where, over the next six years, she carried out the study discussed here, of secondary school progress of children in the National Child Development Study (1958 cohort). She is currently a teacher-researcher, working both as a teacher in an inner London secondary school and as a researcher concerned with secondary schooling, literacy/numeracy and educational broadcasting.

Nils Tomes is a research fellow at the Centre for Educational Sociology, University of Edinburgh, working on the design and analysis of the Scottish Young People's Surveys, a series of longitudinal and cross-sectional surveys of 16–19 year-olds which focus on experiences of education, employment and training. Between 1981 and 1984 she was research officer at the University of Lancaster working on two DES-funded projects concerned with multi-ethnic secondary schooling.

Graham Vulliamy has been a Lecturer in Education at the University of York since 1972. Prior to this he taught Sociology and Liberal Studies for two years at Cambridgeshire College of Arts and Technology and also played the drums in various semi-professional rock groups, one of which he managed. His work in the Sociology of Music Education developed out of a thesis submitted for the MSc in Sociology of Education at the London Institute of Education in 1972. He is an executive editor of the *British Journal of Sociology of Education*, and of the *International Journal of Educational Development*. His most recent research work has been on education in the

Third World, obtaining his PhD for a thesis on the implementation of an educational innovation in Papua New Guinea.

Geoffrey Walford is a lecturer in sociology and education management at the Management Centre, Aston University. Following two degrees in physics he taught in schools in Kent, Oxfordshire and Buckinghamshire. A part-time degree in sociology and education was followed by an MPhil in sociology at the University of Oxford. SSRC fellow, St. John's College, Oxford, 1976–78. He has researched and published widely on science education, higher education and sociology of education, and is author of *Life in Public Schools* (1986) and *Restructuring Universities* (1987), co-author of *Teachers into Industry* (1983), and editor of *British Public Schools: Policy and Practice* (1984) and *Schooling in Turmoil* (1985).

Judith Byrne Whyte is author of *Girls into Science and Technology: the story of a project* (1986) and editor of *Girl Friendly Schooling* (1985). She is Senior Lecturer in the School of Education at Manchester Polytechnic where her main teaching interest is educational innovation and evaluation. She is currently on part-time secondment to Manchester Business School, and hoping to complete there a study of the promotion interview in large public and private sector organizations.

Index